Jimmy Greaves was an outstanding forward for Chelsea, AC Milan, Tottenham Hotspur, West Ham United and England before becoming a popular TV pundit on *Saint and Greavsie*.

GREAVSIE

THE AUTOBIOGRAPHY

JIMMY GREAVES

A *Time Warner* Paperback

First published in Great Britain in 2003
by Time Warner Books

This edition published by Time Warner Paperbacks in 2004

Copyright © 2004 Jimmy Greaves

The moral right of the author has been asserted.

A CIP catalogue record for this book
is available from the British Library.

ISBN 0 7515 3445 5

Typeset in Janson by M Rules
Printed and bound in Great Britain by
Clays Ltd, St Ives plc

Time Warner Paperbacks
An imprint of
Time Warner Books UK
Brettenham House
Lancaster Place
London WC2E 7EN

www.TimeWarnerBooks.co.uk

My autobiography is dedicated to
my ten grandchildren. Known to Irene and me
as the 'Kling-ons'. Live long and prosper!
(Old Vulcan proverb.)

CONTENTS

ACKNOWLEDGEMENTS

I would like to thank the following who by way of expertise, access to memorabilia, friendship or detailed recollection where my own personal memory was sketchy have helped significantly in the writing of my autobiography: Julian Alexander and all at Lucas Alexander Whitley; Gordon Banks; Ken and Jean Bolam; Chelsea FC; John Crockett, Phill Dann, Greg Dyke, Norman and Michael Giller; Alan Gilzean, Stanley Jackson and all at F4 Group; Cliff Jones; Janice Hallam; Keith Lindsay, Jimmy McIlroy; Dave Mackay; Don Mackay; Manchester United plc in particular Mike Maxfield; Arthur Montford; Ian St John; Alan Samson and all at Time Warner; Gill Shaw; Tottenham Hotspur FC; Steve and Deb Waterall; West Ham United FC.

I would like to express my sincere thanks to my good pal Les Scott who worked with me on my autobiography. He has collaborated with Sir Stanley Matthews, Gordon Banks and George Best on their respective books, and when I made the decision to write my autobiography it was Les to whom I turned for a helping hand. Sir Stanley Matthews said of him,

'Les's knowledge of the game is profound. His sense of time and place, exact. He writes beautifully about the beautiful game.' I'll go along with that.

Thanks, Les, it was great fun!

For Sal, Lauren and Ruby.

Jimmy Greaves, 2003

CHAPTER ONE

ONCE UPON A TIME

All these years on I can still hear them. When the ball hit the back of the net the terraces, quiet a moment before, erupted. As if on cue 50,000 supporters lifted themselves three inches off the ground and arms raised, mouths wide open to the heavens, filled the air with a roar that could be heard for miles across the rooftops of north London.

Sometimes they were so tightly packed together there wasn't a fag paper's width between them. On such occasions, in winter, after heavy rain, you could see great clouds of steam rising off their backs and billowing up towards a battleship grey sky. It must have been bloody uncomfortable, but no matter how cold or wet it was their spirits never dampened. They loved to see me scoring goals. Me? I didn't like it. I loved it.

I don't know why, but I found it easy. Scoring goals came naturally to me. I never felt tension, nerves, any sort of pressure and I never lacked confidence. I'd been scoring goals regularly since I was a boy and I had it in my head that it was something I had been born to do.

I'm a laid back guy. I'm always relaxed. Perhaps that had something to do with it. Some people have told me I was so cool in the penalty box they thought I had ice in my veins. Truth is, I just don't get excited about anything. A lot of players worry about missing a goal. I never did. If I scored all well and good. If I didn't, I knew I'd be there again later in the game. Once that ball went in I never jumped in the air or ran over to the supporters and gyrated my body before them. What a waste of energy that would have been. My team-mates would run up to congratulate me. I'd just sigh softly to myself, as if all cares had been lifted from me. Outwardly I never showed any emotion, but inside I felt a deep contentment, not just about that particular goal, more from the knowledge that I could still do it. That I still had the gift. Contentment at the fact that nothing had changed, that life was still going on the same, with me scoring goals.

I don't miss playing too much. What I do miss is scoring goals. My idea of heaven would be to score goals all night, having spent all day scoring goals. The football writer Geoffrey Green once said I scored goals 'like someone closing the door of a Rolls-Royce'. My laid back attitude enabled me to do it with clinical efficiency and without fuss. But I loved it all right. I used to compare it to a shooting star. Because even on the greyest winter afternoon the ball kissing the back of the net was as if a brilliant light had suddenly illuminated the ground, a moment that passed just as quickly as it had come.

In the 1956–7 season, when I was playing for Chelsea Youth team, the first team players rarely saw the manager in the course of a week, let alone the youth team. So I was surprised to see Ted Drake show his face at training one wet and windy Monday morning. More so when I realised he was coming in my direction. I was with the rest of the Chelsea Youth team, training as usual on the dog track behind one of the goals at Stamford Bridge.

'I hear you scored seven on Saturday, son,' Ted said, referring to the previous weekend's game against Crystal Palace.

'Yes, Mr Drake,' I replied.

I was a bit surprised. I'd been with Chelsea for something like six months and this was the first time the manager had ever spoken to me. I didn't think he knew I existed.

'Do you know that I once scored seven goals in a game, son?' he asked.

'Yeah, Mr Drake. Everyone knows about the seven you scored at Villa,' I replied.

Every young lad did. In December 1935, Ted Drake achieved legendary status in football when he scored all the Arsenal goals in a 7-1 victory over Aston Villa at Villa Park. What's more, he also had a couple of efforts that hit the woodwork and his feat was all the more remarkable as he had played the entire game with an injury to his knee.

'Scoring seven goals in a game happens for a very, very select few,' he told me, 'and it happens just once in a lifetime. Can you remember your goals?'

I told him I could.

'Then keep running them through your mind. Like a film,' he said. 'That way, when your playing days are over, you'll always have the memory of your greatest day in football to look back on.'

He placed a hand on my shoulder. 'Cherish the memory, son,' he told me. 'Cherish it forever. That day will never come again.'

In our next game, against Fulham, I scored eight. After Fulham, we played West Ham and I didn't score at all.

Funny old game.

'It's a funny old game' is a phrase everyone associates with me. Like old-time comedians always had a catchphrase, that has become mine over the years. In the eighties, when I was working on a football programme for Central TV, the producer thought it would be a good idea if I was interviewed by my *Spitting Image* puppet. It sounded like a bit of fun, so I went along with the idea. On the day of the recording, I found myself sitting opposite a grotesque but witty caricature of myself, the voice of which was provided by a young, chain-smoking impressionist. Before the recording we had sat down together and devised a workable script. In the end we had about ten minutes of material, far more than the three minutes allotted for broadcast. The recording went well. I sat there answering questions from my alter ego but when the scripted interview had run its course there was an awkward silence. The tape was still running and the director hadn't called 'Cut'. I didn't know what to say next and neither did the impressionist. The last word had been mine, so I simply waited for him to close the sketch. After a moment's silence, he turned the puppet to face the camera.

'It's a funny old game!' he said.

Although that was the first time I had ever heard the phrase, and it wasn't me who actually said it, it has been associated with me ever since. It was a piece of momentary inspiration on the part of that young impressionist: Harry Enfield has a lot to answer for. But he couldn't have come up with a more appropriate or poignant phrase to describe football. I've been in the game as a player, commentator and columnist for some fifty years and if there is one thing I've learned it's that football is indeed a funny old game.

I was born in Manor Park, east London, in February 1940. Manor Park wasn't home for very long. Six weeks after I was born Hitler's bombers paid our street a visit. In later life my dad Jim told me the story of how he'd been coming home from his work on the Underground when he met a mate.

'Fancy a pint in the Black Lion in Victoria Street?' asked his pal.

'The Black Lion ain't in Victoria Street,' my dad said.

'It bloody well is now!' replied his mate.

They found us another house, in Ivy House Road, Dagenham. I lived there with my dad, my mum, Mary, sister Marion and brother Paul until I was ten. My earliest memories are of that house. Of brown sticky paper crisscrossed over the windows in case German bombers paid us another visit. The outstanding feature of this house was the garden – over three hundred feet long, unbelievably generous by London standards. In those days builders could afford to provide such generous gardens; in the forties Ivy House Road was surrounded by open fields.

Everybody knows about 'The Naughty Nineties', 'The Roaring Twenties', 'The Swinging Sixties'. From my point of view, and I should imagine most other people's as well, the forties and fifties were most definitely frugal. During the war most people in Ivy House Road turned their gardens over to the growing of vegetables as food was scarce and rationing the order of the day. The nearby fields were used mainly for growing potatoes. There was an Italian POW camp nearby and the prisoners of war were assigned to pick them. I had my first encounter with Italians in those 'taity' fields. We kids used to climb over the fence and ask them for a few potatoes to take home. They never refused. I used to come home with loads. When I did, my dad used to joke we would sit down to an Italian POW mixed grill – chips, boiled potatoes and mash.

I was very small as a boy, but every kid I knew appeared to be undersize for his age. There were two reasons for this. Diet, and the fact that we never put on weight because we were always playing outside and our play, in the main, involved running. We were Blitz boys, brought up on powdered egg and milk and tinned corned beef. Proper meat such as beef, lamb, pork or chicken was alien to me. In my early childhood I ate so much corned beef that if anyone had cracked a whip I would have been away at a gallop. Sweets were equally as scarce as fresh meat. Occasionally, an American GI from one of the nearby air bases would give us kids some bubblegum but I can't remember having chocolate or boiled sweets until I was about eight. As for fresh fruit, we had apples most of the year, pears, blackberries and raspberries in season, but I was thirteen before I ever saw a banana.

We kids made, as they say, our own entertainment. Looking back the sheer variety of games we played on the street puts a contemporary evening schedule on BBC 1 to shame. Lord knows who invented them; perhaps they had been handed down from generation to generation. If we tired of one game, someone always had another to play and if we younger kids didn't know how to play it, there always seemed to be an older kid who did. Tin Can Tommy was played with a flattened tin. Someone would hurl it down the street and we'd run after it and touch it before the lad who was 'on' could touch you. If you were tagged you had to stand in a chosen area – usually some paving slabs in front of someone's house – and watch while all your mates ran around the street like Tasmanian devils trying to avoid the lad who was 'on'. Knock Down Ginger was another favourite, but had an element of danger to it: the risk of getting your ear clipped by an irate adult. There was no point in going home and complaining to your old man, because if he knew what you'd been up to he'd give you another clip, only twice as hard.

Like other boys I wore a shirt, pullover, short trousers and hobnail boots. The soles of the boots were reinforced by what we called 'blitheys', small semicircular pieces of metal that were tacked to the toes and heels to protect the soles of the boots. When you skimmed your feet across a paving stone, they produced a shower of sparks. How I never set myself on fire, I'll never know. As for hygiene, it wasn't high on the list of priorities. We were fortunate, because our house in Ivy House Road actually had a bathroom, even if filling the bath was somewhat Heath Robinson as it involved Dad pumping the water up from a boiler situated downstairs. This was a laborious task and one which goes some way to explaining why we only had one bath a week, on a Friday night, and why we all bathed in the same water.

In those days rich and poor had one thing in common. They were cold. Our house had a coal fire in the living room and that was the main source of heat for the entire house. In winter, the bedrooms were freezing. I often awoke to frost patterns on the inside of the windows and more often than not got dressed under the warmth of the bed sheets and eiderdown. From the number of feathers I saw sticking out of the jumpers of my school pals, I obviously wasn't the only lad to do this. As for the bathroom, in winter it was so cold that if we had had fresh meat we could have kept it refrigerated there.

We indulged in what our parents called 'crazes'. We didn't have any hobbies as such, but we did collect things. Most adults I knew smoked, so we kids collected the cigarette cards that came free with a packet of fags. Our interests were dictated by the cards being issued with cigarettes at the time. Some weeks we'd all be collecting film stars, then it would be aeroplanes, then ships and boats. My favourites were cards showing famous footballers or cricketers. For some reason no one I knew ever managed to collect a complete set of football cards. While we would have countless Tommy Lawtons to swap, Raich Carter remained elusive. Rumours would abound of kids in a place like Leeds (it was always somewhere miles away) who had Raich Carter cards by the bucketful but none of Tommy Lawton. That was fairly typical in my childhood. As well as that, it seemed that just about every lad I knew had a father or an uncle who had been a very talented footballer and had been offered a trial by West Ham United; on their way to the trial they joined in a kickabout with their mates, only to sustain an injury that put them out of the game for good.

In those days parents talked a lot of sense, but they could

also talk a lot of nonsense which only served to bamboozle me. If I asked my dad for sixpence to go to the pictures, invariably his response would be, 'Pictures? I'll give you pictures!' Which, of course, he never did. My mum and dad always encouraged me in my schooling, for which I am eternally grateful. 'Stick in at school,' my dad often told me, 'make yourself clever and you'll get a better job in life.' Though should I attempt to walk along a brick wall and fall off, he'd soon be saying, 'Trying to be clever, weren't you? See where it gets you?' By far the most bewildering parentism was heard when I tried something dangerous, such as walking along a wall. 'Get down off that wall,' my mum would say, 'or there's going to be a crying match.'

In my child's mind, the very idea of such a thing as a crying match intrigued me greatly. I had visions of a referee standing in between two kids, who on his signal would suddenly start bawling their eyes out to the encouragement of their respective families. I find it amazing that Dagenham mothers spent so much time encouraging their offspring to talk and, when we could, were either at pains to tell us to shut up or answered our many questions with nonsensical replies. For example, to my question, 'What time is it, Mum?', Mum would reply, 'Time you learned to say please.' I would then ask, 'What time is it, Mum, *please*?' Only for Mum to say, 'Time you stopped asking so many questions.' Even when I showed interest in what Mum was doing, her response would be just as absurd. 'What colour is your new coat, Mum?' 'Skyblue pink with yellow dots on,' she'd reply. Looking back, the amount of times I was discouraged from asking questions, it's a wonder I learned anything at all and did so well at school.

I was football mad as a boy. In that big back garden I'd kick a tennis ball around for hours. Along with the other boys from Ivy House Road, we'd play football in the street with the tennis ball until it was bald. Even when the bald tennis ball split, we still played football with it. When the tennis ball finally gave up the ghost that didn't stop us either. I had countless kickabouts in the street with half a tennis ball.

My dad was treasurer of Fanshaw Old Boys, a local amateur club which derived its name from a nearby school that, in time, would boast Les Allen, Terry Venables and Martin Peters amongst its pupils. Most kids had heroes. Invariably these were footballers such as Stanley Matthews, Tom Finney, Joe Mercer or Tommy Lawton. My heroes were footballers as well, but none you will have heard of. They were the lads who played for Fanshaw Old Boys. I used to accompany my dad to their games and his mates would always make a fuss of me and kick a ball around with me before they played their game, giving me little tips, such as how to head the ball properly or trap it. Dad occasionally turned out for the Old Boys, though he wasn't much of a footballer even at amateur level.

In the late forties leather footballs were as rare as rocking horse shit, but, as treasurer of the Old Boys, Dad was given an old ball the club didn't want anymore. Needless to say, this made me the most popular boy in Ivy House Road. No one had a car and the absence of traffic allowed us kids to spend hours playing football in the street with that old leather 'casey', often on dark nights, by the light of the gas lamp, until our mothers appeared at the door to 'shout us in'.

In 1950 my dad was promoted from a guard on the District Line to a tube driver on the newly extended Central Line which offered (and still offers) the longest possible journey on the London Underground without changing, from Epping in the east to West Ruislip, a distance of just over thirty-four miles. The days when Essex folk would make a special trip into London were nigh on over. By the early fifties all they had to do was stay put and wait for London to come out to them. The extension of the Central Line included branch lines and it was to Hainault, on one such branch line, that we moved so that Dad could be nearer his work.

When I was about ten we moved to a newly built house in Huntsman Road on a brand new estate in Hainault, which to me appeared to be in the middle of nowhere. Having been used to a long garden in which I could play football, I was disappointed to find that the garden at our new house was no more than rubble. Fortunately, most of the houses were occupied by young families and I quickly made friends with other boys and the street football recommenced until our parents laid turf in the back gardens, enabling us lads to play there.

The old leather football eventually gave up the ghost. Towards the end of its life, the leather peeled off and hung from the casing in strips, making it dangerous to play with. Every time you jumped to head it, it gave you fifty lashes, so we eventually laid it to rest and reverted to a tennis ball. It wasn't ideal but, looking back, those games with the tennis ball really helped develop my ball skills. The size of the tennis ball meant that I really had to concentrate when it was at my feet. When shooting, I had to hit it just right, otherwise I might not make contact at all. As a consequence, my foot to eye coordination improved immeasurably and my general ball technique came on in leaps and bounds. When I came to play for the school with a proper leather football, I found making contact with the 'sweet spot' was relatively easy. Likewise when it came to a one touch pass or getting the ball quickly under control. Football today is no better or worse than it was in my day; it is just so very different. However, I often hear old pros and seasoned supporters claim that the general level of skill in contemporary football isn't as high as it used to be. Perhaps this might have something to do with the fact that in the old days boys spent so much time playing with a tennis ball, whereas you rarely, if ever, see kids of today kicking one about. The Brazilians are renowned for their ball skills and football technique; as kids they play Futebol de Salao, a game played with a ball much smaller than a conventional football. Players such as Pele, Jairzinho, Rivelino, Romario, Juninho and Ronaldo were all brought up playing this game. Futebol de Salao is a lot more refined and sophisticated than tennis ball football, however, and I'm sure you will see the point I'm making.

There were no schools on our estate, so I travelled to and from school in Dagenham by bus, a distance of just over eight miles. I attended Southampton Lane Junior School and it was here that I played my very first game under supervision for the school team. I can't remember who it was against but I do remember I scored twice. Little did I realise that scoring on my debut for a team would be something I would continue to do, at all levels, until I stopped playing football.

Two teachers in particular, Mr Bakeman and Mr Jones, both Welsh, took a great interest in my development as a footballer and gave up a lot of their time to coach me and my team-mates. I played at inside right (in a five-man forward line, the inside left and inside right flanked the centre forward) and even at the tender age of ten scored a lot of goals, helping my school team to win the Dagenham Junior League league and cup 'double'. What I remember most about those days was our shirts. We played in red and yellow quartered shirts which were made of heavy cotton; they had buttoned collars and cuffs and long tails, which we tucked into our underpants. When it rained, the shirts soaked up water like sponges and in really heavy rain felt as if they weighed about two stone. When it was both wet and cold, my fingers were so numb by the end of a game, that I couldn't undo the shirt buttons. On hot days, with the heat generated by those shirts, long baggy cotton shorts and thick woollen socks, you almost passed out at the end of a game. This type of strip was commonplace at all levels of football and had been for donkey's years. Only when the great

Hungarian team of Puskas and Hidegkuti arrived on the scene in 1953 and trounced England both home and away did kit manufacturers realise that lightweight strips might perhaps be more practical.

Their sublime football apart, with their lightweight shirts, shorts, socks and boots the Hungarians made England appear a team from another age. The football writer John Moynihan summed it up perfectly at the time when reflecting on the two teams taking to the pitch for the return match at the Nep stadium in Budapest. Wrote Moynihan, 'We had always thought of them [England] as gods. But when the two teams took to the field, compared to Hungary, they looked so old fashioned and jaded and their kit was laughable. We felt sorry for you.'

Rarely had the state of English football in the mid-fifties been so succinctly summed up as by those damning words by Moynihan. Individually the England team was talented; although Stanley Matthews was unavailable through injury for the second match in Budapest, the eleven England fielded were the best they could select. In terms of world football, England's kit was as out of date as their style of play. The Hungarians showed us that individual talent, though essential to the game, could be used to much greater effect when tactics turned it into collective talent. The Hungarian team of 1953 with its sublime mix of individual flair and collective organisation were showing England the way ahead in football, though it was to be a good few years before those who ran our game took their heads out of the sand – not that all of them did. If Moynihan felt sorry for the English players before the game, his emotional state must have been akin to that of Paul Gascoigne at Italia '90 come the final whistle. Hungary won 7-1.

When I was eleven I moved up to Kingswood Secondary, a modern purpose-built school that had just opened in

Dagenham. Again I was fortunate because in Charles Dean and Tony Storey, Kingswood had two teachers who took a very keen interest in my footballing development. I played in a very good school team that won every competition it entered. The school took great pride in our achievements, so much so that we were often excused lessons late in the afternoon in order to play for the school team. Now that, to my mind, was really something. Being excused lessons in order to play football? It was the stuff of my dreams.

Like my team-mates, I seemed to have boundless energy. Many was the time after playing for the school that we would spend our bus fare on a bag of chips and a bottle of pop. Failing that, the bus fare went on what really was my favourite, a doorstep of bread and dripping. That eaten, we would then either kick a ball between us on the eight mile journey back to Hainault, or punctuate the journey by running and walking alternatively between chosen landmarks, such as pubs and shops. Once home, I'd gobble down my tea while listening to the wireless before meeting the other lads again for another game of football in the street or the back garden.

Football was everything to me but I did take an interest in my schoolwork and other things. I used to listen to the nature programmes on the wireless in which some kid would go out for a walk with his father or an uncle and find all sorts of interesting wildlife in fields and parks. There were plenty of fields around where we lived, but in all my time spent playing there I never came across a fox, an owl or a badger sett, as they always did on the wireless. I read a lot but I never found the secret gardens and old empty houses the characters came across in the stories and in which their adventures took place. So for all that I had a very happy childhood, both supposed fact and fiction were often a disappointment to me. Neither bore any relation to my life in Hainault and I was convinced that life happened somewhere else for other kids. I lived in my own world, one which revolved around football, but I loved it because football gave drama, excitement, thrills, friendship and a sense of achievement and purpose to what was a safe, secure, albeit at times mundane childhood.

As a family, we never went on what these days we would consider a conventional holiday. Our annual summer holiday was hop picking in Kent. For decades, hop picking had been undertaken by most East End families, and though strictly speaking we were no longer an East End family as such, the habit remained with us. We called it 'hopping', and though it involved hard, often arduous labour for long hours, I used to look forward to it immensely. Hopping was a hark back to the rustic England of the past, to the short stories of H.E. Bates and in particular the Bates character, Pop Larkin. I encountered many Pop Larkins during my time spent hopping as a boy, lovable rogues, always on the make, with a great love of life and a simple philosophy based on fairness and common sense.

Come the end of August, the whole family, along with a gaggle of relatives, would pile on to a lorry along with personal belongings and head off towards the Blackwall Tunnel and Kent. We took everything bar the kitchen sink. Pots, pans, cups, plates, cutlery, bed sheets – you name it; under Mum's supervision it was all loaded aboard the lorry. It took us six to seven hours to drive from Hainault to the hop fields of Kent, which, as a small boy, appeared to me to be forever. Given the sheer volume of traffic one encounters in London nowadays, this is much the same feeling I get now when I make that journey today. I don't know how my parents did it. Like all other East End hoppers, we lived for two weeks in a small tin hut with no electricity or running water and slept on mattresses filled with straw. There was only one toilet on the farm and one stand-by pipe for water. Toilet is too grand a word to describe the receptacle for what Dad euphemistically referred to as 'our ablutions'. It was, in reality, a midden, nothing more than a toilet seat above a hole in the ground. Even after only a couple of days of use by the hoppers, you didn't want to hang about on that toilet seat reading the newspaper, that's for sure. After a few days of use, the stench rising from that hole in the ground was such that even when you walked by some five yards away your eyes spun round like a fruit machine. I think I'm right in saying it was never emptied. Come the end of the fortnight, with all the hops in and the pickers on their way home, it was simply covered over with soil and a new site selected for the following year.

In the main, the menfolk only came down to the hop fields at weekends, as they continued to work at their normal jobs during the week. I always looked forward to the arrival of Dad, who usually travelled in the sidecar of a motorbike owned by my Uncle Fred. On a Friday night, at the sight of Dad and Uncle Fred swinging into the field, I'd immediately rush over to them, knowing that some sort of adventure would be in the offing that weekend. I remember one Saturday night being awoken by Dad who told me to go and get dressed because he and Uncle Fred were going to take me on 'an adventure'.

The adventure turned out to be scrumping in a nearby orchard. Farmers took every precaution to protect their apple crop and this particular orchard was ringed by a large fence. Dad and Uncle Fred, however, had 'discovered' a small hole in the fence that was just large enough for me to squeeze through. Under their instructions I was to clamber through the hole, climb the trees, throw as many apples to the ground as I could, then throw them over the fence to Dad and Uncle Fred. I don't know how many apples I managed to scrump, but it was a lot. We loaded them into Uncle Fred's sidecar and the following day Uncle Fred headed back to the East End, because, I was told, 'he had some work to do on the Black'. The sight of Uncle Fred on his motorbike with his sidecar jammed full of apples remains with me to this day. He wore a leather flying type helmet and goggles, a long worsted overcoat and there was so much weight in the sidecar that he drove away with his body and the bike tilting at a precarious angle.

We East End kids never played with the local children; perhaps they thought of us as urchins and ruffians, whatever, it was a case of never the twain shall meet. We kept ourselves to ourselves. We had our own identity of which we were very proud and, of course, our own way of doing things and our own language. In sitting down to write my autobiography, I have found myself remembering some things that I have not thought about for years, others that I never gave any thought to at all. In recalling the days spent hopping, it occurred to me that I no longer hear many of the phrases and expressions my parents and fellow East Enders once used. The East End has changed, the people have changed and so too has their language. When emphasising a point, people would conclude by saying, 'and well you know it'. A father's mild admonishment of his son would end with the dad saying, '. . . now, go on, hop along'. When someone had been asked his opinion, usually on what should be done on a matter, he would end with, 'and I can't say fairer than that'. On hearing news that met approval – 'And a good job too.' Whereas indecision about a matter would produce 'Well, I don't rightly know.' Surprising news – 'Well, I'll be blowed.' The female response to an apology given for a minor indiscretion – 'Doesn't matter, I'm sure.' Such phrases were common to the everyday language of East Enders; they helped give us our identity and were, I suppose, part of the reason we were thought of as 'Chirpy Cockneys'. Many East Enders may have been rough and ready, but in the presence of children adults never swore. The fact that I no longer hear the sort of expressions mentioned above is proof to me that the East End I knew as a child has long since gone. Perhaps the demise of that culture and its people was in part started by families such as ours, who had, in stages, gradually moved away from the heartland of the East End. Whatever, London's East End is all so different now from what it used to be. BBC TV's *EastEnders* came along thirty years too late.

For all it was dusty and dirty, hard, often arduous work, I loved our annual summer holiday. I will never forget some of the images of hopping. Hop vines, hanging heavy with their crop, coated in the dew of an early September morning. The staggered line of bushel baskets, each tilting at a jaunty angle, that flanked each row of vines. Women and children, their faces contorted by the sheer effort of carrying a full load, heading towards an even larger basket where the tallyman would make his note of who had picked what. Hands so black they looked as if they had been dipped in printer's ink. Though the staining of the hops turned hands to ebony, this only served to accentuate the palm lines, so that the palms of the pickers resembled a Victorian map of the railway network of South East England. The red-brick farmhouse, so weathered it gave the impression of having been faded by years of continual sunlight to a pleasant shade of orange rose.

The work was labour intensive and there was little in the way of motorised transport or mechanisation on the farm. At the rear of the farm was a row of stables, all in the same agreeable shade of brick, where horses were kept. Above them was a row of lofts that were full of ancient bedsteads, hip baths, frayed hop baskets, some beer jars, rusting scythes and mottled poles with gnarled hooks that had been stored indefinitely, rather than thrown away, by the hop farmer and his wife over the course of their, quite literally, fruitful years.

When not playing football for my school on a Saturday morning, I loved to go to the cinema. In Barkingside alone there were six cinemas, the most popular being the ABC, the

Odeon and the Gaumont. With no television except for a privileged few, the Saturday morning trip to the pictures was the only time we kids ever saw cartoons. At the ABC Saturday morning viewing consisted of, to begin with, cartoons such as Mickey Mouse, Donald Duck and Felix the Cat, followed by an adventure serial that always concluded with a cliffhanger to encourage you to come back the following week. More often than not, there would also be a Laurel and Hardy short, or a Flash Gordon adventure, the latter always with an alliterative and evocative title such as 'The Planet of Peril', 'The Tunnel of Terror' or 'Captured by Shark Men'. Even more memorable and just as alliterative was Flash Gordon's main enemy – Ming the Merciless of Mongo, who was to Flash what Moriarty was to Sherlock Holmes.

The morning's entertainment was always rounded off with a film usually made by the Children's Film Foundation, whose output was prodigious. These films lasted about three quarters of an hour and always featured kids in the lead roles. The subject of the stories invariably concerned kids creating their own entertainment, such as a soap box derby or a concert. The line 'There's an empty barn, we can put the show on there' was always the mainstay of the latter. When they weren't devising their own entertainment, the kids would stumble across the hideaway of a gang of criminals or spies, which led them to i) Solving a mystery that had baffled the police, or ii) Saving the nation. Gripping stuff that always had me, as a ten-year-old, on the edge of my seat. As a member of what were called the ABC Minors, I was given what in those days was considered by us kids to have only marginally less value than a ruby – a luminous ABC Minors badge. The badge was round with a red triangle and set boldly within that were the letters ABC in vivid lime green. In the dark of the cinema, the luminosity of the badge came into its own, so that viewed from the front of the cinema, the audience of kids appeared like fireflies. The Saturday morning picture session was hosted by the manager of the cinema, who always alluded to himself as your uncle, and was punctuated by community singing to the accompaniment of the cinema organ that rose from the depths of the pit. Every cinema had its own club song and to this day I can still remember every word of a song the ABC Minors used to sing, with great gusto, to the tune of the military march, 'Blaze Away':

> We are the boys and girls well known as
> Minors of the ABC
> And every Sat-ur-day all line up
> To see the films we like and shout aloud with glee.
> We like to laugh and have our sing-song
> Just a happy crowd are we-eee
> We're all pals to-gether
> We're Minors of the ABC!

Because the words never changed, the song was easy to sing. It has remained with me to this day and I suspect there's many a person of forty or over who can rattle it off just as easily as I can.

I became captain of the school team and in my senior years was made head boy. My best pal was a lad called Dave Emerick, still a very good friend to this day. I would later be best man at his wedding and, when Dave married for a second time, I was a witness. While I played football and cricket in the summer, Dave proved himself to be a very good athlete, something he continued into adult life. To date, Dave has competed in over eighty marathons.

For all it was a secondary modern school, I received, to my mind, a good education at Kingswood. The curriculum covered maths, English, geography, history, science, PE, religious studies and, in my final years, woodwork. Woodwork was considered by the school to be a bit of a luxury, a reward for good behaviour. I have to say it was wasted on me. I'm not a practical person. I can change a light bulb and fix a plug, but that's about the limit of my practical skills. My *pièce de résistance* from two years of woodwork lessons was a teapot stand and a very dodgy stool, too small to be of any practical use. Such were my skills in woodwork that when I took them home my dad had trouble working out which was which.

With no television at home my daily source of entertainment was the wireless. I say daily because every evening at 6.45 I could be found sitting in front of the wireless ready for another adventure with 'Dick Barton – Special Agent'. That fifteen minutes before seven o'clock was the only time, prior to bedtime, when no kids were to be found outside on Ivy House Road. Another popular radio series featured the Ovaltineys: a light, story-driven series which, as the title suggests, was a veiled promotion for Ovaltine under the pretence of being a club for young listeners. Ovaltine was promoted as a drink which helped you sleep; let's face it, which parent wouldn't buy a drink that not only helped their kids do that but also counteracted what they called 'night starvation', a phrase obviously dreamed up by Ovaltine's marketing johnnies. The notion was that kids asleep for eight hours were obviously not eating and eight hours without grub would make us wake up at some ungodly hour screaming for food. That was 'night starvation' and the answer to it was Ovaltine. It was all nonsense, of course, but parents who wanted wholesome drinks for their kids, and didn't want their own sleep interrupted, went for Ovaltine in a big way. Why they called it Ovaltine was a constant source of mystery to me. After all, the tin was round and so was the mug you drunk it from.

I wasn't the only member of our family fascinated by the wireless. Dad was always fiddling with it. On the front of the wireless was a glass plate and on that plate, according to their respective frequency, were the names of certain radio stations. The only British stations on offer were the Light Programme, the Third Programme and the Home Service, all supplied by the BBC and the forerunners of what are now radios Two, Three and Four. Another radio station whose name always appeared on the front plates of wirelesses was Hilversum. I now know that to be in Holland but as a child Hilversum was another source of mystery to me. I didn't have a clue what it was or where it was and, for all Dad's attempts to locate it, never did find out. When he wasn't trying to tune into Hilversum, Dad would take the back off the radio and probe the mind-boggling network of wires, bulbs and circuits. He spent hours fiddling with that wireless, even when there was nothing wrong with it. In pre-barbecue days, fiddling with the wireless was how the man of the house asserted his position in the family. The provider of money and food also felt he had to be the provider of entertainment. On a Sunday morning, I'd walk with Dad to a football pitch behind the Merry Fiddlers pub in Dagenham. This was a weekly pilgrimage. There was no official Sunday football in England because the FA refused to sanction it, but there were quite a number of Sunday sides in our area who initially played friendlies against one another before forming an unofficial league. There were a lot of very good players on show and, for Sunday morning teams, the standard of football was surprisingly high. I used to love standing next to Dad and his mates listening to their banter as they passed judgement on one player or another. Through those Sunday morning trips to the Fiddlers I not only learned about football, but developed a sense of humour.

Though West Ham United was not very far away from our home, I rarely went to Upton Park. In fact as a boy I never went to see any of the big London teams such as Arsenal, Spurs or Chelsea. I preferred to watch one of the many top amateur teams whose grounds were only a bus ride from where I lived. There were four major amateur leagues in the London area – Isthmian, Athenian, Spartan and Corinthian. I don't know the origins of these leagues, but their classical names suggest they were formed in the early twentieth century by former public school boys.

The Isthmian League contained teams such as Walthamstow Avenue, Wycombe Wanderers, Wimbledon, Dulwich Hamlet, Ilford, Barking, Leytonstone and Clapton. The latter four were within reasonable travelling distance for me. The Athenian League contained a lot of teams from north London, such as Finchley, Hendon, Enfield and Barnet, but I saw a lot of games in this league because Leyton were also members. As the Spartan and Corinthian Leagues primarily comprised teams from west London and the Home Counties, they were out of my range, though by way of the occasional trip to Ford Sports I did manage to see a few Spartan League matches. Attendances for the top clubs at this level were very healthy. You'd get a crowd of around 3,000 when Ilford played Wimbledon or Walthamstow Avenue. On one occasion, when Ilford Boys played Swansea Boys in the English Schools Trophy Final, there was a crowd of 17,000. The mark of how popular football at this level was with supporters can be taken from attendance of the Amateur Cup Final itself, which in the fifties was always a 100,000 sell out at Wembley.

In 1952, when I was thirteen, Leyton played Walthamstow Avenue in the Amateur Cup Final at Wembley. Avenue took a very strong team to Wembley trained by two fine coaches, Jim Lewis, an old Avenue player, and Freddie Cox, who was a successful player with Arsenal and didn't see his charges in action at Wembley because he was playing for the Gunners that day against Manchester United at Old Trafford. Jim Lewis was at Wembley and so too was another Jim Lewis, his son, who was the Avenue centre forward. The Avenue were without their inspirational inside left, Ron Horsley, who had a cartilage injury. Horsley's place had been taken by a twenty-year-old lad, Dennis Hall, who only had five first team games under his belt. Walthamstow Avenue won 2-1 after extra time and when the victorious Avenue players returned to their dressing room, something happened that for me characterises the sporting nature of amateur football at this time. Dennis Hall had scored the winner for Avenue in front of 100,000 spectators at Wembley. To have an Amateur Cup winner's medal was the dream of every player at this level, but when he got to the dressing room Dennis handed his to the injured Ron Horsley whose goals had been so instrumental in Avenue reaching Wembley.

'Here you are, Ron,' said Dennis. 'It's really your medal. I was just glad to be called on to help out.'

Only recently I heard a TV pundit say that with the advent of the Premiership, improved facilities for spectators and television's coverage of the game, football today is more of a sporting spectacle than it was years ago.

In recent years football has changed irrevocably. I wouldn't say it's any better or any worse than the game I knew as a boy and a player. It is just very, very different. If there is one thing I mourn the passing of, it is the simplicity of football gone by. I miss the simple ways and pleasures I knew as a child. Football has always reflected society and it occurs to me that everything about the game, and about life, was much simpler then. Although computers, the Internet, mobile phones and texting are supposed to make life easier for us, to my mind they've just made it more complex. For all their apparent sophistication, I still think there is a lot to be said for the simple things I knew as a boy.

Comics were king when I was a child. Most popular amongst us kids were the *Beano*, *Dandy*, *Topper* and *Beezer* from which, as we grew older, we graduated to *Rover*, *Hotspur* and

Wizard. With ten grandchildren I occasionally see kids' comics nowadays. The most striking difference between contemporary comics and those I knew as a boy is not only the content, which in keeping with the times is more sophisticated now, but the nature of the contents. For all that *Rover*, *Hotspur* and *Wizard* did contain comic strips, a surprising amount of their content was solid text. I don't know how many ten-year-olds of today would happily sit down and read a short story of four pages of small print, illustrated by a single line drawing, but at that age I certainly did. The stories in comics such as *Rover* or *Wizard* were high on adventure, often about the war and had titles that made your eyes pop, such as 'The Tankbusters of "B" Troop', or, 'The Day the Earth Was Invaded by Shark Men' all as enticing as those Flash Gordon titles at the cinema.

As well as adventure stories every comic always had a football story. The most famous, of course, was 'Roy of the Rovers' in *Tiger*. Roy first appeared in 1954 and played regularly for Melchester Rovers until *Tiger* disappeared from the newsstands in 1994. If Roy made his debut as a sixteen-year-old in 1954, that means he was fifty-six when he finally hung up his boots. Not a bad career. While 'Roy of the Rovers' tried to portray the reality of life as a footballer and what went on behind the scenes of a club, albeit in an idealistic way, rival comics made no such concessions. The football stories in *Rover* and *Wizard* were quite literally fantastic. One of my favourites was 'The Mysterious Hooded Centre Forward of Hodnet Town'. Whenever Hodnet Town were in trouble in a game, out from the crowd would appear a mystery player whose identity was never known because he wore a black hood. As soon as he appeared, the Hodnet manager would whip off the regular centre forward and on would come the mysterious hooded player who would go on to turn the game around by scoring a hatful of goals. Hodnet's regular centre forward never complained about being yanked off every week and the opposition never took umbrage either. I never questioned why, when substitutes were not allowed in football, this mystery man could leap from the crowd and take part in a game. I just accepted it. Such was my naivety, but then again most people were very naive in those days, adults included. One of the most popular programmes on the wireless was *Educating Archie* which featured the ventriloquist Peter Brough and his dummy, Archie. How naive can you get? A ventriloquist on the wireless! From time to time, the comics we read would contain a free gift, invariably something simple. The 'banger' was a popular comic giveaway and was no more than a triangular piece of brown paper which you held at one corner then, with a sharp turn of the wrist, flicked. The triangle of brown paper would suddenly open, in so doing making a mini sonic boom, hence the name. Another toy was a rubber parachutist whose hands were connected with fine cotton to a small plastic parachute. We kids would spend countless hours chucking these parachutists in the air simply to watch them float back down again. Invariably the time would come when they didn't, and for years after there'd be the sight of numerous rubber parachutists hanging forlornly from the telephone wires that increasingly cut across the streets of east London. Another popular toy was the diver in a bottle. This was a tiny toy frogman, with a small hole in his stomach into which you put bicarbonate of soda. You then popped him into a bottle of water and he would proceed to float up and down. We had endless hours of pleasure with these simple, unsophisticated toys.

Whatever the other pleasures, it was always football for me. As soon as one school match ended, I couldn't wait for the next one to come along. For me, the worst thing that could happen was for there to be bad weather which resulted in the school game being postponed. For all that I was to enjoy a very successful career as a professional footballer, some of those school games have stuck in my mind, particularly one match for Kingswood against Eastbrook school. I was a member of a very good Kingswood team that won everything and swept most other school teams aside. For some reason, this game at Eastbrook kicked off late. As the game progressed me and my team-mates became increasingly concerned that we were going to miss our bus home and we voiced our concerns to the master who was refereeing. One by one, he dismissed the boys who had to catch the bus. With five minutes of the game remaining we only had five players left on the field, but still ended up winning the match 6-2!

Though subject to discipline both at home and at school, when I now look back at my childhood my overriding impression is one of great freedom of movement. I went out to play here, there and everywhere, and as far as I am aware my mum and dad never worried unduly about my safety the way many parents do today. Of course, there must have been horrible people about in those days and perhaps, because we did not have the media network we have nowadays, their evil deeds didn't receive nationwide attention. Though I spent much of my childhood playing outdoors, often a good distance from my own front door, I never came across anyone wanting to harm me and I never heard any of my pals who did either.

In my final year at Kingswood in 1955 I had trials for both Essex and London Schoolboys. This fuelled my desire to play football for a living, though my dad was keen for me to take up a trade. Jobs were plentiful then and with the prospect of good exam results my dad believed I would have no problem being taken on as an apprentice plumber or joiner. He was probably right, but as I have said I am not the most practical of people and the thought of learning a trade didn't appeal to me.

Besides, I knew I wouldn't make a very good joiner or plumber. I assume Dad realised this as well, because one day he came home, told me he had had a word with a friend of his and that there was a job at *The Times* as a compositor that was mine for the taking. I paid lip service to Dad's aim for me, but when a Chelsea scout showed an interest in me after a game for Essex Schoolboys, there was only one career for me.

That scout was Jimmy Thompson, a diminutive man who always wore a bowler hat, an anachronism even in the mid-fifties. Jimmy was a larger than life character who, because he had run foul of the football authorities on a number of occasions for poaching young players, used a variety of aliases. When he approached me, he told me his name was Mr Pope, though I soon found out his real name. Jimmy earned his living scouting for young players and by placing bets for racehorse trainers and jockeys as they, of course, weren't allowed a flutter. West Ham United and Tottenham Hotspur had also shown an interest in me, but for all my dad had great reservations about me taking up football as a career Jimmy just wouldn't take no for an answer and kept turning up on our doorstep.

In 1955 I played for London Schoolboys at White Hart Lane. It was a game in which a young lad by the name of David Cliss stood out head and shoulders above everyone else. By comparison I had a quiet game, which served to make me think perhaps Dad was right after all. A few weeks after this game I was due to leave school. Dad told me he had arranged an interview for me at *The Times*. Jimmy Thompson, however, had other ideas. One afternoon he turned up outside our house in a blood-red Sunbeam Talbot. Although it was his car, Jimmy couldn't actually drive and his daughter was at the wheel. He asked if I would 'go up town' with him and his daughter for a chat, which I readily agreed to do. They took me up West, to the Strand Palace Hotel where we had afternoon tea. I'd never been in such a grand place before and was mightily impressed and not a little overawed by the surroundings and clientele. Jimmy told me that Chelsea were very keen to sign me and that should I be keen too, he would have a word with my dad to straighten things out. I told him I was keen and when we got home Jimmy had a long chat with Dad. The end result of which was that Dad agreed to let me give it a go at Chelsea. As he left, Jimmy reached into his car and presented me with a brand new pair of football boots.

'Tools of your new trade,' he said.

I was embarking on a trade after all.

A couple of days later, Jimmy called again to tell me everything had been sorted out with Chelsea and that I was to report in two weeks' time, at nine o'clock on Monday morning, underneath the big clock in Liverpool Street station. We would go to Stamford Bridge from there.

Come the day, I caught the train to Liverpool Street feeling very excited and not a little self-important. That self-importance quickly evaporated however when I got off the train and walked along the platform to the big clock. There were seven other young lads standing there, a number of whom I recognised from schoolboy representative games such as Ken Shellito, Mickey Block, Mel Scott, Brian Legge and Billy Wall. The sheer quality of these players made me realise I was about to embark on a very competitive career. I was just coming to terms with the fact I would no longer be a big fish in a little pond when another lad walked up and joined us: David Cliss, who had dominated my last London Schoolboys game at White Hart Lane. I thought I was going to be the only lad meeting Jimmy Thompson that morning but a word with the others established they too thought the same thing. Eventually Jimmy himself appeared and, after counting heads, led us down to the Underground and on our way to our first day at Chelsea.

When we arrived at Stamford Bridge, we followed Jimmy into the club office.

'Here they are,' Jimmy announced proudly, 'here's your future. Drake's ducklings.'

Drake's ducklings was a reference to the Chelsea manager, the former Arsenal and England centre forward, Ted Drake. We had all heard about Matt Busby's successful youth policy at Manchester United. The press had dubbed Busby's young charges 'The Busby Babes' and not to be outdone Jimmy gave his latest batch of young hopefuls the collective name 'Drake's Ducklings'. Given the name of the manager, this struck me as being more witty and appropriate a term than United's Busby Babes.

Once the paperwork had been processed by the Chelsea secretary John Battersby, Jimmy wished us all 'the best of luck' and went off to be paid. 1955–6: another season, another batch of young hopefuls discovered and brought to the club by the enigmatic Jimmy Thompson, the best scout since Baden-Powell.

CHAPTER TWO

SINGING THE BLUES

Perhaps because I had done well in my studies and exams at school, rather than being assigned to the Chelsea groundstaff I was set to work in the club office where I was to combine my duties as an office boy with training and learning my trade as footballer. I was paid £3 a week plus £2 accommodation money. As I was living at home, I was given a chitty which my mum had to sign before she received the accommodation expenses she was entitled to for my board and lodging. My £3 wage was taxed but after a few months working in the office I soon found ways to make an extra few bob.

At the time the Chelsea first team players used to have lunch in a restaurant called Annabel's which was situated on one side of the Bridge and considered quite a posh establishment. The rest of us headed for Charlie's, a steamy-windowed café where the one spoon for stirring tea was attached to a string on the counter. Charlie's served a smashing plate of bacon, eggs, sausages, beans and fried bread, the sort of daily meal to make Arsène Wenger pale and hardly the diet of a young footballer today. Every lunchtime I'd queue up behind a line of Chelsea reserves and youth team players patiently waiting for my turn with the spoon, until the last ration of sugar ran out and nobody had any need for the spoon any longer. The players were given luncheon vouchers with a face value of 2/6d (12½p) with which to pay for their lunch, and it wasn't long before I discovered the luncheon vouchers were valuable 'black market' currency.

It was part of my job as an office boy to help John Battersby and his assistant Harry Green to issue the luncheon vouchers. They never kept an accurate tally of how many they had and how many were being issued, so when one of the Chelsea first team players, John 'Snozzel' Sillett, approached me with a scheme to make a few bob for myself, I fell in with him.

'I'm not suggesting for one moment that you steal them,' John told me. 'Them luncheon vouchers are imprisoned in that office. I want you to help me liberate them.'

Liberate them I did. John and his brother, the first team full back Peter Sillett, took me under their wing at the club. For want of a better phrase they showed me the ropes, telling me what to do and what not to do in order to get on at Chelsea and in football in general. The luncheon voucher 'liberation' was merely an extension of that. I'd slip John and Peter a few luncheon vouchers every now and again in return for a few bob. John and Peter would then trade the vouchers down at Charlie's at less than their face value for fags. All in keeping with the notion of footballers as consummate athletes! On arriving at the office every morning, my first job would be to run to Charlie's and buy forty Senior Service for John Battersby. Many was the time Snozzel would waylay me, giving me forty Seniors in return for the cash John Battersby had given me for his fags. Chelsea Football Club? It was more like Harry Lime's post-war Vienna.

Another part of my job in the office was to make tea for the office staff and other club officials. The day centre forward Bobby Smith was transferred to Spurs, I ferried tea and biscuits to the board room as Ted Drake, the Spurs manager Jimmy Anderson and respective club officials thrashed out the deal. I made a point of dawdling in the board room when serving tea in order to eavesdrop. Back in the office was a gang of first team players who wanted to know how much Spurs were paying for Bobby. This was the era of the maximum wage, which at the time was set at £16. Some of the Chelsea first team were on less because the club was always pleading poverty. What these first team players wanted to know was Bobby's real fee, not the one the club might put out to the press. That way, those not on the maximum wage whose contracts were due for renewal would know how much of a rise they could push for.

Chelsea was very much a family club where everyone mucked in. For example, quite a number of players, myself included, helped out with the installation of the club's first floodlights. You just can't imagine that happening at a Premiership club today! Not being a practical person, my assistance was more of a hindrance. One day, when helping lay electric cable, I backed the cable through the office window causing all kinds of damage, an action that prompted dear old John Battersby to suggest I concentrate on my office duties and football. 'You're just not cut out for manual work, are you, Jimmy?' he said. Too right I wasn't.

The erection of floodlights was a major step forward for Chelsea. Not only did floodlights allow the club to stage midweek matches at night, as opposed to a Wednesday afternoon when attendances were affected because people were at work, it also allowed the club to play more money spinning friendlies against continental opposition. Chelsea were among the first English clubs to have floodlighting, but even in 1955 floodlights were nothing new. They were commonplace on the Continent and the first ever match to be played under (temporary) floodlights in England had taken place at Highbury in 1878, but for one reason or another the idea of floodlit football was never taken up. That famous Arsenal manager of the 1930s, Herbert Chapman, was all for floodlit football but he was unable to persuade the Football League and the Football Association to take up the idea. Seeing as Arsenal had been long-time advocates of floodlit football, it was somehow fitting that the first official match to be staged under floodlights in England took place at Highbury in the 1951–2 season when the Gunners played a friendly match against the Israeli team Hapoel Tel Aviv. A crowd of over 44,000 turned up to see that game and a month later 62,000, with 10,000 locked out, descended on Highbury for Arsenal's floodlit friendly against Glasgow Rangers. What made Arsenal's matches against Hapoel Tel Aviv and Rangers important was that floodlighting was on official trial. Officials of the Football League, FA and Scottish FA came along to watch this 'new' phenomenon with a view to then forming working committees that would look at the feasibility of every club installing floodlights. Seventy-three years after an experimental football match had taken place in this country under floodlights, and eighteen years after Herbert Chapman had campaigned for their use, the FA and Football League finally came round to the idea! Better late than never I suppose.

As John Battersby had told me, I wasn't cut out for manual work. What I did feel I was cut out for, however, was football. More to the point, scoring goals, which I found came easy to me. The Chelsea Youth team played in the South East Counties League against the youth teams of other League clubs such as Spurs, Arsenal, West Ham, Fulham and Charlton. The Chelsea fourth team, or juniors as they were known, played in the Hornchurch and District League against the teams of boys clubs such as Upminster YC, Glendale, Central Park and Chadwell Rovers. For some reason I more or less skipped the fourth team, playing fewer than a handful of games at that level, and played the majority of my emerging football in the South East Counties League. As a raw-boned fifteen-year-old I did rather well in the goalscoring stakes. In my first season with Chelsea in 1955–6, I scored fifty-one goals. The following season I created a South East Counties goalscoring record when I netted 122.

We walked that league and little wonder: we had a cracking side. Not far behind me in the goalscoring stakes was Barry Bridges, who would go on to enjoy a fine career with Chelsea and Birmingham City and win four caps for England. Also in that team was the mercurial David Cliss, who had given clear evidence of his outstanding ability in my final game for London Schoolboys at White Hart Lane. At right back we had Ken Shellito, a very classy player who became a mainstay of the Chelsea team that enjoyed so much success in the sixties and early seventies. Our centre half was Mel Scott, a tall, imposing pivot and a very good passer of the ball who would also enjoy a fine career at Stamford Bridge before moving on to Brentford. Mickey Block, Mike Harrison and Brian Legge, for all that their impact in the Chelsea first team would be limited, also enjoyed fruitful careers at other clubs, most notably Mickey, who was to become a firm favourite with Brentford fans.

We enjoyed some outstanding results in my first season as a youth team player and the following season was no different. We played our home matches on the Welsh Harp ground, which was situated near Staples Corner in Hendon. The youth team manger was Dickie Foss, a former Chelsea player himself who was a good old boy. More often than not when arriving for a match I'd find Dickie sitting on the bench outside the Welsh Harp pub enjoying a pint. 'My front office' he used to call it. 'I only drink twice a day,' Dickie once told me. 'When I'm thirsty and when I'm not.'

Dickie Foss may have liked his beer, but he loved his football and had a profound knowledge of the game. I learned a lot from him, as did every other Chelsea Youth team player.

If you watch a match involving a Premiership youth side today, you can see four, sometimes five people on the sidelines, each with a role in running the team. At Chelsea there was just Dickie Foss. He trained us, managed us, coached us, attended to our injuries during a match, put out the strips and gathered them up again at the end of a game, and we won just about every competition we entered. More importantly, many of that youth side made it into the first team, which is after all the main aim of any youth policy.

Under Dickie, between 1954–5 and 1964–5 the Chelsea Youth team won the South East Counties League every season but one. There was also success in the South East Counties Cup and the Southern Junior Floodlit Cup. The one trophy that eluded Dickie in my time with the youth team was the FA Youth Cup, though we did go close to winning it. The FA Youth Cup first saw the light of day in 1952–3 and was the brainchild of the then Football League President Joe Richards. Though the competition was new, the trophy wasn't. It was donated to the FA by the Football League who had bought it during World War Two but never used it. For the first six years of its life, the FA Youth Cup had been won every season by Manchester United, but in 1957–8 United's run of success was finally broken when we contested the final with Wolverhampton Wanderers. The final was played over two legs on a home and away basis, as it still is today. I think we created FA Youth Cup history because, having won the first leg at a canter 5-1 at Stamford Bridge, we contrived to lose the second leg 6-1. Our goals in the first leg came from Mike Harrison (2), Mickey Block, Barry Bridges and yours truly. We thought the FA Youth Cup was all but won, but we were to be given a salutary football lesson in the return leg at Molineux. Our goalkeeper Barry Smart had been a virtual spectator at Stamford Bridge, but in the return leg he was a very busy lad indeed against a rampant Wolves side. We couldn't get hold of the ball. The Wolves attacks came in waves and their centre forward Ted Farmer (excuse the pun) had a field day. Farmer scored four, his team six in all and we lost 7-6 on aggregate. The fact that I had scored our consolation goal was no consolation to me at all. To a man, we were gutted. Not only because we had let what appeared to be an unassailable lead slip, but also because we felt we had let the club and its supporters down, and in particular Dickie Foss.

Dickie was never one to throw tea cups around the dressing room, or bawl out certain players. Though obviously as disappointed as we were, after the second leg he was his usual calm, philosophical self. Perhaps more so than usual. Though he did tell us some home truths.

'Lesson one,' he said, 'it ain't over 'til the ref blows. We come here, it was really only half-time, but you buggers thought you had it won. All them big wins before. The big crowd [there was nigh on 50,000]. You're all getting too big for your boots. Lesson two, never go out on to a football pitch with your big heads on! That's all I gotta say on it.'

Our defeat at the hands of Wolves created the first sense of insecurity in my career. Since I had first started playing for my school, I had known nothing but success, both as an individual and as part of a team. What's more, most of that success had been achieved more or less at a canter. Like the school and representative teams I had played for, the Chelsea Youth side invariably swept the opposition aside. I had the winning habit all right, but as with my Chelsea team-mates the ease with which we beat most teams had turned healthy confidence into a lax attitude. No matter how good a player you are, that will always spell disaster on the football field. No matter how much we dominated games, the opposition would always have a little ten-minute spell where they took the game to us. If in that spell they scored a goal, or even two, it never bothered us because we were confident we'd score four or five in reply.

That had been the pattern for just about every game I had played up to that second meeting with Wolves. Again, like my Chelsea team-mates I had it in my head that that was how football was. In the naivety of youth, we believed we would simply carry on trouncing teams. The return match with Wolves proved a real eye-opener. It was a watershed in my fledgling career. In terms of football I realised I had been living a cosseted existence. In losing to them 6-1 I not only realised that we were far from being the best youth team in the land, but also that because Wolves had turned around a four-goal deficit, their players had a mental strength, character and determination that, thanks to overconfidence, our team lacked. And I include myself in that.

Losing the FA Youth Cup Final in such circumstances had a significant bearing on me as a footballer. It was the first time the reality of football has been brought home to me. I realised there and then that, no matter how good a player you think you are, irrespective of the quality of the team you play in you have to work at the game and be on your mettle for each and every match. That skill and physical fitness is only a part of it. That both those attributes can be rendered nigh on useless unless you also possess mental fitness. For me, our defeat against Wolves was a lesson in the learning. After that FA Youth Cup Final I always took to the pitch with the right attitude, fully mentally tuned to the task ahead.

The club was very disappointed we had failed to win the FA Youth Cup, in particular our manager, Ted Drake, whose disappointment, I learned, had much to do with the fact that he didn't get on with the Wolves manager Stan Cullis. Consolation for Ted, the club and Dickie Foss in particular came two years later when Chelsea eventually won the FA Youth Cup by beating Preston North End with a side that included Peter Bonetti, Terry Venables, Bobby Tambling and Bert Murray, all of whom went on to enjoy fine careers with

Chelsea. By way of a bonus for Dickie, Chelsea then retained
the Youth Cup in 1960–61 with a fine win over a very talented
Everton Youth team.

The words spoken by Dickie Foss after our heavy defeat at
Wolves hit the nail on the head. We had been used to sweeping
teams aside by big scorelines and, four goals to the good after
the first leg, we thought we only had to turn up at Molineux to
collect the trophy. When I say we won games by big scorelines,
I mean big. In the preceding season, 1956–7, my second year
at Chelsea, our goalscoring feats as a team were phenomenal.
We started the season in the South East Counties League
modestly enough with a 2-0 win over West Ham. What
followed, however, was nothing short of remarkable. We then
beat Spurs 11-1, Watford 8-0, Millwall 5-0, QPR 9-0,
Bexleyheath 12-0, Portsmouth 10-0, Fulham 6-1, QPR 6-0,
Charlton 8-0, Crystal Palace 7-3, Arsenal 6-2, Brentford 12-1
and 8-2, Fulham 9-0 and Millwall 10-0, a set of results that
were interspersed with victories of more modest nature, such
as 1-0 against West Ham and 3-0 against Portsmouth. In the
South East Counties League Cup it was no different.

In the two-legged first round we beat non-League
Bexleyheath 9-0 and 7-0, and in round two Arsenal 6-0 and 6-1.
Though we were to be beaten by Arsenal in round four of the
FA Youth Cup, the earlier rounds saw us enjoy 10-1 victories
over both Fulham and Peterborough United and an 8-0
success at the expense of Southend United. In the Southern
Junior Floodlit Competition, similar handsome victories were
posted, most notably against QPR (6-1), Luton Town (5-0)
and Charlton (9-0). I found myself amongst the goals in
no uncertain manner, thanks to excellent service from my
team-mates. I was in my element, banging in goal after goal.
I found it came easy to me and remember Dickie Foss once
telling me, 'The genie's outta the bottle. Who's to know what
you can go on and achieve?'

I wasn't the only member of that Chelsea Youth team pulling up trees. We enjoyed the services of some of the most talented youngsters in English football at the time. Of all the players in that team, the one I thought would go on to make a big name for himself in the game was David Cliss. Oddly, though he did go on to play a number of games for the first team, David never did.

Towards the end of the 1956–7 season Ted Drake called me into his office. I'd spent two years in the club office while playing for the youth team and I was about to find out if the club were going to offer me a full-time contract. I'd created a South East Counties League record by scoring 122 goals that season. I didn't think too much about that, the only thing occupying my mind was the hope that Ted Drake would offer me professional terms.

If a young player scored 122 goals in a single season today, his respective club would be falling over themselves to get him to sign on the dotted line. Agents would be beating a path to his door promising a Porsche and a weekly salary far in excess of what the average person earns in a year. In recognition of my efforts that season the club presented me with an illuminated address, which was unframed. As for awarding me a full-time contract, Ted Drake informed me he was undecided. I don't know if this was a ploy on Ted's part to ensure my feet stayed on the ground, but he said he wasn't 100 per cent sure about me and, if he did decide to offer me terms as such, there would be no signing on fee.

I was concerned. Some twelve months earlier Ted Drake had released a young player called Joe Baker. To my mind, Joe was a very good centre forward who had shown he had all the necessary to make it in the game. Ted obviously thought otherwise and this worried me. As it was to turn out, Ted was to be proved very wrong regarding Joe Baker. On being released by Ted, Joe Baker signed for Hibernian, from where he moved to Torino before coming back to England in a big money transfer that saw him join Arsenal. Joe also went on to play for Nottingham Forest and Sunderland and won eight caps for England. Football, as the guy standing next to you in the pub would no doubt disagree, is a game of opinions.

That Ted Drake didn't consider Joe Baker good enough to make the grade made me think that, for all my goals, he might think the same of me. Our meeting ended with Ted casting doubts on my ability to make it as a full-time professional and reiterating that if he did 'take a chance' on me there would be no signing on fee coming my way.

I was courting Irene at the time and had arranged to meet her outside the ground before going to the pictures. When I came out of Ted's office Irene was there waiting for me. We were walking across the club car park towards the bus stop when Jimmy Thompson pulled up in his Sunbeam – driven by his daughter as he still hadn't learned to drive. Pleasantries over, Jimmy sensed I was down and asked me what was the matter.

'It's Ted Drake. He don't wanna sign me,' I said.

Jimmy pulled the face of someone whose foot has just been run over by a steamroller while sucking on a lemon.

'Leave this to me,' he said, and leapt out of the car.

Jimmy had just returned from a horse racing trip to Ireland, but sensing my career could well be at the crossroads he told Irene and me to get into his car and made a beeline for Ted Drake's office. He meant business all right. Through one of the windows of the main office you could see the door of Ted's office. Jimmy marched straight in without even knocking. Ten minutes later, he came back out.

When he got back in the car, Jimmy told me 'there was no doubt about it'. I was definitely going to be awarded a full-time contract. Needless to say, I was delighted and not a little relieved. I suggested to Irene we skip the pictures and go home and tell my parents the news. Jimmy came with us and when I told Mum and Dad my news they were delighted. Especially when Jimmy told them I was to be paid £8 a week and £7 as a summer retainer.

'What about a signing on fee?' my dad asked. 'The boy's done enough to deserve one. Other clubs would pay it willingly.'

For a moment Jimmy was thrown, but it was obvious from the expression on his face that he knew Dad was right. Jimmy excused himself, went out to his car and when he returned gave my Dad a brown envelope.

'Signing on fee's in there,' said Jimmy.

When Jimmy left our house my dad opened the brown envelope. Inside was £50 – in Irish fivers.

Dad changed the money down at the bank, but the fact remains that Jimmy Thompson, the man who discovered me, paid my signing on fee out of his own pocket. I think.

At the end of that season, along with David Cliss, Barry Bridges, Mickey Wall and Mel Scott, I was added to a squad comprising a mixture of first team players and reserves for a tour of the Netherlands. It was my first trip abroad and, football apart, I was very excited at the prospect of seeing another country, and with it being Holland, of at last being able to tune in to Hilversum.

At the time the standard of Dutch football was nowhere near as high as it is today. Our squad contained a good quota of reserves and youth team players and we proved too strong for our opponents. Many of them, for all that they were top sides in Dutch football, were part-time professionals. I scored in our first game against PSV Eindhoven and netted twice in our second against Vitesse Arnhem. I didn't think too much of it and never for·one moment believed I was actually on the verge of breaking into the first team. I had, after all, only become a full-time professional a few weeks earlier.

On returning from our tour of Holland, like many other footballers of the time I took a summer job. Today there is effectively no close season for football, especially for our top players. The burgeoning World Cup and European Championships which take place every four years but respectively have a two year interval between them, the play-offs, the InterToto Cup and tours to the Far East to help generate commercial sales mean that many of today's players have no real break from competitive football except for a fortnight's summer holiday. But in 1957 the close season was very much as the name suggests. Players received a retainer during the summer break which was less than their normal weekly wage, so many took summer jobs to supplement their income. I spent eight weeks working on the shop floor of a local steel company in Hainault, which in itself exemplifies another era. A steel industry in Hainault!

After finishing work, most evenings I'd meet up with Irene. Irene and I had been courting for some months. As they do now, teenagers went around in groups and, though Irene was not one of our lot, I had seen her out and about with another group of young people we were on nodding terms with. One of my mates was conscripted into the army and we all went along to wave him off. As chance would have it, this lad also knew a few of the people Irene went about with, in particular, Maureen, Irene's younger sister by one year. Irene turned up at this lad's farewell and after it was over I asked if I could walk her home. That was the beginning of it. We were both seventeen, although like any other couple we've had our fair share of problems, forty-six years on we're still together, enjoying our life immensely and more in love than ever.

I can remember that first summer with Irene, 1957, particularly well. Myxomatosis reached epidemic proportions in the UK. I remember seeing rabbits lying all over country roads, either dead or in the throes of death. Rabbit had been very popular in the forties and fifties largely because of meat rationing. That summer, myxomatosis nigh on wiped them out. Rabbits' breeding habits being what they are, they of course came back in numbers, though to this day they have never come back as a popular source of meat. Myxomatosis put paid to that, which I suppose was a back-handed bonus for rabbits.

Irene and I spent a lot of time that summer going to the pictures or dancing at the many dance halls that existed then in the Dagenham area as there was still bugger all in the way of entertainment in Hainault. Few people owned a television, so the cinema was the place to go for entertainment. The big films that summer were *Twelve Angry Men*, and *Gunfight at the OK Corral*. It was also the summer when Oliver Hardy died. In those days a trip to the cinema was an experience in total entertainment. As well as the main film, there was also a B movie and a documentary-style magazine programme called *Look at Life* that featured such things as the making of shoes in Northampton or cider in Devon. There was also Pathé News which offered a digest of the news from the previous week. Pathé News was the only source of filmed news we had.

The bonus for me of watching Pathé News was that it often showed clips from football matches. Even if we had had a television, rarely did TV show a football match as the Football League and the FA believed even televised highlights would be detrimental to attendances. The only way to see football on any sort of screen was in the cinema courtesy of Pathé News. That summer, England beat Denmark 4-1 in Copenhagen and I readily recall seeing the goals and clips from that match at the cinema. This game marked the last appearance for England by Stanley Matthews, who at forty-two still gave the Danish defence the runaround. When I was a kid every boy interested in football aspired to be Stanley Matthews and I was no exception. He was *the* great footballer, *the* great footballing ambassador. Watching him weave his own particular brand of magic up there on the cinema screen, the furthest thought from my mind was that I would soon be playing against him. Furthermore, come his retirement, amazingly still some eight years away, the great man would invite me to play in his farewell game, his testimonial at Stoke City.

The summer of 1957 was idyllic, unless you were a rabbit that is. Madly in love with Irene, I was also looking forward to my first season as a professional at Chelsea. That summer, Bill Haley's 'Rock around the Clock', a number one hit the previous year, became the anthem of the Teddy Boys and further widened the gulf between young people and adults that became known as the generation gap. I was never a Ted, though I did adopt certain aspects of their dress that found their way into mainstream fashion. From my wages at the steel company I bought myself a pair of silver-buckled crepe shoes, though they were nowhere as garish as those worn by devout Teddy Boys. These shoes seemed more crepe paper than crepe rubber and were just about acceptable to Dad who frowned on the new fashions and anything related to Teddy Boys. My generation was the first to dress differently from their parents. The first to listen to a different form of music. We shunned parental favourites such as Dickie Valentine and Guy Mitchell for the new music, rock'n'roll. Many parents saw that as a sign of disrespect. Because we didn't want to wear the same clothes as our parents or listen to the same music, many of them felt that young people were shunning their lifestyle and all the principles and standards they held dear. They didn't realise we were simply exercising our rights to be individuals, albeit ones who dressed alike! Such a misunderstanding caused all manner of arguments within families. For the first time in society the young went their own way and it was a different one from their parents'. The prevailing attitude amongst many young people was that within reason we could do whatever we wanted in life. An attitude I was to take with me on to the football field.

When I returned to Chelsea I was subjected to a medical, and I was passed fit to begin pre-season training as a pro. Compared to the rigorous medicals that today's players undergo, which involve exploration of muscles, tendons and joints as well as measuring such things as cholesterol and heartbeat, the medical I underwent was cursory but par for the course at the time. My only other experience of medicals had been at school and they had consisted of either the nit nurse looking at my hair and fingernails or the 'cough and drop nurse', who simply held my testicles while asking me to cough. You don't get nit nurses visiting schools anymore, though as a grandparent I know you still get nits. As for the 'cough and drop nurse', I could never work out the reason for her visit. I suppose she came to make sure our testicles were hanging properly, but to this day I ain't sure why they had to know this. I mean, even if they weren't, what were they going to do about it?

The school nit nurse was not only on the lookout for nits, but for all sorts of other minor ailments which, happily, we don't see much of these days. When was the last time you saw anyone with a boil? In the fifties, boils were commonplace. They could be such a problem they even sidelined footballers. The most celebrated case – though no doubt he didn't celebrate it – involved Manchester City's Bill Spurdle. He was smitten with boils of such a debilitating nature that he was forced to pull out of City's FA Cup Final win over Birmingham City in 1956. Boils were such a common complaint, but not much was made of it at the time. Though I shudder to think what the headlines in the tabloids would be today if David Beckham missed out on a Cup Final because of boils.

There was a clearly defined pecking order regarding the players at Chelsea, and nowhere was this more obvious than where the players changed for training. Most training took place at Stamford Bridge, with the first team changing in the home team dressing room while the reserves and youth teams changed in the visitors' dressing room. You knew when you were making progress if you were told to change in the home team dressing room. Conversely, if you had been playing in the first team, you knew you were out of favour as soon as you were told to report to the visitors' dressing room. Such a situation created a 'them and us' attitude amongst the players and was, I am sure, detrimental to collective spirit.

After my medical, such as it was, I headed straight for the visitors' dressing room only to be told by our trainer, Albert Tennant, to 'move up to the home team dressing room'. This came as a big surprise to me. I'd done reasonably well on the club tour of Holland but never expected to be promoted to the first team squad.

I have to admit that at first I was a bit overawed to be in the company of such players as goalkeeper Reg Matthews, Peter Brabrook, John Mortimore, Ron Tindall, Derek Saunders, Les Stubbs, John McNichol, Frank Blunstone and Jim Lewis. The Sillett brothers I already knew! Chelsea had won the League Championship in 1954 and Saunders, McNichol, Stubbs, Lewis, Blunstone and Peter Sillett had all been members of that great team. They were heroes to me. I'd read about them, seen their photographs in *Charles Buchan's Football Monthly* and that mainstay of a boy's Christmas pillowcase, *The Big Book of Football Champions*. However, because of the 'them and us' situation that existed at the club, the Sillett brothers apart, I'd never had any contact with them. They were part of some fantastical, fictitious world.

We spent the first fortnight of pre-season training running around Battersea Park. We went on long runs and short runs.

We sprinted between trees. We ran up and down the steps of the monument and when Albert Tennant discovered a hill in the park, we ran up and down that as well. To break the monotony, we'd go down to the Chelsea Embankment, where we did more running.

The initial 'welcome back' over, we then played five-a-side games on the dog track behind the goals at Stamford Bridge and set about building strength and stamina by lifting weights. Then, in case any of us were suffering from withdrawal symptoms, we did more running.

Chelsea had forty-six full time pros at the time: eighteen in the first team squad and twenty-eight in the visitors' dressing room. The only sense of democracy was provided by the training. We all did the same.

The club was always pleading poverty, but compared to many it was somewhat of a go-ahead club, one that readily embraced new innovations and developments in the game. Chelsea's Championship success of 1954 coincided with the inauguration of the European Cup. As English First Division Champions, Chelsea readily accepted UEFA's invitation to take part in the first European Cup that was to be launched the following season. The club, and to his credit, Ted Drake, were all for European competition, not only because they saw it as a money-spinner, but primarily because they believed it was the way forward for football. In the first round Chelsea were drawn against the Swedish Champions, Djurgaarden, but the draw was as far as they got. The Football League and in particular the FA intervened and put pressure on the club to withdraw, which they eventually did. It was the considered opinion of the FA that the newly formed European Cup was an inconsequential distraction from the important business of our domestic league. One FA official of the time even went on record as saying that the European Cup was, 'a gimmick that will never catch on', an attitude typical of many who governed the game at the time, who believed England still to be the masters of world football, and that anything other than English football was of secondary importance. It's worth noting, especially in light of the current state of Scottish football, that the Scottish FA were all for this new European competition and gave full backing to the entry of the Scottish Champions, Hibernian. Hibernian did themselves and Scottish football proud in the inaugural competition, reaching the semi-finals where they were beaten by Stade de Reims of France, having beaten Chelsea's proposed first round opponents, Djurgaarden, along the way. There are very few questions in life that one can answer with a degree of certainty. Except, of course, the one on the front of a packet of Walker's crisps that asks, 'Is there a £20 note inside this packet?' No one can say for sure if Chelsea would have done well in the first European Cup, but given the quality of the team and the progress achieved by Hibernian, I'm inclined to think they would have done England proud.

Perhaps the club should have taken a firmer stance on this issue, stood their ground and argued their case and that of European football with the FA. Then things might have been so very different. In 1955–6 the Football League Championship was won by Manchester United and their manager Matt Busby locked horns with the FA on the subject of the European Cup. Busby was a man of vision. He realised that the post-war burgeoning of the commercial air industry meant Europe was shrinking, that travel between European countries was no longer the arduous task it had been pre-war, and that increased commercial flights would enhance the prospects for European competition. He also saw the European Cup as the way forward for football, whereby English clubs could learn new methods and technique. In short, that the European Cup would not only be a highly competitive competition, but a melting pot for the many new ideas that were coming into the game at the time on the Continent. Busby argued his case articulately and forcefully. Where Chelsea had given way to the FA on Europe, United stood firm. As a consequence, in 1956–7 Manchester United became England's first representatives in the European Cup and, like Hibernian the previous season, reached the semi-finals where they were narrowly beaten by the holders, Real Madrid.

Chelsea did, however, have some representation in the newly formed European competitions, though it was to be a tenuous one. In 1956–7, while I was learning my trade with the youth team, the first team skipper, Ken Armstrong and left back Peter Sillett were pioneers in Europe. The Inter-Cities Fairs Cup was the forerunner of the UEFA Cup. The 'Fairs Cup' as it was commonly known, was of secondary importance to the European Cup and was originally open to cities that had staged European Trade Fairs, hence the name. The 'Fairs Cup' was a bit of a dog's dinner to begin with because it comprised teams such as Barcelona, Birmingham City and FC Basle, along with representative teams from other cities such as London, Frankfurt and Copenhagen. The London team was a mixture of players from Arsenal, Spurs, West Ham, Fulham and Chelsea.

Ken Armstrong, who skippered the London team, and Peter Sillett flew the flag for Chelsea in Europe and though the players didn't know each other too well, the London XI did all right. Having seen off Basle and Frankfurt, they then beat Lausanne in the semi-finals. That pitched them against Barcelona. London drew the first leg 2-2 but were soundly beaten 6-0 in the return in Catalonia. Oddly, though not international games, the FA decided to award caps to any player who completed five appearances for the London XI. Ken Armstrong achieved this feat when he captained the side against Frankfurt, one month before hanging up his boots for good. The fact that Ken received a cap for playing for a

London XI and not England was considered by some at the time to devalue international caps. Knowing what collectors pay for items of football memorabilia these days, I should imagine the value today of Ken's unique cap would be anything but cheap.

I mention Ken and Peter's involvement with London and the Inter-Cities Fairs Cup because it was indicative of how Chelsea readily embraced the new innovations that were coming into the game at the time. In the same season, and for all my efforts to the contrary, Chelsea erected their floodlights and in March 1957 I went along to see them turned on for the first time, for a friendly game against Sparta Prague. It was quite a night. The club waited until most of the crowd were in place before switching on the lights and, when they did, a slack-jawed 'OH—!' resounded around Stamford Bridge from the 30,000 plus who had turned up to witness this auspicious occasion in the history of the club. What was arguably just as innovative was the decision by the club that season to fly the first team to certain away matches in the Football League. For reasons best known to themselves, the Football League chose to ban clubs from taking advantage of the domestic commercial flights that were now, quite literally, taking off around England. However, following requests from a number of clubs that they review the ban (in particular Chelsea and Manchester City) in March 1957, the Football League rescinded its ban on clubs flying to away games. Chelsea were the first to take advantage when they flew up to the North East for their Good Friday match against Newcastle United. The alternative to flying was an all-night trip back to London by train and, with it being Easter, Chelsea had a home match against Everton the next afternoon.

Chelsea's desire to take part in European competition, the willingness to release players for the Fairs Cup, the installation of floodlights and the pioneering trip to

Newcastle by air, all in the same season, contrived to make me believe I was part of a very go ahead and modern club with a fine future ahead of it. That was very much the case in 1957, but, in little over three years, such great ambition was to be turned on its head.

In keeping with most clubs in 1957–8, Chelsea started their pre-season with a public trial match and a series of internal matches, all of which were played on a single Saturday afternoon. These games were known as Blues v Whites, simply because one team would wear our first choice strip of blue, whereas the opponents would wear white shirts and shorts, the kit we wore away when there was a colour clash. The Blues v Whites pre-season run-out comprised three games, for which the Chelsea fans were charged an admission slightly less than that of a normal first team home match. The first game was a thirty minute match between teams comprising first year youth team players, new amateur signings and lads who had been offered a trial. The second match involved a mixture of reserve team players and established youth team players. The final game took place between two sides made up of first team and fringe players.

The gates would open at one o'clock and the crowd grew in number as the afternoon progressed. By the time the first team appeared a healthy crowd of some 15,000 had usually gathered. Some clubs called these internal though public pre-season games Possibles v Probables. They were useful run-outs for players eager to get a match of any sort under their belt after weeks of running, and supporters liked them because it gave them a chance to run their eye over and form an opinion of the talent, or lack of it, at their club. Besides, there was always the appeal to the supporters of being able to spot a diamond in the making. My eyes must have deceived me when I played in my first Blues v Whites game at Chelsea. I thought there were about 15,000 supporters in the ground, but judging from the number of people who, over the years, have told me they were present when I played in my first Blues v Whites match and were first to spot my emerging talent, the crowd must have been nigh on a quarter of a million.

I was selected to play in the game involving the first team players and fringe players. The game was only minutes old when I latched on to the ball just inside the opposition's half. I took it forward and heard Ted Drake shout 'Get rid!' I'd been used to dancing my way through defences in the South East Counties League and for all I was up against first team players I didn't think of doing anything different than trying to go it alone. I managed to sidestep a couple of tackles and was aware Ted Drake had left his seat on the bench and was standing on the touchline.

'Get rid of it. Get rid!' I heard him shout.

I carried on. An opponent came alongside me but I accelerated away from him.

Ted Drake was now running down the touchline tracking my progress.

'Get rid! For Gawd's sake pass the bloody ball!'

Centre half Ian McFarlane came across to check me, but I managed to sidestep him and found myself with only Reg Matthews to beat.

'Get rid! Pass the bloody ball!' the voice from the touchline bellowed.

Reg did what he had to do: he came rushing off his line to cut down my vision of the goal. I dropped my left shoulder, Reg went down and I swerved away to my right. It was a simple matter of rolling the ball into an empty net.

I turned and began to trot back to the halfway line and glanced across to the touchline. Ted Drake was standing, hands on hips a look on his face that appeared to me a mixture of frustration and disbelief.

'You never told me who to!' I shouted.

*

I felt I'd given a decent account of myself in the pre-season build up and had high hopes of being included in the reserves' first game of the season at home to Bournemouth. I had played just two games for the reserves in the previous season, scoring on both occasions, and though still only seventeen was keen to claim a regular place for myself in the Chelsea second string.

Players found out which team they'd been selected for after training on a Friday morning when Ted Drake pinned up the team sheets on the club noticeboard. Immediately after training, along with the rest of the lads I made a beeline for the noticeboard. I looked at the reserve team for the Bournemouth game and my heart sank. I wasn't in it. I then happened to glance at the first team line-up for the game at Tottenham Hotspur. I couldn't believe what I saw. There was my name, at inside right. I was seventeen, I'd played only twice for the reserves and was about to make my debut in the First Division, in a London derby against mighty Spurs. It was like kissing Jesus.

CHAPTER THREE

MAGIC MOMENTS

Should you ever be able to get near the players' car park on the day of a Premiership match (which sadly today's supporters can't) you would see a procession of Ferraris, Lamborghinis and Mercedes. Even young Premiership squad players own sporty, upmarket cars these days. On 24 August 1957, the day I made my first team debut for Chelsea at Spurs, I travelled to White Hart Lane first by Underground, then bus.

It would be unthinkable nowadays for a Premiership player to make his own way to an away match, even a London derby. In 1957, however, it was all so very different. Clubs had no anxieties about their players making their own way to nearby grounds for an away match. For a start, even top players in the First Division, though readily recognisable on the street, were not afforded star status. Though players didn't walk around in anonymity, their every step was not tracked by hordes of admirers and well wishers, fawning agents, image managers and certainly not by a rat pack of journalists and photographers from the tabloids. One of the differences between players then and now is that in the fifties clubs saw their players as commodities to be bought and sold. Today, the top clubs view their players as capital assets. The value of a player to a club appears on the balance sheet. As a consequence, clubs are much more protective towards their players. If a player is valued at ten million pounds or more, clubs feel the need to protect their asset. Even if a top player has come through the ranks, a club will have invested heavily in him, in time, coaching expertise, attention to diet, fitness and general wellbeing. For all that, the protection afforded to today's top players is understandable though sad. Where once players could have a chat and a laugh with supporters and build a relationship with the people who paid their wages, today's top players rarely get to meet ordinary fans. The gulf between modern stars and the supporters who watch them is vast. Because of their wealth, few of today's top players live in the same neighbourhood as their supporters. That, and the shepherding of players to and from grounds, has resulted in many of today's players losing touch with their supporters, and when people never meet that often results in distrust.

In the fifties, even in London, football was community based. Though subject to the maximum wage, footballers still earned more than the average working man, but the difference was nowhere near that of today. Players were held in some esteem, but our financial and social status was only marginally higher than that of many of the people who watched us play. Footballers in the fifties and sixties were not icons. We were not millionaire superstars. We were, to many, simply working-class heroes, and the vast majority of players derived great satisfaction from that.

As I made my way from the bus along Tottenham High Road and down Paxton Road to the players' entrance in the East Stand at White Hart Lane, I may have been working class but I was anything but a hero. I passed unnoticed amongst the supporters milling about on the streets. No one wished me luck. Not one said a word to me because no one knew who I was. Not even Chelsea fans apparently. When I arrived at the players' entrance, understandably the old guy on the door eyed the scrawny seventeen-year-old arriving on his own with some suspicion. As is the case with every player today, Chelsea had issued me with a club book for identification purposes. This book, which entitled the holder to admission to any ground, was about the size of a box of Swan Vestas and in addition to containing the holder's name and signature, verified by our secretary John Battersby, detailed both First Division and reserve team fixtures as well as the club rules for player conduct and training.

I produced my club book from my wallet and, with a raised eyebrow, the old guy stepped aside to allow me entry.

'I know what you're thinking,' I said. 'You know you're getting old when every season the players look younger.'

He huffed and nodded. 'I know I'm getting old when the popes look younger,' he told me. Although I profess to being a laid back guy, I have to admit that I was a bag of nerves when I first entered the Chelsea dressing room. I had confidence in my own ability but nagging away at the back of my mind was the thought that my ability might not be sufficient for me to make my mark against a very good Tottenham team. Spurs boasted players of the quality of Danny Blanchflower (who was to be marking me), Peter Baker, Maurice Norman, Tommy Harmer and Bobby Smith. When a player knows he's going to be up against quality opposition, what he invariably does is take a look around his own dressing room. Which is what I did. Getting changed alongside me were Reg Matthews, Peter Sillett, John Mortimore, Derek Saunders, Peter Brabrook and Ron Tindall. Seeing them made me feel a whole lot better. They were also quality players. I knew that I would receive good service and support; it would be down to me as to how well I was going to fare.

Generally, the higher the quality of his team-mates the better a footballer will play. Spurs were a quality team, but I had no real qualms about facing them because I knew we had players to match. I was down on the team sheet to play at inside right, but that's all I knew. Ted Drake hadn't spoken to me on the Friday to offer any words of advice, or to tell me what role he wanted me to play in the team. I had expected him to take me to one side in the dressing room and give me my instructions, but he never did. The in joke within the club was that Chelsea were the 'all the best' team, because invariably that was all Ted would say to the team before a game. He wasn't given to tactical talks, devising gameplans or informing players of any specific role he wanted them to fulfil in a game. That's no slight against Ted as a manager. Under him Chelsea had, after all, won the First Division Championship. Ted's hands-off approach to management was in fact typical of many managers of this time.

I remember Jack Charlton telling me the story of his debut for Leeds United, at the time managed by Raich Carter, one of the all time greats of English football. As a player in the thirties and forties, Raich Carter proved himself to be a supreme entertainer. He was a stylish artist whose brushes were his perfectly weighted and incisive passes and whose canvas was the pitch. In the colours of Sunderland, Derby County and Hull City he proved himself to be the most mercurial of inside forwards. He wasn't a workaholic, far from it. He often took to the pitch with a casual air and maintained the pose throughout many a match. He had supreme confidence in his own ability and what ability he had. He didn't try to cover every blade of grass on the pitch, he made the ball do the work for him. Carter possessed great vision and with the ball at his feet would dribble, dodge, twist and turn in the space of a hearthrug to send bewildered defenders sniffing madly along false trails. To look at him when he casually strolled out on to a pitch you'd never think that here was a player touched by football genius, though he definitely was. Possessor of the Midas touch on the pitch, as a manager Carter never really struck gold. As with me

on my debut for Chelsea, Jack Charlton was hopeful of
guidance from his manager when he made his debut against
Doncaster Rovers. As the minutes ticked away and five to three
came ever closer, the debutant Jack expected at any moment to
be approached by his manager. But Carter all but ignored him.
As the Leeds team left the dressing room, an anxious young
Jack seized the initiative.

'What do you want me to do, boss?' he asked.

Carter, at first startled that a player should be wanting
specific instructions, thought for a moment.

'See how fast their centre forward can limp,' he told Jack.

At least Jack Charlton was given some sort of instruction as
to what to do on his League debut. All Ted Drake said to me
as I left the dressing room was 'All the best.'

I followed the blue-shirted crocodile of team-mates along a
corridor where the noise of our studs on the wooden floor was
like a dozen cars with tappet trouble. We turned a corner and
before me, at the end of a cool tunnel with whitewashed walls,
was a rectangle of light. As I made my way down the tunnel
that rectangle of light grew bigger and bigger until I stepped
out on to the cinder track and it suddenly disappeared to be
replaced by the sight of White Hart Lane flooded in gold leaf
sunshine. I couldn't have wished for a finer setting for my
League debut. On the packed terraces the supporters stood at
ease in bright short sleeves or rayon blouses, enjoying the
banter that passed between the rival rattle squads. On seeing
the Chelsea team take to the pitch, those Blues fans present
roared their approval, whereas the Spurs fans delivered
nothing more than polite applause.

That's how I remember it. I don't think I'm wrong in that.
In the fifties, though people were no less avid supporters of
their respective team than they are today, they were first and
foremost supporters of football. It didn't occur to people to
shout or do anything that would besmirch the name of their

club, or football in general. They loved the game and their club too much to do that. If their team lost a match, say, 4-3, supporters would be disappointed, but if it had been a good, entertaining game of football they would derive more satisfaction from that than from seeing their team win a dull, drab game 1-0. That is yet another difference between the game then and now. That said, it was just as well a lot of Chelsea supporters preferred to see us lose in glorious fashion rather than shoehorn a narrow victory out of a sterile match, because, as I was to discover, that was often to be the case during my spell at the club.

During my career, a trademark of mine was the baggy shorts I wore. As with the catchphrase 'It's a funny old game', the baggy shorts came to me by chance. Being the youngest member of the Chelsea team that day and a debutant to boot, I kept a low-key presence in the dressing room. Our strips had been laid out in rotation around the changing room, but some of the senior pros had been unhappy with the shorts they had been given, so went around the room looking for a pair that was more to their liking. I didn't feel it was my place to question this, even when Derek Saunders took the shorts that had been placed below my peg and left a baggy pair in their place. When it came to getting changed, I simply put on the baggy shorts Derek had left me. These days Premiership teams have a new strip for every game, but I don't think I wore more than two different strips during my four years as a Chelsea player. I was to go on and enjoy nigh on ten years as a Tottenham player and in all that time only wore four different strips. At one point as a Spurs player, I remember complaining that my shirt had holes in it and was almost threadbare, only for old Cyril Pointon, who doubled as our physio and kit man, to say, 'It ain't the strip, son, it's the player inside it that counts.' In subsequent games at Chelsea I was always given these baggy shorts to wear, and on those rare occasions when new kit was issued I was always given baggy shorts because the kit man thought that's what I preferred. That is how my trademark baggy shorts came about.

More often than not, the first game of a season is tight and our game against Spurs was no exception. Irrespective of how well or badly a team had fared the previous term, the first game of a new season represents a clean slate. Everyone is equal at three o'clock with everything to play for. As a consequence, players tend to apply themselves with more verve and vigour than they might demonstrate in, for example, November, when a few defeats have rattled confidence and given rise to previous misgivings about the team's chances of success. Spurs went into the lead, but we stuck to our task of harassing and hustling in the hope we might force them into a mistake that would produce an equaliser. Being up against Danny Blanchflower, I could have wished for an easier debut but I kept working and during the second half that graft paid off. I managed to escape from the shackles of Danny for a few brief seconds but that was all the time I needed. When the ball was played through to me I took full advantage of the space I'd created and headed off for the Spurs goal. The Spurs keeper Ron Reynolds came off his line, but I saw a gap and planted the ball in it. A goal on my debut, something I managed at every level of football I was to play.

The game ended in a 1-1 draw. I thought I'd done all right and I was delighted to have scored, but nothing could have prepared me for the write-ups I was to receive in the Sunday papers. In the now defunct *News Chronicle*, Charles Buchan wrote, 'Young Jimmy Greaves gave such a brilliant display on his debut that I think he may rival the performance of Duncan Edwards, Manchester United's left half who became the youngest player to play for England. Only seventeen years old, Greaves showed the ball control, confidence and positional strength of a seasoned campaigner. It was the finest first-ever League game I have seen from any youngster.'

When Dad read that he was not best pleased. Don't get me wrong, he was proud of me, delighted I'd done well, particularly of the fact that I'd scored, but he was at pains to ensure the good write-ups didn't go to my head. 'You did very well,' he told me, 'but every game will offer a new and different challenge. You gotta make sure you're up to it. You gotta work hard at your game, don't let those press boys make you think it's gonna be any different.'

Mindful of the consequences of the FA Youth Cup Final at Wolves, I knew Dad was spot on. A lot has been written about my supposed laissez-faire attitude to football, in particular to training. Most of what has been written is bunkum. I knew I had a talent for scoring goals, but I also knew that in itself was not enough. I scored the goals I did because I worked at my game and approached every match with the right mental attitude. I wasn't the best trainer in the game, but I fully applied myself to what was appropriate to me. I've read articles saying that when the Chelsea players were sent on a long run I'd hitch a lift back to the ground on a milk float or a dustbin lorry. I can't remember ever doing that. What would I want to hitch a lift on a dustbin lorry for? It would stop at every bleedin' house and even the slowest runner would be back at Stamford Bridge hours before me. The same for a milk float. Express parcel delivery van, perhaps. Milk float or dustbin lorry never.

I didn't like long-distance running because I didn't think I benefited from it. Where I did apply myself fully to training was in sprinting and shuttle runs. The greatest asset a striker can have is sharpness and speed off the mark. From a standing position or a trot you have to explode. The first three or four yards is crucial to a goalscorer and that first yard is in your head not your legs. Whenever Albert Tennant had us sprinting at Chelsea, I was always first off the mark and out in front for the first six yards or so. I'd even leave a flyer like

Peter Brabrook in my wake. Over longer distances, Peter and one or two others would eventually overtake me, but that was okay because I'd done what was necessary for me. Likewise at Tottenham in the sixties when we were asked to sprint over fifty or a hundred yards. The race would invariably be won by goalkeeper Pat Jennings or left winger Cliff Jones, but for the first ten yards it would have been me out in front. In the fifties and sixties there was no specialist training, even for goalkeepers. Every player did the same training: some of it was appropriate and of great benefit to you as a player and your role in the team, some of it wasn't. I simply channelled my efforts towards the training best suited to me and my needs.

Topsy-turvy would be the expression used to describe the fortunes of Chelsea during my maiden season in the first team. Following our highly creditable draw at Spurs, we then entertained Manchester City at Stamford Bridge and lost 3-2, though I did manage to score once again. Birmingham City were then beaten 5-1, only for us to lose the return against Manchester City, 5-2. We followed that with a 3-0 defeat at Everton, and subsequent matches saw us win 3-1 at Newcastle United, 6-1 at home to Burnley (more goals for yours truly), lose 5-2 at Preston, beat Aston Villa 4-2 and Leicester City 4-0, draw 3-3 with Bolton and lose 4-2 at home to Tottenham Hotspur. That was very much the pattern of the 1957–8 season as far as Chelsea were concerned. We scored plenty of goals but we conceded a lot as well. The emphasis was on attacking football, as evidenced in February and March when, after 3-2 and 3-1 victories over Sheffield Wednesday and Aston Villa respectively, we rattled in four goals at Highbury, only for Arsenal to score five in reply.

Such open and cavalier football was not the sole preserve of Chelsea. Every team played an attacking game, with the emphasis on scoring goals. I always remember Stanley Matthews saying, 'At Blackpool when we scored a goal, it would never occur to us to shut up shop and try and defend our lead. When we scored one goal we were hungry for a second. When we scored a second, we'd go all out for a third. And that's why, at Blackpool, we lost a lot of games 4-3!'

You still see entertaining games these days but it's a different form of entertainment. Like other forms of entertainment and society in general, football today is more sophisticated than it was when I started playing. Goal-glut matches are a rarity nowadays. In 1957–8, such games were commonplace.

A little is lost and gained in living every day and the same applies to football. When I started out, attacking football was very much in vogue; no one gave a monkey's how many goals you conceded, the aim was to score one more than the opposition. The game has indeed changed. In comparing fifties football to the modern game, both eras have their pluses and minuses, but I know which style I prefer.

Though only seventeen, I took to football in the First Division and continued scoring goals at that level. My performances for Chelsea earned me more than a few headlines in the press and after only eight matches earned me something else. A call up for England Under 23s.

As was so often the case in those days, the press boys knew the England Under 23 team before the players did. I arrived at Stamford Bridge one September morning to be confronted by a gaggle of football writers who wanted my reaction to my selection for the England Under 23 team due to play Bulgaria at Stamford Bridge in a little over a week. It was the first I'd heard about it and the news came as a complete surprise to me. To be honest I think the press lads had played a part in my selection because they had been talking me up in their columns, saying my performances for Chelsea merited a chance at Under 23 level. Everything was happening so quickly for me, it was all going over my head. What do you know at seventeen?

In my case, next to nothing, certainly not how to handle a barrage of questions from the press about my supposed first appearance as an Under 23 international. I mumbled something about not having had official notification, and should that come through I would be delighted to represent my country and would do my level best not to let anyone down. I tried to remain calm. I didn't talk about my possible selection for England to anyone but those press boys and even then I'd been guarded. I'd only received the news from them. At the back of my mind was the thought that they might be wrong.

They weren't wrong. The following morning an envelope dropped through our door bearing the crest of the Football Association. I was immediately made aware of the respect and esteem the Football Association had for footballers when I read that letter. It began 'Dear Greaves'! The letter then went on to inform me that I had been selected to play for England Under 23s against Bulgaria at Stamford Bridge on 25 September 1957, and, as there were no pre-match get-togethers for the players in those days, what time I had to report to the ground. The formal and strict tenet of the letter was further emphasised by several paragraphs under the headings 'What You Must Do' and 'What You Must Not Do'. What I must do was report wearing a jacket, collar and tie with shoes suitably polished, in keeping with a player who has been afforded international recognition at Under 23 level. Another must was that I was responsible for my own boots, which had to be 'in pristine condition and studded in such a way as to make them most suitable for play at this level, with the laces washed bearing no unseemly marks of mud'.

As for what I must not do, there was a list only a little shorter than the waiting list for council houses on Dagenham's Becontree Estate. This included players not being allowed to follow any other employment without the sanction of the Football Association, and informing the trainer after the match of any injury sustained (I had been hoping to limp away unnoticed with a torn tendon or something similar). Also, players were not to bring friends into the ground or dressing room under any pretext whatsoever. Seemingly enemies yes, friends, no. I still have that letter amongst my collection of personal memorabilia. Looking back at it now, it seems like the sort of letter Scrooge might have written to Bob Cratchitt. Travel to the game was to be by 'Third Class' rail. Living in London, this didn't apply to me, but the very wording regarding the expenses of such travel – 'Players will be recompensed for any disbursement occurred regarding travel to and from the stadium as long as such expenditure accrued is deemed to be of exactment' – is pure Micawber. Such correspondence now appears like a letter from a master to a slave. Given that footballers were tied to the maximum wage and contractually bound to their clubs until their club thought fit to get rid of them, that to all intents and purposes was what we were. The Football Association was riddled with snobbery and they often treated players as little more than working-class riffraff, an attitude that was prevalent even where the full England team was concerned.

When I was first selected at full international level, for a tour of South America in 1959, the touring party assembled at Heathrow Airport. To kill time before boarding our plane, the Blackpool full back Jimmy Armfield and I went into the airport cafeteria for a cup of tea. I bought a small cake with my cup of tea and was just about to take the first bite when the secretary of the FA, Sir Stanley Rous, and an entourage of FA blazers passed our table. Rous backtracked two steps and eyed me sternly.

'Greaves, put that cake down,' he said tersely. 'You will be fed on the plane!'

My admonishment for daring to eat a cake apart, it was the sentence, 'you will be fed on the plane' that got to me. In particular the word 'fed'. As a player I wouldn't be having a meal on the plane and seemingly to Rous's mind I certainly wouldn't be dining. I would be fed, like a horse or some other such animal.

Another young player on that trip to South America was the Manchester United wing half Wilf McGuinness who recalls eavesdropping on a conversation between a stewardess and a member of the FA touring party. The stewardess was serving canapés to the FA officials who were dining while we players were being fed. The stewardess asked the FA official in question if she should serve the same to the players. 'Canapés? No, no,' replied the FA official, 'it would be like feeding strawberries to donkeys.'

The nature of the FA's letter apart, I was, of course, greatly honoured to have been selected to play for England Under 23s. I only had eight league matches and two games for Chelsea reserves to my name. All my other football had been played with the Chelsea Youth team in the South East Counties League. Though I was very inexperienced, I felt I could do well at this level of football. I was certainly not overawed by the occasion and in the days leading up to my debut I was looking forward to the match immensely. The fact that it would be taking place at Stamford Bridge before what would largely be a home crowd for me further fuelled my confidence.

The England Under 23 team were managed by Walter Winterbottom. I don't know what sort of salary Walter was on at the time, whatever it was he earned it because he was also manager of the full England team, the England Youth side and Director of Coaching for the Football Association.

Selection of the full England team was still largely in the

hands of the FA Selection Committee to which Walter had an advisory role, though never at any time had he the final say. Regarding the Under 23 team I think Walter had a little more influence where selection was concerned, which was appropriate because the inception of an Under 23 team that could groom players for full international level had been his idea.

By coincidence, the first England Under 23 match had taken place at Stamford Bridge in January 1954. What's more the opposition had been Chelsea. The game had been staged as an experiment and was played behind closed doors. The result, which was 1-1, is inconsequential. What was important was the fact that Walter Winterbottom's plan for building for the future in light of England's double humiliation at the hands of Hungary a year earlier was implemented.

As Winterbottom said at the time, 'The formation of an England Under 23 team is proof we are entering a new era of long-term England team building with our finest young talent. The Under 23 team is not an England 'B' team, nor is it England reserves. Should all proceed to plan, it will be the future of English football at International level.'

Following that experimental match behind closed doors, an England Under 23 team then played their counterparts in Italy some weeks later, losing 3-0 in Bologna. A year later, England won the return against the Italians at Stamford Bridge 6-0 with a side that included Chelsea's Frank Blunstone and Peter Sillett, along with goalkeeper Reg Matthews (who at the time was with Coventry City), Bill Foulkes and Duncan Edwards (Manchester United), Johnny Haynes (Fulham), Ron Flowers (Wolves) and Harry Hooper. Hooper scored two of the goals and has the distinction of being the first player ever to score for England at this level.

Following that first match in Bologna, England Under 23s had played ten games prior to the Bulgaria game and were unbeaten. The team Walter Winterbottom chose for what was my bow at international level against the Bulgarians was as follows:

Eddie Hopkinson (Bolton Wanderers), Don Howe (West Bromwich Albion), Gerry Harris (Wolves), Maurice Setters (West Bromwich Albion), Trevor Smith (Birmingham City), Stan Crowther (Aston Villa), Peter Brabrook, myself (both Chelsea), Brian Clough (Middlesbrough), Johnny Haynes (Fulham), Alan A'Court (Liverpool). There were no substitutes, but the travelling reserves were goalkeeper Gerry Cakebread (Brentford), Ken Taylor (Huddersfield Town) and Derek Kevan (West Bromwich Albion).

I'll spare you the Bulgarian team, suffice to say, with the exception of goalkeeper, Derventski, it contained four 'evs' and six 'ovs'.

We had too much quality for the Bulgarians. The final score was 6-2 in our favour and, cheered on by the many Chelsea fans in the 56,000 crowd, I began my fledgling career at international level by scoring after only eight minutes. I finished with two goals to my name, but it could have been a debut hat-trick, only yours truly messed it up by missing a penalty. Penalty miss apart, I was pleased with my debut for the Under 23s and so too were the newspapers, who, as usual to my mind, went overboard in their praise of me. Jim Gaughan in the now defunct London newspaper the *Star* was typical. Wrote Jim: 'More than 56,000 people at Stamford Bridge were shown that Johnny Haynes and Jimmy Greaves are natural partners. There has been nothing quite like this from an England pair since the great days of Raich Carter and Wilf Mannion.' Carter and Mannion? I had only played one game for England Under 23s and already the press boys were equating me with players who, to my mind, lived in the pantheon of the football gods.

The following month I received another of the FA's chummy letters, this time informing me I had been selected to play for the Under 23s against Rumania. Naturally I was delighted, more so when I read the letter properly and discovered the game was to be played at Wembley. It was to be my first appearance at Wembley, to my mind the most famous football stadium of all. This was where Matthews had entered football history. Where, in 1928, a diminutive Scottish forward line dubbed 'the wee blue devils' had given England a footballing lesson by winning 5-1. Wembley was the home of the FA Cup Final, the oldest cup competition in the world. History seeped from its every brick. Not only had countless games passed into legend while being staged there, just about every part of the stadium itself enjoyed legendary status, from the Royal Box and the tunnel to the twin towers and the pitch itself. I was looking forward to the Wembley experience immensely, especially as the Rumania game had the added novelty of taking place under floodlights.

For the game against Rumania, Walter Winterbottom made four changes to the team that had won so convincingly against Bulgaria. Alan Hodgkinson of Sheffield United replaced Eddie Hopkinson in goal, with Jimmy Armfield (Blackpool), Bill Curry (Newcastle) and Ray Parry (Bolton Wanderers) respectively replacing Howe, Clough and Haynes.

Though Wembley had staged a floodlit match two years earlier, when it hosted the Inter-Cities Fairs Cup match in which the London XI beat Frankfurt 3–2, our game against the Rumanians was to be only the stadium's second full game under floodlights. At this stage of their existence, cost-effective they weren't.

The game against Rumania was a lot tighter than our match against Bulgaria. The Rumanians showed a lot of skill and weren't afraid to take the game to us, as the final score of 3-2 to England suggests. Again I managed to feature on the scoresheet and the following day's newspapers were full of praise for my performance.

My embryonic international career had started well, as had my career with the Chelsea first team, though the same could not be said of the fortunes of the Chelsea team itself, for we continued to be as inconsistent as the batter mix in Charlie's café. At no time was our inconsistency more evident than during the fixtures over the Christmas holiday period. In 1957–8 it was still the norm for clubs to play on Christmas Day in a 'double-header' that saw them play the same opponents again on Boxing Day.

Our opponents in the double-header were Portsmouth, and we went into the first encounter at Stamford Bridge off the back of a 4-2 home defeat at the hands of Spurs. We played Portsmouth on Christmas morning in front of a crowd of over 45,000. I find it amazing now to think that so many people, the majority of them men, left the comfort of their homes on a Christmas morning to attend a football match, but they did. Heaven knows what sort of ructions would ensue in countless homes on a Christmas morning these days if a man said to his wife, 'Have fun with the kids, love, and get on with the Christmas dinner, I'm off to the match.' The thought of what a modern woman's response to that line might be makes me shudder.

Portsmouth were scrubbing about at the bottom of Division One but in players such as Jimmy Dickinson, who played a record 764 games for the club, Johnny Gordon, Phil Gunter, Ron Saunders and goalkeeper Norman Uprichard they possessed enough quality to cause problems to any team. Like us, Portsmouth were given to playing an attacking game while taking chances at the back, and taking chances was something I was very good at. I was hungry for this game because Ted Drake had rested me for a number of games, fearing that as a seventeen-year-old the rigours and physical demands of First Division football would take their toll on my body and I might suffer burn-out. Ted was protecting me, in much the same way as certain managers protect emerging young players today. He was also concerned about the gushing praise my efforts had induced in the press. He was worried that it might go to my head, and suggested I took a rest for four weeks during which I would only do light training. That four-week sabbatical turned into six weeks and I was becoming very restless when he eventually took me aside and told me I'd be returning to the first team on Christmas Day for the Portsmouth game.

In what turned out to be a ding-dong battle, we did more donging than Portsmouth did dinging. We beat Pompey 7-4. The festive crowd were treated to a classic game of open, attacking football and I marked my return to the first team by scoring four of our goals. After the game Peter Sillett said to me, 'Four goals after a six-week lay off? Just think how many you might have scored if you'd been match fit!' Immediately after the game I went home to enjoy Christmas dinner with my mum, dad, Marion and Paul. Suitably stuffed, I then went around to Irene's, where a sumptuous Christmas tea awaited me.

In the Christmas double-header the Football League always tried to pair teams that were within a reasonable travelling distance of one another, so that players could at least have Christmas night with their families. It didn't always work out that way. Many was the team that had to travel to a Boxing Day away game on Christmas night. What's more they would travel by train. Few people had cars in those days and travel by motor coach in a pre-motorway Britain was often arduous and slow. When it came to travelling any distance, the train was your best mode of travel. As odd as it may seem now, even though it was Christmas British Rail, as it was then called, adhered to the quaint policy of wanting to provide a service to the public. Eight o'clock on Boxing Day morning found me below the rampant red lion that dominated the portals of what gigantic red letters proudly claimed to be Waterloo Railway Station. I

walked with my Chelsea team-mates down a platform so wet
from the residue of steam engines it took on the appearance of
black glass. Once we'd settled into our carriage the cards came
out. I heard the shrill tone of a guard's whistle. The engine at
the head of our train chugged into life and our carriage jerked
forward, kept on going and the concrete support pillars of the
station's roof passed by with increasing speed. The thin light
of a winter morning somehow managed to pierce the grime of
the carriage window as we emerged into daylight. Peter Sillett
announced that hearts were trumps and we settled back into
our seats, on our way to a 3-0 defeat against the team we had
scored seven against the day before.

The contrasting fortunes we experienced in those two
games against Portsmouth were in keeping with Chelsea at the
time, but typical of many clubs as far as the Christmas double-
header was concerned. In the days of two points for a win,
rarely did a team collect all four points. Why? I don't know.
Maybe it's because one or two of the players overindulged at
Christmas. Christmas games were different. On the terraces
there would be more miniature cigars than fags and those
supporters who did smoke cigarettes would produce them not
from the regular pack of ten or twenty but from a box of fifty
given to them as a Christmas present. From a player's point of
view the crowd seemed different at Christmas. They appeared
to rustle in their new clothes. On more than one occasion,
when near the touchline, I'd catch a whiff of Bell's or Teacher's
cutting through the crisp, frosty air. Perhaps it had something
to do with the season of goodwill, but the atmosphere in the
ground on Christmas morning or Boxing Day was also
different from that of a normal league game. The attitude and
general frame of mind of the supporters seemed more convivial
than usual, and occasionally more irreverent. If we won, all
well and good. If we lost, there was always the compensation
of a damn good turkey dinner at home, presents and a few

drinks to rekindle the spirit. Such was the attitude of supporters at this time. If Chelsea lost, as long as it had been a good, entertaining game of football, most supporters returned home happy enough. Now you may well be given to thinking such an attitude is not conducive to winning trophies. All I can say is, supporters don't win trophies, players do, and at Chelsea, as with every other club, the players always took to the pitch hell bent on winning the game.

For Chelsea to have beaten Portsmouth 7-4 at Stamford Bridge, only to then lose 3-0 at Fratton Park the following day was not an extraordinary set of results. In 1957, Charlton Athletic were 2-0 down at home to Huddersfield Town at half time and ended up winning 7-6. On Christmas Day in 1935 Oldham Athletic beat Tranmere Rovers at Boundary Park. In the return match on Boxing Day, Tranmere won 13-4 with their centre forward, Bunny Bell, scoring nine. As I will later tell in more detail (since I had a personal involvement) on Boxing Day in 1963 sixty-six goals were scored in ten First Division games. On that day Fulham beat Ipswich Town 10-1, only to lose the return at Ipswich two days later 4-1.

The writer and broadcaster Michael Parkinson remembers seeing a Boxing Day match at Barnsley in the fifties when, after twenty minutes of running around, a Barnsley player appeared unsteady on his feet, dropped to his knees and was sick. Parky recalls the club later issued a statement saying that the player in question had been suffering from an 'emotional disturbance'. Contrasting fortunes from one day to the next and the occasional player suffering from an 'emotional disturbance' during Christmas double-headers may well have been the result of the magic of the festive season. What was not an influence, I am sure, was the fact that in the fifties the normally strict licensing hours were relaxed over the Christmas period!

*

Come January, Chelsea were lying mid-table. There was no danger of us being sucked into the relegation battle. Nor, because of our topsy-turvy form, was there any danger of us winning the Championship which was being contested by Wolves, Preston, Tottenham and West Bromwich Albion. Our only chance of a trophy and glory was the FA Cup. In round three, Chelsea were drawn away to Doncaster Rovers, who at the time were propping up Division Two.

As did every club, we would travel to an away game by train and on arriving at our destination a coach would then take us on to our hotel. For a trip such as Doncaster we would travel north on the Friday, stay over in a hotel and the coach would return on Saturday and take us on to the ground after lunch. It was on that trip to Doncaster that I realised just how important a player I was to Chelsea. After lunch on the Saturday the team travelled to Doncaster's ground and left me behind.

The team had assembled in the hotel foyer. I nipped to the loo and when I came back they'd gone. Being only seventeen, I was in a quandary as to what to do. I hung about for ten minutes and was on the point of asking the hotel receptionist if I could phone for a taxi when, to my great relief, I saw our coach swinging into the hotel car park. Apparently a couple of the lads had eventually noticed I wasn't on board and alerted Ted Drake to the fact.

The FA Cup was *the* trophy to win. There was more glory attached to winning the Cup than the League Championship. If you didn't play for England, the only way you could ever play at Wembley was to appear in the FA Cup Final. There were no play-off finals, no League Cup (at that stage) and the very thought of Wembley being hired out for an FA Cup semi-final or a European Cup game would have been anathema to football's governing bodies. There was next to no football on television. The only time people who owned a TV set ever had an opportunity to watch a live game on television was when it broadcast the Cup Final. In 1955 it was estimated that only 250,000 people in the UK owned a TV set. Only three years on, well over half the households in the UK owned a television and the vast majority of those settled down in front of theirs on Cup Final day.

The Football Association Challenge Cup – its proud and correct title – appeared to have an ivy-clad venerability about it. As befits the oldest cup competition in the world it was steeped in tradition. Its story was one of heroics. Of agony and ecstasy. Of workaday mudlarks rising to the occasion to galvanise the nation's factory floors and shipyards. Of crowns set squiffy on majestic heads. It was the competition that offered honest journeymen a chance to make an indelible mark on the game. An opportunity for some players to achieve everlasting fame. The FA Cup embraced a tremendous story of the most dramatic kind. It enjoyed a strong command of our affections and a profound influence on the game. The FA Cup was all that and more. Every club from Altrincham to Arsenal wanted to win it and part of its allure was that every club had an opportunity to do so.

The FA Cup also has a language of its own; the clichés are trotted out and invariably mean something quite different from what was intended. For example:

'We'll be relying on our fans to lift us': 'We haven't got a cat in hell's chance of winning this one.'

'It would be nice to get Manchester United in the next round': 'The club is nigh on bankrupt.'

'The whole town is buzzing': 'The local butchers have put a rosette in their shop window.'

'This club is no stranger to giant-killing': 'Who can forget 1921?'

'We'll be happy to come away with a draw': 'We'll be happy to double our money.'

'In cup football, anything can happen': 'Except that is, us winning today.'

'On the day, it'll be eleven against eleven': 'On the day it'll be eleven no-hopers against eleven internationals.'

'We're looking forward to a good cup run': 'We're battling against relegation.'

'The Cup is a great leveller': 'My players have taken one look at the weather and the pitch and I don't think they're up for it.'

'We're just going out to enjoy ourselves': 'We haven't a hope in hell.'

On the subject of FA Cup clichés, the press saw our game at Doncaster as a potential banana skin. We didn't slip up though, winning 2-0 on a pitch that had more than a passing resemblance to Passchendaele. In the Doncaster team that day was Charlie Williams, who had just started doing a little comedy routine and who, in the seventies, found fame as a comic on the ITV programme *The Comedians*. Charlie was a decent player and when he later took to comedy in a big way would often refer to Doncaster's cup match against Chelsea as part of his routine. According to Charlie, Ron Tindall hit a shot of such power the Doncaster goalkeeper caught pneumonia from the draught the ball created as it flew past him on its way into the net.

'I was up against young Jimmy Greaves that day,' went Charlie's routine. 'He twisted and turned me so many times, I came off that pitch suffering from spiral blood. Me and the goalkeeper had to see the doctor every week for a month. Every time I went, I'd ask the doctor for a prescription for cotton wool. At the end of the month, the wife had enough to fill six cushions.'

Charlie wasn't the only player of the day to venture into the world of entertainment. Colin Grainger was a winger with Sunderland who had previously played for Sheffield United. At

United he won seven caps for England, his most memorable appearance being his debut when he scored two goals in England's 4-2 win over Brazil in 1956. Colin was a good singer and at the time of Chelsea's Cup match at Doncaster was combining his football with substituting for Ronnie Hilton on a tour of British theatres because Ronnie had taken ill. You can't imagine a club of today allowing a player to take off every night to sing in theatres and dance halls up and down the country.

No matter how good a team is, to win anything in football you need a bit of luck. With the draw for the fourth round of the FA Cup, it appeared luck was with Chelsea. We were drawn against Darlington, who at the time were struggling near the foot of Division Three (North).What's more, we were drawn at home. What everyone saw as a straightforward tie for Chelsea proved anything but. The game ended in a 3-3 draw. I didn't score and Ted Drake obviously thought I hadn't had the best of games because he dropped me for the replay at Feethams.

There were three football league grounds that enjoyed a close affiliation to cricket. The pitches at Sheffield United's Bramall Lane and the County Ground at Northampton Town actually formed part of the cricket pitches used by Yorkshire and Northamptonshire respectively. Darlington's Feethams ground also aligned itself to cricket, as it still does today, though the pitch itself is not part of the Darlington cricket club pitch occasionally used by Durham CCC. Though part of one complex, the Darlington football ground backs on to the cricket ground, in much the same way as the Leeds Rhinos' rugby league ground backs on to Headingley, the spiritual home of Yorkshire CCC.

American tourists might be given to saying Feethams is a 'must see'. There is an aura of prim conservatism about the place which is untypical of most football grounds. To one side of the main gates there are almshouses. On the east side, the River Skerne flows idly past weeping willows opposite which is a row of fine Victorian villas which, if situated in London, would cost an arm and a leg. To the west of the ground, the cobbled Polar Lane runs to an ornate footbridge that leads over the river to a Victorian lodge and a leafy park. When you pass through the ornamental gates, in winter you find the cricket pitch given over to hockey. On the far side of the cricket square lies the pavilion and groundsman's house. To reach the football ground you carry on, part circumnavigating the cricket pitch, until you reach another set of ornamental gates, beyond which is Feethams. It is a unique setting for a football ground, one far removed from the congestion and hurly-burly of Stamford Bridge on a match day. Yet in this Victorian urban idyll, Chelsea were to be given a footballing lesson by their supposed inferiors.

It was the first ever time I had been dropped from a team. Having been named as the travelling reserve, I journeyed north to Darlington with my team-mates, knowing that barring sudden illness I would have no involvement in the replay whatsoever. When the game kicked off, I sat huddled in my worsted overcoat in Darlington's East Stand, yearning to be part of the action. Come the final whistle, the score was 1-1 and my mind had changed. I thought, 'Perhaps this might not be a bad one to miss after all.' At the end of extra-time, when Darlington had rattled in three further goals without reply to win the tie 4-1, I was thinking, 'Thank God, I wasn't a part of it.' Ted Drake, needless to say, was not a happy man. Far from it. In the dressing room after the game, I stood in a corner and kept my head down as he tore into my Chelsea team-mates. Normally, following a mid-week match in the north of the country, we didn't hang about. The players would wolf down some sandwiches and grab a cup of tea while trainer Albert Tennant gathered up the muddy kit and threw it into the

whicker skip in double-quick time as there was always a train
to catch. Not on this night. Albert didn't dare busy himself in
front of Ted Drake, because Ted 'had one on him'. Ted was
blazing mad. He systematically went through the team, telling
each player exactly what he thought of their performance. At
one point, John Battersby sheepishly put his head around the
door to remind Ted we had a train to catch.

'I don't care if they [the players] spend the night on
Darlington station or have to walk back to London,' Ted
bellowed without looking at John. 'They ain't leaving till I've
told them some home truths!'

In such a situation as I found myself in you become very
much aware of human nature. I was, of course, disappointed
that we had lost in the Cup, but deep down there was a little
part of me that was pleased. Don't take that the wrong way.
Don't be given to thinking that I wasn't 100 per cent behind
the cause of the club and my team-mates. I was. But like any
other player who has been dropped, when the team then loses,
self-preservation takes over. It may well have been that my
presence in the team might not have made one iota of
difference to the result, but the fact that I had had nothing to
do with the debacle induced in me not only relief but a degree
of cheer. That's the way it is with players. When they have
been dropped, deep down they're torn between wanting the
team to do well and not so well in order that they might regain
their place in the side. If you were to ask any player of any
generation at any level of football about this, if they were being
totally honest they'd tell you the same. Anyone who says
otherwise is lying. That said, there seem to be a number of
contemporary players who seem content to play reserve team
football or even spend their Saturdays sitting in the stand as
long as they continue to earn very good salaries. It would
appear such players would not only rather watch games but
also watch their career tick by from some grandstand, rather

than take a drop in money and play regular first team football
at a lower level. Such an attitude is alien to me, but it seems to
exist in some nowadays. In the 2001–2 season, Titi Camara,
though fit, played just six minutes of first team football for
West Ham. At Aston Villa, Bosko Balaban's first team
appearances were so limited that, against the £5 million Villa
paid for him, they worked out at £30,000 a minute. They are
just two examples. Another can be found at my old club,
Chelsea, where in 2001–2 Dutchman Winston Bogarde,
reportedly on £30,000 a week, played not one minute of first
team football. Come September 2002, Bogarde still hadn't
featured in the Chelsea first team, his last game having been in
2000–2001. When asked by a journalist to comment on his
situation, Bogarde was reported as saying he was 'very happy
at Chelsea'. I bet he bloody was. Thirty grand a week for not
having to put your ability as a footballer on the line is, as the
old song says, 'nice work if you can get it'. I'd be willing to sit
in the stands and watch games for half the money Chelsea are
paying Bogarde. In many respects, his contribution to the club
is much less than that of the Chelsea supporters who have to
pay to watch.

In my time as a player I never came across a footballer who
was happy to sit out games and pick up his money. I wanted to
be playing in the first team and, after our defeat at Darlington,
felt I had a good chance of doing just that in our next match
against Burnley. Ted Drake, or so I believed, couldn't attach
any blame to me for the Darlington defeat. In truth he
couldn't, but having lambasted every member of the team who
had lost at Feethams, he wasn't going to let me out of that
dressing room scot-free.

Having said his piece, Ted told everyone to get a move on
as we had a night train to catch and he didn't want to be
stranded in Darlington overnight. I heaved a sigh of relief
when he stormed out of the dressing room, because I felt

relatively safe, only for Ted to step back into the room and focus his eyes on me.

'As for you Greaves, Mr bloody England Under 23. Some bloody player you are, you can't even get in this side!'

I was seventeen, on my way to coming to terms with the realities of life as a footballer, and to realising that defeat can do strange things to people, even a gentleman such as Ted Drake.

I was back in the team for our next match at Burnley. Though we lost 2-1, we gave a good account of ourselves against what was a very talented Burnley team that included Colin McDonald in goal, who a few months later would be called up for England, that mercurial inside forward Jimmy McIlroy, Jimmy Adamson, Ray Pointer, Tommy Cummings and Brian Pilkington. Quality pros one and all. In the following match, we lost 2-0 at home to Preston North End in a game in which I had the honour of playing against one of my boyhood heroes, the great Tom Finney. After that, normal topsy-turvy service was resumed: we enjoyed consecutive away wins against Sheffield Wednesday (3-2) and Aston Villa (3-1) only to then come unstuck again, at home to Arsenal in that 5-4 thriller.

On away trips, I roomed with Peter Brabrook. Peter was a fellow East Ender, with whom I had much in common, and he had the distinction of being the first Chelsea player to own a car considered worthy of owning. Few Chelsea players of the day owned a car, myself included, and I'll never forget the day Peter drove into the car park at Stamford Bridge in his pride and joy. The car was a light blue Vauxhall Victor with a bench seat in the front and a column gear change. Peter loved that car and so did me and the Sillett brothers. We now had transport to and from the ground!

Late on a Saturday morning prior to a home match, Brabbers would pick up the Sillett brothers and me, and we would head for Moody's café in Canning Town where we would order our pre-match meal of roast beef and Yorkshire with all the trimmings, or pie and mash followed by blackcurrant crumble and custard.

It's now incredible to think that as professional footballers we would eat such a meal just before a match. That we did is down to the fact that no one in the game understood the importance of diet, let alone the function of digestion. Players were in fact encouraged to eat a hearty meal prior to a game. It was a widely held belief that players would benefit from eating a large steak before a match. No one knew that a steak can take as long as thirty six hours to digest and that the benefits of eating steak would only be felt after a matter of days. Steak, we were told, provided us with protein, strength and energy, so it became the chosen pre-match meal of many a player. In his autobiography *Banksy*, Gordon Banks tells of how, during his time as a Leicester City player in the early sixties, his pre-match meal consisted of a large steak with peas and both boiled and roast potatoes, followed by a large bowl of rice pudding. Though we now know such a diet is not conducive to the life of a footballer, it didn't appear adversely to affect Banksy's performances. He did become the greatest goalkeeper in the world, and arguably, of all time.

When not cadging a lift from Peter Brabrook, I travelled to and from the ground by train. More often than not my companion on such journeys was Les Stubbs, who, like me, lived in Essex. At the time Stubbsy was winding down his career as a Chelsea player. The club had bought him for a five-figure sum from Southend United in 1952, with whom he had begun his career in 1949. He was a lovely fella and had played a significant role in the Chelsea Championship team of 1954. As an inside left he proved himself to be quick, progressive and a constant source of danger to opponents. He was a homely man with a simple homespun philosophy on life and particularly football. Throughout his entire career, he was never booked, for, as he told me during one train journey, 'There are two simple rules for staying out of trouble on a football pitch, Jimmy. Rule One: the referee is always right. Rule Two: in the event of the referee being wrong, Rule One applies.'

I have particularly good cause to remember my first season as a Chelsea player well, for it was during this season that I asked my beloved Irene if she would marry me. To my eternal delight, she said yes. Due to my commitments as a player with Chelsea, we were married in Romford Registry Office on a Wednesday. My best man was my old school pal Dave Emmerick and I have three specific memories of the day: Irene was stunningly beautiful, I was ecstatically happy and the weather was bloody freezing.

We didn't have much money, certainly not enough to put down as a deposit on a house, so we set up home in a flat. The curious thing about this flat was that it was situated in Wimbledon football ground. At the time Wimbledon were one of the crack non-league clubs who played in the Isthmian League and, oddly, within their main stand were two flats. I'd heard that one was coming up for rent and, after viewing it, Irene and I decided it would suit us fine. Living in a football ground never bothered us; on the contrary, we thought it in keeping. Part of our tenancy involved me weeding the Plough Lane terraces – again, something that didn't bother me. It was during this time that I bought my first ever car, a 1937 Opel convertible. I bought the Opel from Irene's brother for the princely sum of £30. In those days as long as you had a provisional licence and displayed L-plates you could drive unaccompanied. I'd never driven a car in my life but somehow managed to drive from my brother-in-law's across London to Wimbledon without causing mayhem. After a few months, we went up-market car-wise. I sold the 1937 Opel and bought a younger car, a Standard 8, built in 1938! That old Standard served me well and other players, too. After training the Sillett brothers and Ron Tindall would pile in to save the bus fare home.

Chelsea's topsy-turvy season finished with a 2-1 home victory over Manchester United. That United had managed to field a team at all in the final months of the season was a tribute to the club's remarkable resilience and fortitude following the Munich air disaster the previous February that claimed the lives of eight of their players and which nearly took the life of their manager, Matt Busby. I don't think there was anyone in the country, let alone football, whose hearts did not go out to Manchester United and everyone connected with the club at the time of this terrible tragedy.

It had been late on a cold February afternoon under the first lighted street lamps that I had caught sight of a grilled newspaper placard bearing the words 'Manchester United In Air Crash'. On reading it I wasn't aware of the true gravity of the situation. That came home to me when I turned on the wireless to listen to the six o'clock news. The normally measured, Reithian voice of the announcer seemed to have all the gravitas of a lump hammer as he disclosed the shocking list of fatalities and casualties. There is no greater truism in football than it is a young man's game. The fact that so many young players of promise, many of whom I knew personally, had had their lives taken away at such a tender age shocked me.

The aircraft carrying the United party and a group of journalists crashed when taking off from Munich airport where it had stopped to refuel en route from Belgrade where the team had played a European Cup match. More than half the forty people on board lost their lives, including the United players Roger Byrne, Geoff Bent, Eddie Colman, Mark Jones, David Pegg, Tommy Taylor, Bill Whelan and, after later succumbing to his injuries, Duncan Edwards. Also among the dead were the

United coach Bert Whalley, club secretary Walter Crickmer and trainer Tom Curry. Those journalists who lost their lives included Don Davies, who wrote for what was then the *Manchester Guardian* under the pseudonym of 'The Old International', and the former Manchester City and England goalkeeper Frank Swift, who was working for the *Sunday People*.

The whole country was in deep shock. The football world mourned the loss of so many lives, but like their manager Matt Busby in a German hospital, Manchester United fought on. Busby's assistant manager, Jimmy Murphy, had missed the trip to Munich because he was managing the Welsh national team. Following the Munich tragedy, Murphy took charge of the team for the remainder of the 1957–8 season, hastily drafting in some experienced players and promoting the reserves. In little under a fortnight, when United played their first game following the disaster, the match programme for their FA Cup tie against Sheffield Wednesday contained eleven blank spaces on the United team page, simply because no one had any idea what sort of team Murphy would be able to turn out.

Though severely pained by the tragedy of it all, the club galvanised and rallied, aware that, despite their great loss, life and football had to go on. Many clubs rallied to their cause. The Blackpool inside forward Ernie Taylor was on the point of signing for Sunderland but, as a gesture of support, the Sunderland board allowed Ernie to join Manchester United. Later that year, when the player crisis at Old Trafford had somewhat eased, the United board reciprocated by offering Ernie to Sunderland at a fee perceived to be far less than his transfer market value.

To their credit Manchester United carried on, the mark of their redoubtable spirit the fact they finished the 1957–8 season in ninth place, two places above Chelsea. Even more remarkable, they reached the final of the FA Cup for the second successive season.

United's opponents were Bolton Wanderers, who found themselves in a no-win situation as far as the Cup Final was concerned. The wave of sympathy that swept United to the Cup Final was immense, matched only by the gratitude offered to players such as Bobby Charlton, Alex Dawson, Dennis Viollet, Ronnie Cope and Freddie Goodwin on to whose young shoulders United's future had now been transferred.

Although, like everyone else, Bolton were deeply touched by and sympathetic to United's plight, they had to do a job on the day and could not let their sympathies cloud their judgement or affect their professionalism. That old warhorse Nat Lofthouse, 'The Lion of Vienna', put Bolton ahead after only three minutes. Early in the second half, after a Bobby Charlton piledriver had hit the post then bounced into the waiting arms of the Wanderers goalkeeper Eddie Hopkinson, Bolton caught United on the break. The ball was swung into the United penalty area just under their crossbar. Though facing his goal, the United goalkeeper Harry Gregg appeared to have collected the ball comfortably, only for Nat Lofthouse to come racing in and shoulder charge Gregg. The ball spilled from Gregg's hands and over the line to put Bolton two up and the final out of the reach of United. Though the referee, Jim Sherlock of Sheffield, had no hesitation in awarding the goal, Nat's effort was considered highly controversial at the time. From the moment the ball crossed the line, the arguments raged as to whether Mr Sherlock should have allowed the goal to stand or not. At the time a shoulder charge was considered a legitimate challenge in the game. When contesting a ball, I had often gone shoulder to shoulder with an opponent, sometimes winning the ball, sometimes not. Press photographs and film footage of the incident were analysed in great detail. That a shoulder charge was a legitimate form of challenge, no one had any doubt. The burning question was, had Nat Lofthouse met Harry Gregg shoulder to shoulder, or simply barged into the goalkeeper's back with his shoulder, causing Gregg to drop the ball. Opinion was split. On seeing the incident the words of Les Stubbs came readily to my mind. Rule One: the referee is always right. Rule Two: if he is wrong, Rule One applies.

Harry Gregg was not happy about Nat Lofthouse's challenge in the 1958 Cup Final but accepted it because physical challenges were part and parcel of the game in those days. Indeed, after the initial inquest was over, Nat's challenge became the subject of much levity. When he retired from the game, Nat took over as the licensee of the Castle Hotel in Bolton. For years, another hotel in Bolton displayed a photograph of Nat's second Cup Final goal, under which a caption read:

> Harry Gregg after t'final
> Went into Nat's for a beer
> Who returned his money
> And telt 'im
> We don't charge goalkeepers here!

I mention all this because I want to emphasise not only how different the game was in terms of how it was played when I started out, but how different the attitude of the fans and players was to physical play. In the fifties, if a player was dumped on his backside by an opponent, more often than not it would induce ripples of laughter amongst the spectators. Should that happen now, fans would be on their feet, incensed and hurling abuse at the perpetrator who they would view in much the same way they would a criminal who has committed a particularly heinous crime. Football was still very much a game when I started out, albeit a very tough one. Nowadays,

in the eyes of many fans, football is nothing more than a
conflict. As for the players, whenever I was sent sprawling, I
didn't roll and wriggle about on the pitch like some skewered
worm. If I'd done that, my team-mates would have given me
short shrift, saying something like, 'Get up, you big Jessie and
stop being so bloody dramatic.' Likewise the Chelsea fans
would have taken a dim view of such antics and I would have
quickly found my popularity on the wane. When supporters
saw a player making what they believed to be too much of a
tackle, it was he they gave stick to and not the perpetrator of
the tackle.

In thirty-five matches for Chelsea in 1957–8, I scored twenty-
two goals. I was the club's leading goalscorer and I derived a
great deal of satisfaction from that, especially as it had been
my first season as a professional. The leading goalscorer in
the First Division that season was Bobby Smith of Spurs,
whose transfer from Chelsea I had eaves-dropped when
serving tea and biscuits in the board room. Regarding the top
scorers in the First Division, I was a good way down the
pecking order, eleventh to be exact. Ahead of me were such
notable goalscorers as Tommy Thompson and Tom Finney of
Preston North End (34 and 26 respectively), Gordon Turner
(Luton Town, 33), Jimmy Murray (Wolves, 30), Joe Hayes
(Manchester City, 25), David Herd (Arsenal, 24), Bobby
Robson (West Bromwich Albion, 24, yes, Sir Bobby, as he
now is), Norman Deeley (Wolves, 23) and Ronnie Allen
(West Brom, 22). Hot on my tail were no fewer than fifteen
players who had scored seventeen goals and more for their
respective clubs. From that you might be given to thinking
that a lot of goals were scored in the First Division that season
and you'd be right. As I have said, the emphasis at this time
was on attacking football and just about every team in every
division of the Football League boasted one player who

scored twenty plus and at least one other who hit double figures.

Three teams, Champions Wolverhampton Wanderers, runners-up Preston and fifth-placed Manchester City, scored more than one hundred league goals. Spurs, Leicester City and West Bromwich Albion all scored over ninety goals and four other teams hit eighty plus. Even bottom club Sheffield Wednesday scored a healthy sixty-nine goals. That managers did not place too much emphasis on the quality of their defence, however, can be evidenced by the fact that in scoring 104 goals Manchester City conceded one hundred. I'm well aware that such cavalier football would induce in the coaches and supporters of today accusations of teams being unorganised, even unprofessional. But what do supporters like to see when they attend a game? Goals. In 1957–8 they saw plenty of them. Manchester City's forty-two league matches produced 204 goals. If that isn't a case of supporters getting value for money, I don't know what is.

In 1953 England had been beaten 6-3 at Wembley by Hungary, the first time England had ever lost to foreign opposition on home soil. The real shock came not in the margin of defeat, but the manner of it. England were totally outplayed and found wanting in just about every department, from the kit to the tactics they employed. Just under a year later when England played Hungary again in Budapest, an almost identical English team tried to play exactly the same style of football they had attempted at Wembley, a style that had changed little in three decades. This faithfulness to tradition and the folly of such was shown in the result. England lost 7-1. Portsmouth's Jimmy Dickinson, who played in that game, later said, 'The gulf between the two teams was so great, Hungary might easily have scored ten.'

As with fifties society, English football was very reluctant to release its hold on the traditions which had brought so much power and success in the past. But as with society in general, come 1958–9 football, albeit tentatively, was about to enter a period of great change and modernisation. These transformations filtered down through society to football and touched the lives of individuals, myself included.

CHAPTER FOUR

HERE COMES SUMMER

In the close season of 1958, many newspapers had been touting my name for possible inclusion in Walter Winterbottom's England squad for the World Cup Finals taking place in Sweden. In the season just ended I had added to my England Under 23 caps in games against Scotland and Wales. We beat Scotland 3-1 at Everton, but in April had gone down 2-1 against the Welsh at Wrexham. I thought I'd given a reasonable account of myself in those two games, in truth, more so against the Scots than the Welsh. Quite a number of the press boys were of the mind my performances for Chelsea and England Under 23s made me worthy of inclusion in Winterbottom's squad for Sweden. It wasn't to be. England set off for the World Cup without me and Stanley Matthews.

I was a tad disappointed. Though I had only one season in the First Division to my name, I felt I was ready. In the days leading up to the announcement of the squad, I was expecting to be included. When I wasn't, my initial disappointment was tempered with the thought that should I continue to score goals for both Chelsea and the England Under 23s, my time would come, and soon. The reason given for my non-inclusion was that, at eighteen, I was too young to make a significant contribution to the England cause in a major international competition. I didn't see it that way, but of course I accepted it. The Brazilians obviously didn't hold such a view. They included Pele in their squad for Sweden. He was some months short of his eighteenth birthday and would be the star player of the tournament.

As for most people, the 1958 tournament was the first World Cup I ever saw on television, though the coverage was nothing compared to that of today, consisting in the main of edited highlights from selected games. The '58 World Cup had great interest for the UK because England, Scotland, Wales and Northern Ireland all qualified. The first and, to date, only time that has ever happened. England were in a tough group, their opponents being Brazil, the USSR and Austria. England gave a decent account of themselves, finishing second behind Brazil, but level on points with the USSR which meant they had to meet in a play-off. For this game the press were calling for Bobby Charlton to play at centre forward, but Winterbottom (more probably the England selection committee) stuck with West Bromwich Albion's Derek Kevan. England lost their play-off against the USSR 1-0, and not for the last time an England World Cup team returned home cursing their bad luck.

In winning the World Cup, Brazil gave Europe, in particular the English game, a lesson not only in football but in modern tactics. I was in awe of that Brazilian side which included the 'magnificent 7', Garrincha; that little Napoleon who orchestrated their every attack from midfield, Didi; Vava, one of the tidiest and sharpest football brains there has ever been; and of course, the sensational Pele. Every member of that Brazil team displayed a complete mastery of the ball and sublime skills. They also demonstrated to me, from Didi's midfield dominance to Pele's precocious and predatory skills in the penalty box, the benefits of collective talent. England and the other Home Countries seemed pedestrian by comparison. Our football, though reasonable in terms of international standards, was colourless. That said, the performances of the Home Countries in the 1958 World Cup, in terms of pure football, were not as anachronistic as they had been four or five years previously. The quest to modernise the English game had begun and over the next few years would continue apace.

I spent much of the close season of 1958 enjoying married life. Irene and I were blissfully happy and, with my football career seemingly moving in the right direction, I was very optimistic about the future. I found myself on a voyage of discovery, not only with regard to my marriage and life in general but in my fledgling career as a footballer. I received no coaching as such other than the odd tips from Albert Tennant and senior pros at the club. The training at Chelsea, as in pre-season, consisted in the main of various forms of running, followed by small-sided games. Some days we never saw a ball at all in training. My real football education took place out on the pitch during actual games. I'd try something in a game and, if it didn't work, I'd try something else. It was hit and miss, but fortunately, more often than not, when presented with a good opportunity in front of goal I'd hit the target. The increasing availability of easy travel by air saw a number of First Division clubs opting to tour abroad as part of their pre-season build-up. In the lead-up to the 1958–9 season, Spurs went to Holland, Sunderland to Spain, Arsenal played a game in Italy, Wolves toured Switzerland and France, while Manchester City sought the delights of both the South of France and Austria. Chelsea too embarked on a mini-tour abroad during which the players had an opportunity to sample the style and delights of chic continental living. We went to communist Bulgaria.

All I have to say in favour of our visit to Bulgaria is that the weather was hot. It occurred to me that Bulgaria in the fifties probably wasn't much different from Bulgaria in the twenties. The country seemed to belong to another age. This was the first time I was ever made aware that many of the things we took for granted in Britain, such as electricity, were not common to certain other countries. We were based in the capital, Sofia, as we were scheduled to play two games in the city. Our hotel was basic, the food – well let me be diplomatic and say it was not what we were used to. We were there for just over a week and in that time Sofia suffered numerous power cuts. I was rooming with Peter Brabrook who at the time had a Remington electric shaver and an adaptor for use on the Continent. The first night Peter produced the shaver from his bag I begged him not to use it.

'If you plug it in you might get electrocuted,' I told him. 'Failing that, knowing the grid system over here, the power that thing uses could plunge half of Sofia into darkness.'

Bulgaria was my first experience of a communist country at work and my overall impression was that communism didn't work.

The first of our games was against CDNA Sofia who were Bulgaria's reigning Champions. The club were the unofficial team of the Bulgarian Army and secret police, which may go some way to explaining why they had won the Bulgarian Championship in eight of the previous nine seasons. Perhaps they were given the pick of the players; whatever, they weren't a bad side and on the day beat us 2-1 before a crowd of 50,000. As John Sillett said afterwards, '25,000 watching the game, and 25,000 secret police watching those watching the game.'

We fared much better in our second and final game of the tour, beating Levski Sofia, 2-1, with yours truly amongst the goals. Levski weren't a bad side either, having been runners-up to CDNA the previous season. I learned that the influence of the communist state touched every walk of life, including football, as each club in the Bulgarian First Division was under the control of one official body or another. Each team was aligned to the army, the police, the secret police, railway workers or other state industries. Levksi, I discovered, were an offshoot of the Interior Ministry. Their players, as with all the top players in Bulgaria, were supposedly amateurs. The Levski lads, we were told, worked for the Interior Ministry, though they couldn't have done much in the way of government work as they trained full-time. They may have done a little office work occasionally, but their role in the Ministry was really a sham. That said, it was no more of a sham than some footballers in England, subject to the maximum wage signing for a club for the same wage, but receiving another wage for supposedly working for a company owned by a director of their new club.

The most famous case of this involved Tommy Lawton. Tommy was a star turn, a strongly built centre forward whose powerful shooting and incredible strength and timing in the air made him one of the greatest centre forwards of all time. He made his debut as a seventeen-year-old with Burnley in 1936 and four days later, against Spurs, gave ample evidence of the great goalscorer he was to be when he became the youngest player ever to score a hat-trick in the Football League. After only three months he joined Everton where he had the unenviable task of taking over from Dixie Dean. Tommy wasn't overawed, however, and in the last two pre-war seasons he was the First Division's leading goalscorer. In wartime football he scored 337 goals in major matches and when he signed for Chelsea in 1945 enjoyed star billing. Two years later, while still England's centre forward, he caused a sensation by moving from Chelsea to Notts County, who were then in the Third Division South. In contemporary terms, it was like Michael Owen choosing to leave Liverpool for Notts County. No one could understand why Tommy did it. Because of the maximum wage County couldn't pay him any more than Chelsea and Tommy's move to the Third Division South didn't do him any favours career wise. While at County he only played four more games for England, the

FA seemingly taking a dim view of England's number nine plying his trade against the likes of Aldershot and Newport County, rather than Arsenal and Spurs. Behind Tommy's sensational move was, of course, money. Tommy had been on the maximum wage of £14 a week at Chelsea and though Notts County couldn't offer him any more, a County director put him on the payroll of a company he owned at a further £14 a week. That doubled Tommy's weekly wage and, believe me, £28 a week in 1948 was serious money. His 'second job' supposedly involved him doing some clerical work in the offices of the company owned by the County director, as well as doing promotional work as and when required. According to Stan Matthews, who knew him very well, Tommy never set foot inside those offices and it is questionable if he ever did any promotional work.

Such bogus jobs were not uncommon to players during the era of the maximum wage; while making a name for myself at Chelsea I too was the subject of such an 'under-the-counter' offer.

In many respects the sham amateurism I encountered during our tour of Bulgaria bore a certain similarity to the situation a number of top players found themselves in at home. Both systems, though seemingly worlds apart, involved some players having bogus jobs in addition to their career as a footballer. I wasn't sad when our mini-tour of Bulgaria came to an end. My only previous experience of another country had been Holland. Communist Bulgaria in the fifties was a culture shock to me. There was little on the shelves in the shops and to me the people always seemed to be wary and constantly looking over their shoulders. The players and officials of both CDNA and Levski were hospitable and friendly enough, but I was always aware that here was a people fearful of what they said and did. As such, every conversation was carefully measured and stilted, to the point of being dour. (Believe me, when you have spent time chatting to Bulgarian communists of the fifties, never again will you think of Belgians as boring.) Our visit to Bulgaria was only a brief one, but in that time I saw enough to know communism wasn't for me.

Chelsea kicked off the 1958–9 season against the same opponents we had played on the final day of the previous season, Manchester United. Only this time, we met at Old Trafford as opposed to Stamford Bridge.

In 1958, society was changing, football was also changing and so too was my life. Irene was expecting our first child. We were gloriously happy, coming to terms with married life and looking forward immensely to being a family.

The influence of American popular culture was beginning to take a hold on the British way of life. More and more people had televisions and American stars such as Perry Como, Jack Benny, Phil Silvers as Sgt Bilko, and Lucille Ball and Desi Arnaz in *I Love Lucy* entered the living rooms of the nation. Nowhere was the American influence more profound than in popular music. Rock'n'roll in the form of Elvis Presley, Buddy Holly, Fats Domino, Jerry Lee Lewis and Chuck Berry captivated a whole generation of teenagers, myself included. Along with Bobby Darin, Ricky Nelson, Paul Anka and the Everly Brothers, they changed the musical tastes of my generation overnight, as a result of which the likes of Eddie Calvert, Winifred Atwell, Alma Cogan and even the king of skiffle, Lonnie Donegan, found their stars on the wane.

These new pop stars brought with them new fashions in clothes, at least new to us British youngsters. Brightly coloured shirts appeared under suit jackets, T-shirts under what were known as college jerkins. Every young person seemed to own a pair of jeans, and on our feet we wore black baseball-type boots with sixteen eye-laceholes to each boot and a white circular rubber logo on the ankle. These boots were so popular that most footballers even wore them for training.

Hairstyles also changed as young people discovered a youth culture for the first time. The generation gap which had started to open in the early fifties continued to widen. One of the popular new hairstyles for young lads was the crew cut, or the Tony Curtis, named after the film star who had first sported the look, disassociated it from the US Army and popularised it. It was short at the sides and bullet-like on the top, with the hair brushed up so it appeared to stand on end. I liked the crew cut so much that on the opening day of the 1958–9 season at Old Trafford I ran out for the first time sporting this hairstyle. I still have the match programme from Chelsea's game there. The front cover was particularly poignant because it showed a photograph of Matt Busby back with the United players for the first time since the Munich tragedy. Inside was a very moving message from the United chairman, Mr Hardman, which also proved to be prophetic. In making mention of how, in the aftermath of Munich, United had reached the FA Cup Final and the semi-finals of the European Cup, Hardman wrote: 'Were these boys inspired? Inspired yes, not only by the memory of their comrades but by the inspiration they derived from our supporters. In asking once more for your cheers in victory we ask also for your tolerance in defeat. Give us your loyalty and United will be great again.'

Tolerance in defeat. As I have been at pains to point out, many people, though naturally wanting to see their team win, were tolerant of defeat, as long as they had witnessed a good, entertaining game of football. That work was plentiful at this time can be evidenced from some of the advertisements that appeared in the United programme. Metropolitan Vickers Electrical Company took out a half-page advertisement listing immediate vacancies for nine different trades and occupations.

One wonders just how many bar turret lathe operators and boring mill operators there are in the country these days, let alone the Manchester area. A company called Handley Page 'urgently required fitters and fitters mates', offering them a wide range of benefits including 'a wide range of sports and social activities'. The National Coal Board were in need of miners for 'this rapidly growing industry', while Edward Wood and Company had 'immediate vacancies for constructional engineers and all associated trades and non trades'. Britain was getting back on its feet. After a decade and more of frugality and slow growth following World War Two, the nation was beginning to rebuild in no uncertain fashion. In just about every town and city I visited with Chelsea, the bomb sites were being built on. The town and city landscapes of the nation were changing dramatically. New buildings were going up. Wages were going up. The standard of living was rising as were people's expectations. The only thing that didn't appear to be going up was Chelsea. We were about to embark upon another topsy-turvy season that would see us finish in the bottom half of Division One.

On a personal note I started the season well. I scored twice against a United team that included Harry Gregg, Bill Foulkes, Dennis Viollet, Bobby Charlton, Wilf McGuinness, Alex Dawson and my namesake, Ian Greaves. Unfortunately, United proved too strong on the day and in reply to my brace scored five! Having conceded five on the opening day of the season, in true Chelsea fashion we then contrived to beat Spurs 4-2 at home. Our third match was against the reigning League Champions Wolverhampton Wanderers, whose captain, Billy Wright, was four appearances short of creating a record 100 games for England. When it came to scoring goals, Wolves had no equal. They would go on to score 110 in the league that season. The previous season, they had scored 103, while the forty-seven they conceded made the Wolves defence the meanest in the entire Football League. Well marshalled by Billy Wright, they also possessed players of similar high quality in Peter Broadbent, Bobby Mason, Jimmy Murray, Bill Slater, Ron Flowers, Eddie Clamp, Eddie Stuart, Norman Deeley and goalkeeper Malcolm Finlayson.

Wolves were a real class act and had to some extent redeemed English football after 1953–4 by staging a series of floodlit friendlies at Molineux against crack continental opposition such as Real Madrid, Moscow Dynamo, Moscow Spartak and Honved. Honved had been the Hungarian Champions and included in their ranks several of the players who had put England to the sword in '53 and '54. Wolves were voracious hunters of the long-ball game, while Honved, with Puskas, Kovacs, Kocsis and Czibor, were the masters of short passing. This clash of contrasting styles produced a game of searing speed, pounding power and consummate skill. It also produced something else – the restoration of English football's pride and reputation. It may only have been a friendly, but so keen were Wolves and English football in general to put one over on the Hungarians who had humiliated England that a crowd of 55,000 turned up at Molineux. Wolves did not disappoint, coming back from two goals down to win 3-2 to restore, in our minds at least, the reputation of English football abroad.

An even bigger crowd, of over 61,000, turned up at Stamford Bridge to see if we could beat the Champions. We didn't get off to the best of starts. Bobby Mason put Wolves ahead after only two minutes, but we were far from being fazed by that. There were certain games when I took to the pitch and just knew I was going to have one of those games when everything would go my way. From my first touch of the ball, I felt comfortable. I was relishing the big match occasion, confident of my own ability, sure that I would feature amongst the goals. In our first real attack of note, I corkscrewed past Ron Flowers and Gerry Harris before playing a one-two with

Peter Brabrook. Though shackled by Bill Slater, when receiving the ball back from Peter I felt confident enough to hit it first time. I'd seen a gap just to the left of Malcolm Finlayson and aimed for that. Whenever I was presented with such an opportunity, I never hit the ball with all the power I could muster because I didn't have to. When I saw an opening, I would simply 'pass' the ball through the space knowing no one could reach it. Malcolm Finlayson couldn't and we were level. Most of the goals I scored were like that. Rarely did I hit a spectacular shot from thirty yards. It was all about ghosting into space and hoping a team-mate had spotted me on the run and would thread through a well-weighted pass. If not that, then I attacked the ball. That is, I'd run into the penalty area taking up a position where I thought the ball was going to end up from a cross, a pass, or even from a block by an opponent. Rarely did I score with a thunderbolt from great distance, I wasn't that sort of player. I was a predator of the penalty box who made space to score goals. I'd pass the ball, stroke it, side-foot it, chip it or drive it into the net depending on the situation and the circumstances I found myself in at the time. As a result, goals I scored that could be termed spectacular were few and far between. I scored what I called bread and butter goals. I had no coaching to speak of. What I did in front of goal came naturally to me. Quite often I didn't even think about it. I just did it. I never panicked, never snatched at the ball, and because of the position I had taken up was always confident I had sufficient time in which to apply the killer touch. Sharpness and speed off the mark were crucial to my play. I was always looking to create a 'now you see me, now you don't' presence in and around the penalty box. Against Wolves that worked well, because I scored a second, then a third. When the second half got underway, the Wolves manager Stan Cullis had obviously been at pains to try and counteract my presence because that wily campaigner Bill Slater had been detailed to mark me rather than Ron Flowers. As things were to turn out, however, this was to be my day. I found Wolves very square across the back and by timing my runs to get on the end of some superb passing from Peter Brabrook and Mickey Block ended the day with five goals and had another disallowed for offside. If I remember correctly, Bill Slater pulled a goal back for Wolves from the penalty spot, to make the final score 6-2 to Chelsea.

The press went overboard about my five-goal haul against the Champions, but praise was also forthcoming from Stan Cullis, who after the game told the London *Evening News* – 'What a player. Someone's just said he [me] doesn't run around enough; he wouldn't have to do that for me.' You score five goals and all someone can find to say is, 'he doesn't run around enough'. It's a funny old game.

It certainly is. Following Chelsea's sensational six goal romp against the meanest defence in the Football League, we lost our very next game at Tottenham 4-0.

That game against Spurs was one of the few occasions that season when Chelsea failed to score in a game. Following our disappointment at Spurs, we then picked up a point in a 2-2 draw at Portsmouth, and were then involved in a match that produced another sensational scoreline when we beat Newcastle United 6-5 at Stamford Bridge, where once again I added to my goals tally. Our seesaw fortunes in the league were also mirrored in the club's first venture into European competition. Qualification for entry into the Inter-Cities Fairs Cup had changed. UEFA had agreed to individual clubs from cities taking part in the competition, rather than representative sides. To this day I'm not sure why Chelsea took part in the Fairs Cup rather than Tottenham, who had finished the previous season in third place. I assume, because we were situated in a principal city, we were simply invited. Birmingham City, who had finished the previous season in thirteenth place, also took part, again simply by virtue of the fact that they had received an invitation.

Chelsea's first sally into Europe started well but, as was our wont, we couldn't find consistency. In the first round we were drawn against Frem Copenhagen and won 3-1 in Denmark before emphasising our superiority by winning 4-1 at Stamford Bridge in the second leg. In round two we beat Ville de Belgrade 1-0 at the Bridge, but any hopes we had of European glory were scuppered in Yugoslavia when we lost the second leg 4-1. Having outplayed Belgrade at home, for us then to be outplayed in turn by them was very disappointing. I'd thought Belgrade very unadventurous at Stamford Bridge. They fell back in defence, seemingly content to soak up all the pressure we exerted. Having been used to English games in which both teams went out to attack, I found Belgrade's tactics baffling. Though I wasn't aware at the time, I was receiving my first lesson in European competition whereby teams would play it tight away from home then go all out to win on their own turf. Which is exactly what Belgrade did. We, of course, approached the away leg in much the same way we would any other match – all-out attack. For their part, Belgrade showed their experience of European competition by catching us on the break – four times!

In October I became a father when Irene gave birth to our first child, Lynn. In the weeks leading up to the birth, friends who were already parents themselves told me that with the arrival of a baby my life would never be the same again. They were right. Irene and I were happier than we had ever been. Irene proved to be a wonderful mother. Me? Somehow I managed to muddle through thanks to Irene's guidance and advice and a little bit of common sense on my part. With the birth of Lynn I became very much aware that my life, in particular my lifestyle, appeared to change overnight. I was ready for bed at half past nine. At the first sign of a cough from

Lynn, I'd be consulting the medical book. I learned how to change a nappy, this at a time when nappies consisted of a cotton sheet and safety pins. I was in danger of finding conversations about wallpaper and curtains interesting and became a devotee of the BBC World Service at two in the morning. I was now Daddy and I loved every moment.

There were occasions when Chelsea's inconsistency, in particular our tendency to concede soft goals, frustrated not only the Chelsea supporters but the players themselves. In November, following a 5-2 win over Leicester City and a 2-0 defeat of Leeds, we travelled to Manchester City with high expectations of gaining at least a point. The game took place in thick fog and, though we enjoyed a lot of the play, City romped home 5-1. I'd scored our goal with a left-foot volley from a corner but found little consolation in the fact. In the dressing room, no one could hide their disappointment at having conceded five. Peter Sillett muttered something to the effect that we should have made more of the chances we had in front of goal, only for Ron Tindall to spin around and say, 'What bloody difference would it have made? If we'd scored five, you buggers in defence would have conceded six.' No one took issue with Ron on that.

That was the first occasion I was ever made aware of an element of discontent amongst the Chelsea players, the first time I had the greenery of my salad days as a footballer removed from my eyes. Up to that point, win, lose or draw, the relationship between the players and their attitude, particularly to one another, had always been convivial. Up until this defeat, I too had been fired by enthusiasm for the cause, believing the next game would be the one when we embarked on the wonderful run of results that I thought our individual talents were capable of. Results that would bring the club its second Championship, or first FA Cup. That defeat at Manchester City was the first time I became aware of questions being asked. What's more, it was the first occasion on which I started to ask myself questions about Chelsea's pedigree and ability to achieve real success on the pitch. The spirit in the dressing room and the camaraderie between the players was still topper, but the seeds of doubt and discontent that would eventually result in me leaving the club were beginning to germinate.

Following our defeat at Manchester City, Les Stubbs, who so far that season had only played two first team games, was transferred to Southend United along with Alan Dicks, who was the longest-serving member of the Chelsea playing staff, having joined the club from Southend in 1952. Alan's and Stubby's exits signalled that Ted Drake was to pin the future hopes of the club on youth. The club's youth policy was one of the very best, but blooding so many inexperienced players in the First Division within such a short space of time proved to make us even more inconsistent with regard to both our performances and results.

An experienced pro rarely has a bad game. He may have a game in which his performance and contribution fall somewhat short of normal, but rarely will it be poor. Young players, on the other hand, are wildly inconsistent. They can be on fire in one game and anonymous in the next. Ted Drake's policy of blooding youngsters was Hobson's choice. The financial situation at the club was tight, there was certainly no money to splash out on big fees for proven players of quality, so Ted had little option but to call upon the services of the products of Chelsea's fine youth policy. I imagine Ted was well aware of the detrimental effect so many young players would have on results, but I think he believed that in time the ship would right itself and we young players, having gained experience of First Division football, could be moulded into a team capable of mounting a serious challenge for trophies. Some players and supporters may have had misgivings about the club pinning all its hopes on youth, but Ted was optimistic.

But that was Ted Drake. He was the supreme optimist; in 1958
he still believed Glenn Miller was just 'missing'.

In addition to myself, other young players such as Mel
Scott, Tony Nicholas, Mickey Block, Les Allen, Cliff Huxford,
Mike Harrison and Peter Brabrook were to feature regularly
in the Chelsea first team. Other youngsters such as David
Cliss, Ken Shellito, Pat Holton, Bobby Tambling and Barry
Bridges featured intermittently.

Our results seesawed more than ever. Of our forty-two
league matches, we won eighteen, lost twenty and drew only
four. In the Christmas double-header we faced Blackburn
Rovers. A crowd of 32,149 turned up for our Christmas Day
meeting at Ewood Park and most of them went away
disappointed. We played Blackburn off the park, winning 3-0.
Two days later, in the return at Stamford Bridge, over 46,000
saw goals from Peter Dobing and Roy Vernon give Blackburn
a comfortable 2-0 victory.

And so it went on. In January we proved ourselves to be
Wolves' bogey team in beating the Champions 2-1 at
Molineux. We followed that with a 4-1 victory over
Newcastle United in the third round of the FA Cup and a
2-2 draw with Portsmouth in the league. We thought that
with the new year we'd turned the corner, only then to lose
twice against Aston Villa in both the FA Cup and the league.
We bounced back, winning 3-2 at home to West Ham and 3-1
at Nottingham Forest, only to lose 3-1 at home to Burnley
and 6-0 at Bolton Wanderers. The *Daily Sketch* dubbed
Chelsea 'the Jekyll and Hyde' of the First Division and few
argued with that description. Our form was a constant source
of frustration to both players and supporters alike and
occasionally some Chelsea fans couldn't hide their
frustration. Following our 3-1 defeat at home to Burnley,
John Sillett, who at the time still didn't own a car, made his
way to the bus stop a hundred yards away from the ground.

Most supporters had long since made their way home, but on arriving at the bus stop, Snoz found four middle-aged Blues fans.

'Been to the match?' one supporter asked Snoz.

Snoz nodded.

'What about that bloody John Sillett, he was bloody rubbish, wasn't he?' one of the supporters remarked.

Snoz had no alternative but to agree. Thankfully, from his point of view, the four supporters hadn't recognised Snoz, who then had to stand and listen as the supporters heaped abuse on his ability as a footballer. With little or no football on television, the vast majority of supporters only saw players from the terraces. The fact that he hadn't been recognised was a great relief to Snoz, because those four Blues really had it in for him. When the bus eventually arrived, the supporters headed upstairs so Snoz tactfully sought a seat downstairs. As Snoz said at the time, 'My critics are like London buses. I don't come across one for some time, then four come along at once!'

Though the 1958–9 season was very frustrating for many people connected with Chelsea, it was very successful for me. I finished the season with thirty-two goals. I was not only Chelsea's leading goalscorer, but joint top goalscorer in the First Division alongside Bobby Smith of Spurs. To be the leading goal scorer in the First Division at just over nineteen gave me immense satisfaction and, of course, the newspapers went overboard about it.

My goalscoring exploits in 1958–9 brought me to the attention of both the press and the England manager Walter Winterbottom, and also to someone else. Stan Thomlin was an agent. He wasn't the sort of agent one comes across in football today, far from it. In 1959 football agents were thin on the ground. Stan was one of them, but, as with the other agents, never handled the contract a player had with his club. Stan and his like handled what were then termed 'peripherals'. That is, the opportunities players had for making money outside the game. The first football agent was Bagenal Harvey, who at one point in my career represented me for a time. Bagenal was a dapper man, a gentleman of impeccable manners who often wore a worsted jacket and open-necked shirt from which billowed a red cravat like a June rose. Bagenal was a friend of Denis Compton, who played cricket for Middlesex and football for Arsenal and represented England at both. In the late forties, Denis Compton was a star, one of the few English sportsmen whose face was readily recognisable to all. His sporting prowess made Denis very popular with men and boys, while his matinée idol looks made him a hit with girls. As a result, Denis Compton received fan mail by the sackload. He never had time to reply to all his fan mail, so he asked Bagenal Harvey to deal with the mail on his behalf. When Bagenal saw the sheer volume of mail his eyes nearly popped. He immediately realised Denis's commercial potential. Bagenal had heard that County Perfumery, a company based in Stanmore in Middlesex, were looking for a model to promote Brylcreem. Bagenal approached County Perfumery suggesting they use Denis Compton and the company jumped at the idea.

Denis was paid £1,000 for three days' photographic work and permission to use his image to promote Brylcreem in newspaper and magazine adverts and on hoardings throughout the country. A thousand pounds doesn't sound like a lot of money today, but in the late forties it was considered a small fortune.

That was the first time a footballer ever made serious money outside the game, the first time a player's image had been used to promote a commercial product. Denis was quids in, so was Bagenal Harvey and the sales of Brylcreem went through the roof, so everyone was happy, with the possible exception of Arsenal and the FA. Neither Arsenal nor the FA would give permission for Denis to appear in the Brylcreem ads wearing an Arsenal or England strip. Both the Arsenal board and the FA believed that to do so would vulgarise and denigrate the strips in question, which is why Denis appeared in the advertisements for Brylcreem wearing a nondescript, plain white football shirt that bore a strong resemblance to a cricket shirt, together with black shorts and stockings. This is another indication of how football has changed. Today all clubs, not least Arsenal, and the FA itself, see the sale of strips as an integral part of their business.

I knew Stan Thomlin vaguely. In his younger days he had been a good enough runner to represent Great Britain and later turned to sports writing. When I made it into the Chelsea first team, Stan had earned me a few bob (literally a few bob) by ghosting a story in a Sunday newspaper that detailed my thoughts on my breakthrough into league football. The headline was, 'My First One and a Half Games of Success', or something equally pithy. Like Bagenal Harvey, Stan was a gentleman. Because of my previous dealings with him over the ghost-written article, I agreed to meet him when he rang me up one day and said he might have a little business to put my way.

'Look,' he said, 'you're making a name for yourself in the game. There might be a few bits of business where you might make a bit of money. How about me looking after those bits of business and being your agent?' I didn't know what 'bits of business' these might be, but with Irene and I now parents, I was keen to earn as much money as I could.

The first 'bit of business' Stan Thomlin put my way was promoting Bovril. I secured permission from Ted Drake and Chelsea to lend my name and image to a series of advertisements promoting Bovril under the heading, 'Dynamic footballer Jimmy Greaves trains and scores on Bovril'. Of course, I didn't train on Bovril (how can you?) and this beef drink certainly had nothing to do with the goals I scored, but

I did like Bovril as a drink and still do. I was paid something like £100 for the Bovril ads, which involved me spending an afternoon at Stamford Bridge running about with a ball and shooting at an empty net while a photographer snapped away. Those Bovril ads appeared in newspapers up and down the country and for a time formed the back page to the match-day programmes for England games at Wembley. Of course, when my Chelsea team-mates saw them, they took the micky. If I didn't score in a game they'd say things like, 'You ain't had your Bovril today, have you, Jimmy?' Following a 5-0 defeat at Blackpool, where I had missed a couple of chances early in the game, John Sillett remarked, 'Jimmy, son, your performance today and that Bovril has made you a laughing stock.' It's the mark of the quality of the gags of my Chelsea team-mates that that joke from Snoz was the best of those about me and Bovril!

The jokes and the ribbing concerning my involvement with Bovril never bothered me. I'd been paid five times my normal weekly wage for a couple of hours work. To me that was fantastic money.

'Dear Greaves', the letter began, 'we are contacting you to ascertain your availability for the forthcoming tour of South America and the United States to be conducted by the senior England International football team . . .' For once I didn't take exception to the Dickensian nature of the correspondence I had received from the Football Association. I had been selected for England at full international level and I was delighted. Within minutes of receiving the letter I was on the telephone to the FA, informing the Dickensian character on the other end of the line that 'Greaves is willing'.

The England tour comprised four matches, against Brazil, Peru, Mexico and the United States. At the time I was unsure of the exact nature of the touring squad, but having been selected I was certain I would feature in at least one match.

Less than two years after making my debut for Chelsea, I had made it into the England team. Things were really taking off for me and I was confident that, irrespective of who I might be selected to play against, I could play at what was the highest level in the game.

I'd been a little disappointed not to have been called up sooner to the England squad. When England played the USSR in October, many newspapers had put my name forward for selection and I certainly thought I was ready for international football. Unfortunately from my point of view, Walter Winterbottom and the England selection committee had chosen to overlook me for the USSR game. England won that match 5-0 with a team that must have created some sort of record, as not one of the eleven players England fielded that day had cost a fee. They had all come up through the junior ranks of their respective clubs, a situation I could never imagine occurring these days.

The fact that England had beaten the USSR so handsomely meant nothing when it came to selecting the team for the next international against Wales a month later, however. Winterbottom and the selectors made four changes to the team that had walloped the USSR, but again I was overlooked. England had posted reasonable results in their next two games in the spring, a 1-0 victory over Scotland and a 2-2 draw against Italy, both at Wembley. I lived in hope of being selected for the summer tour of South America, but I didn't expect it. The news of my selection wasn't a shock, more a pleasant surprise. Obviously my thirty-two goals in the league for Chelsea had earned my selection to the England team, thanks in no small measure to my Chelsea team-mates who gave me such good service, in particular Peter Brabrook, Ron Tindall and Mike Harrison.

Peter Brabrook was an East Ham lad who, like me, had played for both Essex and London Schoolboys. Peter had also

played for England Schoolboys, his most memorable
appearance being against West Germany in front of a 40,000
crowd at Highbury. England Schoolboys won that game 2-1,
and Peter scored both England goals, one a half-volley from
thirty yards and the other a spectacular diving header. Wally St
Pier, the West Ham scout, was at that game and proceeded to
pursue Peter with a view to him signing for the Hammers.
Peter wanted to join the West Ham groundstaff, but the club
told him they didn't have a spare place for him. While West
Ham deliberated, Jimmy Thompson came knocking on Peter's
door and, from that moment, Peter's future as a Chelsea player
was never in doubt.

Peter started his career at Stamford Bridge as an inside
forward, but when Ted Drake saw his speed he switched him
to the wing at outside right. I think Peter found playing on the
right wing a lot easier than in the centre of the park. That
tends to become congested and Peter relished the room he
found out wide, which afforded him more time on the ball and
the opportunity to use his pace to run at opposing full backs.
He was a tricky winger, nimble of foot and, once in full flow,
very direct. I always liked to receive the ball early, and the
earlier the better. Peter knew this and in games would release
the ball quickly, either threading a perfectly weighted pass
through the opponents back line for me to run on to, or
hitting a telling cross for me to control, rather than head.
Peter's service created a lot of the goals I scored in those early
days with Chelsea. As well as being a good team-mate we were
close friends. When Tommy Docherty took over from Ted
Drake as Chelsea manager in 1962, one of Tommy's first acts
was to sell Peter to West Ham. Tommy didn't fancy Peter's
style of play, though at first he was reluctant to sell him to
another London club. Everton came in for Peter but he was
about to marry a London girl, Doreen, and didn't fancy a
move North. In the end, West Ham, who could have signed

him for nothing if they had only created a place on their groundstaff, paid £35,000 for his services, a sum that in 1962 equalled the record fee for a winger that Spurs had paid Swansea for Cliff Jones.

Peter's career took off again at Upton Park. He was a member of the West Ham team that won the FA Cup in 1964 and only injury denied him a place in the Hammers team that won the European Cup Winners' Cup the following season. He ended his playing days with Leyton Orient in 1971 and for a time coached at Cambridge United. In 1995, Harry Redknapp asked Peter to go back to West Ham where he remains today, running the club's Under 16 and 17 teams. As for his pedigree in that line of work, suffice it to say that Peter has played an influential role in the development of such players as Joe Cole, Michael Carrick, Frank Lampard and Rio Ferdinand. Should you ever see those players in action, you might notice one thing they all have in common – they are all excellent distributors of the ball.

Ron Tindall had been a key member of the youngest forward line in Chelsea's history when he lined up alongside Peter Brabrook, Les Allen, Tony Nicholas and Frank Blunstone against Leeds United in September 1956. There is a photograph in existence of another young Chelsea forward line, one that took to the field at West Ham in 1958. That photograph shows Peter Brabrook, myself, Ron, Tony Nicholas and Mike Harrison. In comparison to the others, who appear physically strong, I look like the stripling I was. It wasn't a bad forward line, on the day we scored twice against West Ham, but, in keeping, conceded four. Ron Tindall was a great help to me in those days. He was a dual sportsman who played cricket for Surrey in the summer. Football teams comprise all manner of different types of people and Ron Tindall belied the notion that all footballers are thick. Ron was the most intelligent player in the Chelsea dressing room at that time. He was a well-read, cerebral man, who knew a great deal about all sorts of subjects. He came from a sporting family and went to Camberley Grammar School. On leaving school Ron played his football with a local amateur team, Camberley Wanderers, but such was his talent that it wasn't long before a string of scouts from league clubs were beating a path to his door. Ted Drake offered him the chance to join Chelsea, but he was undecided as he had just signed as a professional cricketer for Surrey. The fact that Surrey's home, Kennington Oval, was just downriver from Stamford Bridge, played a significant part in Ron's decision to sign for Chelsea. Today, because of the demands of both sports, it's unimaginable to think of someone playing both professional football and cricket, but in the fifties when the two respective seasons were more clearly defined, even though they did overlap it was not uncommon to find dual sportsmen.

Again, it's unthinkable today, but Ron negotiated an arrangement with Ted Drake that allowed him to play for Surrey for the entire cricket season, which meant he was unavailable to Chelsea from mid-April until early September. Chelsea were keen to have Ron on their books and so went along with this arrangement. That it suited Ron fine was due in part to his love of both sports and the fact that, as a First Division player on the maximum wage, there wasn't a great deal of difference between his wages at Chelsea and Surrey. I don't know what a county cricketer earns today, but it is nowhere near the money a Premiership footballer earns. The near parity of wages between footballers and cricketers and, indeed, the supporters who watched them play, meant there was no gulf between these respective bodies of people.

Today, Premiership players drink from a different well. They have much less contact with players from other sports such as cricket, and with their supporters. This lack of contact saddens me and has given rise to some players having an inflated sense of their own importance. I often wonder if some of today's top players truly understand what their club means to the supporters and how a win or a defeat affects them. I knew how our results at Chelsea affected our fans because they told me. I lived in the same neighbourhood as many Chelsea supporters. I met them socially at supporters club functions and at Ron Tindall's charity and benefit cricket matches. Quite often on the train home from an away match my team-mates and I would have a natter with Chelsea fans who were also journeying home. We'd share a beer or a cup of tea, we got to know them and they got to know us. There was an affinity and understanding that I don't think exists today because players don't have that level of contact with supporters. Perhaps it still exists in the lower divisions, but sadly not in the Premiership where too many players have erected barriers to separate them from supporters.

In the summers of '57, '58 and '59 I played a lot of cricket at the request of Ron Tindall, as did Mike Harrison, Peter Brabrook, Tony Nicholas and the Sillett brothers. Surrey always seemed to be involved in a charity game or a benefit match for one of their players on a Sunday to which Ron would extend an invitation for us to play. There were no official cricket matches on Sundays, so these charity and benefit matches attracted sizeable attendances. More often than not they would take place at some village cricket club in Surrey and would always end with everyone having a good few pints and a singsong. I used to enjoy these games as they afforded an opportunity for me to play either with or against some of my cricketing heroes such as Alec and Eric Bedser, Tony Locke, Peter May, Jim Laker and Ken Barrington. Though the games were taken seriously, they were always played with tremendous spirit and humour which carried on after the match and well into the night. In the pavilion of one village club I remember standing next to the great West Indies batsman Everton Weekes as we queued for tea. One of the ladies serving tea took one look at Everton's six feet plus frame and stepped back in awe.

'You're a very tall fellow, aren't you?' remarked the tea lady.

'Yes, ma'am, I am,' replied Everton.

'Just how tall are you?' the lady enquired.

'Six feet three, ma'am,' Everton informed her.

'Ooooh,' purred the woman, nudging her tea-lady companion, 'and are you all in proportion?'

'No,' replied Everton, grinning, 'if I was, I'd be eleven feet six!'

The transition from cricket to football wasn't always seamless for Ron Tindall. Following our opening day defeat at Manchester United, Ted Drake telephoned Ron asking if he was available for our second game of the season, a midweek match at home to Spurs. Not having kicked a ball since April, Ron was very apprehensive about returning to the side for such an important game. He expressed doubts about his match fitness, but Ted convinced him cricket had kept him reasonably fit and that he would get through the Spurs game without a problem.

Ron did a little light training on the morning of the Spurs match and that night ran out in front of a packed Stamford Bridge not having played a football match at any level for five months. In the opening minutes Ron was running around as if he hadn't missed a game or a training session all year. He was on fire. After twenty minutes we were two goals up and he had scored both of them. Now, quite often when a player has given his all in a speedy and tempestuous game, come the final few minutes he can have trouble talking. Strenuous physical exertion takes its toll on body and mind. His body is tired, he's panting for breath and the lack of oxygen affects the brain and consequently speech. Ron had survived on adrenalin in those first twenty minutes, but his lack of training and match fitness quickly told. At one point I looked across to Ron and saw him pointing to his left.

'Jimshy, jish drop in heesh fafeesh mish,' Ron blurted, his face contorting with the sheer effort of trying to speak.

I looked across to Peter Brabrook.

'Ron's gone, for God's sake don't play to him,' I told Peter, before turning to Ron and telling him to take a few deep breaths and get his rest while play was deep in our end of the field.

Ten minutes later, Reg Matthews was injured diving at the feet of Bobby Smith. After receiving treatment, Reg declared himself fit to carry on. Five minutes later, Bobby Smith sent a thunderbolt of a shot into Reg's ribcage. Reg winced with pain, but gamely scrambled to his feet and dived at the rebounding ball. Johnny Brooks came racing in and there was a sickening thud as Johnny's outstretched leg made contact with Reg's ribcage as he tried to clear the ball. Reg was in severe pain and it was obvious to all there was no way he could continue.

John Oxberry called for a stretcher. As there were no substitutes in those days, we looked at one another wondering which one of us would take over from Reg in goal.

'Anybody up for it?' asked Peter Sillett.

Suddenly, there was Ron Tindall, pushing his way past the knot of blue-shirted players.

'Ish shall do it. Gish me sish shershy.'

The game was thirty-five minutes old when Ron took over in goal from Reg Matthews and we were two goals to the good. To be fair, Ron did all right in goal. Despite a lot of pressure from Spurs he managed to keep a clean sheet until the fifty-first minute when Bobby Smith pulled a goal back for Tottenham. I was just about to restart the game from the centre spot when the referee's attention was drawn to some activity on the touchline. I looked across and there was Ted Drake with Reg Matthews by his side. Reg gamely returned to the fray and a suitably rested Ron Tindall once again joined me in attack. Minutes later, Tony Nicholas played the ball into Ron who then laid it off for me to run on to: 3-1 to Chelsea. The drama, however, was far from over. The Spurs goalkeeper Ted Ditchburn then dislocated a finger and their left back Ron Henry took over in goal. The Spurs winger Terry Medwin then scored a super goal to make it 3-2. Ten minutes later, Ted Ditchburn came back on to the pitch with his fingers taped up and took over in goal from Ron Henry. The game ebbed and flowed; it was there for the taking for either side. Then, with just under ten minutes remaining, Tony Nicholas scored to give us a 4-2 lead. In the dying embers of the game, Bobby Smith hit the bar for Spurs while at the other end I had an effort rebound off the post. It ended 4-2 to Chelsea. As I was leaving the field I walked across to shake hands with the referee.

'What a cracking game of football that was,' he said. He wasn't wrong.

Nothing hurts when you win. Ron Tindall hadn't played a match or done any serious training for five months. He'd come straight back into the first team, scored two goals and taken over in goal. When Ron entered the dressing room immediately after the game, he didn't whoop and holler or punch the air. He took a cup of tea from the tray and went over to see how Reg Matthews was before taking off his strip and sliding quietly into the plunge bath. A few of us were going for a drink and I asked Ron if he was coming along.

'Thanks, Jimmy, but not tonight,' Ron said. 'I'm feeling a little tired, I could do with getting to bed.'

It was the mark of the man. Ron Tindall was one of the game's quiet, unsung heroes with no pretentions whatsoever. And was so versatile: in the following season he also played for Chelsea at left back and left half.

Mike Harrison, like Mickey Block, was a well-built, speedy

winger who joined Chelsea on the same day as me. Mike was an Ilford lad who had been spotted playing for Newby Park Boys Club by Jimmy Thompson. Mike made his first team debut at Chelsea against Blackpool in 1957, a week short of his seventeenth birthday. Like Mickey Block, Mike had the misfortune of competing against Frank Blunstone for a place on the left wing and as such his appearances in the first team were restricted. He always did a good job when he came into the side and gave me sterling service. Though his outings with the Chelsea first team were intermittent, Mike was good enough to play for England at Under 23 level. With his newfound status, Mike felt it an appropriate time to go and ask Ted Drake for a rise.

'How much are you looking for?' Ted asked.

'An extra two pounds a week,' said Mike.

'An extra two quid a week!' said Ted aghast. 'What you trying to do, Mike, bankrupt this club? Two quid a week! Are you playing for money or a love of football?'

Ted spun Mike the hard-luck story of the club and, when he had finished, Mike had been made to feel so bad about asking for a rise, he was on the point of telling Ted he'd take a drop in wages to help the club out!

When Tommy Docherty took over from Ted, he and Mike never saw eye to eye and he moved to Blackburn Rovers for a fee of £18,000. Mike made more than two hundred appearances for Blackburn before moving on to Plymouth Argyle, then Luton Town, ultimately enjoying two successful seasons with Dover in the Southern League. I wonder if Mike ever tells his grandchildren about the day he scored for Chelsea against Arsenal with a thirty-five-yard piledriver past the Arsenal keeper Jack Kelsey? If he does, I hope he doesn't fail to mention that it was me who set him up for that shot, with a perfectly weighted pass from two yards.

In mentioning some of my Chelsea team-mates who were

instrumental in my success at the club, I shouldn't forget Reg
Matthews. The fact that we conceded a lot of goals may give
the impression that Reg was not the best of goalkeepers. On
the contrary, Reg was a very good goalkeeper and we would
have conceded even more had it not been for him. Reg won
five caps for England while at Coventry City and has the
distinction of never having played in a losing England team.
When he joined Chelsea from Coventry he quickly
established himself as one of the best goalkeepers in the First
Division. He was brave, agile and on more than one occasion
gave the Stamford Bridge faithful a demonstration of the finer
points of the game's most spectacular art. For all that, I have to
say he was the worst kicker of a dead ball I ever came across.
On those dreadful mid-winter pitches with a heavy leather case
ball, when it came to taking a goal kick Reg was so woeful that
Ron Tindall, Peter Brabrook, Mike Harrison, Frank Blunstone
and myself used to drop so deep we were lining up just outside
our penalty area. Reg would run up to the stationary ball and
emit a loud grunt as he kicked it. For all his efforts the ball
would bounce before it left his penalty area, then bobble for a
few yards before all hell broke loose as players from both teams
descended upon it some three yards outside the box. For all the
pressure it put us under, Reg still insisted on taking the goal
kicks. In the end, we had to gang up on him in the dressing
room and collectively persuade him to let the Sillett brothers
take our goal kicks.

His dead-ball kicking apart, Reg was a good goalkeeper
and a grand lad who possessed a keen wit. Following the six-
goal drubbing at Bolton Wanderers in 1959, Mel Scott was
bemoaning the lack of cover he had at centre half,
complaining that a number of the Bolton goals had come
about because he had been exposed. Reg, who in playing for
Chelsea knew a thing or two about being left exposed at the
back, was unimpressed.

'Don't bother telling team-mates your troubles,' Reg told Mel, 'because the way it is in football, half of them don't care, and the other half just reckon you had it coming.'

The 1958–9 season ended on a high note. I received notification of my selection for England's forthcoming tour of South America, and Chelsea rounded off the season with a 4-1 defeat at Birmingham City. As was often the case in those days, Ted took the opportunity of a fag end game whose outcome had little bearing to blood one or two players who had been on the fringe of the first team. For the Birmingham game, Ted replaced Reg Matthews in goal with Bill Robertson. Having signed for Chelsea in 1946 from the Scottish junior club Arthurlie, Bill was coming to the end of his career as a player and though he was to remain at Stamford Bridge for another season did so as second choice to Reg. Ted also brought in Pat Holton at left back. Pat had only been at Chelsea for a matter of weeks, having been signed by Ted from Motherwell. The other two changes of note from the team that had played much of the season were at wing half, where Sylvan Anderton and Stan Crowther had established themselves since their respective transfers. Stan Crowther was a tough-tackling wing half whom Ted had signed from Manchester United, a Midlands lad who had been born in Bilston and played his early football with Aston Villa. He had moved from Villa to Manchester United in the dark days after Munich and went immediately into the United team for that epic first post-Munich match in the FA Cup against Sheffield Wednesday and repaid the faith Jimmy Murphy had shown in him by scoring one of United's goals. He went on to appear for United in the FA Cup Final against Bolton Wanderers but when Wilf McGuinness and Nobby Stiles began to establish themselves at Old Trafford, Stan found himself out of favour and moved to Chelsea.

Stan earned himself a unique place in football history while at Manchester United. Having previously played for Aston Villa in the FA Cup that season, the FA gave United special dispensation to play Stan against Sheffield Wednesday. Thus he became the first and, so far, only player ever to appear for two teams in the FA Cup in one season.

Stan Crowther spent two seasons at the Bridge before signing for Brighton, but after a season at the Goldstone Ground left in mysterious circumstances and announced his retirement at the age of twenty-seven. Stan is on record as saying he was sacked at Brighton. He had been left out of the team for some time and announced his retirement 'as a matter of principle'. His old Villa boss Eric Houghton was in charge of non-league Rugby Town and Houghton persuaded Stan to return to the Midlands and see out his playing days with Rugby. He retired far too early from league football but the general feeling is that he fell out of love with the professional game. Sadly Stan has little interest in football now. In 1975 he gave an interview for the Aston Villa match-day programme in which he said, 'Football for me was wasted years and as far as that is concerned I want to forget it.' Stan went on to say that if he could have his time all over again 'football would be the last business I would choose as an occupation'.

I don't think I have ever heard a former player talk in such frank terms or so acidly about the game. Again, I find that very sad. As for why Stan felt that way, I can only assume that, like every other player of his time, he was deeply in love with the game but the harsh realities of football, such as finding yourself out of favour with a particular manager and not achieving the goals you have set for yourself, served to make him bitter. He later said he left the game at twenty-seven because 'football and Stan Crowther didn't get on. Some of the things I saw going on would break your heart.' Perhaps it was a case of football not living up to Stan's ideals. Perhaps here was an example of a man who found he had a talent for a job he'd rather not be doing. Whatever, Stan left the game in his prime.

At right half against Birmingham City in that last game of the season was Sylvan Anderton. Sylvan was a a super lad whose rich Devon accent would immediately conjure up for me images of cream teas, the chocolate-and-cream-coloured railway carriages of BR's Western Region and evocatively named towns and villages such as Combe Martin, Woolacombe, Ottery St Mary, Appledore and Westward Ho!. Through no fault of his own, Sylvan has often found himself being referred to in somewhat less than flattering terms with regard to him joining Chelsea. This is unfair, because the circumstances surrounding his arrival at Stamford Bridge had nothing at all to do with him.

That season Ted Drake had been tipped off about a wing half who had been turning in some terrific performances for Hearts in the Scottish First Division. At the time Ted was eyeing Sylvan Anderton who was playing for Reading, the club Ted had managed before taking over at Chelsea. The reports from Chelsea's Scottish scout about the Hearts wing half kept arriving on Ted's desk, each one more glowing than the last. Keen to see for himself this player who was so exciting our Scottish scout, Ted travelled north to see Hearts play. The press got wind of Ted's interest and on his return asked for his impressions. Ted told the press boys that, having seen the Hearts player in question, he was of the mind that Sylvan Anderton was a far better player and promptly went out and signed him from Reading.

That Hearts wing half was Dave Mackay and I will leave you to draw your own conclusions as to the quality of Ted's judgement. Dave Mackay eventually signed for Spurs and became not only one of Tottenham's all-time greats but a colossus of the English game. As for Sylvan? Well, he had a decent enough game against Birmingham City. Who knows what impact the arrival of Dave Mackay would have had on the fortunes of Chelsea. Of course, no one can say for sure. What I will say is, should Ted have signed Dave and not Sylvan, such would have been his contribution to the team that I would probably not have been so keen to move on in 1961.

The fact that Ted Drake opted for Anderton rather than Mackay had nothing to do with Sylvan. I'm sure Sylvan would acknowledge he was not in the same class as Mackay, but that is no slight against him. Sylvan did his best for Chelsea and in truth wasn't a bad player. He just wasn't a Dave Mackay.

I still have the match programme from our game at Birmingham City. In goal for Birmingham that day was Gil Merrick who had won twenty-three caps for England, the first against Northern Ireland in 1952. Gil gave sterling service to Birmingham City both as a goalkeeper and a manager. He'd won his last cap in England's 4-2 defeat against Uruguay in the 1954 World Cup and, though still a decent keeper five years on, appeared anachronistic. English football was modernising. The players wore short sleeved V-necked shirts and shorts whose length was much shorter than those worn in the days when Gil kept goal for England. Our stockings too were different, cotton instead of wool. Gil Merrick, however, appeared to belong to that other age. This had nothing to do with his goalkeeping, more his general appearance. His hair was short back and sides and slapped down with Brylcreem and he sported a dapper moustache, the sort I had seen worn by English film actors of the forties when playing a Scotland Yard detective. That's how Gil appeared to me: an English film actor of the forties. Birmingham City beat us 4-1 in what was Gil's final bow as their goalkeeper. It was almost as if fate wanted it that way. Gil was a fine goalkeeper but the era in which he had been in his pomp and to which he was so closely associated was at an end. Some months after our defeat at Birmingham City saw the retirement from the game of such great names as Gil, Tom Finney and Nat Lofthouse, with Stanley Matthews, just an occasional player in the Blackpool first team, dropping down to the Second Division to enjoy a swansong with Stoke City. Another all-time English great was also to announce his retirement – Billy Wright, recipient of 105 international caps and a veteran of numerous overseas tours, for whom my first England tour would prove to be one tour too many.

CHAPTER FIVE

WHAT DO YOU WANT TO MAKE THOSE EYES AT ME FOR

Prior to joining the full England squad for the tour of South America and the USA, I was also chosen for two other representative sides. Oddly, though I had played all my football in the Chelsea first team in 1958–9, I was chosen to play for the Football Combination Representative XI, which was the league the Chelsea reserves played in. I can only assume my selection for this team, together with my team-mates Reg Matthews, Peter Sillett and Sylvan Anderton, had much to do with the fact that this representative XI was to be managed by Ted Drake with John Oxberry as trainer. We played a Dutch Select XI in Amsterdam, a closely contested game which we ended up winning 4-3 with me scoring a hat-trick.

My other representative honours came when I was selected to play for England Under 23s against Italy in Milan, a match that took place two days before I was due to fly out to South America with the full England team! We beat the Italians 3-0 and I scored two of the England goals. There was no opportunity for celebration, however. Immediately after the game, Walter Winterbottom, the Blackpool full back Jimmy Armfield and I caught a night train from Milan to Zurich from where we flew to Heathrow to join up with the rest of the England touring party. It was while at Heathrow that I was admonished by Sir Stanley Rous for having the audacity to eat a cake with my cup of tea. Welcome to the England team!

From Heathrow we flew to Lisbon then on to Recife in north-west Brazil where we caught a connecting flight to Rio de Janeiro. When we arrived in Brazil I was absolutely shattered. Our passage from Heathrow had taken twenty-six hours and before that I'd travelled to London from Milan via Zurich by train and air. When Walter Winterbottom announced the team to face Brazil and I wasn't in it, I have to say I was somewhat relieved not to be making my full England debut as I still hadn't recovered from the journey.

The tour did not get off to the best of starts and from that moment on it gradually deteriorated. We played Brazil in front of 150,000 fervent home supporters in the Maracana stadium, and I watched from the dugout as England went down 2-0. The Brazilian team included seven members of the side that had won the World Cup a year before and we were a goal down after only three minutes. Jimmy Armfield, who was making his international debut, got into a muddle with Billy Wright. They both left the ball for one another and in nipped the Brazilian outside right Julinho to send the packed terraces into raptures. Pele and Didi were running the show and after twenty-eight minutes Pele left Billy Wright gasping as he sprinted into the England penalty area before squaring the ball for the outstretched leg of Henrique to make it 2-0.

To our boys' credit they gave it a go in the second half. Their football in the second period was much more fluent and, but for the woodwork which denied both Bobby Charlton and Johnny Haynes, we could have got something out of the game. Though the overall performance was satisfactory everyone was disappointed to begin the tour with a defeat, albeit against the World Champions. What no one knew, however, was that the performance against Brazil was to be England's best of the tour. After Rio, it all went downhill.

I was never comfortable when flying. From Rio we flew to

Lima, not over the Andes but through them. Apparently the plane was carrying too much weight and, as such, flying over the Andes could have caused problems. Whatever those problems might have been, from my point of view they couldn't have been any worse than seeing vertical mountainsides through the windows on both sides of the aeroplane, and for the plane to be confronted by seemingly hurricane force winds that roared down the valleys, causing the plane to constantly roll and often to lose height. With us on board was a film crew from BBC television sport that included Ken Wolstenholme, Paul Fox and Brian Cowgill. The latter two would go on to carve out influential careers in television, while Ken, of course, was to achieve broadcasting immortality by virtue of a few well-chosen words in 1966.

At one point in the flight I asked a stewardess why we were carrying so much weight on the plane and she told me it was because of the sheer amount of baggage and equipment the BBC party had with them.

'Then tell those BBC boys to dump some of their baggage! Their cameras for a start,' I informed the stewardess, more from nerves than anything else. Ken, Paul, Brian and the other members of the BBC team turned and gave me disapproving looks.

'You're starting out on your England career, Jimmy; you should be grateful for our presence,' said Ken Wolstenholme. 'There's no such thing as bad publicity.'

'Except an obituary notice,' I replied.

Peru were coached by the Hungarian Jorge Orth and had recently drawn with Brazil and beaten Uruguay in the South American Cup, so I knew they would prove difficult opponents. I also knew I wasn't along for the ride and following our defeat against Brazil, had a very good chance of making my full England debut in Lima. I wasn't wrong.

Walter Winterbottom was the first manager of England,

having been appointed in 1946. He was thirteen years into the job, but still didn't have overall control when it came to selecting the England team. Though by 1959 Walter's influence on selection had grown, he still hadn't managed to wrestle it from the blazer brigade at the FA. The England team was chosen by Walter and a selection committee. (I have travelled all over the world and on my journeys have walked through numerous cities and countless public parks but I have yet to see a statue to a committee.) Selection for England was not solely based on ability or merit. Quite often a player was awarded a cap by the selectors in recognition of his services to football. Even more disturbing was the fact that some players had been chosen for England because, as Walter once remarked, one of the selection committee said, 'It's really time we gave this deserving chap a cap as he is a damn decent fellow.' This happened with Leslie Compton of Arsenal in 1950. According to Walter, when he sat down with the selection committee to choose the England team to face Wales at Sunderland, one member said, 'Compton is doing well at the Arsenal, he's a gentleman and a sportsman. Isn't it time we honoured him? Why not give him a chance?'

Walter had to tread carefully. In the late forties and in the fifties, he diplomatically suggested the Football League Representative team as a means of 'honouring' good sorts rather than the England team. Slowly but surely his influence over team affairs was growing.

When he was first appointed, Walter had had to sit down with an eight-man selection committee, every member of which would put forward nominations for the forthcoming England game. Sometimes that would involve half a dozen players being nominated for a single position. Walter then had to agonise while each player nominated was subjected to a series of votes until they came up with one player for the position in question. On one occasion, five players were nominated for the position of goalkeeper. It turned out that none of the committee members had actually seen any of the goalkeepers in action. Walter knew such a system was ridiculous and insisted the committee see a player in recent action before nominating him for the England team. That only provided him with another problem.

A number of the FA selection committee were directors of league clubs and obviously watched their own team in action every week, which created a bias. In the mid-fifties, Walter set about persuading all members of the selection committee to watch teams in action other than their own. That was a step forward, except that the committee members now began to report back with their heads filled with the comments of the particular manager they had been talking to who had invariably been singing the praises of one of his own players. As far as Walter was concerned, the changes he had managed to instigate made little difference to his plan to create an England team over a four-year period in preparation for a World Cup. The England team still changed from one match to the next, sometimes wildly so. This goes some way to explaining why, when England could call upon such great players as Stan Matthews, Tom Finney, Nat Lofthouse, Len Shackleton, Wilf Mannion, Jackie Milburn, Roger Byrne and Billy Wright, in the mid-fifties we never cemented our traditional reputation as being one of the world's strongest international teams. With the exception of Billy Wright, the majority of the aforementioned, Matthews included, were in and out of the England team and some, such as Shackleton, were only awarded a handful of caps. With all due respect, who would prefer Portsmouth's Jack Froggatt to Stanley Matthews; Bolton's Malcolm Barrass to Blackpool's Harry Johnston; Sheffield Wednesday's Redfern Froggatt to Len Shackleton; and Ivor Broadis of Manchester City to Stan Mortensen of Blackpool? The England selection committee, that's who, for the game against Scotland in 1953. Walter Winterbottom would have one team for one match then find himself with a completely different side for the next game. It frustrated the hell out of him, not least because, in 1959, he was looking to introduce a number of young players to the England set-up with a view to creating a side for the 1962 World Cup, and one of those young players was me.

I was given the chance to prove what I could do at international level in the game against Peru, though I could have wished for a happier debut. The England team for my debut as a full international was: Eddie Hopkinson (Bolton Wanderers), Don Howe (West Bromwich Albion), Jimmy Armfield (Blackpool), Ronnie Clayton (Blackburn Rovers), Billy Wright, Ron Flowers, Norman Deeley (all Wolves), myself (Chelsea of course), Bobby Charlton (Manchester United), Johnny Haynes (Fulham) and Doug Holden (Bolton Wanderers). Before the game I was very nervous, but Walter Winterbottom eased my nerves somewhat by stressing that I was under no pressure whatsoever and that my future England career would not hinge on this one performance alone. Walter told me to go out and enjoy myself, to play my normal game and to make sure I was always available to outside right Norman Deeley and right half Ronnie Clayton. He also stressed that I would play off Bobby Charlton and that the pair of us should stay relatively close together. It was a revelation to me to hear Walter talk to each and every player in that dressing room, informing them of what he expected from them. At Chelsea, Ted Drake still more or less confined himself to 'All the best'!

Though Walter's words of encouragement eased my nerves somewhat I was still very anxious as I joined the line of England players behind Billy Wright as we left the dressing room. We created a little bit of history that day as the shirts we wore were royal blue; this was the first time England had ever taken to the field for an international match wearing anything but their white shirts, or, in the event of a colour clash, red. But any idea that this new strip was to herald a new beginning for England was to be quickly dispelled.

As we made our way down what seemed like a hundred concrete steps that led to the tunnel the palms of my hands felt clammy. My mouth was as dry as sandpaper and my stomach felt as if it were doing cartwheels. On the signal from a Peruvian official, Billy Wright stopped some two yards from the mouth of the tunnel. Though I couldn't see them I could hear the buzz of a very sizeable crowd outside. The Peruvian team, in white shirts with a red trim, arrived at our side. The guy standing next to me smiled and nodded, then extended his hand. I smiled and shook it. I felt a little embarrassed. His hand was dry and clean; mine, by comparison, was coated in a film of sweat. From somewhere in the distance a tinny band was playing a military-type tune, only it was a military tune the style of which I had never heard before. That tune bounced along. Pump ah pump; pump-ah-pump-ah-pump. Pump appa pump ah pump. Trumpets shrilled. Cornets came in unexpectedly. A tuba inopportunely gatecrashed. I remember thinking, 'It was never like this in "Peter and the Wolf".' The tunnel echoed to the sound of Spanish voices. Peruvian officials in red blazers and white cotton trousers buzzed about our midst brandishing clipboards and talking to one another in what appeared to me to be excessively loud voices. The shrill of a referee's whistle cut through the air. The Peruvian players started to bounce up and down. They shouted at one another. It felt like a world away from Stamford Bridge, Wembley even. I felt like a stranger in a strange land.

Normally, when I crossed that white line whatever nerves I was feeling immediately disappeared. I'd run around the pitch feeling any anxiety draining from me. But that didn't happen this time, because it couldn't. Rather than running when we hit the white line, we continued to walk. A slow, irritating walk that made my legs feel like lead. In contrast, the alp-like terraces that surrounded us were alive with flailing humanity. The noise that came down from those terraces was deafening. I couldn't focus on any one aspect of the open terraces, but I didn't need to do that to know there was not a single friendly voice amongst them.

'Pear-roo! Pear-roo! Pear-roo!'

The chant was incessant, and it was unchallenged as it resounded around this bowl of a stadium.

When we reached the centre circle we turned to face our opponents. I looked across and found myself staring into the inscrutable face of one of their defenders. His expression never altered. I felt transparent because he appeared to be looking not at me but straight through me.

Billy Wright walked down our line, introducing each of us to a besuited man and a general who was wearing so many medals you would have thought he'd fought in every war there had ever been. I shook the hands of both and nodded to each man. Billy then handed over these two VIPs to the Peruvian captain who took some time introducing them to his team-mates. I again glanced across at the inscrutable Peruvian defender. He didn't appear to be looking straight through me this time. Though his face did not move a muscle, his eyes ran the rule over my body. That done, we eyeballed one another with the clear, innocent eyes of a couple of used-car salesmen.

The Peruvian players appeared muscular and strong. I felt thin and weedy in comparison. 'What the hell am I doing here?' I asked myself, only to quickly tell myself, 'I'm here to score goals.'

The formal introductions over, the tinny band struck up again. The Peruvian national anthem was a strange tune, or so it seemed to me. Very grand, very up-tempo, but just when it sounded as if it was settling down to a jolly tune, the mood changed and the overall feeling became one of foreboding, only for the tune to pick up again before concluding on a high note with every brass instrument jockeying for pole position.

Immediately the band finished, a volatile roar of pride and aggression swept down from the terraces. Then the tinny band struck up once more and silence immediately descended on the terracing. The band were playing our national anthem, but in a style I had never heard before. They were playing almost up-tempo. They appeared to be in so much of a hurry that the final notes of each line were cut short. (Throughout my career, wherever I was to play overseas, I never heard our national anthem played the way a British military band plays it. The renditions were always respectful, in keeping, but somehow they always appeared different.) Whether it was nervous tension or what, I don't know, but I found myself singing our national anthem with great gusto.

'Lo-oh-oh-oh-ong to reign oh-ver us, Gor-ohd saaaaaaaaave are queeeeeen!'

When the band had finished, the stadium erupted once more. I thought I felt my ears pop. Ron Flowers and Ronnie Clayton peeled away and like the rest of my team-mates ran to one end of the field. They weren't in front of me for long. I turned and sprinted after them, overtook them and carried on running at full pelt. I jumped through the air and when I landed back on the bone hard ground, I threw my arms out wide, then did it again. I felt all the tension, irritation and anxiety that had built up inside me in the previous half hour rush from my body. I trotted into the penalty area, Bobby Charlton passed a practice ball to me and I hit it straight at Eddie Hopkinson. Eddie clutched the ball into his midriff, threw it back, only for me to hit it straight back at him. So we continued, like a little machine, both of us getting a good feel for the ball.

I turned away from Eddie in order to give Bobby Charlton

and Norman Deeley the chance to fire some shots at goal and surveyed the scene. As Billy Wright exchanged pennants with the Peruvian captain, I became aware of an air of expectancy all around the stadium, as if the teeming masses crammed on to the mountainous terracing knew something I didn't. I knew nothing at all about this Peruvian team except what little Walter Winterbottom had told us. Apparently they had a very good left winger in Seminario who was direct, tricky and capable of whipping in dangerous crosses. What Walter failed to mention about Seminario was that he also had a very good eye for goal. Something England, and in particular our right back Don Howe, would soon discover at some cost.

Seminario was not the only member of the Peru team who could play a bit. In the opening exchanges Seminario, Sanchez, Mosquera, Loyaza and Joya proved themselves more than a handful for the England defence and to the delight of the fanatical home crowd we found ourselves chasing the game. The game was only ten minutes old when an error from Billy Wright enabled Seminario to give Peru a lead from which we never recovered. Don Howe, who later in his career would prove himself to be one of English football's finest coaches, was given the runaround by Seminario. As for Billy Wright, he offered only glimpses of past glories. Billy's performance against Peru was from the school of Wright rather than the work of the master. In the opening twenty minutes, Don Howe dug himself a pit and promptly climbed in, by half-time he had eased himself down into that pit and scraped the earth over his head. Seminario helped himself to a hat-trick, made another goal for Peru and just for good measure also rattled our woodwork.

At the final whistle, Peru were worthy 4-1 winners; in truth, we hadn't been at the races. Consolation for me came from the fact I had scored our solitary goal. A great through ball from Johnny Haynes had put me in the clear. I simply had to keep going and keep my cool, which I did to maintain my record of having scored on my debut for every team I had played for.

It may have been my first tour with the England team, but I didn't have to be an experienced international to know that from the team's point of view it wasn't going well. Defeat against Brazil was disappointing though not unexpected. To follow that defeat, however, with a 4-1 drubbing at the hands of Peru served to make the press boys sharpen their pencils. We felt we had a chance to rectify the situation and redeem some of the pride of English football in our next match, against Mexico. The Mexicans were considered to be 'third rate' in terms of international football, but the rot had set in as far as this tour was concerned. In Mexico City, things went from bad to worse.

Mexico had taken part in five World Cups but had never won a single game. Their team was devoid of star names, even in terms of football in Central America, but on the day they proved too hot to handle for England.

For the Mexico game, Walter Winterbottom reverted to a more orthodox forward formation rather than the one he had asked us to play against Peru, whereby Doug Holden, Johnny Haynes and Norman Deeley had occupied the middle of the field behind Bobby Charlton and me. Against Mexico, Walter made one change to the defence, playing Wilf McGuinness instead of Ron Flowers; up front, Doug Holden switched to outside right in place of Norman Deeley, with Bobby Charlton taking Doug's place on the left and Derek Kevan taking over from Bobby at centre forward.

The game was played in blazing heat and, with Mexico City being 7,500 feet above sea level, we also struggled in the rarified air. Not having had the benefit of any real acclimatisation, the altitude quickly told on the England players. I was puffing and panting after half an hour and Eddie Hopkinson in goal had trouble adjusting to the speed of the ball in the thin air. That said, we made a good start in the game and took the lead courtesy of a textbook header from Derek Kevan, who got on the end of a cross from Bobby Charlton and headed the ball low and to the left of the Mexican goalkeeper. In what were for us difficult conditions to play in, Mexico gradually ground us down and eventually won the game 2-1. What had initially been a tide of criticism from the English press suddenly turned into a raging torrent.

When we moved on from Mexico to Wrigley Field in Los Angeles for our match against the USA we knew that no matter how handsomely we beat the part-timers of the USA, such a result could not redeem us. The barbs were out. The English press had it in for England, whom they saw as a declining force in international football.

The day after our defeat against Mexico we made the 1,500-mile flight to Los Angeles where we were feted handsomely. On our first night in LA, the British expats in Hollywood held a reception for us that was attended by a number of British actors such as David Niven and Pat Cutts who were working in Hollywood at the time.

The following day I joined the rest of my England team-mates for an afternoon's racing at the famous Hollywood Park racetrack. The day after that we trained, but in the evening took off to see Sammy Davis Junior perform in what was billed as a one-man show. Some one-man show this turned out to be. He took to the stage with the Nelson Riddle Orchestra! Sammy Davis Junior gave a terrific performance that night. I doubt whether he knew anything about football, but he, or one of his writers, had done his homework, because at one point in his show he turned to our party and said:

'The England soccer team are here tonight. They're on tour and have lost to Brazil, Peru and Mexico. In fact they haven't won a game yet. If you guys think you've got some explaining to do when you get home, spare a thought for me. I'm a one-eyed Jew who also happens to be black!'

Sammy's act went down a storm and the England party joined the rest of the audience in showing our appreciation of his rare talent by giving him a ten-minute standing ovation. As I applauded wildly I couldn't help but wonder who Sammy Davis Senior was and if he felt any chagrin at being one generation removed from world fame? That's the way my mind works at times. I find myself dwelling on those who just missed out on fame and immortality for probably no other reason than fate. For example, what about the penultimate Mohican?

Between training we also enjoyed seeing the LA Dodgers in action after which Bobby Charlton came out with a comment that would have done Sam Goldwyn proud.

'I don't take to baseball, cricket is much better,' said Bobby, when asked to comment, 'and I hate cricket.'

A friend of Billy Wright, the comedian and singer Dave King, who was a big star in the UK at the time, flew in from Florida to watch our game against the USA and must have been amongst only a handful of England supporters present at the Wrigley Field Stadium for a game that did not start well for England. For a time against the USA it looked as if this match was going to be the biggest disaster of the entire ill-fated tour. The USA took the lead and only a goal from Bobby Charlton enabled us to go in at half-time on level terms with a team who had not won an international of any note for nigh on five years. Any fears of us recreating unwanted football history by suffering another ignominious defeat at the hands of the USA, as had happened to England in the 1950 World Cup, were quickly dispelled in the second half when another goal from Bobby Charlton put us ahead. With our second goal, the USA crumbled. Bobby helped himself to a hat-trick and further goals from Warren Bradley of Manchester United, Derek Kevan, Johnny Haynes and a brace from Ron Flowers gave us a convincing 8-1 victory.

Only the English press were far from convinced about the value of this win.

Having failed to feature on the scoresheet in a game that produced eight goals for England, you might be given to thinking I had a poor game. To my mind, however, I came off the Wrigley Field thinking I'd done all right. My forte was scoring goals, but as was often to be the case during my career some of the games in which I didn't score gave me as much satisfaction as when I did. For the USA game, Walter Winterbottom had asked me to hold the ball up and then lay it off to Johnny Haynes when he arrived to support our attack. This task I carried out dutifully, so for all that I didn't manage a goal against the USA myself, I thought I'd made a telling contribution to our team play. Walter certainly thought so, because he made a point of complimenting me on my performance after the game, saying I had been 'unselfish' and that I had indeed 'made a telling contribution to the team'. I felt I'd done the job that had been asked of me. In many respects the role I fulfilled went against my natural inkling to turn and run for goal when the ball was played into my feet and I found myself with some space. But I stuck doggedly to the task I'd been given and found satisfaction in the fact I had played Johnny into the game on several occasions.

Apart from my personal achievement of having made it into the full England team, there was little to be gained from this tour. Our trouncing of the USA was only to be expected and the only momentous incident came during our game against Mexico when England used substitutes in an international match for the very first time. The use of substitutes had yet to be officially recognised, but FIFA had given permission for countries to use them in international friendly matches on an experimental basis as long as the two respective teams were in agreement. Against Mexico, Ron Flowers and Warren Bradley created a little English football history when they respectively replaced Wilf McGuinness and Doug Holden. Some FA officials on that tour had expressed doubts about the validity of using substitutes in international matches. As absurd as it may seem, their main concern was whether or not part participation in an England game merited the award of a cap. English football was being dragged kicking and screaming into the modern world.

It makes me smile when I read today of how some managers and players believe they receive a bad press. The criticism levelled at contemporary players is nothing compared to what it used to be. In his autobiography *The Way It Was*, Stanley Matthews wrote, 'Many modern players would wither if they received some of the criticism that was levelled at individual players in the thirties and forties. The sports writers of that time did not hold back and you had to have broad shoulders in order to carry the burden of what was often damning criticism of your performances.'

In 1959 it was little different. I returned with the England touring party to a barrage of criticism aimed at Walter Winterbottom and many of the players who had taken part in the tour, but in particular at the FA who were seen to be, as one sports writer put it, 'light years out of touch with what is happening in the modern game'.

John Moynihan described the tour as 'a slight against the reputation of English football'. Eric Batty talked of 'the poverty of England's performances' and went on to say that, 'the lack of fight by some players, in particular from those with not a little experience under their belts, was unforgivable'. Arguably the most damning criticism came from the sports writer son of the former Bolton Wanderers and England inside forward David Jack. Writing in the *Empire News* Jack referred to the tour as, 'undoubtedly the most disappointing tour ever to be undertaken by an England team'. He continued, 'The defeats on this tour emphasised once again that, unless changes are made at the top, English International football will continue to deteriorate until we are unfit to compete against the great soccer nations of the world.'

Jack went on to say, 'Of the eighteen players on tour, not one justified the great honour paid to him as a representative of his country. In such poor company, Johnny Haynes had useful games in Rio and Lima and Jimmy Greaves, although not yet ready, did enough to reveal promise for the future. Bobby Charlton, denied the opportunity of playing in his correct position, should, for that reason, escape criticism. As for the defence, only Ron Flowers and Ronnie Clayton emerged with any credit . . . the men at the top chose players who were not the best at England's disposal. They took poor performers to South America and left good players at home. That simple fact tells the whole story. The England selectors have much to answer for and the abject failure of this tour brings into question their very worth as decision-makers regarding the composition of our national team.'

In many respects such criticism only served to strengthen Walter Winterbottom's hand. He wanted sole responsibility for the England team so that he could build a side over a four-year cycle that could win the World Cup for England. The press criticism of the FA served to make them relinquish their power with regard to the selection of the England team, but only fleetingly so. Walter Winterbottom was to be given a more or less free hand when selecting an England team for an international match later that year. But when Walter's youthful England team, of which I was a member, failed to impress, it was back to square one and Walter's dissatisfaction and frustration with his role as England manager began to take root.

When the football fixtures for a season that bridges two decades are first produced, the printing of the season in question always looks odd and somehow unreal. 1959–60. The appearance of those numbers on the cover of my Chelsea book of training rules and players' instructions emphasised to me the passing of time. I'm sure everyone feels that way when they see the numbers indicating a new decade appear on a fixture list for the first time. I'd become so used to seeing the fifties that 1960 seemed inappropriate, almost as if it were a printing error. For all it felt strange at the time, we were indeed about to embark upon the sixties, a decade in which society and football would change dramatically and forever, the events of which would have an equally dramatic effect on my career and, ultimately, my life.

My thirty-two goals in the season 1958–9 was a new club record for Chelsea, beating Bob Whittingham's record of forty-eight years. In recognition of that feat, in the summer of 1959 the Chelsea chairman, Joe Mears, presented me with yet another illuminated address. Rather than being the number of our Wimbledon flat in lights, this was a scroll of parchment beautifully handwritten in the style of olde English and detailing my thirty-two goals in that season. Although the power and influence of the Football Association and Football League can be further gauged from the fact that Chelsea had first to seek permission from both bodies before making the presentation, and despite the fact that as a professional footballer I wanted to be paid a wage in keeping with my efforts and achievements, I derived a great deal of pride and satisfaction from the presentation of this illuminated address. To me, like every other player of the time, football was all about the pursuit of sporting distinction, not money and power.

One of football's abiding attractions is that events rarely pan out the way you expect them to. As I prepared for a new season, in my heart of hearts I knew Chelsea wouldn't win the

Championship, though I was hoping for a more than decent run in the FA Cup. On a personal note, I felt fitter and stronger than ever and I was confident that with some experience now behind me, I would continue to score goals for Chelsea and, should I be selected, for England.

The way I saw it in the summer of '59, I felt Wolves were going to emulate the Huddersfield Town side of 1923–6 and Arsenal of 1932–5 and win three First Division Championships on the trot, an opinion I am sure was shared by many players and supporters of the day. When it came to scoring goals, Wolves were the master blasters, having scored 307 league goals in the three seasons I had been a professional footballer. Wolves were a formidable team; they had won the Championship in the two previous seasons and their strength in depth was evidenced by the fact that their reserve and youth sides had also won their respective leagues two years running. But that summer Billy Wright announced his retirement from the game. It came as no surprise. The rumours had been circulating for weeks but with the confirmation came the realisation that Billy's retirement signalled the end of an era for English football. As Eric Batty wrote in *Soccer Star*, 'The retirement of Billy Wright is significant. The old guard are making way for the new in English football. As we prepare to enter a new decade we do so heralding the emergence of new talent such as Johnny Haynes, Bobby Charlton and Jimmy Greaves. New talent produces new deeds; can those emerging players achieve or even surpass the achievements of Wright, Matthews and Finney? Only time will tell. The only thing we know for sure is, English football will never be quite the same again.'

Batty was thinking along the right lines, but the changes that were to come about and revolutionise English football in 1960 had little, if anything, to do with the retirement of such legendary figures as Wright and Finney or the winding down of the career of Stan Matthews.

Even when I heard of Billy Wright's retirement, I still thought Wolves would be at the forefront of the race for the Championship. The other two teams I thought to be in the reckoning were Manchester United and Arsenal, with the dark horses being Spurs and West Bromwich Albion.

When Manchester United had been beaten 6-3 at Bolton in November of the previous season, they were only four points off the bottom. It looked as if relegation might have to be one of the many prices United would pay for the Munich air disaster nine months before. United, however, rallied in no uncertain fashion and in their next twelve league games only dropped a single point and in beating us 3-2 at Stamford Bridge in December had looked a very competent outfit indeed. Like us, United's strength was their ability to score goals – 103 in 1958–9 – though unlike us, they could also boast a defensive record that had been bettered only by Wolves. At one point, the press were calling for Walter Winterbottom and the FA selection committee to pick United's inside forward trio of Dennis Viollet, Bobby Charlton and Albert Quixall for the England team. Fortunately for me they didn't otherwise I might not have been given my England debut so early. Albert Quixall cost United a then record fee of £45,000 from Sheffield Wednesday in September 1958 and with Viollet and Charlton formed a free-scoring spearhead that was well serviced by wingers Albert Scanlon and Warren Bradley.

Arsenal were beginning the new season strengthened by the inclusion of Mel Charles, the brother of John, whom the Gunners had signed from Swansea Town the previous season but couldn't play because he had been signed after the March transfer deadline. Arsenal had finished third in 1958–9 but many believed they could have improved on that but for suffering from a crippling crop of injuries. Arsenal had a very good first team squad that included goalkeepers Jack Kelsey and Jim Standen, the veteran Len Wills, Dave Bacuzzi, the Northern Ireland internationals Ted Magill and Bill McCullough, John Barnwell, Vic Groves, David Herd, Gordon Nutt, Alan Skirton, Geoff Strong, Dave Bowen and a tough-tackling, no-nonsense wing half by the name of Tommy Docherty. That was a decent First Division squad but that summer Arsenal were boasting something we at Chelsea didn't have: a specialist coach. In July the Arsenal manager George Swindin appointed a first team coach who was creating a name for himself in the London area with what were at the time very modern and radical views on how the game should be played. The coach in question had played his football with Brentford and Bradford Park Avenue but, like most of his generation, had lost his best years as a player to the war. When he finished at Brentford as a player, he got a job coaching the Oxford University football team from where he moved on to coach the amateur club, Wealdstone. I'd heard on the football grapevine that he believed in purist football where the ball was passed out of defence rather than simply kicked. Swindin was so taken with this guy that he gave him overall responsibility for all the Arsenal first team training and tactics, and there was even talk at the time of Walter Winterbottom giving him a coaching role with England Under 23s. What with Arsenal's good showing in the previous season, their strong squad and the addition of a specialist coach, I felt the Gunners were going to be a force to be reckoned with in the coming season. Incidentally, the name of this coach, who in the summer of '59 enjoyed a meteoric rise from amateur football to one of the biggest clubs in the country, was Ron Greenwood.

Without doubt, West Bromwich Albion were capable of brilliance. They had achieved the double over Chelsea the previous season and, if anything, could boast an even stronger squad than Arsenal. In goal they had Ray Potter, a Beckenham lad who was being tipped as having a great future in the game. West Brom had an embarrassment of riches at full back where the Williams brothers, Stuart and Graham, contested the two positions with England's Don Howe and Bobby Cram. In players such as Charlie 'Chuck' Drury, Ray Barlow, Maurice Setters, Derek Kevan, Bobby Robson, Ronnie Allen, John Lovatt, Alec Jackson and Derek Hogg, the Baggies boasted real quality and were a side capable of putting any First Division team to the sword. There is one other West Bromwich Albion player worthy of mention: David Burnside.

David Burnside was a stylish and gifted inside right, and he was also the great entertainer of the time. There was seemingly nothing that David Burnside couldn't do with a football. His juggling and ball skills were unbelievable and in the pre-match kickabouts, he'd do one or two party pieces to the delight of the crowd. Initially he displayed his ball juggling at the Hawthorns before home matches, but when word got around and his confidence grew, he began to do one or two tricks before Albion away games. Wherever West Bromwich Albion played, the home supporters shouted for him to perform and rarely did he refuse. Today it seems the top players only display their party piece ball skills when appearing on TV advertisements for Nike or some other such manufacturer of sportswear. David Burnside displayed his ball skills for the benefit of those who paid his wages.

It seemed too that every team possessed at least one character who captured the imagination of the crowd. West Bromwich Albion were a good side and, as such, pulled crowds wherever they played. But even so-called unglamorous teams seemed to have someone whose very presence added spice and flavour to a game, such as Allan 'Bomber' Brown of Luton Town; those graduates of the school of hard knocks, Jimmy Scoular and Bob Stokoe at Newcastle United; the former German POW, the great Bert Trautmann of Manchester City;

Mark 'Pancho' Pearson of Manchester United, so called because of his Zapata moustache and Teddy Boy sideburns; and the enigmatic and outspoken Derek Dougan of Blackburn Rovers. That's to say nothing of great crowd pullers such as Stan Matthews, Danny Blanchflower, Bobby Collins (Everton), Johnny 'The Phantom' Fantham (Sheffield Wednesday), Peter Broadbent (Wolves), Johnny Haynes of Fulham and a bevy of larger than life team-mates such as Maurice Cook, Jim 'The Gentleman' Langley and Trevor 'Tosh' Chamberlain. More about them later.

How many contemporary players, or, for that matter, footballers of the past two decades have there been whose antics and characteristics have earned them a nickname? Trevor 'Tosh' Chamberlain, Jim 'The Gentleman' Langley, Johnny 'The Phantom' Fantham, Charlie 'Cannonball' Fleming, Cliff 'Snakehips' Jones and John 'Snoz' Sillett may well have been given their nicknames by team-mates, but they were also widely known as such by the supporters. The general usage of such nicknames was indicative of the familiarity that then existed between players and fans. Though the majority of supporters didn't know the players personally, they felt as if they did. How many supporters of today feel they have such familiarity with Ryan Giggs, Patrick Vieira, Jimmy Floyd Hasselbaink or any Premiership player?

I wasn't alone in thinking Wolves, Manchester United, Spurs, Arsenal and West Bromwich Albion would be at the forefront of the race for the 1959–60 League Championship; the bookies too had them all among the favourites. Now it's par for the course for me to get such things wrong, but rarely are the bookies way out when offering odds. They were on this occasion, however. Burnley had a very talented side but few people saw them as serious contenders for the Championship. As things were to turn out, not only did Burnley mount a serious challenge but they kept the momentum going until the very last day of the season to finish as Champions.

Having played in the curtain raiser to the new season, the public trial match, which on this occasion was billed as Blues v Reds, Chelsea set off for Holland for a friendly against Ajax. Today a match against Ajax would be a formidable task for any team, but in 1959 Ajax comprised mainly part-time players and, having finished some way behind Sparta Rotterdam, Heerlen and Fortuna Geleen, were not considered to be one of the top teams in Holland. Football had yet to take off in a big way in the Netherlands, and though the national team had competed in the 1934 and 1938 World Cups, it had played very few matches with the exception of twice-yearly games against Belgium. It was not until the mid-sixties, coincidentally with the emergence of Ajax as a force in Dutch football, that Holland truly entered the international scene.

When we arrived in Holland, their national league, the Eredivisie, was only two years old and full-time professional football had been sanctioned only recently. Ajax were obviously getting their act together, however, because they gave us a very tough game, though we won 3-2 in the end with me scoring twice.

Unbelievably by today's standards, the public trial match and our friendly against Ajax was the sum total of our pre-season games. Six days after the Ajax match, we opened our First Division campaign with a home game against Preston North End.

1959–60 was the second season of the Football League's reorganisation whereby the regionalised Third Division's South and North had formed a Third and Fourth Division. Having experienced national travel for the first time, and incurred greater travelling expenses, a lot of smaller clubs such as Exeter City, Torquay United, Gateshead United and Aldershot had spent much of the summer lobbying the

Football League. The increased costs of travel and the fact that some teams had to face the further expense of overnight accommodation was stretching budgets to the limit. Just about every club in the newly formed Third and Fourth Divisions had become increasingly dependent on funds raised by their supporters' clubs to meet the crippling costs of what were seen as being far distant away games. In the previous season Gillingham had stayed in the North-East to play Darlington, Hartlepool and Gateshead United within a five-day period in April. Those three games had been watched by fewer than 7,000 people. Gillingham's total outlay for the trip was £430 whereas their share of the gates came to only £105. At Chelsea we enjoyed an average attendance of over 30,000 yet the club were always pleading poverty. I remember thinking that if we were on our uppers with an average gate of 30,000 how on earth would the Gillinghams and Gatesheads of the game survive? The answer, or part answer, came that summer from the Football League themselves in what was the first real piece of commercial enterprise conducted by the body that ran our domestic football. In July the Football League established the copyright on all their fixtures. The football pools companies had been going for the best part of the century, during which time there had existed a gentleman's agreement between them and the League that allowed fixtures to be used for the purpose of the pools. That summer it all changed. In order that they continue in business, the pools promoters were forced into an agreement whereby they agreed to pay the Football League a minimum of £250,000 a year for ten years for the rights to reprint fixtures on their coupons.

A quarter of a million pounds a year was a lot of money in 1959. The Football League allocated a sizeable percentage of that money to the clubs as a royalty payment for their 'involvement' with the pools industry. I think the gross annual payout to clubs was something in the region of £130,000.

Again, when you consider there were ninety-two league clubs, it may not sound a lot, but it meant each club would receive in the region of £1,400 per season. Not a lot to Arsenal or Manchester United perhaps, but a godsend to Gillingham who received £105 as their share of gate receipts from three games in the North-East and returned from that trip having made a loss of £325.

The deal the Football League struck with the pools promoters was the start of the situation we now have in football, with the game besieged by the forces of commercialism. Of course no one at the time saw this deal as the advent of commercialism in football as we know it today. It was to all intents and purposes a knee-jerk reaction on the part of the Football League who didn't want their fixtures used by the pools companies for purely their own gain, and as a quick shot in the arm for the finances of smaller clubs who were finding the increased travel costs of reorganisation a burden on their budgets. The pools companies agreed to the deal purely as a means of continuing their business.

Those who filled out a football pools coupon in 1959 didn't put an 'X' next to the game they thought would be a draw, they put a zero. Indicating a possible draw with an 'X' on a coupon came into being in 1962. I don't know how many pools punters had our opening game of the 1959–60 season against Preston down on their coupon as a zero, but those who did got it right.

The 1959–60 season can be said to be the final year in football's age of innocence, the last in which just about every game was played in a very open and attacking manner. Football was about to change rapidly and irrevocably. The new decade brought with it the first rumblings of the massive upheaval that would change the face of football forever with the introduction of specialist coaches and their desire to make teams collectively more efficient and better organised. Chelsea didn't have a coach in 1959 and neither did Preston North End, which may go a long way to explaining why both sides kicked off the season hell-bent on throwing just about every player forward. The game ebbed and flowed and the Stamford Bridge crowd were treated to a fine exhibition of attacking football from both sides, who, in the end, shared eight goals.

I was pleased to get the new season under way by featuring on the scoresheet myself. Any disappointment I may have felt at Chelsea not having started the season with a home win was tempered by the fact that at least we hadn't lost against what was a very talented Preston team who, that season, included Tom Finney in its ranks for the very last time.

Along with Stanley Matthews, Tom Finney had been one of my boyhood heroes. Tom was to announce his retirement later in the season, and English football was to be denied the services of one of its all-time greats.

A mark of the respect and esteem in which Tom was held by all clubs and their supporters can be gauged by the fact that, for years, a photograph of Tom in action hung from one of the walls inside Stamford Bridge. All these years on I can still see that photograph of Tom in my mind's eye. It was an action shot taken of him playing for Preston in a game at Stamford Bridge in 1956. Tom is at an acute angle, his left arm outstretched in an attempt at preventing him going to ground. The amazing thing about the photograph is the state of the pitch, which is waterlogged. Surface water is clearly visible and in showing Tom losing his footing, the backdrop to him is a wave of water and spray through which one can just make out the blurred profile of a grounded Chelsea defender getting a complete soaking. Though a still photograph the scene is all action, which is fitting because that is what Tom Finney was as a player.

In many respects, Tom Finney *was* Preston North End. He was their captain and so versatile that he could play in any position in the forward line. He took all the Preston throw-ins, free kicks, penalties and corners. Such was his devotion to

North End, he would have manned a turnstile and taken admission money if they'd let him. Tom Finney was a player of exceptional and unique ability. As a youngster he played for Preston in the 1941 Wartime Cup Final only then to be conscripted into the army. Unique? I can't think of another player who played in a Wembley Cup Final and then had to wait five years before making his league debut for the same club! During World War Two he served with the 8th Army in North Africa under Field Marshal Montgomery. Tom fought against Rommel. Suffice it to say that Rommel lost. He won seventy-six caps for England, forty at outside right, thirty-three at outside left and three at centre forward, scoring on his debut in each position. He played 433 games for Preston between 1946 and 1960, scoring 187 goals along the way. He was twice voted Footballer of the Year, in 1954 and 1957, and was awarded an OBE in 1961 and a CBE in 1992 before being knighted for his services to football.

Earlier I mentioned the nicknames many footballers had at this time. Tom's was 'The Preston Plumber', for the simple reason that while he was a pro with Preston he ran a successful plumbing business in the town under the name of Tom Finney Services, which still thrives to this day. Of course Tom's 'other job' as a plumber gave rise to all manner of jokes and jibes but Tom was not shy of making humour of his situation himself. In 1958, when Wilf McGuinness made his debut at wing half for England against Northern Ireland in Belfast, Tom Finney 'talked' a nervous Wilf through the game. After the final whistle, when the players were leaving the pitch, a grateful Wilf thanked Tom for his help and guidance, saying, 'If there is anything I can do for you, Tom, just ask.'

'Be at my place on Monday afternoon,' said Tom jokingly. 'I've a bathroom to install and my labourer's reported sick.'

Tom Finney was one of English football's all-time greats who played in an era when even footballers of his lofty status were kept firmly in their place. When he travelled to England matches, he did so by second- and sometimes third-class rail travel. In 1952, when his mercurial talent was at its height, he was offered £10,000 to sign for the Italian club Palermo. Ten thousand pounds in 1952 was an unbelievable amount of money, though entirely in keeping with his talent. Palermo were so keen to sign Tom that they also offered him a wage of £130 a month plus bonuses, a villa and a sports car. Tom was earning £18 a week less tax with Preston so naturally he was interested in the deal on offer, but any thoughts he might have had of playing in Italy were crushed when he went to discuss the possible move with the Preston chairman Mr Buck, who told Tom, 'Tha'll play for us, Finney, or tha'll play for nobody.' Tom never did play for any club other than Preston North End. Though he missed out on what was then a small fortune, when he now looks back I am sure Sir Tom wouldn't have had it any other way.

Tom Finney was the complete player. He was blessed with a marvellous natural ability and was so adept with either foot that I could never make up my mind which one was the most effective when it came to shooting, passing, crossing or dribbling. Tom Finney possessed another highly laudable attribute, loyalty. Though the Preston chairman had put his foot down when Tom informed him of the approach by Palermo, I doubt whether he would have taken them up on their offer even if it had received the blessing of Mr Buck. Tom's loyalty to his home town club was unswerving, unlike his daring runs. His body swerves and feints mesmerised countless defenders. He could beat any opponent, find the space to make a telling pass when under pressure and possessed a thunderous shot. When I was a boy my dad and his mates were constantly debating who was the better player, Tom or Stanley Matthews. I don't want to get into that debate; suffice it to say, what a choice! Without doubt, Tom Finney was the more versatile of the two and it says much for him as a player and man that, following his appearance for Preston against Arsenal in the Wartime Cup Final of 1941, the resultant loss of five years of his playing career as a result of his military service did not prevent him going on to achieve legendary status. I played against him twice in 1959–60 and both were terrific games of football. As I've said, we drew 4-4 with Preston at Stamford Bridge on the opening day of the season and in the return fixture at Deepdale in December Chelsea won 5-4. That season, Tom decided to call it a day at the age of thirty-eight. Preston's last game of the season was against Luton Town. Preston were safe in the top half of the First Division whereas Luton were already confined to relegation. To all intents and purposes it was a meaningless fixture at the fag end of the season, but 31,000 turned up at Deepdale to say goodbye to Tom. The following season Chelsea took three points off Preston and I remember thinking how that Preston team sorely missed the presence and wizardry of their talisman. Come the end of the season Preston were relegated from Division One and the locals felt they knew the reason why.

Following our thrilling opener against Preston, my hopes of Chelsea enjoying a successful season were boosted when we travelled to Old Trafford and came away with a 1-0 win. My initial optimism was quickly tempered, however, for in Chelsea's very next game at Leicester City goals from Albert Cheesebrough, Willie Cunningham and Ken Leek cancelled out a fine solo effort from Peter Brabrook to consign us to our first defeat of the season. A crowd of over 66,000 turned up at Stamford Bridge to see the return fixture against Manchester United. Both teams went at it hell for leather in the first half, which, at the interval saw United leading 3-2. We gave it our all in the second period and enjoyed the lion's share of possession but a United defence well marshalled by Bill Foulkes soaked up all our pressure and hit us on the break. The game ended 6-3 in United's favour, which, given we had enjoyed the majority of the play, I felt flattered them somewhat. We bounced back straight away with a fine 4-1 win against a Burnley side destined to be Champions. Thereafter, we stuttered and spluttered. Though we were to enjoy some fine wins and I was to continue my goalscoring exploits to even greater effect, for the first time in my embryonic career the defeats that were inflicted upon Chelsea outnumbered the victories.

After our 4-1 success over Burnley we travelled to St Andrews for a midweek match against Birmingham City. We drew that game 1-1 but our promising start to the season was soon to evaporate. Though we were to chalk up some notable wins at Fulham and West Bromwich Albion (both 3-1) and at the Bridge against Birmingham City (4-2) and Blackburn Rovers (3-1) it soon went pear-shaped. Following our victory over Blackburn in early November, from then to mid-February we were to enjoy just one more victory in the league, 5-4 at Preston, a game in which I scored all five of our goals. What's more, Chelsea made a quick exit from the FA Cup.

In the third round of the Cup we were drawn at home to Bradford Park Avenue, who at the time were a mid-table team in Division Four. Mindful of our Cup exit the previous season at Darlington we set about Bradford in no uncertain fashion. In front of a crowd of 32,000 Frank Blunstone gave us an early lead when, after a mazy dribble that took him past three Bradford defenders, he unleashed an unstoppable shot into the top left-hand corner of the net. Frank also made our second, crossing for Peter Brabrook to head home. Minutes later, following a free kick from Peter Sillett, Brabbers put us three up with a brave diving header. In the second half, I joined the goalscorers when I hit a shot from eighteen yards to put us four goals up, then had a hand in setting up Charlie Livesey for our fifth and final goal. All of which set us up for another home tie in round four against Aston Villa.

In his programme notes for the Villa game, Ted Drake described the match as 'the most attractive tie of the round'. Somewhat prophetically, he also mentioned the fact that Chelsea had never beaten Aston Villa in a cup tie. By ten to five that afternoon, that record was still intact. Villa put an end to any hopes we had of a good run in the Cup by winning 2-1. In their side that day at centre forward was Gerry Hitchens, who would soon be on his way to Inter Milan. Little did I know at the time that within eighteen months I too would be joining Gerry in Milan, albeit with AC, rather than Internazionale.

I wanted to achieve success in football. I wanted to win trophies with Chelsea, not just for myself, but for the club and its supporters. Following our exit from the FA Cup and with no chance of doing anything special in the league, it was now becoming increasingly apparent to me that such hopes were forlorn. It would be wrong of me to say I was becoming increasingly disillusioned with life at Chelsea. I still loved the club and its supporters and really enjoyed playing with my team-mates, but something was nagging away at my insides. With each defeat we suffered, my frustration, rather than disillusionment, grew. In my heart of hearts I think I knew then that matters would come to a head, only I didn't think it would take another eighteen months.

It was around the time of our defeat in the FA Cup that Irene, Lynn and I moved out of the Wimbledon flat and into a club house in Great Nelmes Chase in Hornchurch. The house was a bungalow which Chelsea purchased for £1,700 and Irene and I rented it from the club. It was in a lovely spot, between Emerson Park and what is now the A127 Southend arterial road and was surrounded by plenty of fields. There was even a farm nearby called Lillyputts Farm, which I am happy to say still exists today. I'd made it known to the club that Irene and I wanted to move back to Essex and, to be fair to Chelsea, they made that happen. Players living in club houses was common in those days. Due to the maximum wage a lot of footballers, particularly those in London where the cost of housing was high, simply couldn't get a mortgage. To retain the services of a player and to keep him happy a club would buy a house and rent it to the player concerned. In many ways such a situation was indicative of the fiefdom of the clubs. Players were treated like serfs and many lived in houses owned by the lord of the manor, which was, of course, the club. Players were beholden to the club that owned their contract, kept them tied to a maximum wage and, in the case of me and many others, also owned the houses in which they lived. Though club houses still exist today, particularly for players with lower division clubs situated in an area of highly priced housing such as the south east and south west, their numbers are nowhere near as high as they once were. Most Chelsea players I knew lived in club houses. In one respect it was good that the club helped players out in this way. Then again, they wouldn't have had to if players had been paid a decent wage. Today it's unthinkable that a top player would rely on his club for somewhere to live. Today's top players can afford a home of their own, which can only be a good thing.

Chelsea agreed to help Irene and me acquire a home in Essex in the hope of keeping me happy at the club. I wasn't unhappy exactly but I was becoming increasingly frustrated, though just when I felt I was on the point of giving vent to my frustration by asking for a transfer, we would enjoy a decent sequence of results and I would keep my thoughts to myself. Like the fisherman on the verge of packing up who gets a nibble, I'd hang around in the hope that we were going to land a trophy in due course. In March, we lost 6-1 at Everton. We then lost 3-2 at home to Blackpool, then 1-0 at Blackburn Rovers. I was on the point of making my frustration known to Ted Drake, only for us then to beat Manchester City 3-0 and follow that home win with a super 4-1 win at Arsenal. It's amazing what a win can do to your hopes and confidence, back-to-back victories in particular. My spirits soared. I thought our win at Arsenal was going to be the turning point. My frustration disappeared. I convinced myself that at last we were getting it together as a team, and, though too late to do anything in this particular season, we were going to end on a high note, one that would bode well for the future. For a time, I almost convinced myself that our days of conceding soft goals were behind us, but of course they weren't. Following our success at Arsenal, I was brought straight back down to earth when we lost 3-1 at home to Spurs.

Prior to our next game, at home to Nottingham Forest, I experienced something very disconcerting, something I had never come across in football and, happily, was never again to experience in my career. Though in the bottom six of the First Division, Chelsea had no real fear of relegation. Nottingham Forest, however, were embroiled in a relegation dogfight with Leeds, Luton and Birmingham City. There was no Players Lounge at Chelsea at this time, but the players did have a room above the club office that we used for leisure purposes and meetings. This room had a snooker table and many was the time I'd join some of the other lads for a game and a chat. Before our game against Forest, our captain Peter Sillett called a team meeting in the snooker room. I had no idea what this was about but when Peter told us, my jaw dropped. Having ensured that every player was present and the door closed, Peter then commenced to drop his bombshell.

'Listen lads, I don't know how to put this too you all,' he said gravely, 'but a couple of the Forest players approached me. They're worried about being relegated and are desperate for points. The long and the short of it is, they tell me they have £500 to be shared amongst us if we throw the game and let them win. Personally I'm totally against the idea, but as your skipper I feel I ought to let you know of the situation. Now you're all big boys, old enough to make up your minds. Needless to say, whatever you think, this "offer" as I'll call it, must not go beyond this room.'

For a few seconds there was complete silence. I glanced about the room. Every player was nervous and edgy. Then Peter's brother, John piped up.

'Well, I ain't up for throwing any 'king match. Think of our supporters,' said Snoz.

A chorus of 'nor me' swept the room, punctuated by the odd, 'Tell 'em to stuff it.' Peter Sillett told us he would make contact with the two Forest players concerned and inform them that 'the deal *wasn't* on'. As things turned out Forest gained a valuable point that day: we drew 1-1, with me getting the Chelsea goal. There were three games of the season remaining and Forest did just enough to preserve their First Division status. They ended the season third from bottom, one point ahead of Leeds United, who along with Luton Town were relegated to Division Two. I have never discovered the identity of the two Nottingham Forest players who approached Peter Sillett with the offer for us to throw the game. Peter is now no longer with us, so I suppose I never will know who they were. Nor do I know if the £500 we had been offered had come from the Forest team, a club director or a wealthy supporter. All I do know is that we were offered a bung and rejected it outright, the first and only time I ever came across such a situation in my entire career as a footballer. I never mentioned this offer of a bung to anyone, nor have I revealed the fact until now. It was sordid, unpleasant and totally out of keeping with football at the time. Two years later, however, a number of players, including two of my England colleagues, would have their careers brought to an abrupt and premature end by foolishly accepting similar bribes in a scandal that rocked English football to the foundations.

Perhaps one or two of my Chelsea team-mates might have been tempted by the £500 on offer, though, as Snoz said as we left the room, 'We wouldn't know how to throw a game anyway.' The maximum wage at the time was £20 less tax. The divvy up from the amount on offer was just over £45 per man, the equivalent of just over two weeks' wages. No one seriously considered accepting the bung; it was against everything we held dear. Apart from the consequences if we were caught, we were pros and the very thought of deliberately losing a game was anathema to every one of us. Apart from all that we had dignity, pride and a strong sense of loyalty to the club and its supporters.

The offer of the bung was a by-product of the maximum wage which gave rise to all manner of under-the-counter dealings. In December 1959, Chelsea played a Christmas double-header against Newcastle United. On Boxing Day we drew 2-2 at Stamford Bridge and, two days later, 1-1 at St James Park. After the second game a director of Newcastle United approached me with a view to signing for his club. It was an unauthorised approach but such approaches were quite common so I heard him out. The director in question told me that should I sign for Newcastle United he would arrange for me to be given a 'jolly job' with a Tyneside company he was connected with. I wouldn't have to do any work for this company, but would appear on the payroll as being a 'consultant' for which I would be paid £25 a week. There was also talk of a car and a club house with some arrangement to be made that would involve the company paying the rent. In essence what they were offering me was more than twice my weekly wage at Chelsea, plus a car and rent-free accommodation. I said 'thanks but no thanks' to that offer. In the first instance, I didn't fancy a move to the North-East and I didn't think Irene would have been up for it either. Secondly, I was ambitious for myself. I wanted to win trophies and play in a quality team that would improve me as a player. Newcastle were above Chelsea in Division One but were pulling up no trees, and I felt at the time that they were a team in decline. I was proved correct in my thinking because the following season Newcastle were relegated. I wasn't unique in being offered an under-the-counter deal by another club; many players were 'tapped up' during this period. Football's governing bodies and club directors had imposed the maximum wage structure, and in so doing had created fertile ground for illegal dealings. That such illegal deals were nearly always proposed by club directors themselves only further served to make a mockery of the situation, to say nothing of portraying many directors as hypocrites.

The 1959–60 season ended for Chelsea not with a bang but a whimper. Our final game of what had been a very disappointing season was against Wolves at Stamford Bridge. It was a generally held view that a team which had reached the FA Cup Final, as Wolves had done, would have the Cup on their minds when it came to fulfilling their remaining league fixtures. With an appearance in the FA Cup Final considered to be the pinnacle of any player's career, no one wanted to sustain an injury in a league match at the fag end of the season that would mean him missing the Cup Final. As such, it was not unknown for players due an appearance at Wembley to pull out of a tackle in a match they might otherwise be fully committed to. Any notion we may have had of Wolves not being up for the game at Stamford Bridge went out of the window because they were also embroiled in a fight for the Championship with Burnley and Spurs (at least two of my predictions were right).

Should Wolves win the Championship, they were in with a great chance of becoming the first team in the twentieth century to win the League and Cup double. I knew we were in for a very hard battle and that Wolves would give this game their all. What I wasn't prepared for was how easily Chelsea would capitulate.

In our previous game, though we lost 2-0 at Bolton Wanderers as a team we had demonstrated a lot of character and determination. With no fear of relegation, Ted Drake had used the remaining games of the season as an opportunity to blood some of our younger players. He had given Peter Bonetti a run of six games in goal in which Peter amply demonstrated his developing talent. Unfortunately, in the early stages of our game at Bolton, Peter picked up an injury that resulted in him having to leave the field. As there were no substitutes, Ron Tindall took over in goal from Peter and we played out the remainder of the match with ten men. Ron did a good job as Peter's deputy and to a man we battled against Bolton and but for some good saves from their goalkeeper, Johnny Bollands, could have taken the lead before half-time. Unfortunately the extra man told in the end. Bolton scored twice in the second half to take the points but, given the circumstances, we felt we had acquitted ourselves well on the day and were a tad disappointed not to come away with a point.

The application and motivation we had shown at Bolton were conspicuous in their absence against Wolves. From the outset they tore into us. Billy Wright had retired but in Eddie Clamp they had a robust ball winner at right half. Time and again Clamp won the ball in midfield, fed it to Bill Slater or Ron Flowers, who threaded it up front to their inside trio of Barry Stobart, Jimmy Murray and Peter Broadbent who proceeded to lead our defence a merry dance. When it wasn't a long ball through the middle, it went wide to their wingers, Des Horne and Norman Deeley, who were equally bent on absolute destruction. Old gold shirts seemed to be everywhere. We couldn't get into any rhythm of play because we couldn't get the ball off them. Ron Tindall and I dropped deeper and deeper into our own half. We succeeded in mounting an occasional retaliatory attack but Wolves were in determined mood and it wasn't long before Reg Matthews was picking the ball out of the net. Reg did that five times that afternoon, his opposite number, Malcolm Finlayson, only once. Wolves played us off the park but their efforts proved to be in vain. Burnley, the team Wolves had beaten 6-1 only weeks previously, won 2-1 at Manchester City to clinch the Championship. Spurs blew their chance by losing at home. It was Burnley's first Championship since 1921 and their success was a tribute to their style of play, pure football with the accent on attack. The amazing thing about Burnley's title success was they had not been at the top of the First Division until their last league game. Wolves had been favourites and for all that they had whacked Chelsea 5-1, a couple of points dropped in the final run-in proved their undoing. Consolation for Wolves came a week later when they beat Blackburn Rovers 3-0 to lift the FA Cup.

And Chelsea? Our final league position of fifth from bottom was a disappointment to everyone connected with the club, in particular myself. Our penchant for conceding soft goals and our inability to mount a concerted challenge for honours served to make me more restless. Our defeat against Wolves, especially the manner of it, convinced me that we were nowhere near good enough to be considered a force in the First Division. For the first time in my fledgling career I found myself asking if my future in football would be best served at Stamford Bridge. Such thoughts were further fuelled by a number of articles that appeared in the press at the time. The *Empire News* ran a story under the heading 'CHELSEA – A CLUB IN CRISIS'. The *Daily Sketch* ran a piece essentially saying I'd be better off at another club and suggested that Spurs and Manchester United would be keen to acquire my signature. Our performances that season prompted all manner of journalistic jibes, even from the *Manchester Guardian*, which carried a less than complimentary piece about Chelsea in which it said, 'Even with the goalscoring feats of young Greaves, Chelsea remain as they have always been, free to peruse the tenor of their unpredictable ways, staunch in the belief that waywardness in front of their own goal has its part to play in the human comedy as well as reliability.'

In *Soccer Star* Graham Payne wrote, 'If it's goals you want to see, see Chelsea. Goals are what Chelsea deliver unfailingly, at either end of the pitch.'

When you read such stuff it does make you think and question. The thing was, Chelsea's ailing fortunes on the pitch and the press they were receiving were in direct contrast to what was happening to me as a player.

CHAPTER SIX

SAVE THE LAST DANCE FOR ME

I ended the 1959–60 season as Chelsea's leading scorer with twenty-nine league goals, three fewer than the First Division's leading goalscorer, Dennis Viollet of Manchester United. I'd also scored several goals in money-spinning friendlies the club had staged that season against such teams as Entente Royale Anversoise of Antwerp, Atletico Bilbao and the British Olympic XI. My loyalty to the club had been such that when given the opportunity of a rest when the first team played friendlies against non-league teams such as Ashford and Sittingbourne, I'd travelled anyway to give the lads some support. Though I had been somewhat restless, no one could say I had been anything less than 100 per cent committed to the Chelsea cause.

The fact that I had continued to score goals in the First Division further cemented my appearances at international level. I added to my eight caps for England Under 23s with appearances against Hungary, Scotland and Holland and won full caps against Wales (one goal) and Sweden. I had also been selected by Walter Winterbottom for the England squad to play close-season internationals against Yugoslavia, Spain and Hungary. On the personal front everything was great; only at Chelsea, things were not too rosy.

When England played Sweden at Wembley in 1959 I'd

lined up in what was one of youngest, if not *the* youngest, England teams ever to have taken the field for an international match. Walter had managed to persuade the England selection committee to go along with his idea of picking a youthful England team. He picked what he believed to be an outstanding crop of young players to face the Swedes, most of whom were under the age of twenty-one. Tony Allen (Stoke City), Trevor Smith (Birmingham City), John Connelly (Burnley), Brian Clough and Eddie Holliday (both Middlesbrough) joined a twenty-two-year-old Bobby Charlton and me in a team facing a Swedish side managed by George Raynor, the first Englishman to have taken a team to a World Cup Final. Sweden were without some of their key players such as Hamrin, Gren, Liedholm, Skoglund and Gustavvson, all of whom had played in the 1958 World Cup but were on duty with their respective Italian league clubs. Sweden, however, still proved too strong and won the game 3-2. It was only England's second home defeat by overseas opposition and it went down like a lead balloon with the FA. The FA selection committee made it known to Walter in no uncertain terms that they were opposed to his policy of promoting young players to the full England team and went back to the old regime. In so doing, they took English football another giant step back in time.

In May 1960 I played for England in our 3-3 draw with Yugoslavia and managed to help myself to one of our goals. As international friendly matches go, our game against the Yugoslavs had little bearing and even less effect on the development of football in this country. In the same month, however, another match took place on these shores, the consequences of which were to change the face of English football forever. Oddly for a match that revolutionised our game, it didn't take place in England but in Scotland, at Hampden Park in Glasgow. What's more, neither of the two teams in the contest was British. They were German and Spanish, but the game they contrived to produce set the agenda for the future of English football.

On the night of 18 May 1960, I sat and watched on television the greatest ever performance from the greatest club side football has produced. On a sultry Glasgow evening, Real Madrid, inspired by the brilliance of Alfredo Di Stefano and the mercurial talents of Ferenc Puskas, beat Eintracht Frankfurt 7-3 to win the European Cup. It was Real's fifth European Cup success in the five years since the competition began, but it was the manner of their victory which stunned everyone. Real's performance that night sent shock waves through the British game. It was as if the football they played had come from another planet. The margin of their victory could have been even greater such was their domination. As it was, one might be forgiven for thinking Frankfurt were a second-rate team, but nothing could have been further from the truth. The Germans were in fact a very good side. In the semi-finals they had beaten Glasgow Rangers 6-1 and 6-3, a team considered one of the best sides in Britain!

Real enthralled, enraptured and, at the end, stunned the biggest ever crowd to witness a European Cup Final, in excess of 134,000. Come the final whistle a packed Hampden was so mesmerised by what they had seen that for a moment they stood in silence, only to then burst out into huge and spontaneous applause in appreciation of the brilliant football they had witnessed. The crowd refused to leave until the Real players did a lap of honour and an hour after the final whistle the ground was still packed to the rafters with incredulous Scots.

I was with England in Hungary at the time and along with my team-mates watched the game on television in our hotel in Budapest. Because of the involvement of Ferenc Puskas (who had fled the country), the communist government in Hungary had banned any broadcast of the game. Fortunately the manager of our hotel was both a football fan and a wily old bird and had managed to get hold of a TV aerial that could pick up Swiss television. To a man the England team watched Real in disbelief. The football they produced that night was of a kind we had never seen before – fluid, pure, consummately entertaining and devastatingly effective. Seeing such cavalier, attacking football I thought I'd been transported to football paradise. To describe Real's football that night as being brilliant cannot do it justice. To say their performance was magnificent would not do it credit. It was as if one had discovered Shakespeare, Picasso and the Beatles for the first time and all on the same night. A stunningly formative experience from which there was no going back.

Real Madrid's superlative performance in the European Cup Final had an immediate and galvanising effect on English football, in particular on Walter Winterbottom's fledgling FA coaching school at Lilleshall which suddenly found itself inundated with applications from managers and players as English football went hell-bent on modernisation.

Among Walter's school of 1960 were such names as Tommy Docherty, Billy Bingham, Peter Taylor, Don Revie, Dave Sexton, Bob Paisley, Frank O'Farrell, Malcolm Allison, Jimmy Adamson (Burnley), Phil Woosnam and Bert Johnson (Leicester City), who, when they became coaches or managers, would change the face of English football in the sixties and forever. What's more, the contribution of these coaches would prove to be a decisive factor in the success of English clubs in Europe and in England winning the World Cup in 1966.

I began the 1960–61 season as a Chelsea player basically for two reasons. First, after a summer which saw me play for England against Yugoslavia and Spain, after which I had a complete rest from the game, come July I found my enthusiasm for another season with Chelsea had been rekindled. I was happy to give it another go at Stamford Bridge in the hope that the team could put the disappointment of the previous season behind us and challenge for honours. Secondly, though the newspapers had been full of speculation about a possible transfer, as far as I was aware no official offer had yet been made to the club for my services.

After three weeks of pre-season training and the annual medical which once again proved I had not succumbed to any dreadful disease such as malaria, Chelsea began their programme of two pre-season friendlies with the public trial match. Usually this series of games, on this occasion billed as Blues v Reds, took place on a Saturday afternoon. In 1960, however, the Blues met the Reds on a Monday night. A healthy crowd of 11,565 turned up to see the Blues triumph by 3-1. I played for the Blues and scored our opening goal, with the other two coming from Charlie Livesey. In the Blues side that night was a young Terry Venables, Peter Bonetti and our new signing, Bobby Evans, who had joined us from Celtic. Ted Drake had either transferred or released a number of senior pros such as Bill Robertson, Dick Whittaker and Derek Saunders and the two sides which took to the field and subsequently formed the first team squad had a distinctly young look about them. For the Reds that night were two teenagers destined to become legends at Stamford Bridge: Bobby Tambling and Barry Bridges.

Our other pre-season game was against an Edinburgh XI. Where neighbouring teams are concerned today, too often the relationship between the two respective groups of supporters is blighted by moronic tribal rivalry. This wasn't the case in 1960. Where there were two teams in one city, supporters would often watch one club one week and the other the next. This was very much the case in Edinburgh where the

Representative XI Chelsea played was made up of players from Heart of Midlothian and Hibernian. Fans from both Edinburgh clubs mixed happily on the terraces, which was, of course, the whole idea. By fielding a combined Edinburgh side against us the respective clubs were assured of a much bigger attendance.

The Edinburgh side ran out 5-4 winners in what was a cracking match, though I didn't manage to feature amongst the Chelsea goals scored by Peter Sillett, Frank Blunstone and Charlie Livesey (2). Chelsea opened the 1960–61 season at Aston Villa in front of a sun-kissed crowd of over 44,000. Villa were newly promoted, having regained their First Division status at the first time of asking, and on the day were worthy 3-2 winners. With players in their ranks such as Gerry Hitchens, Stan Lynn, Vic Crowe, Pat Saward, Ron Wylie and Peter McParland, Aston Villa were a decent side but I knew they weren't going to set the First Division on fire. More importantly, our performance on the day gave me ample reason to believe Chelsea's old problem of shipping goals at the drop of a hat hadn't been resolved. We were one game into the new campaign but already I sensed we were to be in for a long, hard season of disappointment.

Four days later, those thoughts were compounded when Leicester City beat us 3-1 at Stamford Bridge. Our next game was another home match against the mighty Wolves. A crowd of 42,000 turned up, probably fearing the worst, but as was our wont we suddenly found a rich vein of form against free-scoring Wolves and showed we could score goals ourselves. This proved to be the game when my season really took off. Up to this point I still hadn't scored, but against Wolves I got my goalscoring underway with a hat-trick.

I relished the big occasion and a game against Wolves was always just that. I always made sure I arrived at Stamford Bridge for a Saturday game at around one o'clock. Usually I passed small knots of spectators, mainly boys making their way to the ground in order to secure a place on the perimeter fencing. When I arrived at the Bridge there would be a scattering of supporters milling around the car park, most of them brandishing autograph books or scrapbooks bearing pictures of the Chelsea players mounted on pages of coloured sugar paper.

When I made my way towards the ground on the day of the Wolves game, however, there were far more supporters about than normal. A lot more. All along the Fulham Road there were men, men with women and men with boys all heading in the same direction and with the same ambition. As was normal at the time, the men wore collars and ties to the match. It was a warm, sunny lunchtime in late August and the perennial mackintoshes and worsted coats of the men had been left in the wardrobe. Instead, the men wore jackets, of either the worsted or sports variety. Now and then, you saw the occasional blazer bearing the badge and arms of some army regiment or RAF command. The men wore slacks, some cream, some light grey but mostly what Millets described as light tan. Various styles of shoes were also in evidence: brogues, suede, brown leather winkle-pickers, black and brown crepe shoes. Amongst that lot you could pick out the shoes of small boys: black 'Empire' pumps, white sandshoes or brown leather shoes scuffed and in desperate need of Dad's weekly polish. Just about every boy I spotted under the age of twelve was wearing short trousers and a good many in their early teens were, too.

The nearer I got to the ground, the more the pace of the supporters seemed to quicken, as if when catching sight of the floodlight pylons their hearts pumped faster, making their legs quicken accordingly.

The Fulham Road then was on the up, but still some way from the boutiques, smart bars, expensive terraced houses and dolly birds that would make its name only a few years later. In

1960 the Fulham Road was lined with tired houses that had
seen better days but would, in fact, see even better ones. On
the sides of some of the end-of-terrace houses were metallic
hoardings advertising Bisto and the *News of The World*, the
latter promising that within its pages we'd find 'all human life
is there'. All human life, or a good part of it at least, seemed to
be heading towards Stamford Bridge that roasting day. Now
and then a supporter would recognise me and without
breaking step, call out, 'Good luck today, Jimmy, son!' 'Watcha
Greavsie! Stick it to the Wolves today.' 'Up the Pensioners!'

Heads turned to look at me. Heads with short back and
sides. Greased hair in the DA style. Quiffs matted down on to
foreheads with the palm of the hand and water. Quiffs combed
back off the forehead to form a miniature surfers' wave of hair
and Brylcreem. Pale young men. Some just out of National
Service and no doubt cursing their luck at having been born
two years too early, for conscription had just been abolished.
Fags doing a balancing act on the lower lip. Trouser creases like
knife blades. Sullen lads firing jets of spit through gritted teeth.

Many of the older men wore trilbies, unlike at grounds in
the North where flat caps were still the order of the day. Young
girls with hair bundled into a beehive, their eyelashes twin
miracles of mascara. Men, women, boys, young women, swept
along on a tide of optimism. Hopeful of seeing their team win
and maybe, just maybe, witnessing their heroes fashion Iliads
and Odysseys before their very eyes.

'Pro-grammes! Pro-grahmmes! Pro-graaaahmmes o' the
match!'

On seeing the programme sellers, the smooth, snaking
throng of supporters suddenly disintegrated. Those who didn't
want a programme had to make a detour around those who
did. The knot of programme buyers safely circumnavigated,
those supporters with no need of match information fell back
into step, marching inexorably towards the Bridge.

I turn the car off the Fulham Road where red London Transport buses deposit more supporters on to the pavements before crawling off to all points west London for more. And there will be more and more. Multiples of thousands, not one of whom would ever describe football as simply twenty-two grown men trying to get a piece of leather filled with air between two sticks. To their minds, that would be tantamount to saying the Bible is only so much pen and ink.

Team-mates' cars are already in the car park. A Ford Prefect. A Vauxhall Cresta. An Austin Westminster. A Ford Zephyr. I pull up alongside and get out.

'Sign here, Jimmy, please.' 'Can you sign this, please? Can you put, "To Arnold"?'

I'm looking at grainy grey newspaper photographs of myself playing against Leicester. There is one of Ron Tindall and me in aerial combat with Gordon Banks. I sign. One of me against Spurs. I sign. A head and shoulders shot in Chelsea strip. I sign. I'm walking towards the players' entrance; hurriedly I sign more. One by one the autograph hunters peel away looking at my signature with some satisfaction.

I hastily scratch my name on a blank piece of lined paper.

'I saw your first game down here. Public trial match. I said to me mates, "He's got it." I was the first one to spot you,' the voice says.

'Thanks.'

Inside is a haven of peace. I make my way down the corridor and into the home dressing room. In the centre of the room is an old physio bench whose leather cover is tattered and torn. On the bench there is a battered metal tea tray and on it a large brown metal teapot steams gently. I pick up a chunky white china cup and pour myself some tea. Strong tea so hot I have to purse my lips and sieve it into my mouth.

Charlie Livesey is whistling the Shadows' 'Apache'. There are players in vests, some plain cotton, others string. String vests are new. Who would have thought a vest with holes in it would actually be warm? Bobby Evans is getting changed. His mop of ginger hair stands out like a fire beacon on top of a body that appears whiter than white.

'He wants straightening out, he does,' says Snoz.

'Who?' says Terry Venables rising to the bait.

'Oliver Twist!'

Snoz roars with laughter, not at the joke but at having caught Tel out again. In numbered sequence blue shirts hang from pegs around the room. I move to one side the shorts and socks that are beneath the number eight shirt and sit down. Every player has his own regular place in the dressing room. When you first arrive you simply sit in the place vacated by the player whose place you have taken in the team. It now becomes your place. Your little bit of territory in the dressing room where you can conduct your pre-match ritual in peace. To either side of me sit Peter Brabrook and Charlie Livesey. We chat away as we get changed but it always seems to be on the other side of the room where all the tomfoolery and high jinks take place. Where the Sillett brothers and young Venables get changed. You know how it is on bonfire night when, no matter how much you spend on fireworks, the next door neighbours' fireworks always seem more spectacular? That's how it is in the dressing room. It's always on the other side of the room where the interest is and the fun takes place. Yet I know if I was to go and sit across there it would be nothing special.

Time moves on. Those who have been glancing at but never reading the match programme have cast it aside or stuffed it into a jacket pocket for the nephew or neighbour's son. Balls are being bounced on the floor. Boots stamped. John Oxberry, on one knee, shifts from Brabbers to Charlie Livesey and begins massaging liniment into Charlie's legs with fingers as thick as bananas. I never had liniment applied to my legs.

Never felt a need for it. Without averting his eyes from Charlie's legs, John engages me in conversation.

'You had any more trouble with that calf, Jimmy, son?'

'Nah.'

He presses his thumbs deep into one side of Charlie's thigh, his fingers pummel the muscles. There is silence for thirty seconds or so.

'Fancy you for one today, Jimmy, son.'

'Hope so.'

'That Ron Flowers. He don't like ya taking him on the inside, ya know.'

'Nah.'

'Use that speed o' yours.'

'Yeah.'

'Other leg, Charlie, son.'

Twenty minutes to three. Ted Drake comes into the room.

'Down in five, lads,' he says, helping himself to what must now be cold tea.

The five minutes pass. Arms folded, legs stretched out before me, I await Ted's team talk.

He doesn't say much. Ted has a brief word with the Sillett brothers about the Wolves wingers Norman Deeley and Des Horne. Tells Bobby Evans to stay tight on Jimmy Murray, the defence as a whole to make sure they 'get there first'.

Ted claps his hands. 'All the best!' he says. A buzzer sends a rather pathetic shrill sound ricocheting around the room. Like a bee trapped in some old tin can.

'All the best.' 'Good luck.' 'Have a good 'un.' 'Let's go.' 'Come on!'

No one is in a hurry at this point. There is the slow, careful click-clack of studs on the floor. We make our way down the corridor where staff caught unawares press themselves against the wall to allow us passage. One nods and offers a half smile. Another stares at us with the wonderment he'd reserve for aliens landing from another planet. There is so much liniment vapour in the air my eyes are almost watering. Through the liniment I can smell a fag. We turn a corner and head down the tunnel. We start to run. I can see daylight. I can see the Wolves players on the pitch. I can hear the crowd and what a crowd it is. Forty-four thousand spectators roar their approval of our arrival on the pitch. Somewhere, off in the distance, is the sound of Connie Francis singing 'Robot Man'.

The song immediately enters my head. It becomes part of my breathing. Heavy breathing as my legs pummel to take me around the pitch in double-quick time. I stop running and join Charlie Livesey and Frank Blunstone. We form ourselves into a makeshift triangle and begin to pass between us an old leather case ball. Breathing softly, I sing to myself, 'I want a robot man to hold me tight, keep me lardee dee-dah through the night . . .' I'm not singing to myself really. It's more of a mumble. The song is riding out of my body with each exhalation of breath.

I look around. Peter Sillett has disappeared. I look to the centre circle and see him shaking hands with Bill Slater and Tom Hanger, the referee. Moments later Peter is back in our midst.

'As we are,' he informs us and we stay in the same half of the pitch.

I walk downfield and stand on the right of the centre circle. I rub my hands together. I jump up and down. I take up the stance of a Victorian sprinter. One foot forward, ready for the off when given the say-so. Tom Hanger checks his watch. He waves to both his linesmen. He puts his whistle to his lips and blows it with gusto. The packed terraces are suddenly animated. A thunderous roar sweeps down on to the pitch. Jimmy Murray taps the ball to Peter Broadbent. Broadbent makes a half turn and passes the ball back to Ron Flowers and I go after it . . .

*

The headlines were good. At least they were for me: 3-3 against the Wolves, our first point of the season and I scored a hat-trick. Any disappointment I may have felt at us not having won the match was tempered by the thought that at least I had done my job. My job was to score goals and I derived a great deal of pleasure from having scored three. In all probability more pleasure than if I had scored one and we had won 1-0. That's not just human nature, it's how a forward thinks and feels. It was certainly how I felt about goals.

Yet again the newspapers went overboard about my performance. The *Sunday People* even went as far as to say, 'Young Jimmy Greaves displayed ample evidence that he is a star of the sixties in the making.' I don't know about me being a star of the sixties but those who were to become synonymous with fame in the sixties, such as Bobby Charlton, Bobby Moore, Cliff Richard, Mary Quant, even The Beatles, were, in fact, all products of the late fifties but were to become the cult of the young as the new decade unfolded.

And as the 1960–61 season unfolded my goalscoring continued apace. Following my hat-trick against Wolves I scored in seven of our next ten league games, including a hat-trick against Blackburn Rovers and a brace against Blackpool. Sandwiched in between those games were another couple of goals in Chelsea's 7-1 romp at the Den against Millwall in the League Cup.

This was the first ever season for the League Cup which had been introduced by Alan Hardaker, the dreadnought secretary of the Football League. Though Hardaker had been the driving force behind the introduction of the League Cup he had in fact borrowed the idea from his old adversary, Sir Stanley 'Put That Cake Down' Rous, the secretary of the FA. Even then, one could hardly say it was an original idea from Rous as Scotland had had a League Cup for years. Indeed, Rous's original idea for a League Cup was for it to comprise

qualifying groups, the winners of which would then progress
to a straight knockout. Hardaker refined the idea, making it a
knockout competition from the outset and included the idea in
his 'Pattern for Football', a revolutionary blueprint for the
future of the game in which he wanted the Football League to
reorganise into five divisions of twenty clubs, the balance of
which would be made up by eight top non-league sides.

The clubs threw out all of Hardaker's proposals with the
exception of the League Cup which, rather than being staged
at the start of every season, the clubs demanded should take
place throughout the season, thus adding to the fixture
congestion Hardaker was trying to overcome by reducing each
division to twenty teams. Hardaker was furious with the clubs,
and more so when he saw his baby less than enthusiastically
received, with Arsenal, Spurs, Sheffield Wednesday, Wolves
and West Bromwich Albion refusing to take part.

When the draw for the first round was made, the little
wooden balls rattled around in the velvet bag with no sense
of history. That was another problem. The League Cup was
new and did not have the venerability of the FA Cup. What's
more, this new competition was to be a creature of the night.
It was to be played midweek, under floodlights, and would
not bask in a single ray of sunshine, not even on the occasion
of the two-legged final itself. Many thought of the League
Cup as being an untidy tournament that would lurch
through the season making way for its elders and earning
more money than respect. Though it would in time enjoy
a golden period in the seventies and eighties, a lot of
supporters and a number of participating clubs didn't
take this new upstart seriously. We did at Chelsea. The club
prided itself on welcoming innovations and Chelsea's
acceptance of the offer to participate was one of the first to
be received by the Football League. As players we also took
the competition seriously, because with a number of big

clubs refusing to enter, we thought we had a good chance of winning it.

The draw was kind to us. Following our 7-1 demolition of Millwall, Chelsea were given a home tie against Workington Town in round two. The fact that Chelsea fans were less than enamoured with this new competition was reflected in the attendance for this game. Only 5,360 turned up at Stamford Bridge to see Chelsea win 4-2 in a game that I missed out on due to a niggling injury. I was also to miss our third round tie at Doncaster Rovers, though the lads managed to scrape through without me, winning 7-0 in front of 10,000 at Belle Vue.

I resumed League Cup action in mid-December. We were drawn away to Portsmouth and it proved not to be the happiest of nights for us. A goal from Jimmy White in the second half gave Pompey the lead and, for all we tried, we couldn't manage an equaliser.

With Chelsea ensconced in mid-table there was no fear of us winning the Championship and all we had to look forward to was the FA Cup in January. We were drawn at home to Crewe Alexandra who at the time were a mid-table Fourth Division team. We went into the tie with Crewe desperate for a good result. On a personal note I was doing all right with, at this stage of the season, twenty-seven goals to my name for Chelsea. In mid-November I scored another hat-trick in Chelsea's 6-3 win over Manchester City and followed that up a fortnight later with five goals in a 7-1 hammering of West Bromwich Albion. I'd also scored eight times in four appearances for England and three for the Football League against the League of Ireland. I was flying but Chelsea were to come down to earth like a bag of hammers. Following our victory over West Bromwich Albion on 3 December we failed to win any of our next five league games. Just before the Crewe game we were beaten 6-0 by Manchester United and 6-1 by

Wolves. Ted Drake was beginning to come under a little pressure as manager. For the first time there were murmurings about him in the press with, in particular, Desmond Hackett of the *Daily Express* wondering if Chelsea's interests would be best served by a new manager and a fresh approach. Ted Drake needed a bad result against Crewe in the Cup as much as he needed a hole in the head. Cue the drill.

In the previous season Crewe had suffered the ignominy of being beaten 13-2 by Spurs in a fourth round replay. Even in the long traditions of the FA Cup this was an extraordinary result and real humiliation for Crewe. Oddly, when the Crewe team left their home town by rail, their train had departed from platform two on Crewe station. On the return journey, they left Euston on platform thirteen! Though no one expected us to run up double figures against Crewe every Chelsea supporter amongst the crowd of 32,574 did expect us to win and handsomely. The game, however, turned out to be a nightmare from our point of view. The Crewe team only contained three members of the side that had lost so heavily to Spurs in the previous season: their skipper and left back, Don Campbell, right half Stan Keery and their left winger, Mervyn Jones, who like Campbell had once been on Liverpool's books.

In the first half Frank Blunstone scored for us but Crewe went into the half-time interval with their tails up courtesy of goals from Barrie Wheatley and Billy Stark. In the second half on what was a gluepot of a pitch we just couldn't find an answer. Their centre half Eric Barnes played a blinder and when we did breach the Crewe rearguard, their goalkeeper Brian Williamson, who had signed from Gateshead United, stopped everything we threw at him. Crewe managed to hold out to secure one of the most famous victories in their history. The press boys were scratching the words 'giant-killers' in their notepads but were in effect writing the first draft of Ted Drake's obituary as manager of Chelsea. Though he was to continue for another year, our Cup defeat against Crewe was really the beginning of the end of Ted's reign at Stamford Bridge.

I wasn't happy and I told Ted Drake as much. I don't think there has ever been a player who at one time or another hasn't intimated to his manager that he would like a move. I never put in an official transfer request in all my time at Chelsea, but I did tell Ted I was unhappy, that I wanted out. Ted did his best to persuade me that things were going to get better. He asked me to 'give it a go'. I did but things didn't get better for Chelsea. They got worse. We won only six of our remaining eighteen league matches to finish just below halfway in Division One. At twenty-one I became the youngest ever player to score one hundred league goals. There were some notable highlights in that second half of the season: a 4-4 draw at reigning Champions Burnley, where I managed a couple of goals, and in March a great 6-1 win at Newcastle United with Ron Tindall scoring twice and yours truly getting four. But those two results were an oasis in what was ostensibly a dry and barren run-in to the end of the season.

Though the goals flowed I had become increasingly unhappy with life at Chelsea and my role in the team. I felt as if I was carrying the team on my shoulders, that I was constantly baling water out of a sinking ship. It was draining me both physically and emotionally. I was scoring goals, as were the other forwards, but we were also conceding them. I found myself holding my head in my hands in anger and frustration as the defence let in another soft one. Though we finished the season in the bottom half of the table we scored a highly creditable ninety-eight goals and were the fourth highest scoring team in the First Division behind Spurs, Wolves and Burnley. The problem was, we conceded a hundred.

A lot of players who ask for a transfer do so half-heartedly, which is why they don't put it in writing. They're partly fishing, hoping a better offer may be out there. Partly hoping the manager will tell them they are an invaluable member of the team so that they feel wanted. Football is a very insecure profession and you'd be surprised just how many players need that sort of reassurance every now and then. When I first told Ted I wanted to move on, I did so half-heartedly, but on the second occasion, I meant it. What's more, Ted knew I meant it.

There were meetings. One such meeting took place at the home of the Chelsea chairman, Joe Mears. I was accompanied by Irene, and also present were Joe, his son Brian, Ted Drake and John Battersby. We talked at length. Though I had put nothing officially in writing to the effect, I told those assembled that I wanted to move on. Chelsea were strapped for money. Joe and Ted never put up a great case for me to stay, and I was of the mind they wanted me to go because the transfer fee would be a godsend to the club. Joe Mears, however, was not keen on me going to another First Division club, where I might end up scoring goals against Chelsea. There had been talk of Tottenham Hotspur being interested in me and Joe made it plain that he was desperate for me not to join Spurs. For me to join a rival London club would also incur the wrath of the Chelsea supporters. Even in 1961 there was a keen rivalry between the respective supporters of both clubs.

'If I agree to you moving to Spurs, the supporters will want to lynch me,' Joe said, adding in true Sam Goldwyn fashion, 'so there's no way I'm going to put my head on the block.'

I knew my time as a Chelsea player was up. I wanted to go and the club wanted to sell me. That much I knew. What I didn't know was who to. What I also didn't know was that Joe Mears had a card up his sleeve.

In 1961 the Italian FA decided to lift its ban on foreign players. Footballers from overseas were once again to be allowed to ply their trade in the Italian League as from the

In the back garden of our home in Ivy House Road at four years of age. The strip is that of Fanshaw Old Boys, to whom Dad was club treasurer. Alongside me is my pal Freddie Little and stealing the show is his younger brother Bruce. *(Jimmy Greaves)*

Class photograph at Kingswood School. I'm on the front row to the left. On the far right is Glyn Bateman, one of several teachers who encouraged me both in my studies and at football. *(Jimmy Greaves)*

Leaving the Chelsea office where I worked as an office boy, following a pre-season Blues v Whites trial match in 1957. The state of the brickwork and pointing says much about the financial situation of Chelsea at this time. *(Daily Express/Edward Wing)*

Making my debut as a 17-year-old for Chelsea against Spurs at White Hart Lane, August 1957. I scored Chelsea's goal in a 1-1 draw and would make a scoring debut for every team I played for at senior level. *(Popperfoto)*

My second game for England Under-23s against Romania at Wembley in October 1957. Floodlit games at Wembley in the fifties were a rarity, though not as rare as a headed goal from Greaves! *(Popperfoto)*

A very happy moment in my life. Irene and I on our wedding day, February 1958. I'm carrying Irene over the threshold, since when she has carried me! *(Daily Mirror)*

England 9 Scotland 3, April 1961. I'm flanked by Bobby Shearer and Bertie McCann, while goalkeeper Frank Haffey has an inkling as to what sort of day it will be – he's already wearing a black armband! *(Colorsport)*

Arriving in Milan with Irene in 1961, following my transfer from Chelsea. You can tell from the size of the suitcase that I wasn't planning on staying too long. *(Hulton Getty)*

Milan three months on and still scanning the skies for a London-bound plane. The security fence ran the entire perimeter of the AC Milan training ground, but I still got out. *(Daily Express)*

Bill Nicholson stuffs the Tottenham cheque book back into his pocket as I arrive at White Hart Lane in December 1961, following my record transfer from AC Milan to Spurs. *(Hulton Getty)*

A scissors-kick volley brings me the first of what would be a hat-trick of goals on my Spurs debut against Blackpool in December 1961. From left to right, Tony Waiters, Les Allen, Glyn James, me and Roy Gratix. *(Popperfoto)*

The 1962 Cup Final is only four minutes old when I give Spurs the lead against Burnley. From left to right, Alex Elder, Adam Blacklaw, Tommy Cummings, Bobby Smith, Jimmy Adamson and, sliding in on me, Brian Miller. *(Popperfoto)*

A very proud moment for me and Tottenham Hotspur Football Club – parading the FA Cup following our 3-1 victory over Burnley, May 1962. From left to right, Ron Henry, Cliff Jones, Dave Mackay, me, Maurice Norman, Bobby Smith and goalkeeper Bill Brown. *(Popperfoto)*

Losing my marker Ramiro and firing past goalkeeper Madinabeytia to give Spurs the lead against Atletico Madrid in the 1963 European Cup Winners' Cup Final. Spurs became the first British team to win a European competition. *(Popperfoto)*

Displaying the European Cup Winners' Cup along with, left to right, John White, Bill Brown, Ron Henry, Cliff Jones and 'Man of the Match' Terry Dyson. *(Popperfoto)*

Pre-season 1963 and Spurs manager Bill Nicholson (far right) goes back to basics. 'This is a ball, Jim,' he tells me, to the amusement of, left to right, Cliff Jones, Terry Medwin, Peter Baker, John White, Danny Blanchflower and Bobby Smith. *(Popperfoto)*

following season, 1961–2. The top Italian clubs were thus scouring Europe for talent, a fact that had not escaped the attention of the wily Joe Mears. A move for me to Italy would be perfect for him and Chelsea. The club would receive a sizeable transfer fee, I couldn't come back and haunt the club with goals and Joe would not incur the wrath of Chelsea supporters for having sold me to a rival club. It would be the perfect move for everyone. Except me.

A few days later, Joe Mears sounded me out about a possible move to an Italian club. I have to say that straight away such a thought appealed to me. The maximum wage was still in force. I was earning £20 a week, and although I didn't know much about Italian football I knew their players earned a damn sight more than that. At the time Irene and I were trying to come to terms with a personal living hell, while simultaneously feeling joy at the fact she had another baby on the way. Our living hell was the result of the loss of our second child, Jimmy junior. Jimmy was a beautiful boy but he contracted pneumonia when four months old. His condition worsened and for a child so young there was nothing anyone could do. Jimmy's death devastated us. It nearly drove us out of our minds. We were inconsolable. If ever there was a time in my life when I had wanted to call back yesterday, it was the day young Jimmy died. Though we had Lynn, our grief lay before us, our joy seemingly behind us. You grieve for the death of any loved one, but when it is for your own child, no words can describe that grief. As parents you expect your children to outlive you. When that doesn't happen, you become an empty shell. Jimmy junior's time on this earth was all too brief. Time heals all, they say, but not this. To this day, the pain remains.

We were still struggling to come to terms with our loss when Irene told me that she was pregnant. The thought of a move to Italy appeared to offer us a new beginning, a fresh start. Besides, with another child on the way, the extra money

I would earn would be crucial to me achieving the quality of life I wanted to provide for my family. Joe Mears swore me to secrecy and it was at this point that the waters started to get a little muddy. I say that because to this day I'm not sure whether Joe acted as an *agent provocateur* or not.

I was approached by a guy purporting to be a journalist from an Italian newspaper. He told me he was acting as an 'undercover agent for a major Italian club' and asked if I would be interested in talking to him about a move to Italy. It was an illegal approach but I went along with it as I wanted to hear what might be on offer, and arranged to meet a few days later at a restaurant in Soho. At this meeting the journalist cum agent cum James Bond revealed to me that the club he was representing was AC Milan and that they were very keen on signing me. At this stage of the proceedings I told him that I wanted to play it straight. If Milan were indeed interested in me they would have to make an official approach to Chelsea via Joe Mears. To this day I'm not sure whether this journalist had approached me at the sole behest of Milan or whether Joe Mears had a hand in it too, simply to gauge my enthusiasm for the move.

Milan did make an official approach to Chelsea and Joe Mears, though it was all kept under wraps. Joe informed me that a lucrative move to Milan was a real possibility and asked me to report to a hospital in central London to undergo a medical. I thought the medical would involve me being at the hospital for an hour or so, but I was to learn just how thorough Italian clubs were when it came to signing players. I was in that hospital for two days! When I came out I bumped into a pal of mine, sports journalist Tony Stratton-Smith. 'Where you been?' Tony asked, 'I've been trying to get hold of you for days.' I told him I'd been in hospital for a couple of days.

'What's wrong with ya?' Tony asked.

'Nothing.'

'So why'd you have to go into hospital?'

'Because the hospital wanted to satisfy themselves that there was nothing wrong with me.'

'There's nothing wrong with you, so the hospital ask you to go in for a few days so that they can satisfy themselves there's nothing wrong with you. And we have people who are ill waiting for a bed. What sort of health service is that?'

'Ours.'

What a tangled web we weave . . . The hospital I'd checked in to was actually a private hospital run by Italians, but I couldn't tell even a good pal like Tony that, because the cat would be out of the bag and I'd been sworn to secrecy.

As it turned out, and much to my surprise, the hospital in question did find something wrong with me. I had been subjected to numerous X-rays, one of which revealed I had a couple of small interlocking bones in my back. When I was a kid full of rough and tumble, I'd broken these two bones and they had somehow interlocked in the process of healing. They never caused me any discomfort and had certainly never affected my performances as a footballer. I was completely unaware of the fact that they had interlocked. It was intimated that these two interlocking bones, though of no concern at the moment, could prove to be a problem later in my career. As such, I appeared a dodgy investment. The Milan officials were very concerned, but not as concerned as me. For a time I had visions of myself in my mid-thirties in a wheelchair.

The X-rays were referred to a Harley Street specialist who, having studied them, announced there was nothing to worry about. According to the specialist the abnormality was common; there were loads of people with the same condition and it wouldn't in any way affect my ability to play football at the highest level.

The Milan officials told me they were very relieved to hear this news. I assured them they weren't as relieved as I was to hear it. I was passed 100 per cent fit to play and the transfer was back on. As for the deal itself, that was conducted on behalf of Milan by their representative, Gigi Peronace.

In 1961, Mario Puzo was in the process of writing *The Godfather*, which, looking back, is somehow appropriate because Gigi Peronace looked as if he could have stepped from the pages of Puzo's novel of Mafia family life. If a crocodile could talk it would sound like Gigi Peronace. He was an imposing figure, one to be wary of, yet he could charm a bracelet. To first look at him you were immediately wary of the man. When he first spoke, your reservations were seemingly confirmed, but as his conversation unfolded he displayed great charisma and charm, and you ended up being enchanted by the man. Like most Italians, Peronace was a smart dresser. No matter what you wore, even your Sunday best, you felt you were wearing rags when standing next to Peronace. Some people acquire a sense of how to dress themselves, others look as if their clothes have been thrust upon them and a few are born to it. Peronace belonged in the latter category. He wore Cerruti suits and when he removed his jacket he folded it like origami. His shirts were made to measure. They fitted him like bark on a tree. He wore Gucci shoes, so highly polished you could have shaved in them. He always appeared to have a cigar the size of a chair leg protruding from his mouth. The only time he seemed to remove it was when he laughed, and when he laughed, he sounded like a hyena that had just heard a bloody belter from another hyena.

Peronace had taken up temporary residence in a salubrious apartment in Knightsbridge, a corner kick away from Harrods. You could just about walk across the deep pile carpet without the aid of snowshoes, and on the walls and dotted around on antique tables was a collection of artwork that could have put the Tate to shame. Peronace didn't just look the part and live the part – he was the part. Fluent in five languages, he was articulate, educated and more cosmopolitan than a comet. His knowledge of football and, in particular, footballers, was profound and matched by his financial acumen. Be of use to him and it was as if you were his only son. Should he have no use for you, he wouldn't recall your name if it was chiselled on your forehead. He was Milan's missionary in the world of football. He was the wheeler-dealer, and the deal he struck with Joe Mears was for me to join AC Milan in the close season for £80,000.

The Milan manager, Giuseppe Viani, was a super guy whom I took to straight away. Viani arrived in London to clinch the deal and, guided by Peronace, came up with my personal terms. I was told I would receive a £15,000 signing on fee, payable over the three years of my contract, with £1,000 up front. I was to earn a basic weekly wage of £130 but with win bonuses that could increase considerably. It was the stuff of my dreams. At Chelsea I was on £20 a week, less tax, in the football season and £16 a week, less tax, as a summer retainer. What's more, Irene and I were to be given a luxury apartment on the outskirts of Milan. The job was a good 'un, or so it appeared.

As the 1960–61 season was still in progress and Italy's embargo on foreign players would not officially come to an end until the beginning of the following season, Milan took an option out on me and I continued to play for Chelsea.

My initial euphoria about the prospect of playing and living in Italy quickly subsided and, as the weeks passed, I began to have doubts about the move. I'm a home boy, Essex born and bred. The thought of living away from the London area in another part of England didn't appeal to me, let alone living in another country. I began to re-evaluate. I liked my creature comforts. I enjoyed London life and the London lifestyle. I was a young family man so I didn't frequent the night clubs or West End restaurants; moreover it was the simple pleasures of

London life that appealed to me and I knew I would miss them when I went to Italy.

Leading up to our final game of the season, Chelsea won two and lost five. Come the last game, at home to Nottingham Forest, I was hopeful of making that match a swansong to remember. As a gesture of thanks for the service I had given the club, I was made captain for the day and felt pride and gratitude when shaking hands before the game with the referee, Mr Pickles from Stockport, and the Forest captain, Bob McKinlay. My final game in Chelsea colours couldn't have gone any better from my point of view. We beat Forest 4-3 and I scored all four of our goals, the second a right-foot volley into the top left-hand corner of Peter Grummitt's net. Come the final whistle, Chelsea supporters ran on to the pitch and carried me shoulder high around the ground so that I could wave goodbye to those for whom I had given my all during my time at the club. It was a very emotional moment. I did feel sadness at the fact that I was leaving Chelsea, but deep down I knew it was the right thing to do. Though just as deep down I didn't feel the proposed move to Milan was the right one for me.

Some people, no matter how hopeless they appear to be at decision making, occasionally get it right by sheer chance. Even a broken clock is right twice a day. Others prefer to give considered thought before making a decision. In the final weeks of the 1960–61 season I gave a lot of considered thought to my proposed move to Milan. I wasn't so much wondering if this was the right move for me; rather, I was trying to convince myself that it was the right move. But on each occasion I came to the same conclusion. I didn't want to move my family to Italy and I didn't want to play football there. I couldn't lie to Irene and I couldn't lie to myself. I asked for a meeting with Joe Mears, Ted Drake and John Battersby and during this meeting I made my feelings known. I told them I didn't want to join AC Milan.

They were horrified. As part of the option agreement Chelsea had already received £10,000 up front. I was informed by Joe Mears that, although Milan had not officially taken up the option on me, it was inevitable that they would.

I knew Chelsea were strapped for cash, but I didn't realise just how much. Joe and Ted did a better selling job of Italy than the Italian Tourist Board. They tried to persuade me that I would love the Italian lifestyle. That my personal game was suited to Italian football and that I would improve as a player. That I would love the weather and everything Italy had to offer. I had no agent or adviser and I was twenty-one. What do you know at that age? In my case, not a lot. What I did know, however, was for all that I'd verbally committed myself to joining Milan, my heart wasn't in it. I told them I didn't want to go and stuck to my guns. So did they.

'There's no ifs or buts about it,' John Battersby informed me, 'you gotta go, Jimmy. You gotta go.'

I felt like some young lad who had consented to marriage only because he didn't want to upset anyone. It was arranged I would fly out to Milan where the final details would be sorted out.

The story of my transfer was now public knowledge. As far as the newspapers were concerned, the deal was done. I was, they said, 'now an AC Milan player.' With that sort of pressure on me, I felt I had no option but to fly out to Milan, though even at this late stage in proceedings I tried to get out of the deal and for good reason.

For some time the footballers' trade union, the Professional Footballers' Association, had been battling with the Football League for the abolition of the maximum wage and 'slavery' contracts which bound a player to a club for life until such time as the club thought fit to get rid of him. In a meeting between the Football League and the PFA at the Ministry of Labour, the League agreed to abolish the maximum wage and contracts binding a player to a club for life. This had happened only recently and its effects were yet to be realised, but it would mean footballers would receive a wage in keeping with their talent. This victory was down to the work of the PFA chairman, Jimmy Hill, and the secretary, Cliff Lloyd, a former solicitor. Their victory on behalf of all footballers would open the door for me to earn more money in England, which further undermined my initial decision to join Milan. I not only asked Joe Mears to do all he could to get me out of the Milan deal, I entreated him, pleaded with him and eventually begged. But I stopped at that; after all, a man must have some pride. To be fair, Joe Mears seemed genuinely sympathetic to my plight. He told me the club would hire one of the very best lawyers their money could buy, which, given Chelsea's perilous financial situation, worried the hell out of me.

The barrister Chelsea hired did indeed turn out to be one of the very best in the legal profession. His name was R. I. Lewis and I am convinced to this day that John Mortimer based his fictitious barrister, Rumpole of the Bailey, on R. I. I met R. I. at his chambers. He was a large, colourful character with a smile like a dirty-minded cherub. Lewis was sometimes bombastic, occasionally blustering but in his thinking always sharp as a razor and, I thought, probably just as accommodating when rubbed up the wrong way. He was charming to me, always at pains to play down his role and status. But I couldn't help but think that even barristers who try not to behave like barristers just end up behaving like barristers trying not to behave like barristers.

I had asked my pal Tony Stratton-Smith to accompany me on the trip to Milan. R. I. Lewis informed me he would follow us out and, when there, would do everything in his power to have the deal annulled. When I got home and looked up the word 'annulled' in the dictionary, I felt a whole lot better. A few days later Tony and I flew out to Milan and the following day were joined by R. I. On the morning of the meeting that would decide my future, I debated what to wear. There was gold-leaf sunshine in the sky. It was ninety-eight degrees, so I decided that smart casual was to be the order of the day. I opted for a short sleeved polo shirt, light slacks and slip-on shoes, and, once dressed, went down to the hotel foyer to meet Tony and R. I. Tony arrived wearing very similar clothes to me. When R. I. turned up I was flabbergasted. The weather was blazing hot, but R. I. was wearing a dark woollen three-piece suit, a starched wing-collared shirt and a bowler hat. In one hand he was carrying a furled umbrella, in the other a bulging briefcase and over his arm was draped a heavy worsted overcoat. Tony and I looked at one another in amazement.

'You're having a larf, Mr Lewis, ain't ya?' Tony asked.

He wasn't.

I know this may seem unbelievable today, but as a player I wasn't allowed to attend the meeting that was going to determine my future in the game. Instead, while R. I. met with the AC Milan president Mr Spaddicini, their manager Giuseppe Viani and other club officials, I was left kicking my heels outside with Tony.

The meeting took place at Mr Spaddicini's home in Alassio, a sumptuous icing-cake-walled villa with a terracotta tiled roof and white stone trim from which tumbled a salmon-pink bougainvillea as wide as a decent-sized waterfall. Tony and I sat on a veranda overlooking a surprisingly green lawn, flanked by three white acacias that were worth seeing. As it turned out, I didn't do much sitting. I was very anxious about the outcome of the meeting and spent most of the time pacing up and down. After twenty minutes, R. I. emerged from his meeting.

'Well?'

'Good news and bad news, Jimmy,' said R. I. 'I'm afraid I've been unable to get you out of the deal. They've taken up their option. You're an AC Milan player.'

My heart immediately sank.

'So what's the good news?'

'I've got you an extra tenner a week,' R. I. said.

I thought he'd done everything he could to try and get me out of the deal, but from the point of view of Milan it was 'watertight'. I was more than disappointed. I was gutted.

On the way back to our hotel, dark clouds swamped the sky and the rain came down like stair rods. R. I. simply smiled, donned his overcoat and put up his umbrella. Tony and I got a really good soaking and our polo shirts clung to our bodies like another skin.

'Everything watertight, my arse.'

CHAPTER SEVEN

MOON RIVER

There could not have been a greater contrast between the club I was leaving and the one I was to join. Chelsea were strapped for cash. For Milan, money appeared to be no object. At Chelsea we invariably trained on the dog track behind one of the goals. Milan had their own training ground offering first-class facilities, including a players' restaurant, and also owned a training retreat in the mountains that was fully self-contained. Chelsea travelled to away games by second-class rail; Milan never put a foot outside their stadium unless they were travelling executive class. Stamford Bridge was a cavernous stadium that, at the turn of the twentieth century, was England's second largest sporting venue after Crystal Palace. Major development to improve the stadium had taken place in the 1930s, primarily a cover at the rear of the Fulham Road terracing which later became known as 'The Shed'. That development took place not with football in mind but greyhound racing, the aim being to provide cover for bookies on greyhound nights. More improvements to Stamford Bridge should have followed the club's Championship success of 1955 but never did. Stamford Bridge was still a large stadium, but apart from the installation of floodlights, no real development had taken place since the thirties and in 1961 it was a tired old stadium that in parts was downright shabby.

Milan's San Siro stadium was in direct contrast. It too was cavernous, boasting a capacity of 87,000, but the stadium itself was, for 1961, state of the art. Though the San Siro still had terracing, many of the supporters were seated and enjoyed the benefits of on-site bars, top-quality catering stalls and a café. The favourite pre-match snack for Milan supporters was a pizza and Peroni. Stamford Bridge, like every other English league ground at the time, did not serve beer and the pre-match menu of tea, Bovril and hot pies hadn't changed for decades. There's nothing wrong with Bovril and a pie. Bovril, after all, was supposedly what 'Jimmy Greaves trains and scores on' but the pre-match fayre on offer to English supporters lacked the cosmopolitan variety and sheer quality of that offered to supporters at the San Siro.

I was leaving a club that was in decline for one very much in the ascendancy. Though I had wanted to move on, initially I was saddened to leave Chelsea, where I had made a lot of good friends. My eventual departure, however, was acrimonious. Following the last game of the season against Nottingham Forest, deemed to be my last game in Chelsea colours, the club then insisted I accompany them on a close-season tour of Israel that was to start on 1 May with a game against Hapoel in Haifa. I couldn't see the point in me going on what was in essence a meaningless tour, so refused to go. The club took umbrage at this and suspended me. Given the circumstances I wouldn't have been bothered but the two-week ban imposed on me by the club prevented me from playing for England against Mexico at Wembley.

I was furious. I had given five seasons of loyal service to the club. In 1960–61 I was once again the club's leading goal scorer with forty-one league goals, which also made me the First Division's leading goalscorer by a long chalk. I finished the season twelve goals ahead of my nearest challenger, David Herd of Arsenal, and thirteen ahead of four other players, including Aston Villa's Gerry Hitchens. Chelsea sold me to Milan for £80,000 which, given that I had cost them a £10 signing on fee, meant I had realised a profit of £79,990 for the club. I was on my way to Milan, somewhat reluctantly it has to be said, and for the club to suspend me for not wanting to go on a meaningless close-season tour was despicable behaviour on their part.

The club had arranged to play three games in Israel. Apart from the game against Hapoel they were also due to play an Israeli Select XI and Maccabi, with the latter two games taking place in Tel Aviv. The only reason I can imagine the club insisted I play in those games was that they had guaranteed my appearance as part of the fee they were to receive. This was common practice at the time and still is today. In the fifties Blackpool earned a lot of money from playing friendlies in which the fee the club received was tied to a guarantee of Stanley Matthews playing. Like every other footballer, Stan's contract meant he played in friendlies for nothing while his club raked in money. Stan was even asked by Blackpool to return from his coaching in South Africa to play in a lucrative friendly Blackpool had arranged in the Republic of Ireland. Stan was reluctant to leave his coaching role in the townships, but out of loyalty to Blackpool travelled back to the UK and played in the friendly in Ireland, returning to South Africa the very next day. Blackpool earned a lot of money off the back of Stan's good name and fame in football. However, when the time came for Stan to leave Bloomfield Road, the directors didn't see fit to award him a testimonial after fourteen years during which his name on the team sheet guaranteed a full house wherever Blackpool played.

At Chelsea the players weren't paid for playing in friendly matches either. I remember coming back on to the pitch for the second half of a friendly at Stamford Bridge as the band that had been providing the half-time entertainment was

marching off. I remarked to Frank Blunstone that the band
were being paid more than us.

'That ain't difficult, considering we are being paid bugger
all,' said Frank.

'The board must obviously think the band play better than
us.'

The fact that I wasn't to be paid for the tour of Israel was
not an issue with me. Even if the club had been paying me, I
still wouldn't have gone because I felt it unnecessary. What
really annoyed me was that the fourteen-day suspension
coincided with England's game against Mexico. I was loath to
miss this one, because England were really flying.

In 1960–61 Walter Winterbottom was creating an England
team I felt were good enough to go on and win the 1962
World Cup in Chile. The old guard had gone and Walter had
created a young England team that was finely balanced and in
tune with one another as players. One which played well as a
collective unit while at the same time allowing individuals to
express themselves. We weren't just beating other teams, we
were steamrollering them.

England's great run of results began in October 1960 with
a 5-2 win over Northern Ireland in Belfast. I scored twice that
day, England's other goals coming from Bobby Charlton,
Bobby Smith and Bryan Douglas. A fortnight later we won
9-0 in Luxembourg where there were hat-tricks for Bobby
Charlton and myself and further goals from Bobby Smith (2)
and Johnny Haynes. A week later, Spain were beaten 4-2 and
in the following month we enjoyed a 5-1 win over Wales. That
was four international games in the space of six weeks, and
players complain about having to play too many competitive
games these days. Those four games produced twenty-three
England goals, but our best performance was still to come.

The annual meeting between England and Scotland was the
biggest match in the international calendar of both countries,

and had been since the very first meeting had taken place between the 'auld enemies' in Glasgow in 1872, which was in fact the very first international football match of all. Most English clubs had a good smattering of Scottish players on their books and the ribbing in the dressing room following an England–Scotland game was something terrible. If England lost, those Jocks never let up for weeks. We English feel passionate about a game against the Scots, but our zeal is only there on the day and, while our feelings are strong, they're not fundamental to our being. With the Scots it's different. For them the dedication to this fixture seeps down into the soul and becomes part of instinct.

And it was like this from the moment one match ended until the return fixture the following year. If Scotland won at Wembley, the joy of the Scots was unbridled. When they eventually returned to their homes, they'd do so hell-bent on saving two bob a week for the next trip to London in two years' time. The 1961 meeting between the two countries was my first experience of this fixture at full international level. I have never forgotten it, and such is the story of this particular game, I am sure the memory of it will remain with me even when I am old and grey and full of sleep and nodding by the fire.

'What's the time?' 'Nearly ten past Haffey!' That was the joke doing the rounds following England's 9-3 demolition of Scotland at Wembley in 1961. Poor Frank Haffey. The Celtic goalkeeper's performance was anything but breathtaking, but England's performance that day definitely was.

England had been posting good results under Walter Winterbottom. I had scored eight goals in the previous four international matches. I didn't think my international career could get any better. I was wrong. On 15 April 1961, it did.

When the two teams emerged from the Wembley tunnel I thought I was in Glasgow. Well over half the 100,000 crowd were Scots and the noise they made was deafening. The massed bands of the Irish and Grenadier Guards and the pipes and drums of the 1st Battalion Scots Guards were playing Haines' march, 'The London Scottish', but I could hardly hear them. It was tartan bedlam. Wembley seemed to be soaked in Scotland that afternoon and as my boots touched the famous Cumberland turf I felt the full force of the Scottish supporters' two years of anticipation.

I can't envisage two sets of supporters of today indulging in community singing for half an hour before kickoff. But they did in 1961, as they had done at Wembley since it first opened its doors to football in 1923. The songs the bands played made no concessions to the pop music of the day. They were old music-hall favourites or traditional tunes. 'I Belong to Glasgow', 'The British Grenadiers', 'Bonnie Dundee', 'Ye Take the High Road', the perennial Wembley favourite, the hymn 'Abide with Me' and oddly, for a crowd that was by and large male, 'I'm A Lassie From Lancashire'.

The Scots were confident of success, but England were on a great run of results. Our confidence and team spirit were sky high and though I expected us to beat Scotland, I thought it was going to be tight.

Walter Winterbottom decided on a 4-4-2 formation, but really we were playing with five forwards, as of old: Blackburn's Bryan Douglas, myself, Bobby Smith of Spurs, the mercurial Johnny Haynes of Fulham and Bobby Charlton. From the first whistle the Scottish supporters got right behind their team. Rangers' Davie Wilson missed a great chance to put Scotland ahead in the very first minute, firing wide when well placed. Roared on by their massive support I thought Scotland were going to give us the runaround but after ten minutes I fed the ball to Bobby Smith out wide. Bobby pulled the ball back into the path of Bobby Robson who slammed it past Frank Haffey.

Ten minutes later, Johnny Haynes produced the sort of pass he was renowned for. Johnny's left foot was so reliable and dependable it could have been used for the delivery of registered letters. From just inside the England half, Johnny hit a beautifully weighted pass that split the Scottish defence in two. I'd timed my run, got on the end of the pass and it was a simple matter of taking the ball on and sliding it past the oncoming Haffey.

Just to show everyone it was no fluke, Johnny did the same again five minutes later and so did I: 3-0!

The England dressing room was cock-a-hoop during half-time. Walter Winterbottom didn't say a great deal; like the supporters I think he was stunned. He just told us to keep playing football, and make certain we kept it tight in the opening ten minutes of the second half because he was certain the Scots would come out all guns blazing and give it a go.

From the kickoff Scotland came at us with a vengeance. They had in their ranks Denis Law, Ian St John, Billy McNeill, Dave Mackay, Eric Caldow, Pat Quinn and Davie Wilson, all quality players. In the case of Mackay and Law, world class.

I knew there was no way that lot would give up without a fight. Within three minutes of the restart Dave Mackay pulled a goal back for the Scots. Minutes later, Davie Wilson made amends for his earlier miss by making it 3-2. Denis Law was causing our defence all manner of problems and was unlucky not to equalise when he rattled our crossbar. It was then that the game changed and in dramatic fashion.

Immediately following Law's strike we gained possession and surged deep into the Scottish half where the referee, Monsieur Lequesne, awarded us a free kick. The Scots were livid. They didn't think Bobby Charlton had been fouled and were still arguing with Lequesne when I took the free kick quickly and dinked the ball to Bryan Douglas who scored to make it 4-2.

If the Scots were livid before the free kick, they were damn well rabid now. Even after they had kicked off to restart the game they were still berating Lequesne, not only for awarding the free kick, but for allowing me to take it quickly as they believed he hadn't blown his whistle.

Our fourth goal and the manner of it knocked the stuffing out of the Scots. They lost all their composure and we set about them in no uncertain fashion. Scotland lost their shape and discipline. In midfield, Johnny Haynes suddenly found more space than Captain Kirk, and had all the time in the world to thread those exquisite passes of his to our front line. We didn't waste them. Bobby Smith made it 5-2 and even though Pat Quinn pulled a goal back for Scotland I knew we would go on to win handsomely. Johnny Haynes helped himself to a couple of goals, Bobby Smith finished with two and I completed my hat trick. My record now stood at eleven goals in five England matches. I even had what I thought was a good goal disallowed for offside, but with the final score at 9-3 was past caring.

It was and still is England's record victory over Scotland. The amazing thing was that when the England players walked off the pitch after the final whistle, we did so to a less than half-empty stadium. The Scottish supporters had vacated it in their droves, having probably gone off to drown their sorrows. History has it that the margin of our victory was entirely down to Frank Haffey in the Scottish goal. It's true he had a poor game, but Frank wasn't the only Scot who didn't perform well that day. In truth, I don't think any international team of the time could have lived with England that day. Johnny Haynes was outstanding. To my mind it was his greatest performance in an England shirt and that's saying something considering his track record at international level. Bryan Douglas, the three Bobbys, Smith, Charlton and Robson, were imperious and we forwards received super support from our defence. To get things into perspective, Scotland were far from a poor team. What wouldn't the Scots give to have the likes of Dave

Mackay, Denis Law, Ian St John and Billy McNeill in their ranks today?

Frank Haffey's name did not appear in the team's line up in the match programme. He was a last minute replacement for Airdrie's Lawrie Leslie who was injured. I wouldn't mind betting that after the match Lawrie Leslie was counting his lucky stars he'd been injured in training because England were unstoppable. The stories surrounding the aftermath of this game are as legendary as those of the game itself. Denis Law told me that the humiliation of the margin of their defeat never sank in with Frank Haffey. After the game, much to the annoyance of his fellow Scots, he was heard singing in the bath. Frank was naive in many respects, not only as a goalkeeper at international level but in the way he allowed himself to be manipulated by the English press. That night, after the players' banquet at the Savoy, Frank went for a walk with some of the other Scottish players to see some of the sights of London. A freelance press photographer caught up with him near Big Ben and had him pose for a photograph in goalkeeping mode. It was a quarter past nine. The following day, many of the late editions of the Sunday papers carried a photograph of a smiling Frank, arms outstretched, fingers pointing in a mirror-image of the hands of the clock behind him.

That did it for Frank with the Scottish supporters. He never did play again for Scotland. Even the Celtic supporters gave him grief. He was ridiculed wherever he played and acquired the nickname 'Hapless Haffey'. Poor Frank, it all got too much for him and a year or so later he emigrated to Australia, which some Scottish fans said was just about far enough away.

There's a phrase amongst footballers: nothing hurts when you win. No player wants to be sidelined when his team is flying. He wants to be part of that. Niggling injuries are ignored for two reasons. A player wants to be part of a winning team and he's afraid that if he succumbs to a minor injury he might lose his place in the side for some time. I was loath to miss England's game against Mexico especially after our historic win against Scotland. But the suspension Chelsea imposed on me for refusing to travel to Israel prevented me from playing at Wembley, and my place in the England team was taken by Derek Kevan of West Bromwich Albion. I was really disappointed as I felt England were going to turn in another blistering performance. I wasn't wrong. England crushed Mexico 8-0. The bandwagon rolled on without me.

Regarding my exit from Chelsea, the suspension left a bitter taste in my mouth. Fortunately, regarding my place in the England team, I returned at the first time of asking. Ten days after the demolition of Mexico, England departed for a three match tour of the Continent. Walter Winterbottom not only included me in his squad, he played me in all three games. The first, a 1-1 draw with a very strong Portugal side in Lisbon, the second a magnificent 3-2 win over Italy in Rome. I scored one of our goals against Italy, the other two came from Gerry Hitchens and his performance that day was enough to earn him a transfer from Aston Villa to Inter Milan. Gerry was going to be playing for AC Milan's great rivals, but I thought once in Milan at least I would have a fellow Englishman to befriend. Little did I know, the regimes of both clubs were to offer little opportunity to go out and socialise.

England's continental tour ended with a blip. We lost 3-1 to Austria in Vienna. Given our previous performances this was a disappointing result but I think Walter Winterbottom saw a lot of positives in it. He used the Austria game as an opportunity to give some of the younger squad members a game, among them the Burnley pair John Angus and Brian Miller. The disappointment of losing was tempered by the notion that Walter was on track to creating a side capable of mounting a serious challenge for the World Cup in Chile.

Unfortunately, fate was to deny him three players who, to all intents and purposes, provided the backbone to the side he had so meticulously created.

A few days after returning home with the England party, I was on my way to Milan. The club had arranged a prestigious friendly against the crack Brazilian side Botafogo and wanted to use this match as a means of introducing me to the Milan supporters. It was another friendly that I wasn't overly keen to play in and for good reason. Irene was due to give birth to our second child and naturally I wanted to be with her. The club informed me that if I played against Botafogo I could return to London to be with Irene. I wasn't keen to be travelling to and fro, but not wanting to appear discourteous and start my career at Milan on the wrong foot, I flew out for the Botafogo game.

I was accompanied on the flight by Desmond Hackett of the *Daily Express* and a photographer for that newspaper, Norman 'Speedy' Quicke. Desmond's reputation amongst players as a football writer was not so much one of fame as one of infamy. He was one of the old school. He wore a brown bowler hat, an anachronism even in 1961, but had an individualistic style about him. His face may have looked like an old boot, but without question it was handmade. He always maintained he found his copy difficult to write, but that can't have compared to the pain of having to read it because no player was above criticism. He went for the jugular, what's more, and by his own admission he never let the facts get in the way of a good story. As such, his copy made for compelling reading.

In 1952, following a disappointing performance by England in Italy, Desmond Hackett wrote a damning piece about the England centre forward that day, Nat Lofthouse. Hackett didn't just want Nat dropped for England's next game in Austria, he demanded he be sent home. When the England squad reached Vienna, Nat Lofthouse managed to telephone his wife at home, who told him about Hackett's piece in the

Daily Express, screaming for Nat to be sent home and for Newcastle's Jackie Milburn to be flown out to Austria as his replacement. Nat Lofthouse kept his place in the England team for the Austria game and the rest is history. Nat played the game of his life, displaying tremendous courage and fortitude in very difficult circumstances. Nat's brave performance and goals in England's famous 3-2 victory against one of the best sides in the world earned him the nickname of 'The Lion of Vienna'. The man who coined that phrase was Desmond Hackett in his match report for the *Daily Express*. Twenty-four hours earlier he had been demanding Nat be sent home, but made no reference to that in a match report that was glowing in its praise of Nat Lofthouse.

That was typical of Desmond Hackett. He could change like a weather vane and didn't give a monkey's about what anyone thought. He was typical of the cigar-chomping sports journo who, along with the BBC dilettante who'd 'had a good war', commented on football in the fifties. Hackett, like most of his contemporaries, knew his onions. He was one of the best football writers of his time. He knew football inside out and his love for the game was only equalled by his love of a good time.

I arrived at Heathrow Airport two hours before my flight to Milan was scheduled to depart. I went into the cafeteria for a cup of tea but when Desmond Hackett arrived with 'Speedy' Quicke he informed me that my inaugural trip to Milan was befitting of something more than a cup of tea.

'You're about to make your debut for AC Milan,' said Desmond. 'My dear boy, that calls for a lobster and champagne lunch. On me. Or rather, on my benevolent employers at the *Express*.'

I was only twenty-one, prey to the advice and smooth talk of more seasoned individuals connected with the game. I didn't know what the form was, I simply assumed a lobster and champagne lunch was par for the course for a football writer of Hackett's esteem. So I didn't say 'No' to his kind offer.

It was, quite literally, a cracking lunch. Lobsters were consumed with relish as were two bottles of champagne. We put the football world to rights and were so involved in our conversation that we lost all track of time. Eventually, 'Speedy' Quicke looked at his watch.

'Bugger! Our flight to Milan. It left ten minutes ago!' Speedy informed us. I was very anxious but Desmond Hackett was unperturbed.

'Is there another flight?' he asked.

Speedy told him the next flight to Milan would be in six hours.

'There you go then,' said Desmond, 'nothing to worry about at all.'

We arrived in Italy six hours late and at the wrong airport. Thirty-four miles away on the other side of Milan, at Linate Airport, a welcoming party from AC Milan were pacing the concourse concerned as to my whereabouts. It was just as well. Desmond had plied me with more drinks during the flight and I arrived in Italy very much the worse for wear. I checked into the hotel and managed to contact the club and get hold of someone who spoke English. I gave him a story about a mix-up in flights and they were so relieved I'd arrived, they bought it. When I woke up the following morning, my mouth was so dry David Lean could have shot *Lawrence of Arabia* in it. I had some toast and orange juice and like most young guys, quickly shed the hangover. When the car arrived to take me to the San Siro for the game against Botafogo, I felt as right as rain.

I felt good when I took to the pitch for my first game in the colours of AC Milan and, as luck would have it, I made another scoring debut. Milan drew 2-2 with Botafogo and, my goal apart, both the officials and supporters of the club appeared happy with what they had seen of their new signing. After the game, the Milan secretary Bruno Passalaqua complimented me on my performance and told me the club would be looking forward to my return in July after Irene had had our baby. Irene was due to give birth on 15 July and I had made plans to fly back to Milan two days later. Babies arrive when it suits them and this one definitely had a mind of its own. The 15 July came and went. I cabled Milan, informing them of the situation, saying I would be staying with Irene until she gave birth and would return two days thereafter, when I was satisfied that Irene and our new baby were both in good health. I concluded the cable by saying 'I hope this is acceptable to you.' It wasn't. Milan got back to me intimating they would fine me £50 for every day that I failed to appear at the club. Their lack of understanding and compassion regarding Irene's situation irked me. My relationship with Milan was not coming on in leaps and bounds, because we had got off on the wrong foot.

We traded cables. I informed the club that, regardless of whatever action they might take, I would not return until Irene had given birth and I was satisfied both her and our new baby were in good health. Milan eventually informed me that they were willing to accept the situation, but I sensed they did so only with some reluctance.

Our baby finally arrived on 6 August, a beautiful girl whom Irene and I named Mitzi. I planned to fly back to Milan four days after the birth of Mitzi, on 10 August, only that didn't go as intended.

During my paternity leave from Milan I received a telephone call from a friend of Bobby Moore, Jack Turner. Jack informed me that he and the West Ham player Phil Woosnam were behind the launch of a new football boot and suggested I might like to lend my name to it. It was a commercial deal and I told Jack that I would be interested. He asked me to fly to Venice to meet the people from the company behind this boot, which I agreed to do.

I contacted AC Milan to confirm I would be joining them for pre-season training but instead of flying direct to Milan caught a flight to Venice. The company was called Vallesport and was one of the leading manufacturers of football boots in Italy. It had plans to trade in England under the name Sports Italia Ltd and had three flagship boots on offer, the Brasiliana, Continental and Roma. The market for football boots in the UK was just opening up and Vallesport were keen to exploit what they believed would be a burgeoning marketplace. For decades the FA and Football League had only given official blessing to three manufacturers of football boots. These were the Wellingbrough Boot and Shoe Company of Northampton which produced the Hotshot, a heavy ankle-length boot with a bulbous toecap that had remained largely unchanged since the thirties; the wonderfully named Streamlined McGregor, which was produced by William Shillcock and worn by Chelsea when they won the First Division Championship in 1955; and the Manfield-Hotspur Continental as made by the Manfield Company of Northampton. Of course, there were other boots on the market – thousands of mothers must have bought their sons a pair of Co-op boots as promoted, but not worn, by Stan Matthews – but the three aforementioned boots had official blessing. The game was changing, English football was undergoing a period of modernisation and its governing bodies no longer wished to give their approval to one type of boot rather than another. But while Vallesport were keen to exploit the new market, they were not so keen to exploit me. For whatever reason, the company decided to have Phil Woosnam endorse the boots their advertising claimed were 'Used and demanded by the world's leading players'. Rather than making me commercially hot, my trip to Venice put me in hot water. Following the meeting with Vallesport, I caught a train from Venice to Milan and arrived a day late for pre-season training where a shock was awaiting me.

I arrived to the news that Giuseppe Viani, the Milan manager who had been instrumental in signing me, had died of a heart attack. The news saddened me because Viani had struck me as being a really decent guy, a man of warmth and understanding. His replacement, I was to discover to my cost, was just the opposite. Nero Rocco was a Neapolitan who was suspicious of the Milanese. He distrusted Romans, didn't like Florentines, disliked Sardinians, loathed Tuscans, despised the Spanish and hated the French. So you can imagine what he thought of the English.

Rocco was a large, burly man whose backside was so big he appeared taller when he sat down. My first impression of him was that he looked like something that would eat its young and I wasn't far out. He was a strict disciplinarian who could have given irritability lessons to Captain Bligh. He made my life hell and I didn't exactly bring sunshine into his.

I arrived in Milan and travelled to the team's training camp at Galaratte, about forty miles outside the city. I was roomed with one of Milan's big stars, Sandro Salvatore, with whom I got on very well. It was Rocco and his strict regime I didn't get on with.

I did try to make a go of it, but it appeared to me that every time I made an effort to immerse myself in the Milan way of doing things, obstacles were put in my path. The daily schedule was regimental in the extreme. Like every other player I received a daily itinerary the content of which detailed our every move from morning to night. The itinerary made the 'Dear Greaves' letters I'd received from the Football Association appear positively chummy.

'You will rise at seven thirty a.m. You will report for breakfast at eight thirty a.m. Following breakfast you will join your team-mates for a supervised walk commencing at nine thirty a.m. At ten thirty a.m. you will train. At noon you will partake of a light luncheon. At two p.m. you will train. At four p.m. you will retire to your room for a rest period', and so it continued until ten thirty p.m. when 'You will go to sleep in your room'.

The Italian lads weren't particularly happy about this regimentation but they were used to it. I wasn't and I hated it. The strictness of the daily routine was one thing, but all the time our training was subjected to the bullying of Rocco who constantly barked orders like some demented sergeant major. It was not in the nature of the man to coerce players into doing something or instil an element of fun and humour into these training sessions. At best he was manic and at worst he appeared to have all the mental stability of Caligula. I was not a happy recruit and he knew it, yet at no time did he ever take me to one side for a man-to-man chat. Man-management came very low on his list of priorities, if it appeared at all. I hold up my hand and say I had been silly to fly to Venice to discuss the proposed boot deal and subsequently arrive twenty-four hours late for pre-season training. Of course, I should have travelled direct to Milan. I was in Rocco's bad books from the moment I arrived at that training camp, but rather than admonish me and be done with it, Rocco's displeasure with me seemed to fester and grow with each passing day.

Nero Rocco was an employee of AC Milan. As the coach his brief was to get the very best out of the players under his charge. To be fair to the man, he obviously believed the strict regime he imposed whereby the players did everything together was the best way to achieve this. He didn't particularly single me out for harsh treatment. He treated every player that way and that was his mistake. Players are individuals and each one reacts and behaves in a different way. To get the best out of some players, you have to bollock them. Others need a more subtle approach. You jolly them along and coerce and cajole them into doing what you want them to do. In order to get the best out of some, you may even have to nurse them along. A good manager will take the time to familiarise himself with the character and idiosyncratic ways of each player and act accordingly. Rocco never did. He treated us all like wayward ragamuffins whose sole requirement was discipline and lots of it. My team-mates put up with it simply because Rocco's regime was merely a more severe form of what they had been used to, whereas the whole Italian approach to training and football was totally alien to me.

We were never allowed to leave our hotel unless Rocco accompanied us. His considerable presence was always there, like a shadow of foreboding, even during meals. He supervised our diet to the extent that he would order our individual meals from the menu. He not only ordered my meals but sat opposite me to make sure I ate them. Smoking was still, to a certain degree, acceptable amongst footballers at this time. Rocco allowed those who liked to smoke two cigarettes a day, one after lunch and one after our evening meal. I was only an occasional smoker but the pressure and anxiety I felt as a result of Rocco's regime at the training camp served to make me smoke even more. One evening, having smoked my ration of two cigarettes, I felt the need for another. The players were passing time together in the hotel lounge and I excused myself on the pretence of going to the loo. My intention, of course, was to have a crafty cigarette outside. When I entered the gents washroom it was if I had walked into the snug of a London pub. A fug of smoke hung in the air and every cubicle was occupied by a Milan player puffing away on a cigarette. In a strange sort of way that made me feel better. I didn't feel so alienated by the strictness of Rocco's regime or so much guilt for having sneaked away for a crafty cigarette; half a dozen other players had done the same.

When our pre-season training came to an end, I returned to my apartment in Milan. At least there I could escape the dictatorial presence of Nero Rocco as even he had a home to go to. The freedom I found living in the apartment would be short-lived, however.

Having moved into the apartment, I was once again prepared to give it a go at Milan. I'd hated the regimentation of the pre-season training but I relished the relative freedom of life in the apartment and decided to put the horrors of the training camp behind me and apply myself to the task of playing for Milan. But for all my good intentions, somebody seemed intent on causing trouble between myself and the club. One morning I received a telephone call from the Milan trainer asking why I had not reported to the training ground that morning. I informed him that no one had told me that we were training that day. No one had but the club didn't accept that as an excuse and fined me £200. Communication between the management and myself was poor. I never knew what I was supposed to be doing. Sometimes I only found out because one of my team-mates told me. I was very homesick and when Irene telephoned to say that she was coming over to see me along with her brother Tom and his wife, Nancy, I couldn't wait for their arrival, especially as their stay was to coincide with the Milan players having a rare day off.

On the day in question we motored down from Milan to Venice and enjoyed a super day out. The following day I was carpeted and fined £400 by the club for breaking city limits. No one had told me Milan players were banned from travelling outside the city, or, more to the point, why. The Italian press got hold of the story and their headlines did not make pretty reading from my point of view. I was made out to be the bad boy in all this, especially as I had already fallen foul of Milan's club rules during an earlier visit from Tom.

On that occasion, Tom had joined me at a hotel in which the Milan team were staying and in the evening the two of us enjoyed a couple of lagers together while sitting on my balcony. The next day two workmen entered my room and without explanation, nailed two planks of wood across the slatted door leading to the balcony. I can only assume someone had seen Tom and me enjoying a drink and tipped off Rocco about it. His response was not only typically uncommunicative, I felt it to be insulting.

The only relief I felt was when I stepped over the white line and played for Milan. Though Milan, like every other Italian team of the day, played the *catenaccio* system which resulted in dour, colourless football, I found the freedom to express myself during games. The *catenaccio* system, whereby a sweeper played behind a four-man defence, stifled open, fluent football. Once a team took the lead the gameplan was to fall back and defend that lead. This resulted in countless games ending 1-0 or even 0-0 as the emphasis was not on scoring goals but on not conceding them. I played in a two-man attack alongside the golden boy of Italian football and a great hero of the AC Milan supporters, Gianni Rivera, though there were games when he played deep, which left me up front as the lone striker. Man to man marking was universal and I came in for some close attention from opponents. My every step was dogged by my marker. Even so, I discovered I could be my own man out there on the pitch. As the striker I wasn't subjected to the strictures of the *catenaccio* system. I enjoyed relative freedom and found a blessed relief in that, even though the price of that freedom more often than not was a two-man attack taking on an eight-man defence.

My debut for Milan in Serie A was against Lanerossi Vicenza in the Romeo Menti stadium and I was fortunate enough to make it a scoring debut. Italian football at the time was a curious mixture of superlative skills and technique peppered with cynicism, niggling fouls and spite that bordered on the vicious. It was a type of football I was not used to, but I dealt with it and continued to score goals. The big game for AC Milan was against their local rivals Internazionale, with whom they shared (and still do) the San Siro stadium. Against Inter, the officials and supporters of AC Milan didn't care how the team played as long as they won. The ends justified the means and many was the Milan player whose reputation had been made solely as a result of scoring a winning goal against Inter. This was not to be in the case of yours truly. We beat Inter 3-1 and I effectively wrapped up victory when I scored our second goal. I felt, however, that still didn't endear me to the Milan supporters and certainly not to Nero Rocco. Nor did success in the local derby endear me to Milan and Italian football in general. I was desperately unhappy. The club were aware of this and did what they always did when they found they had an unhappy player in their ranks. They offered me more money. That was their solution to most problems with players. Initially it had been money that had tempted me to Italy, but by this stage of proceedings no amount of money could make me happy. I was in a bad situation and it was to get even worse.

We were playing Sampdoria and looking good value for both points. I had scored to give us the lead and though Sampdoria later equalised, I had a hand in setting up a second goal. Only minutes of the game were remaining when I tracked back to offer support to our defence in what was surely Sampdoria's last throw of the dice. As I passed one of the Sampdoria players, he spat in my face. Without thinking, I kicked him. The referee saw it and awarded Sampdoria a free kick just outside our penalty area. Sampdoria scored from the free kick to gain a 2-2 draw. Back in the dressing room, Rocco went berserk with me. He ranted and raved for fully ten minutes. Though I had scored one of our goals and helped make the other, that fact was ignored. I and I alone was to blame for us not winning the game. To his mind, I had let everyone down, I was a disgrace to the famous red-and-black shirt. I felt belittled in front of my team-mates and I wasn't going to put up with it.

'Stuff this for a game of soldiers,' I told him. 'I've had enough.'

I had.

If I found one crumb of comfort from my unhappy situation, it was in the knowledge that the other three British players currently plying their trade in Italy were also deeply unhappy and unable to adjust to their new way of life.

My former England team-mate Gerry Hitchens was not enjoying life at Inter Milan. Neither club was keen on the idea of their players socialising with those of the fiercest rival and the consumption of beer was definitely frowned upon. I used to meet Gerry in secret at Milan railway station where, after pouring a bottle of lager, we'd pour out our sorrows to one another. Milan's main railway station may appear to be the most unlikely place to meet, given that it is so public, but there was a quiet room at the back of a buffet that seemed safe from prying eyes. I only met Gerry on a couple of occasions and he was never relaxed at any time. He was forever looking over his shoulder. Though Gerry enjoyed our chats, and no doubt the beer, the pressure was all too much for him. After only a couple of get-togethers, he told me that he wouldn't be able to come anymore as he feared the consequences of being found out. As things were to turn out, Gerry did make a go of his life and career in Italy. He stayed on and when his days at Inter were over played for both Atalanta and Cagliari.

The other two British players in Italy at this time were Denis Law and Joe Baker, both of whom were at Torino. The fact that they had one another's company at the same club did little to make them any happier than me. I never played against Torino during my spell with AC Milan, but did come across Denis and Joe.

Milan were travelling south by train for a league game and I discovered to my delight that Torino were on the same train. I went in search of the Torino party and met Denis and Joe in the corridor of the train. Apparently, they had heard AC Milan were aboard and had set off in search of me.

As soon as I spotted the pair of them, I couldn't wait to pour out my troubles to a friendly face but I didn't get the chance. The initial greetings over, Denis and Joe proceeded to tell me of their deep-seated unhappiness with life in Italy and at Torino in particular. In a strange sort of way, their sorry tale made me feel better. I had been of the mind that they had settled into life at Torino without a problem and that they loved playing in Italian football. I had this notion because that is what I had been told by Nero Rocco and other officials of AC Milan. Whenever I had cited my unhappiness, I'd been told that my attitude and mental state was in direct contrast to that of Denis and Joe, who were very happy playing for Torino. I'd been made to believe that I was the problem. I didn't feel so alienated hearing Denis and Joe say that they were just as unhappy as me with their situation.

'So how long you gonna give all this then?' I asked.

'I'm not,' said Denis. 'Give it a few weeks and I'll be home. I ain't staying.'

'Nor me,' said Joe.

'I'm very unhappy,' I informed them. 'I'll be home before you pair.'

'No, you won't,' said Denis. 'I'll be home before you.'

He wasn't, though it wasn't to be long before he did follow me.

Both the English and Italian press wrote stories about me that were less than complimentary. The Italian press were particularly vindictive, making me out to be a spoiled brat. My every misdemeanour was the subject of a fine from Nero Rocco, though at times some of these misdemeanours were not of my making. One morning I turned up at the training ground only to discover that Rocco and my team-mates were at the San Siro. Nobody had told me I was supposed to report to the stadium that morning, but I was still fined. There were occasions when I did court trouble. Rocco watched me like a hawk and when the team stayed in a hotel he would sit at the foot of the staircase to make sure I didn't come down to the hotel bar for a drink. On one away trip I was joined by Irene's brother, Tom. Fed up with being confined to my room, I persuaded Tom to join me in a bolt for freedom. Though my room was on the third floor we climbed out of the window and edged our way along a ledge to where I thought there was a fire escape. Only we came up against a brick wall and had to edge our way back. We were not to be defeated. We managed to sneak downstairs and, once in the bar, made a big show of ordering a large round of drinks. Rocco received word of this and made a beeline for the bar. When we saw him coming we sneaked out of the hotel via a rear exit. While Rocco was cancelling our order at the bar, we ran across the road and enjoyed a crafty lager in a small bar before sneaking back to my room. That little escapade cost me a fine of £300, which meant that when I played in our next game against Genoa I was playing for nothing. I may have been a brat at times, but I certainly wasn't being spoiled.

Alcohol was not a problem in my life at this time. Though I did enjoy a beer, I don't think I consumed any more than an average, healthy, twenty-one-year-old guy, and I was far fitter than the average. Some people have since made out that I sought solace from my troubles in Italy in drink. I wasn't presented with enough opportunities to drink to have done that, though there were occasions when a jolly was to be had. In the main they took place in the company of the British journalists who arrived in Milan to cover my progress.

Being the naive young man I was, I welcomed the company of any fellow Brit. Members of the British sporting press were frequent visitors to Milan, so frequent that we even formed an informal club, called The Jimmy Greaves Club. Every sports reporter who visited me in Milan automatically became a member and I even went as far as having a special club tie made. The tie had a map of Italy overprinted with a football and my initials, and I gave a tie to every British sports journalist who travelled to see me. Recipients of the commemorative tie included Desmond Hackett and Norman 'Speedy' Quicke of the *Daily Express*, Ken Jones and Bill Holden (*Daily Mirror*), Ian Wooldridge (*News Chronicle*), Maurice Smith (*Sunday People*), Tony Stratton-Smith and Laurie Pignon (*Daily Sketch*), Brian James and Roy Peskett (*Daily Mail*), Brian Glanville (*Sunday Times*) and Peter Lorenzo (*Daily Herald*).

Sometimes I would just chat with the press boys at my apartment, other times we would meet up at La Tampa, a popular restaurant in the centre of Milan. Or at a bar cum club called Porto Dora. It was odd that I could enjoy a meal and chat with a journalist one night, and the following day he might file copy that was less than complimentary about me and my situation at Milan. In the main, however, they knew which comments of mine were intended for print and which were 'off-record' and played the game accordingly.

I was not so fortunate where the Italian press were concerned. One Italian tabloid ran a story saying Irene and I had had a three-in-a-bed romp with another woman. That, of course, was rubbish and I was furious when I heard about it. That scurrilous story came about because a reporter from the newspaper in question had been spying on my apartment with binoculars and caught sight of Irene and her sister, Nancy, walking around in vest and shorts.

Fortunately that trumped-up rubbish never found its way back to the British media, but other stories concerning me that were patently untrue did. At first I couldn't work out where such stories were coming from. I gave the matter considered thought but just couldn't believe the likes of Ian Wooldridge,

Ken Jones or my good pal Tony Stratton-Smith would ever do such a thing. Of course, they wouldn't. It was Irene, more perceptive than me, who finally sussed it.

Irene was of the mind that the scurrilous stories printed in some of the Italian newspapers were finding their way back to the UK via a British journalist who was based in Milan. This journalist was always hanging about in La Tampa and the Porta Dora, although he wasn't a member of The Jimmy Greaves Club. He was always cocking an ear to my conversations so I decided to tell a story within earshot that was patently untrue. If the story found its way back to the UK press, then I would know he was the culprit. I recruited Clive Toye of the *Daily Express* as my fellow conspirator and the ploy worked a treat. While having a drink with Clive, I proceeded to tell him in confidence that AC Milan were buying George Eastham of Arsenal as a playing partner to keep me happy. Clive made all the right noises, acting as if he had just stumbled across a big exclusive, but of course did nothing. Two days later the *Daily Sketch* ran with the so-called 'George Eastham Transfer Exclusive'. I had nailed my man and from that moment on was to give him a very wide berth. My set-up, however, backfired on Clive Toye. He was woken up at three in the morning by a telephone call from his sports editor at the *Express*. He was fuming and wanted to know why, as Clive was in Milan, he hadn't picked up on the story of George Eastham signing for AC. Subsequently George Eastham had the job of denying he was about to move to AC Milan and told countless reporters that he had no idea where the story had come from. Well, you do now, George.

Such interludes of light relief were few and far between. I was not only unhappy at AC Milan, I was becoming depressed. I was coping well enough with the standard of football and scoring goals, but the Italian style of football did not inspire or excite me. Far from it.

As I have said, every team played the *catenaccio* system which resulted in a lot of sterile football. I spoke little Italian but knew that *catenaccio* was Italian for 'door bolt' or 'padlock'. *Catenaccio* was a very defensive system of play, so defensive that if any of the defenders got as far as the halfway line, they would have a nosebleed. It was an overly cautious system of play based on 4-3-3, or 1-4-3-2, which involved a team denying its opponents scoring opportunities by defending the 'scoring space' and adopting man-to-man marking supported by a sweeper. Such a highly defensive gameplan relied on counterattacks and breakaways, and as these by their very nature didn't happen very often, I found there were long periods in a game when I never saw the ball at all. Though *catenaccio* was popular in Italy at the time and resulted in both Milan clubs enjoying success in European competitions in the sixties, the system was anything but new. Nor was it indigenous to Italy.

In the late 1930s an Austrian, Karl Rappan, the manager of Switzerland, introduced a system of play he called, *verrou* which meant 'bolt'. *Verrou* was an innovative system of play at the time and involved Switzerland playing with a sweeper, soaking up extensive pressure from opponents, then breaking quickly on the counterattack. Though it produced uninspiring and dour football at times, *verrou* was highly effective, as England found to their cost when playing in Zurich in 1938. On a tour of the Continent and coming off the back of a historic 6-3 victory over Germany in Munich, they ran up against a brick wall in the form of the Swiss. Though England camped in the Swiss half for lengthy periods in that game, they only had a goal from Arsenal's Cliff Bastin to show for their efforts. Kappan's Switzerland did England that day, scoring two breakaway goals. As Stan Matthews once told me, 'Switzerland strung four defenders across their back line and had a guy behind them who did all the mopping up. It was a completely new style of football, not pretty, but hard to break down.'

Switzerland adopted the *verrou* system during the 1938 World Cup, but it was the Italian club sides of the fifties and sixties that further developed this system of play and refined it, and no one more so than Helenio Herrera, the coach of AC Milan's great rivals, Internazionale. AC Milan had adopted *catenaccio* when winning Serie A in 1957 and 1959, as did Juventus when they won the Championship in '58 and '61. Though *catenaccio* produced football that was as dull as ditchwater, the fact that it proved successful served to make every Italian coach believe this type of football was the way forward. Every team played it. It wasn't what I was used to and I didn't like it, but I got on with my job and like to think I did all right. I only played fourteen games for Milan, but when I did leave I went as the club's leading goalscorer with nine goals.

Once again Irene came over to join me in Milan. I told her I had been to see the Milan secretary Bruno Passalaqua and that I had told him that I wanted to return to England. Passalaqua was a decent guy and genuinely sympathetic to my situation. He tried to persuade me to stay, saying, 'Give it more time.' I was adamant, however. I told him I was going.

'We gotta go home, Irene,' I told her. 'Plain and simple. I can't hack it here.' Irene was with me all the way. But how was I going to go home? I was so deeply unhappy, I made up my mind that if Milan refused to sell me, I would return to England and give up football altogether if need be. Fortunately, it never came to that.

The first inkling I had that Milan were prepared to sell me came one morning when I turned up at the training ground and noticed there were far more reporters and photographers than normal. I asked Gianni Rivera what was going on.

'The press. They here for our big new signing. Rocco, he sign the Brazilian, Dino Sarni.'

Dino Sarni was a midfield player who could also play as a

striker. I knew for certain Milan would never want to sell Rivera, so it was immediately obvious to me that Sarni had been bought as a replacement for me. I was absolutely spot on with that assumption because later in the day Bruno Passalaqua told me that the club had placed me on the transfer list. I can't say I was gutted. On the contrary, my spirits were lifted. I could see a move back to England on the horizon. Passalaqua concluded his conversation by saying, 'Oh, one more thing, Yimmy. We may be needing your apartment.'

A couple of days later while I was training with Milan and Irene was busying herself in the apartment she answered a knock on the door. She opened it to find a thickset man with wavy brown hair that was going grey. He was wearing a tweed jacket, shirt and tie and over his arm he carried a thick worsted overcoat.

'Good morning,' he said, 'is Jimmy Greaves at home?' Irene informed him that I wasn't, that I was training, but that I wouldn't be long and invited him to come inside and wait for me to get back.

'Tea?' Irene asked.

'That would be very nice. Thank you,' he replied.

Irene offered him a seat on the sofa. Over tea they made polite conversation for ten minutes or so.

'Do you know who I am?' the man eventually asked.

'Yes,' said Irene, 'you're Bill Nicholson, the Tottenham manager.'

When I returned to the apartment I was delighted to see Bill Nicholson – there could be only one reason for his visit. Bill informed me that he wanted me to sign for Tottenham Hotspur and that he had already had a preliminary discussion with Andrea Rizzoli, a senior official at the club. At first Rizzoli told Bill Nicholson that I wasn't for sale. When Bill asked why, Rizzoli told him I had not been turning up for training, had broken club rules and must therefore face an internal disciplinary hearing. That was news to Bill – and to me. I didn't know anything about this.

'If I hadn't been turning up for training, believe me, I'd know,' I told him.

Bill was baffled by this claim. Earlier that day he had met with Nero Rocco and never at any time during their conversation had Rocco mentioned to Bill that I had gone AWOL and that I was to face an internal disciplinary hearing. It was all nonsense and Bill Nicholson knew it. I had just returned from training. As for the previous day, I had received permission from the club to take the day off to take Irene's mother and the children to the airport where they were catching a flight back to London. Bill Nicholson was of a similar mind to me. Milan officials were trying it on, throwing a spanner in the works in an attempt to get him to pay the highest possible price for my transfer.

I was heartened when Bill told me that at the end of his meeting with Rizzoli, he had been asked, 'How much are you willing to pay for Greaves?' Milan wanted to sell me all right, but at their price. When Bill left he reaffirmed that Tottenham were keen to sign me and informed me that he would do all he could to find a way out of the deadlock.

A few days later, Dino Sarni moved into the apartment and Irene and I moved out to a room in the Inter-Continental Hotel. As hotels go, the Inter-Continental was decent enough, but far from being the best that Milan could offer. In a strange sort of way, that heartened me. AC Milan never accepted second best for their players. The team always travelled first class and stayed in only the very best hotels. The Inter-Continental was not the best hotel in Milan. I knew I was going to be home soon.

Tottenham had a rival for my signature, my old club Chelsea. Apparently both clubs offered Milan £90,000 for my services. I was flattered, but I didn't want to return to Chelsea.

The club was in decline, whereas Tottenham were very much in the ascendancy. In the previous season they became the first club in the twentieth century to win the League and Cup double. They had a great team and were competing in the European Cup. Chelsea were struggling to maintain their First Division status. There was only one club for me.

To this day I am convinced that Chelsea's bid was a smokescreen. Though the club had received a sizeable fee for me from Milan, it was less than the supposed £90,000 they were now offering to bring me back to Stamford Bridge. As Chelsea were always strapped for cash in my time at the club, I couldn't see how they had suddenly managed to come up with £90,000. The Chelsea supporters were very discontented. They were unhappy with the club's lack of success and peeved at the phenomenal success of Spurs. Many Blues fans were of the mind that either Chelsea had become an unambitious club or had neither the money nor the resources to realise their ambitions. By offering Milan £90,000 I think Joe Mears, rather than being determined to sign me, hoped the offer would not be accepted so he could then appease disgruntled Chelsea fans by saying, 'We tried to re-sign Jimmy Greaves, but couldn't.' That way Joe could deflect criticism and at the same time hoodwink the fans into believing Chelsea were ambitious and that they could compete with a really big club like Tottenham.

Whatever, I didn't want to return to Stamford Bridge. To do so would have meant a return to the problems I had wanted to escape just a few months earlier. Besides, the prospect of playing in what was a great Tottenham team enthused, excited and inspired me.

The bidding edged up to £96,000. When Bill Nicholson returned to Milan he ran into the Chelsea secretary John Battersby. John told Bill he had come to Milan to sign me.

'So have I,' Bill told him. 'It's no use you being here because Jimmy's coming to Tottenham Hotspur.'

For his part, John informed Bill that he would do everything in his power to make sure I rejoined Chelsea. Bill countered that by saying he knew Chelsea couldn't bid any higher.

'We're offering £96,500,' said Bill. 'Don't worry about going over the top. Jimmy has said he wants to come to Spurs, so your club won't be committed.'

Both clubs submitted identical offers to Milan. I received a telephone call asking me to report to the club for meetings with both Bill and John. While I made my way to the stadium, Bill informed John that the Spurs board had not put a restriction on what he could offer for my services.

I had a short meeting with John and made it clear that, while I was flattered by Chelsea's interest, there was only one club I wished to sign for and that club was Spurs.

Aware of my state of mind, John informed Bill that there was no point in him staying on in Milan. Chelsea were out of the bidding, somewhat to the relief, I am sure, of Joe Mears and his fellow directors.

Bill Nicholson and AC Milan locked horns. It was all down to the money. Bill later said that he was never involved in so much haggling over the transfer of a player as he was with Milan regarding my move to White Hart Lane. Just as obstacles had been placed before me to hinder my progress at Milan, every time Bill felt he was near to closing the deal Milan would come up with some reason as to why it could not be finalised. Milan told Bill that should I return to England and publish an article in a newspaper that did not reflect too favourably on their club, they would take action in the courts. Bill circumnavigated that obstacle, only for the negotiations to return to money. Bill was becoming very frustrated.

'This is becoming like a scene from *The Merchant of Venice*,' Bill told Rizzoli, 'with your club wanting its pound of flesh.'

Rizzoli took exception to this comment.

'You are impertinent to bring in Shakespeare,' said Rizzoli. 'You are a very hard negotiator yourself.'

It was becoming very silly and in an attempt to end all arguments Bill Nicholson offered Rizzoli the sum of £99,999 for my signature. Milan accepted and I was on my way home.

The sum Tottenham paid for me was the highest fee ever paid by a club for a player. I became what the newspapers dubbed 'Britain's most expensive footballer', but there was a reason why Bill had offered Milan a pound less than £100,000. Quite simply, as Britain's most expensive player he knew I would be under a constant spotlight, that the pressure would be on me to produce the goods. What Bill didn't want was the added pressure of my being 'Britain's first £100,000 footballer'. Bill Nicholson knew me as a player, but at this stage he didn't know me as a man. Had he, he would have realised that such tags never bothered me in the slightest or in any way affected my performance on a football pitch. Unless it was something outrageous like the 'three-in-a-bed' story, nothing the press wrote ever bothered me. The press could call me 'Britain's first £100,000 footballer' if they liked, it wouldn't affect how I reacted when faced with an opposing goalkeeper and the ball at my feet.

AC Milan finally accepted Bill Nicholson's offer and in December 1961, four months after my arrival in Italy, I was homeward bound. To the very last, however, it seemed that my every effort to return home was to be thwarted. A good chunk of the £1,000 I had received from Milan as a signing on fee I had used to buy a beautiful Jaguar car. I'd had the Jag shipped over to Milan but it had never come out of mothballs. During my spell in Italy I drove around in a Fiat Vicento, but that Jag was to come into its own when the time came for me to return to England.

Irene and I were due to fly back to Heathrow, but on the day of our flight Milan airport was enveloped in heavy fog. All flights had been cancelled and with the weather forecast suggesting the fog was to be around for a few days, the possibility of any flight leaving the airport was remote. I was so keen to be on my way home that I suggested to Irene we pack all our bags into the Jaguar and drive back to England. Irene was up for this, especially when we heard the fog was in the main confined to the Milan area.

My knowledge of the geography of Italy was, at best, flimsy. Having loaded up the Jag we managed to negotiate our way out of Milan but I then took a wrong turning. Instead of heading due north-west towards France and Grenoble at the foot of the Alps, I mistakenly headed south through Novara and Alessandria towards Genoa. In normal circumstances I would have been really annoyed with myself for having made such an error of judgement but I was so happy we were heading for home, albeit by a most circuitous route, that nothing could dampen my joy. When I realised my error I turned the car north-west and headed for Grenoble via Turin. No stopping to pick up Denis and Joe along the way. As far as getting home was concerned, they were going to have to sort themselves out.

Every centimetre of every kilometre of that journey was a joy to drive because it brought us nearer to home and put my nightmare move to AC Milan further behind us. We caught a ferry from Calais to Dover and in seemingly no time at all the famous white cliffs were in view. When we docked in Dover, I was so grateful to be home, I felt like falling to my knees and kissing the jetty.

Her Majesty's Customs and Excise is arguably the most benevolent and understanding of all the departments of the Crown, although that is an argument no one has ever won! I thought I'd left all my problems behind in Milan, but having been back in England for only five minutes I ran into big problems, courtesy of HM Customs.

When I initially had the Jaguar shipped out to Milan, I hadn't paid duty because my move was considered to be of a semi-permanent nature. On returning to England, however, I was told by Customs that I had to pay £400 duty on the car, right there and then, otherwise the car would be impounded. I told the Customs officers that I didn't have £400 on me. And there were no bankers cards or credit cards in 1961. Her Majesty's Customs were very understanding. They told me to unload the car as they were going to impound it.

'How're we gonna get home?' I asked.

'That's your problem, not ours,' I was informed.

Irene and I were in a right pickle, but help was at hand. I had sold the story of my move to Milan and subsequent return as an exclusive to the *Sunday People*. Keen to protect their interests and their exclusive, the *People* had sent one of their reporters, Maurice Smith, to meet Irene and me off the ferry. When we failed to materialise from Customs along with the rest of the passengers, Maurice had gone looking for us and, thankfully, found us.

'I thought you were keen to come back home,' Maurice said.

'I am, but they won't let us back into the country,' I informed him and proceeded to tell him why.

Maurice made a telephone call to his editor who gave the green light to him paying the £400 import duty on the Jag even though it had been bought in London!

'The money will be deducted from the fee we are paying you for your exclusive,' Maurice informed me.

That was fair enough, but as the fee in question was just over £400, it meant I was earning next to nothing from my story. That proved par for the course regarding payments surrounding my move to Milan. I never did make the fortune I had gone to Italy to seek. The initial payment of £4,000 I received as part of my signing on fee was gobbled up by tax bills and legal costs. I never did receive the balance of £11,000 because Milan refused to pay it. The club said my short spell at the club didn't merit payment, that my heart was never in the move from the onset. Well, they weren't wrong on that score.

My four months at Milan took their toll on me, both financially and psychologically. It was a depressing time in my life but it did not, as some have maintained, act as a catalyst to my later addiction to alcohol. That came much later in my life. Financially, I cut my losses and set my mind to rekindling my playing career with Tottenham Hotspur. I was still only twenty-one and felt my best years in football were ahead of me.

From the very start there had been nothing right about my move to Milan. I had attempted to wriggle out of it as soon as I realised that. Milan were employing my feet but what I couldn't give them was my heart. My heart wasn't in the move and never had been. I'm of an age now where most men complain about their memory but never of their judgement. Given that I was only twenty-one, my judgement regarding my move to Milan had been sorely lacking in realism and objectivity. On my return to England I decided to put the whole episode down to experience, and experience is what we men call our mistakes.

The full, true story of my move to Milan doesn't end here, however. Indeed, I wasn't to become aware of the whole story until a couple of years ago.

I was the guest speaker at a sporting dinner and, following my after-dinner speech, was signing autographs for members of the audience when I was approached by a lady.

'You don't know me,' she said, 'but you knew my father very well.'

'Really, who was that then?' I asked.

'John Battersby, the Chelsea secretary.'

We talked for a few minutes about her father, who, the lady informed me, had passed away some years ago.

'Throughout his life, my father always felt very bad about the circumstances surrounding your move to Milan,' she said.

I told her that it was now all water under the bridge, that her father and Chelsea had done everything in their power to try and get me out of the deal.

'They even hired a top barrister, R. I. Lewis, to fly out with me to Milan to try and get me out of the deal,' I said.

The lady looked perplexed. 'Don't you know?' she asked.

'Know what?'

'That's why my father felt so very bad about how you were treated by the club. Chelsea didn't hire R. I. Lewis to try and get you out of the deal. The club were so desperate for the money, they hired Lewis to make sure the deal went through.'

CHAPTER EIGHT

WALKING BACK TO HAPPINESS

The newspapers dubbed me 'Britain's most expensive footballer'. I had joined the best team in the land, Tottenham Hotspur, holders of the League and Cup double, but that cut no ice with the club when it came to somewhere for the Greaves family to live. We had sold our home in Hornchurch and on our return to England had nowhere to live. I had been hoping that Spurs would put us up in a hotel until Irene and I found a house, but the club were a bit slow in coming forward in that respect, and it was Irene's parents who came to our rescue.

Irene, Lynn, baby Mitzi and I moved into a two-bedroom council house in Dagenham along with Irene's mum and dad and her sister. It was cramped but somehow we all managed to get along, which was just as well, as we were to live in that house for four months before Irene and I managed to buy a home of our own. How times have changed. Can you imagine Britain's most expensive footballer returning from a top Italian club to live in a council house nowadays? At the time it never bothered me. More to the point, it never bothered Irene's family either. They were terrific in putting up with the family that had moved cuckoo-like into their home. The only thing that made me uncomfortable was the sight of my Jag parked outside their council house. I often wondered what people thought of that.

Thanks to the efforts of my fellow professionals in the PFA, in particular Jimmy Hill and Cliff Lloyd, the maximum wage had now been abolished. I signed for Tottenham for a wage of £60 a week, very good money in 1961. My joy, however, was not as a result of the wage Tottenham were paying me. The fact that my family were back in England and I would be playing my football in the country I loved made me blissfully happy. I couldn't wait to get going.

Before I made my debut for Spurs, however, there were a few formalities that had to be ironed out which prevented me playing for the first team. On 9 December, I made my first appearance for Spurs in a reserve team game at Plymouth Argyle. A crowd of 14,000 turned up at Home Park to witness my return to English football and just before kickoff the Plymouth chairman Ron Blindell came on to the pitch with a microphone. In what was a wonderful gesture on their part, the Plymouth players lined up and applauded as I took to the pitch with my new colleagues. Ron Blindell announced, 'On behalf of Plymouth Argyle, the people of Devon and Cornwall but not least the whole of England, I say to you, Jimmy, welcome back.' It was a great homecoming for me, one I appreciated very much. I'd received some unflattering press regarding my period with Milan but the reception I got from the people of Plymouth made me feel not only humble, but made me realise that ordinary folk are not always swayed by what they might read in certain newspapers. It was a good homecoming in every respect. I scored twice to help Spurs reserves to a 4-1 victory.

The Football League had refused Spurs permission to play me in a league match until they were satisfied that the deal which brought me from Milan was completely above board. Bill Nicholson and I were summoned to a meeting of the Football League Management Committee, which was taking place on a Friday in the Grand Hotel in Sheffield. We travelled to Sheffield by train and arrived in good time for our meeting. On arrival we were told to take a seat in the corridor as the committee were discussing another matter and we would be summoned in due course.

Bill and I sat in that corridor for two hours. Bill was becoming increasingly agitated at the delay and eventually collared a Football League official and demanded the Management Committee see us.

When Bill and I entered the room we couldn't believe it. There were eight members of the Football League Management Committee sat around a table and two of them were asleep. On the table before them were several bottles of wine, a brandy bottle that was nigh on empty and the remnants of what had obviously been an exceedingly good lunch. No one had entered or left the room during the two hours Bill and I had sat in the corridor, so the Management Committee had obviously not seen anyone else that morning. At the head of the table sat the secretary of the Football League, Alan Hardaker, who, on seeing Bill and me enter, indicated with a lazy wave of a hand that we should take a seat. Without disturbing his two dozing colleagues, Hardaker got the meeting under way.

'Now then. We just want to know, this here transfer from Milan. Was there anything untoward about it?'

'No,' said Bill. 'It was a bit messy, but totally straightforward.'

'No under-the-counter shenanigans?' asked Hardaker.

'No,' replied Bill.

'Then yon Greaves fella is cleared to play,' said Hardaker. 'Good afternoon, gentlemen.'

Another laconic wave of a hand indicated we should leave.

During our journey back to Sheffield Midland station, Bill was not best pleased. 'Did you get a load of that lot?' he asked.

'They weren't interested in the details of your move. They dragged us all the way up here just so they could have a good troughing.'

He wasn't wrong.

'You okay?' Bill asked during the journey back to London. I told him I was.

'Good,' he said, 'because you're playing in the first team tomorrow.'

Blackpool were no longer the glamour team they had been in the fifties, in the days of the two Stans, Matthews and Mortensen. They were, however, a decent side occupying a mid-table position in Division One. Spurs were in fourth place, one of four teams on twenty-five points, trailing Burnley, who occupied pole position with a five point lead. Ominously, rooted to the bottom of Division One were Chelsea.

Blackpool were on a good run. At the beginning of October they had collected only nine points from their first twelve matches, but the measure of their subsequent improvement could be gauged from the fact that they had taken twelve points from a possible eighteen in the nine games prior to their arrival at White Hart Lane. Their captain was my England colleague Jimmy Armfield and in goalkeeper Tony Waiters and centre forward Ray Charnley, Blackpool possessed two England internationals in the making. As it had been only the day before when Bill Nicholson was given the all-clear to play me, my name didn't feature in the team line-ups printed in the match programme. I took Dave Mackay's place at inside left, with Dave switching to left half in place of Tony Marchi.

I couldn't have wished for a better debut for my new club. I scored a hat-trick, the first goal a flying scissors kick which I still rate as one of the most spectacular goals I ever scored. I'll never forget that goal. Dave Mackay was a long-throw specialist who could hurl the ball into an opponent's box from fully forty yards. Dave's ability to achieve such distance with his throw-ins made him unique in football at the time. When he first started to take long throw-ins for Spurs it resulted in quite a number of goals, simply because it caught opponents unaware. Opposing teams would mark Spurs players who had taken up a position within ten to twenty yards of Dave and fail to pick up forwards who had made runs into their penalty box. Even when opponents got wise to this tactic it still produced goals for Spurs because a Dave Mackay throw-in was as good as a dead-ball kick. Against Blackpool I managed to lose my marker Dave Durie for a brief moment by pretending to run one way, only to feint and take off in the opposite course. That gave me a yard or so of space, and it allowed me to get on the end of Dave's throw-in. I'd actually come a little too deep and when the ball arrived·it came at chest height. It's amazing what your mind can take in in a split second. I thought about cushioning the ball on my chest with a view to laying it off to a team-mate, but bit the bullet and had a go at goal. Successful volleying of the ball is all about technique and timing. You have to get it spot-on, especially when you're airborne, which I was on this occasion. Should you get the timing wrong and meet the ball with the toe end of your boot it can result in an injury to the tissue and muscle in the instep, or, as the toe end of the boot takes all the velocity and weight of the ball, the Achilles tendon. Fortunately I got it right. I'd seen a gap to the left of the Blackpool keeper Tony Waiters, aimed in that direction and the ball flew into the net as sweet as a nut. I think that goal did a lot to endear me to the Tottenham supporters; in many ways I had signalled not only my arrival at White Hart Lane, but also my intentions. The fact that I went on to complete my hat-trick didn't do me any harm with the Spurs supporters either, and of course made my first game for my new club an absolute dream of a debut. It was a great start to my Spurs career and quickly erased what few nerves I had felt prior to the game. Two goals from Les Allen gave us a 5–2 victory and a crowd of 43,000 applauded us off the field. It was great to be home. In our next game, away at Arsenal, I came down to earth with a bump. Spurs' great north London rivals turned us over at Highbury by the odd goal in three in front of a crowd of 63,440. Funny old game.

On Boxing Day that year, Spurs travelled to Chelsea. It was strange getting changed in the away dressing room and I did wonder what sort of welcome I would receive from the Chelsea supporters when I took to the field with Spurs. I needn't have worried. They gave me a tremendous reception and even applauded my first touch of the ball. It has to be said, though, that they weren't as vociferous in their support of me when I gave us the lead. The game ended in a 2-0 victory for Spurs, with our other goal coming from Cliff Jones. Four days later, we beat Chelsea 5-2 at White Hart Lane to add to their troubles. Though I had been happy to return to Stamford Bridge and see old friends, I felt no sentiment when out on the pitch. I was a pro, I had a job to do and I did it. Our back-to-back victories over Chelsea, if they did anything, convinced me I had made the right decision in signing for Spurs. Tottenham were the top club in England and Chelsea, sadly, were in decline.

The hat-trick on my debut for Spurs and the fact that I continued to score goals regularly made me an instant hit with the supporters, though initially I wasn't so readily accepted in the Spurs dressing room. Spurs were the holders of the League and Cup double and understandably one or two players wondered 'What the hell do we need Jimmy Greaves for?' They had won the double in some style, too. Spurs posted consecutive wins in their first eleven games of the season and come 31 December had played twenty-five league matches of which twenty-two had been won, two drawn and only one lost. They hadn't just beaten teams, they had pulverised them. Spurs led the First Division from the start and stayed there.

They won the Championship with just under four weeks of the season remaining and scored a staggering 115 league goals. Tottenham's march on the Championship had not been affected by their involvement in the FA Cup. They scored twenty-one goals in FA Cup ties and in the final comfortably beat a very useful Leicester City side 2-0.

The team Bill Nicholson had created was a wonderful blend. Not every player was a top international. Far from it. Right back Peter Baker and winger Terry Dyson were both uncapped, as was left back Ron Henry, though Ron would win his only cap for England in 1963. Goalkeeper Bill Brown had only a handful of appearances for Scotland to his name, whereas Les Allen, who often played centre forward in the absence of Bobby Smith, played just the once for England Under 23s. It was the mark of the time that a team that won the League and Cup double contained uncapped players and players who were not regulars for their country. To balance that, Spurs did have Danny Blanchflower (Northern Ireland), Bobby Smith and Maurice Norman (England), Dave Mackay and John White (Scotland) and Terry Medwin and Cliff Jones (Wales). The blending of these players was instrumental in the phenomenal success of Spurs. They were a team in every sense of the word, though the hub on which every move turned was their skipper, Danny Blanchflower. Danny was a cerebral player who dictated the pace of a game and it was his ability to dictate the tempo of a match that was crucial to Spurs' success. When opponents seemed on the point of seizing the initiative, Danny would put his foot on the ball and slow the game to suit Spurs. There would follow a seemingly meaningless interchange of passes in midfield between Blanchflower, White and Mackay that would lull the opposition. Then, when Danny sensed an opening, the telling pass would be made and Spurs would immediately spring into life and attack to devastating effect.

As the season unfolded, Spurs were always there in the top four of the First Division and for much of the time I harboured the hope we would finish as Champions. But it was not to be. Ask Arsène Wenger, Sir Alex Ferguson or any manager who has won the double what is the hardest thing to do. The answer will always be, 'To win it again the following season.'

We were contesting three trophies, the League Championship, the FA Cup and, as reigning Champions, the European Cup. I don't think the heavy fixture schedule affected us too much. Ask any player what he would rather be doing, playing matches or training, and it will always be the former. Spurs had a good squad that boasted strength in depth, so when a regular first team player missed out through injury, there was always a quality player available to step up from the reserves and take his place. There's never one single reason for a quality team not repeating the success of a previous season; it's down to a number of reasons. If they happened separately these factors could in all probability be overcome, but when they occur simultaneously, they have a detrimental effect on the fortunes of any team.

One important aspect of the Spurs double success of 1960–61 was the element of surprise. Tactically Bill Nicholson's side was innovative and inspirational, but twelve months on teams had got wise to the tactics and ploys that had caught so many sides out during the double season. At Chelsea, Ted Drake rarely ventured out of his office during the course of the week, but a revolution was taking place within English football. Managers and players were becoming more tactically aware and teams better organised. Unlike Ted Drake, other managers were getting out and about watching other teams, in particular forthcoming opponents. If a manager was unable to do this himself, he would invariably send someone else who would then compile a report.

A small but contributing factor to this greater awareness of

Spurs' style was the post-match drink between opposing players. Following a game, the away team would snatch a beer before embarking on the journey home. Players might have only twenty minutes or so in which to do this, but invariably they would get chatting and might pass on a word of advice about forthcoming opponents and the movements of individual players. For example, Spurs' opponents might get warned to look out for Maurice Norman popping up in the penalty box when we won a corner. One tactic that had provided quite a number of goals for Spurs in 1960–61 was to have Maurice make a dummy run to the near post for a corner. Cliff Jones or Terry Dyson would pretend to hesitate over the corner, and Maurice would pretend to be annoyed at the fact he had made a run for nothing and trot back out of the penalty area, seemingly to drop back into defence – only to then run in an arc outside the penalty area ready to attack the far post. While all this was going on, Spurs had positioned three players a few yards from the far post. When Dyson or Jones eventually delivered the corner, those three players would make a dummy run to the near post, taking their markers with them. Maurice Norman would then bolt into the space they had left and power a header at goal. According to Bill Nicholson that tactic worked on numerous occasions for Spurs in the double season. Come 1961–2 they found most teams were wise to their tactics and had come up with ways of counteracting them. Also, our opponents were becoming increasingly adept at playing attacking football themselves. Bill Nicholson had taken his lead from the great Real Madrid side of the fifties. Spurs led the way in English football where tactical innovation was concerned but after their phenomenal success of 1960–61 other teams had fallen into line. All of which meant that Bill Nicholson and Danny Blanchflower continually had to come up with new ideas. This was the beginnings of the situation we now have in football, whereby coaches direct and dictate events on the pitch. In the sixties the likes of Danny Blanchflower, Bobby Charlton, Jimmy Adamson, Jimmy McIlroy and Johnny Haynes, though to a degree subjected to tactics, ran the show on the pitch. Teams were becoming better organised and players more tactically aware, but the power was still with the Blanchflowers and the Charltons, not the coaches, and individuals such as myself were still free to express themselves during the course of a game.

The lessening of Spurs ability to surprise and confound opponents played its part in the team not repeating its Championship success of the previous season, but there were other telling factors. Our heavy fixture burden, though we never found it debilitating, did contribute to our failure to retain the League Championship. In January and February we found ourselves contesting the European Cup and the FA Cup as well as the League. We failed to win the Championship basically because we put our greatest effort into the European Cup. It was the first time Spurs had ever been involved in the European Cup, it became our Holy Grail and it drained us of the mental and physical strength required to maintain a sustained league title challenge. At the time you never think this. Players feel they are in control, fit and ready to produce optimum performances as the games come rolling in. It is only with the benefit of hindsight, I now realise, that continental travel combined with titanic struggles on heavy pitches in both league and FA Cup, make it virtually impossible for a team and individuals to perform to the best of their ability in every match. Such was the case in 1961–2, when from New Year to 24 March, while also involved in both European and FA Cups, we won just one of our nine league matches.

Following the glamour and excitement of playing at a White Hart Lane packed with 63,000 spectators in our FA Cup third round replay against Birmingham City, we failed to reproduce the same mental approach for our next league fixture at lowly Cardiff City, where we were fortunate to come away with a 1-1 draw. The travel, heavy pitches and our penchant for the caviar of cup competition rather than bread-and-butter league games lost us vital ground in the race for the Championship. When the weather improved, pitches dried out and our involvement in the European Cup came to an end, our performances in the league improved. We were still in with a shout of the Championship but even just one defeat in our last ten league games was not enough to ensure Spurs a second successive Championship. Our final three league games were all played away from home, at Blackburn, Birmingham and Leicester. We won all three but the damage had been done in January and February. Though we lost only four more games than in the previous season, we finished in third place, a point behind runners-up Burnley, and four points behind the Champions, Ipswich Town.

To my mind the most telling result of our poor run of league form in the New Year was our 3-1 home defeat in early March to Champions elect Ipswich Town. Just as one reason for the phenomenal success of Spurs in 1960–61 was their ability to surprise opponents, so Ipswich Town took everyone by surprise in 1961–2, not least because they employed tactics that opposing teams had never encountered before.

Alf Ramsey was the Ipswich manager. Ipswich were not known as 'The Tractor Boys' in 1962, they were dubbed 'Ramsey's Rustics'. In guiding what was widely seen as an unfashionable East Anglian team to the Third Division South title in 1956–7, to the Second Division Championship in 1961 and subsequently to the League Championship in their very first season in Division One, Alf Ramsey had worked a minor miracle. His Ipswich team was a collection of honest journey-men and discards. They didn't possess any of the so-called star players of the day, but Ramsey proved himself to be a superb motivator and strategist. He moulded his collection of unsung heroes into a highly effective team, getting his players to believe in themselves and fulfil their potential as individuals. To which he added innovative tactical strategies that blended the Ipswich players into a formidable team.

Orthodox wingers were still the order of the day. Ramsey, however, confused and confounded opponents by instructing his left winger, Jimmy Leadbetter, to play a deep-lying role to the left of the centre of midfield. Jimmy did this to devastating effect in 1961–2. He probed and prodded and used his astute vision and superb distribution to create numerous openings for his forwards. Opposing right backs who had been used to marking orthodox left wingers were unsure as to what to do. Because Jimmy played so deep, right backs were in a quandary. They didn't know if they should forsake their normal position and be sucked into midfield to close down on Jimmy and thereby create space for the Ipswich left half John Elsworthy or stay put. Most opted for the latter and as a consequence Jimmy Leadbetter proved Ipswich's unlikely hero. To look at Jimmy, you'd never think that here was a player blessed with football genius. The comic actor Sid James looked old when he was in his early twenties, but in his sixties Sid didn't appear to look any older. This was the case with Jimmy. His gaunt features, receding hairline and thin, bony frame made him appear more like the man from the Pru calling to collect the weekly insurance money than a top-flight footballer. Appearances, however, can be deceptive. Jimmy was a highly gifted, mercurial player with a very sharp football brain.

There was much more to Ipswich in 1961–2 than Jimmy Leadbetter playing his unorthodox role. Up front Ipswich enjoyed the services of two phenomenal goalscorers, centre forward Ray Crawford, and inside left Ted Phillips. Between them Crawford and Phillips were responsible for sixty-one of the ninety-three goals that Ipswich scored that season. Ray Crawford finished the season as the joint leading goalscorer in

the First Division with thirty-three goals to his name. Ted
Phillips was fourth, with twenty-eight behind Blackpool's Ray
Charnley (thirty) and Derek Kevan of West Bromwich Albion
who tied with Ray on thirty-three. I managed twenty-one goals
in the twenty-two league games I played for Spurs following
my move to the club in December, which, given that I also
scored nine goals in the FA Cup that season, more than
satisfied me.

We played Ipswich on a frosty Wednesday night at White
Hart Lane and the importance of the fixture was reflected in
an attendance of over 52,000. The White Hart Lane pitch may
have looked all right from the terraces but it was in fact one of
the poorest in the First Division at the time. Given the general
state of pitches in winter in this era of football, that's saying
something. White Hart Lane was rutted and, certainly down
the middle, bereft of grass from October onwards. In normal
circumstances in mid-season, the pitch was a difficult one on
which to play fluid football. The fact that Spurs had a
reputation for such is a credit to the skill and technique of the
players of the day. On the night we played Ipswich, the pitch
was a nightmare. It was frozen as well as being rutted which
made the going underfoot particularly treacherous, although
it was, of course, the same for both teams.

Ipswich, however, seemed to adapt to the tricky conditions
better than we did and with Jimmy Leadbetter and his cohort
in midfield, Doug 'Dixie' Moran, in top form we never got into
our stride. Doug Moran was another unsung hero. Few people
other than Ipswich supporters of a certain age will readily
recall his name today, but 'Dixie' Moran was a fine player, what
in the sixties we referred to as a 'schemer'. Dixie was the one
player Alf Ramsey added to the Ipswich team that had won the
Second Division the previous season and in many ways showed
how Ramsey preferred to opt for a player he knew could do a
given job in a gameplan, rather than sign a big-name star

whose style might not be suited. 'Dixie' Moran cost Ramsey £12,000 when he signed him from Falkirk in the summer of '61. At the time his transfer merited just a line or two in the newspapers, if it was mentioned at all. But following Ipswich's 3-1 victory over us at White Hart Lane, along with Jimmy Leadbetter 'Dixie' shared the headlines in most of the national newspapers the following morning.

I managed to score the Spurs goal, but it was scant consolation. The game was a massive one for both clubs and Ipswich, unencumbered by involvement in cup competitions, were able to give it their full attention and approached it with exactly the right mental attitude. In the end Ipswich were worthy winners. Surprisingly, given the tactical nous displayed by Spurs the previous season, on the night we were outthought and outmanoeuvred by 'Ramsey's Rustics'. Ipswich had an answer for most of our ploys and we never got to grips with the unorthodox roles of Leadbetter and Moran in midfield. Having beaten us at Portman Road in October, Ipswich had completed a double over Spurs, who along with Burnley were their major rivals for the title. Though it was only mid-March and there were still some ten league games remaining, Ipswich's victory proved telling, for them and for us. According to Ted Phillips, Ipswich's victory that night boosted their confidence enormously. Conversely, it dented ours. Just how significant that night was to the Championship prospects of both sides can be gauged by the fact that, as results were to turn out, if we had beaten Ipswich at White Hart Lane, Spurs would have been Champions.

Following their victory over Spurs no doubt Ipswich celebrated in some style on the last train back to Suffolk. The Chairman of Ipswich Town, John Cobbold, and his co-directors, who included his brothers Alastair and Patrick, were not only the most generous hosts of all directors in the Football League, they loved to celebrate each and every Ipswich victory.

The Cobbold's family business was a brewery, Tolly Cobbold Ales, and following a game at Portman Road copious amounts of their products were available to both visiting directors and players. A trip to Portman Road was a joy, even if during this era opposing teams usually departed pointless. The hospitality of the Cobbolds began the moment you arrived at Ipswich station where you would be greeted by John Cobbold and his co-directors. I can't recall the directors of any other club meeting an opposing team and its directors off the train. It was unique. Following the initial greetings, the Cobbolds would then take to their cars and escort the opponents' team coach to Portman Road where their hospitality would begin in earnest.

As I say, each Ipswich victory was celebrated in style. When they clinched the 1961–2 Championship, John Cobbold gave an interview to Frank Wilson of the *Daily Mirror*. Frank began the interview by saying, 'John, I suppose this has been one long season of wine, women and song for the Ipswich board of directors.'

'I can't recall us doing much singing,' replied John.

When John Cobbold appointed Alf Ramsey as the manager of Ipswich Town in 1955, he took Alf into the board room, opened the drinks cabinet and poured a couple of stiff ones to celebrate. Having shared a drink, John took to his feet. 'This will be the first and last time I ever offer you a drink in this board room,' John informed Alf. He then threw a key to the drinks cabinet in the direction of Alf. 'From now on, Alf, feel free to come in and help yourself,' said John.

Though Alf did enjoy a glass of whisky, I doubt whether he ever took John Cobbold up on his offer. Alf was too much the pro.

You didn't have to be playing Ipswich to enjoy the hospitality and generosity of the Cobbolds. Having won the First Division Championship, Ipswich qualified for the

European Cup. Their first opponents were Floriana Valletta of Malta to whom they were drawn away in the first leg. John Cobbold invited Brian Mears, the son of the Chelsea chairman Joe, to join them in Malta for his club's first experience of European competition. Brian followed the Ipswich party out to Malta and on arriving at their team hotel found that it backed right on to the beach. Having checked in, Brian went in search of the Ipswich party. He found the players relaxing, playing cards and reading newspapers in a lounge, and asked if they knew where he could find Mr Cobbold. They pointed him towards the sea. The water was very shallow and Brian spotted John Cobbold some twenty yards from the shore, dressed in a short-sleeved shirt and shorts, idly flicking his toes in the blue waters. Brian made his way down on to the beach and, on seeing John Cobbold glance in his direction, responded with a wave of a hand. John waved back and beckoned Brian to come and join him in the sea.

Brian was a little reluctant at first. While John was dressed for the beach, Brian was still wearing his suit and sporting a stylish pair of crocodile shoes. Not wishing to appear disrespectful to his host or ungrateful for the invitation to join him out in Malta, Brian, forever the gentleman, tiptoed over the sands and gingerly made his way through the water to John.

'Good morning, John,' said Brian when he was three or so yards from the Ipswich chairman.

John Cobbold broke off from his musings and a look of great surprise registered on his face at the sight of the Chelsea director in designer suit and shoes with the sea lapping his calves.

'Oh, it's you, Brian,' said John, somewhat taken aback. 'When I saw you wave from the beach, I thought you were the wine waiter.'

John Cobbold was loved and respected by everyone. He enjoyed a good time and liked a party, but he was smart and a

very adept businessman and negotiator. He loved Ipswich
Town and he loved football. John Cobbold was on the board
of Ipswich Town for all the right reasons and you can't say that
about every club director you come across. He was a colourful
character given to more than the occasional eccentricity:
during one particular board meeting at Ipswich he suddenly
stopped co-director Cecil Robinson in full flow to pick up a
telephone that hadn't rung.

'Hello? Hello? Hello?' said John, to the bemusement of his
fellow directors.

'The telephone didn't ring, John,' ventured Cecil Robinson.

'I know,' said John, 'but I never like to leave anything to the
last minute.'

To a man we were all very disappointed to have lost at home to
Ipswich Town. Although Ipswich achieved the double over us
that season, overall I felt Spurs were a better team than
Ipswich. We had more quality in our side but that poor
sequence of league results in the New Year proved to be our
undoing with regard to retaining the Championship.

Our venture into the European Cup provided us with a lot
of pride and, in the end, heartache and not a little bitterness
and recrimination. When Spurs began their quest to win the
European Cup in September 1961, I was of course with AC
Milan. Spurs' first taste of European competition ended
ignominiously when they were beaten 4-2 by Gornik Zabrze
in front of 70,000 partisan Poles. In the second leg at a packed
White Hart Lane, it proved to be a different story. Spurs
pulled back the two-goal deficit from the first leg and
proceeded to wipe the floor with Gornik, winning 8-1 on the
night to go through to the first round proper on an aggregate
score of 10-5. Prior to my arrival at White Hart Lane, Spurs
then accounted for Dutch Champions Feyenoord, winning 3-1
in Holland in front of a capacity crowd of 64,000. The home

leg was somewhat of a disappointment in that Spurs only managed to draw 1-1, but it was enough to see them through to the next round on an aggregate score. When Spurs returned to European football in February even though I had signed for the club in December, UEFA regulations at the time ruled I was ineligible to play. I was disappointed not to have made my bow in European competition, but got behind the lads and consoled myself with the thought that my team-mates would prove too strong for their next opponents, Dukla Prague, and that I could well return to the fold for the European Cup semi-final, which proved to be the case.

Though ineligible to play I flew out to Prague with the Spurs party to lend the team my support. When we arrived at the national stadium I took one look at the pitch and thanked my lucky stars I wasn't playing. The pitch had a light dusting of snow on it and underneath was nigh on frozen solid. I sat up in the stand for the game, seated alongside Les Allen who was the travelling reserve, and remarked to Les that the pitch was so icy both sides would have trouble turning around at half-time. Spurs were never comfortable throughout the game and in the end happy to come away with a single-goal defeat. That scoreline was really a moral victory, and though the Czechs boasted some very good players, everyone was confident the tie would be turned around at White Hart Lane. The attendance for the first leg in Prague had been 64,000 and another cracking crowd of 56,000 turned up to see the home leg. Dukla had been given permission to switch the first leg to the national stadium as that held 64,000, as opposed to their own Juliska stadium which had a capacity of only 28,000. The lads had done well to come away with a 1-0 defeat in front of what was fanatical home support and at White Hart Lane did a thoroughly professional job on Dukla. Two goals apiece from Dave Mackay and Bobby Smith providing us with a 4-1 victory to take us through to the semi-finals.

It would be wrong to say that Bill Nicholson's sole priority was to win the European Cup, but he had definitely set his heart on it. Bill felt we were good enough to win it and, I have to say, so did I. I was champing at the bit to taste the action in the European Cup because European games at night at White Hart Lane had their own very special atmosphere. Singing on the terraces was a rarity among supporters, but when Spurs played their midweek European games White Hart Lane reverberated to the song that had been adopted and adapted by Spurs supporters. To the tune of 'John Brown's Body' they sang 'Glory, Glory Hallelujah, as Spurs go marching on'. The sound of over 60,000 voices giving full vent to their emotions made the hair stand up on the back of the neck. The reason these games had an atmosphere all of their own was because they were played at night under floodlights. Players seemed to perform in a cube of light beyond which there appeared to be another, much darker world, from the depth of which could be heard a legion of sonorous voices singing as one: 'Glory, Glory Hall-eh-lu-jah. Glory, Glory Hall-eh-lu-jah!' It was as if a heavenly choir had taken up residence in the powers of darkness, and as such was a great comfort to me.

Eighty-six thousand people watched our European Cup semi-final first leg against Benfica at the Stadium of Light in Lisbon. Sixty-five thousand were packed to the rafters for the return leg at White Hart Lane. A total of 525,000 supporters had watched Spurs' eight matches in the European Cup, an average of 65,625. Those eight matches produced thirty four goals: that's 4.25 goals per game. The European Cup had captured the imagination of the public. They turned up in droves not only to see if Spurs could become the first English team to win the trophy but to sample the very special atmosphere that they themselves created. The European Cup was seven years old and like any seven-year-old had a character and personality all of its own while still being able to captivate and enthral by way of its innocence and zest for life. Though teams were becoming better organised and more tactically adept, the football played was fluid, open and given to attack. Supporters loved it. The European Cup had in seven years established itself as Europe's premier club competition. The burgeoning commercial air industry had opened up Europe; the Continent had shrunk and English football supporters delighted in the novelty of seeing the Champions of England pit their wits and skills against the very best teams in Europe. The football and the goals were free-flowing, the attendances very big and the atmosphere at matches unique. And to that I say 'Glory, Glory Hallelujah!' The European Cup was not blighted by the problems that would beset the competition in later years when teams playing away from home would go out to 'silence the crowd', or, worse still, play dour and suffocating football in the hope of taking a goalless tie to penalties. The competition was an adventure for both players and supporters alike and the football was by and large adventurous too. That's not to say the cynical side of professionalism was not in evidence at this time. It was, and Spurs came up against it when we first met Benfica in the semi-final.

By this stage of proceedings I had established myself in the Tottenham team at the expense of Les Allen. I'd spent three months under the managership of Bill Nicholson during which I never had cause to doubt his managerial skills or his tactical nous. Against Benfica, however, I feel Bill made the mistake of changing the team and adopting a very cagey and defensive gameplan. In many ways I understand why Bill did this. Benfica were a terrific side who included in their ranks the imposing Germano and Coluna, the wily Aguas, the flying winger Simoes and a young Eusebio. Benfica's home record at the Stadium of Light was formidable: they had not been beaten there in European competition and in domestic football had lost only twice at home in five years.

Against Benfica, Bill attempted to play a tight defensive game. He left right winger Terry Medwin out and played Danny Blanchflower deep in front of a defensive formation of Peter Baker, Ron Henry, Maurice Norman, Tony Marchi and Dave Mackay. I still felt with the quality in the side we could achieve a favourable result, but what I didn't account for was diabolical decisions on the part of the referee and some really shabby tactics from Benfica themselves.

Bill wanted us to soak up pressure from Benfica then hit them on the break, hoping the combination of myself and Bobby Smith would cause them problems. From the very start Benfica made their gameplan obvious to all. They kicked and hacked each and every one of us and to my great annoyance, like the band on the *Titanic*, the referee played on. Why Benfica resorted to such dubious tactics I'll never know because they really were a fine footballing side as suggested by the three goals they scored on their home turf. Bobby Smith replied for us but the story of this game has much to do with the officials, in particular the referee Mr Poulsen from Denmark. Like players referees have good games and not so good games. The mark of a professional footballer is that he will rarely, if ever, turn in a very poor performance in a game. He may not play to his usual standard, but he won't play a bad game. The same applies to referees. On this night, however, Mr Poulsen made a string of decisions that I not only found bewildering but left me feeling downright suspicious. Allowing Benfica to hack and kick at us unchecked was one thing, but when he disallowed what to every member of the Spurs team was a perfectly legitimate goal from Bobby Smith, it really was beyond the pale.

What aroused my suspicions was the fact that when Bobby put the ball in the net, Mr Poulsen blew his whistle and it was only then that his linesman, fellow Dane Mr Hansen, raised his flag to indicate Bobby had been offside. I had a clear view of the incident, and believe me, Bobby wasn't offside when the ball was played to him. Minutes from the end I scored what I believed was a perfectly good goal only to have it disallowed, again for offside. I was too stupefied to protest, I simply stood hands on hips staring in disbelief at the referee. It was as if a bad dream had become a reality.

I had been looking forward to my first taste of European competition with great anticipation, but the way Benfica quite literally tackled the game and the ineptitude of the officials left a bitter taste in my mouth. We felt we had been turned over. We felt aggrieved and bitter but worse was to come in the return leg at White Hart Lane.

Though 3-1 down from the first leg we felt confident that we could tear Benfica apart at home, but if anything we tried too hard and the rhythm of our play was never constant and fluid. We received a setback when, after fifteen minutes, Benfica's captain and centre forward, Aguas, scored to give them a 4-1 aggregate lead. We took the battle to Benfica. We pummelled and pulverised their defence. After twenty-four minutes our pressure paid off. John White curled a beautiful centre around two Benfica defenders. Bobby Smith volleyed the ball into my path and I did what I was paid to do. Mr Poulsen blew up for the goal but there was a problem. The linesman, Mr Hansen, was wafting his flag as if waving off an express from King's Cross. The Benfica players dragged Mr Poulsen across to his linesman and once again, to my utter disbelief and disgust, pointed to the penalty box to indicate offside.

''King offside? Whatdya mean 'king offside?'

I was furious.

'Orf-side,' said Mr Poulsen.

It was the third goal we had had disallowed in the two matches. To the lasting credit of my team-mates, we didn't allow such rough justice to affect our professionalism and performance. Angelo took the free kick for Benfica and as soon as the ball was in play, we picked up the same script and laid siege. Seven minutes from half-time, John White floated the ball into the Benfica penalty area. The beer-barrel chest of Bobby Smith cushioned the ball and it fell to his feet like a dead bird only to then be dispatched with characteristic ferocity into the net. White Hart Lane, which only minutes before had been in black despair, suddenly erupted as 65,000 fans gave full vent to their delight.

The second half was only four minutes old when those voices not only appeared to make the Welkin ring, but seemingly split it asunder. John White, whose skilful repertoire of long and short passes, timed and executed to perfection, once again probed the Benfica defence. He played the ball to Bobby Smith who returned the compliment. Having had the ball returned to him, John took it past Cruz but he didn't go with it. Cruz took John's legs from under him and Mr Poulsen didn't hesitate. Penalty.

As Danny Blanchflower prepared to take the penalty kick it was difficult to believe there were 65,000 people in the ground. White Hart Lane was as quiet as a country churchyard. If Danny had any nerves he certainly didn't show them as he addressed the ball. He was cool as a bank of snow and when he characteristically tucked the ball into the corner of Costa Pereira's net, White Hart Lane was once again a cauldron of noise. That was 2-1 to us, 4-3 to Benfica on aggregate.

While supporters willed and wished and, no doubt in the case of some, prayed, we flung ourselves into attack. To win any trophy a team must have its share of luck. Against Benfica if it wasn't for bad luck we'd have had no luck at all. Terry Medwin, recalled to the team in the absence of Dave Mackay headed goalwards, Germano clearly wafted the ball away with a hand but Mr Poulsen waved play on. Minutes from time

John White roasted and basted Cavem's pig's ear of a clearance. He played the ball into Bobby Smith who smacked a shot against the foot of Costa Pereira's right-hand post. The vital goal remained elusive and a match of surging drama reached, what for us, was a heartbreaking finale.

It takes two teams to create a memorable game of football and the British press were fulsome in their praise of both teams in the newspapers the following day. The consensus was that our game against Benfica was one of the best matches ever seen at White Hart Lane. It had certainly been pulsating football, seen by millions who watched the second half on their TV screens, but I couldn't overcome my anger at what I perceived to have been the injustice of it all. To my mind we'd had three perfectly good goals disallowed and that took some getting over. We had set our hearts on winning the European Cup and I don't think I have felt sadder coming off a football pitch than I did that night at the end of the second match with Benfica. But for those questionable refereeing decisions I'm sure we would have gone on to win the European Cup because Real Madrid, the other finalists, though still a very good team were not the magnificent side they had been when dominating the competition in the fifties. Benfica beat Real 5-3 in the final in Amsterdam, three days before Spurs appeared in the FA Cup Final at Wembley against Burnley. Looking back, thank God we had the FA Cup Final to look forward to, otherwise the pain of our defeat at the hands of Benfica would have lingered in the mind.

I don't think I have ever looked forward to playing against Sheffield Wednesday as much as I did in 1962. The Benfica game had taken place on a Thursday night and we played Sheffield Wednesday at home on the Saturday. Nowadays most managers and players would moan about having to play an important league match two days after an equally important European tie. If we had played Sheffield Wednesday on Friday

morning that would have been fine by me. Whenever we lost
a game I couldn't wait for the next match to come along in
order to get the depression and dullness of defeat out of my
system. In the wake of a defeat I was never personally
depressed but it did tend to dull what was normally a good
sharp edge to my life.

Following a match a football ground takes on a totally
different air. When the vast majority of supporters have left the
scene and the once turbulent and volatile atmosphere has
disappeared into the ether, a football ground becomes a
remarkably empty place. Even in the aftermath of victory there
is a sadness about it. When I left White Hart Lane following
our aggregate defeat against Benfica, this sadness was even
more pronounced.

The litter that blew down the streets indicated that the party
was over. Newspaper hoardings pinned to lampposts that only
a few hours earlier heralded the game and as such had an
immediacy about them, now appeared redundant and
smacked of tired old news. The surrounding streets that once
hummed to the optimistic and hopeful chatter of supporters
were now nigh on deserted. Before the game, these streets had
been alive with colour and brightness. Now their lamps flung
their yellow light against the rows of toy-box Victorian houses
and, with the warmth of massed humanity having departed the
scene, there was a coldness. There always is coldness in streets
around a football ground when a match is over but that night
it chilled to the bone.

The Jag was cold too, but the engine soon kicked into life.
I flicked a switch and the wipers cleared the spots of rain that
had settled on the windscreen. I made my way down the High
Road, then swung into Park Lane, heading for where
Willoughby Lane and Shelbourne Road meet head on. I felt as
the High Road looked at that time of night with the rain now
coming down in barrels. Grim and desolate.

'Fack it. It's only football.'

When has it ever been 'only football'?

Football: life's greatest irrelevancy. Just exactly what is football capable of? It can make me fly home as if on silver wings. It can make me feel that even the most mundane task is a joy. It can put a spring in my step. Dupe me into believing there are no times but good times. And yet tonight football has numbed me, turned me into an empty shell and I hate it. I hate football for making me feel like this. And I hate myself for being so vulnerable to football's fickle ways. Football don't care about me, so why should I care about it? I tell myself I don't. I try to convince myself that I don't. But deep down, way down in the pit of my stomach, there is something that can't be denied. What strange power does football have over me? The Jimmy Greaves the fans see on the football pitch isn't the real me. So who is the real me? I ain't gonna think about this anymore, it's driving me crazy. I don't need this. What I need is a drink. Yeah, that's what I'll do. I'll get home and have a drink. It's the fourth mouthful that does it for me, gives me that lift. Makes me feel happy and good. That feeling of wellbeing and elation don't last for long. Two, three minutes at most. But it's a lifter from all this. I shouldn't wish my life away, but I wish it was Saturday and Sheffield Wednesday. Then all this will be gone. The numbing feeling. The pain of injustice. The irritation from having had no luck. The torment from the fact all the luck was with them. The anger felt from the sheer cruelty of it all. It will all be gone and soon. In time to come, when I look at the result in the record books, there will be no feeling. It'll be just another football statistic. Like all the bloody rest. People who aren't even born yet will look at the result and it will tell them Benfica won. But they will never know what it meant to me and others. They'll never know how it affected me. Know the emptiness. How I let it dictate my emotions and how I feel. How weak I really am.

I tell myself there has to be times like this. Without the bad times, there would be no good times. Let's be realistic, we have a great side and there definitely will be good times. No. Great times. Perhaps some good will come from all of this? Maybe we'll find inspiration from somewhere? Learn from it. We certainly learned a lesson out in Lisbon. They knew how to set their stall out. What to do to stop us playing. What's required to win a European Cup match. Oh, they knew exactly what to do. Maybe we can learn from that. Bill Nich made a mistake out in Lisbon. We all made mistakes. We've got a little bit more experience now. We're wiser. That can only be to the good. We'll not make those same mistakes again. It's as if there has to be this pain. There has to be this night. The saddest night I have known in football.

The pain and disappointment of our European Cup semi-final defeat at the hands of Benfica, and a linesman, was erased by Spurs' success in the FA Cup. While it is true to say that the European Cup had been our main priority, that's not to say that the FA Cup didn't feature prominently in the minds of everyone connected with the club, myself included. Spurs' route to Wembley in 1962 had begun at Birmingham City where, at 3-0 up, we appeared to be coasting. I'd managed a couple of goals and another from Cliff Jones put us in the driving seat, but we reckoned without a spirited fightback from the home side. Birmingham scored, a few nerves set in, we lost our rhythm and before we knew it, it was 3-3. We enjoyed more than our fair share of luck at St Andrews that day. Two minutes from time, with the score still at 3-3, the Birmingham centre forward Ken Leek scored what looked to be the winner. Fortunately for us, the referee disallowed Ken's effort, though to this day I have no idea why. From where I was standing, it looked like a perfectly legitimate goal. You take your luck in football and we certainly did. Back at White Hart Lane we walked the replay. Terry Medwin got a couple and both Les Allen and I chipped in with a goal apiece and, though Birmingham did score twice, the 4-2 result didn't reflect our superiority on the night. I always felt we had another gear and whatever Birmingham produced we would have topped it. In round four I returned to the scene of my very first game for Tottenham reserves following my move from Milan: Plymouth Argyle. It's funny what you remember. I can remember some things from way back which appear to me to be of little importance and consequence in my life. Why I do is a mystery to me. I don't remember much about the actual game against Plymouth other than that we won at a canter. Goals from Terry Medwin, Cliff Jones, John White and a couple from yours truly gave us a very comfortable 5-1 win. I do, however, remember two very minor things from this game.

Home Park was packed with over 40,000 spectators. At the time, one side of the ground opposite the main stand was open terracing behind which stood a number of trees. It was late January when we played the tie and these trees were obviously not in leaf. I remember seeing a number of supporters hanging very precariously from the branches of these trees, enjoying a free view of the match with seemingly no policeman taking it upon himself to order them down lest they fall and injure themselves, or worse, someone at ground level.

Such a laissez-faire attitude to large crowds and safety at football matches was also prevalent within Home Park itself. Supporters were packed like sardines on the open terracing but, amazingly, below them on the cinder track were more supporters seated on chairs and wooden benches. Most of them appeared to be elderly people or young boys, and the sight of overcoated men sitting cross-legged on chairs by the side of the pitch was, even for the time, surreal.

Such a sight, of course, would never be seen today, though as far as I know, none of those chairs or benches was once displaced during the course of the game. The attitude to public safety at football matches was carefree but it was in keeping with the game itself. The supporters were carefree and in many ways so too were the players. In the five years since I had first made my debut as a seventeen-year-old for Chelsea, players had changed because the game was changing. Players were becoming more professional in their approach and attitude to games, but there was still fun and a carefree element to games. Forty thousand packed into Home Park. Supporters dangling from nearby trees. The overspill from packed terraces seated on wooden chairs and benches on the perimeter track. Press photographers at liberty to run on to the pitch during the pre-match kickabout and take photographs of whichever player took their fancy. Carefree? During the pre-match kickabout if I spotted Norman 'Speedy' Quicke of the *Sunday People* squatting on his stool at the side of the goal preparing his camera, I'd purposefully ping a shot at him.

'You bugger, Jimbo,' he'd shout, spectacles askew like Captain Mainwaring from *Dad's Army*.

It was carefree all right.

Following our victory over Plymouth, Spurs travelled to West Bromwich Albion. 'The Albion News', the club's match-day programme, informed spectators 'Spurs have their eyes on the treble, European Cup, FA Cup and League' adding, 'We cannot offer our good wishes in the FA Cup at present, but we would like to see Spurs bring the European Cup to these shores for the first time. In that, we heartily say, "Play up Spurs".' It was a sporting gesture on the part of West Brom, in keeping with what turned out to be a very sporting though fiercely contested cup tie. A crowd of 53,539 saw Bobby Smith and me score a couple of goals apiece to help earn Spurs a 4-2 victory. We felt we were on a roll in the FA

Cup and, as things were to turn out, we just kept on rolling.

In round six Spurs were drawn at home to Aston Villa, a club with a very fine pedigree in the FA Cup. Villa proved to be our most difficult FA Cup opponents to date, they contested every ball, pushed men forward at every opportunity and, when defending, got just about every player behind the ball. For all their valiant efforts, Danny Blanchflower gave us the lead and when Cliff Jones converted a cross from Terry Medwin with a spectacular diving header I knew we were home and dry.

We travelled to Sheffield and Hillsborough for our semi-final against Manchester United. On the last day of March, 65,000 crammed into Hillsborough to see what was for United their most important match since 1958. The opening exchanges were frantic and frenetic, typical cup semi-final football. Only four minutes had elapsed before I managed to get on the end of a perfectly weighted pass from John White and glide the ball past the United goalkeeper Dave Gaskell. Twenty minutes later, Cliff Jones cut in from the left and jinked along United's defensive line looking for the avenue for a shot before sending a fierce, low drive wide of Gaskell's flailing arms. Two goals to the good, the rest, for Spurs, was a victory parade. I thought we were going to sweep past United with all the ease of a Jaguar overtaking a Ford Anglia on its way to a more important destination, but had reckoned without the predatory instinct of David Herd. With eight minutes remaining we appeared to be coasting when Bobby Charlton let rip with a characteristic thunderbolt of a shot. Bill Brown, one of the best shot-stopping goalkeepers in the game at the time, got down quick but couldn't hold Bobby's effort and there was David Herd to give United hope. It was, however, hope of the fleeting variety. Five minutes later, Terry Medwin delivered the killer blow. For a few days there was talk of the possibility of an all London Cup Final. The other semi-finalists, Fulham and Burnley, had played out a 1-1 draw, but in the replay Burnley evicted the Cottagers from the Cup by way of the odd goal in three. We were two well-matched sides. Danny Blanchflower had an equal in the Burnley skipper, Jimmy Adamson, likewise John White in the mercurial Jimmy McIlroy and Bobby Smith in the rumbustious Burnley centre forward Ray Pointer. The press were in agreement, believing a classic Cup Final was in prospect, and for once they all got it right.

The rosetted legions of Spurs and Burnley fans who invaded north west London in their thousands wore the 'we won't be beaten' look on their faces. On the morning of the final they had milled about central London exuding conviviality and friendship, expunging the capital of its rather stern weekday commercial air of John Collier suits, cane umbrellas and tired typists running for the Underground.

The capital's new, refreshing, optimistic air was evident within Wembley stadium itself when I joined my Spurs team-mates for the ritual of the pre-match walk on to the pitch to 'soak up the atmosphere'. In the centre circle the massed bands of the brigade of guards, Scots, Irish, Welsh, Grenadier and Coldstream, played Eric Coates's 'The Dambusters March'. The great alp-like terraces of Wembley were already filling up with the supporters of both teams, dividing the old stadium by way of a colour code. Scarves and shirts, rosettes and rattles, favours and frocks in claret and blue, and blue and white adorned the stadium as the early arrivals hung over the crush barriers like seasick landlubbers on an ocean journey. What I remember most about these fans were their hats. Only at Wembley on the occasion of a Cup Final are people given to wearing hats that normally would be considered ridiculous. Bespoke, homemade hats, hats made of cardboard and stovepipe hats. Ten-gallon hats pasted with brightly coloured tissue paper, their brims as wide as car tyres. Sombreros, stetsons and sun bonnets, garish and precarious on top of heads constantly twisting and turning to see who else was present that they might know.

Back in the cool, cavernous dressing room everyone busied himself with his own pre-match ritual. Before we took to the pitch, Bill Nicholson gave us a little talk, but didn't say too much.

'You are the players who have been good enough to get us here,' said Bill, 'and you're good enough to win it. If each and every one of you does his job, we will win.'

My main job was to score goals and the final was only three minutes old when I did just that. I darted through the Burnley rearguard to get on the end of a header from Bobby Smith and thought I had a clear run at goal. But the Burnley defenders were quick to cover and I checked left on the look-out for an avenue to shoot. I was, however, being forced away from goal. I sensed the Burnley goalkeeper Adam Blacklaw would be constantly adjusting his angle accordingly, so decided to fire a snap shot in the general direction of where I thought an opening might be. I couldn't see the goal because I was heading away from it, so swivelled to shoot on the turn. There was an element of hit and hope about the shot, but I hit it as well as any shot I'd taken and saw the ball evade Blacklaw and enter the net just as I fell to the ground. At that very moment, I felt ten feet tall. The blue and white half of Wembley erupted into life and my ears were assailed by a thundering explosion of noise. Wembley, being the size it is, the roar of the crowd takes a split second to reach the players down on the pitch. Light, of course, travels quicker than sound. I saw the Spurs fans erupt before the noise actually reached my ears. It was one of the unique aspects about playing at Wembley. When a goal was scored, for a brief moment it was as if the terracing had become animated in silence, then it hit you.

It was a final that lived up to pre-match expectations. The game ebbed and flowed throughout the first half. Both teams created chances but a second goal wasn't forthcoming until the fiftieth minute when the Burnley inside left, Jimmy Robson, sent the Lancastrian hordes into raptures with a crisp shot.

The Burnley fans were still celebrating when, twenty seconds after the restart, Bobby Smith latched on to a low cross from John White and slammed a fierce drive into the roof of the Burnley net. Burnley never let up in their efforts, but with our noses in front I felt we were always in control and, nine minutes from time, the cold voice of reason spoke the truth when the Burnley centre half Tommy Cummings prevented what would have been a certain goal when he handled on the line. Up stepped Danny Blanchflower to send Adam Blacklaw the wrong way with a brilliant dummy from the penalty. Blacklaw fell to his right, the ball glided across the lush turf to his left and so ended what had been a magnificent Cup Final.

The newspapers were praising in the efforts of both teams. The consensus of opinion was that it had been a final for the purists, though one or two of the press boys did go overboard in their references to yours truly, in particular my goal. Said Sam Leitch in the *Sunday Pictorial*, 'How he [me] got that goal still mystifies me. A hefty clearance from goalkeeper Bill Brown was nodded down perfectly by Bobby Smith to the galloping feet of Greaves. He charged on to goal but lost control through the momentum of his own pace. Then, wheeling to the left, he blasted the ball all along the ground past five thunderstruck defenders.'

I actually rolled the ball rather than blasted it. As I have stressed, I was never a blaster of the ball, in fact I was always in awe of those who could, such as Bobby Charlton, Peter Lorimer of Leeds and George Mulhall of Sunderland. Even Dave Mackay could hit a shot far harder than I ever could, or wanted to. Of all the goals I had scored in my career to date, my goal against Burnley gave me the most satisfaction and pleasure. Before the final, just to instil confidence in my Spurs team-mates, I told them I would have a goal to my name after five minutes. Not for the first or last time in my life I was wrong with my predictions. My goal against Burnley came two minutes early.

When I first joined Spurs I never felt accepted in the dressing room. The team had just won the 'double' without me and following my move from Chelsea and subsequent spell at AC Milan, some quarters of the press had given me a rough ride. The spirit in the Spurs dressing room was very good and perhaps one or two of the lads thought I might be a disruptive influence. I had respect for all the players but I knew I would have to earn their respect. I knuckled down to training to the best of my ability, did the job I was brought in to do, score goals, and as the months passed I was accepted by the Spurs players as being one of them. Helping them win the FA Cup further cemented the relationship. When I had first walked into the dressing room in December 1961, I was given a polite though guarded welcome. Five months on, it was as if I had always been a member of the fold. That I had played for no other club but Spurs. I felt I belonged, that I had at last found my spiritual home at White Hart Lane. Life was good again.

A footballer is only too aware that his career will be short-lived. Likewise, the lifespan of a team. You're aware of those facts, but you don't dwell on them, just as we never dwell on the fact that we will not live forever. I was now twenty-two and the lion's share of my career as a footballer was still to come. I never dwelt on the fact that some of the members of the great Spurs double side had only a couple of years left at the club. That within two years the side would be dismantled and recreated. I didn't think about that because I lived for the moment. Spurs without Danny Blanchflower was unthinkable.

So I didn't think about it. Though even at this stage, Bill Nicholson obviously did.

Spurs were a super side to play with. Our goalkeeper Bill Brown had begun his career in Scottish junior football where his talent was spotted by Dundee. He played against England at Wembley in April 1959 and gave such an assured performance that Spurs paid £16,500 for his services. Bill was a great shot-stopper, a goalkeeper who belied the notion that all Scottish goalkeepers were of the dodgy variety. If he had a weakness, it was on crosses. He came, but he didn't always collect. His all-round ability as a goalkeeper, however, more than compensated for this slight deficiency in his game. I remember Bill saving our bacon and everything else that Slovan Bratislava threw at him during our successful European Cup Winners' Cup campaign of 1962–3. The weather in Bratislava was so cold, the Danube had frozen over. The Slovan pitch was like a skating rink and we just couldn't adapt to the conditions. Slovan murdered us that day. They won 2-0 but should they have won 6-0 it wouldn't have been an injustice. The fact that they didn't was all down to the heroics of Bill Brown. Bill kept us in the tie and the competition. In the return leg at White Hart Lane we swept Slovan Bratislava aside and quickly wiped out the two-goal deficit.

Invariably whenever people analyse successful teams they overlook the important roles played by the full backs. Full backs rarely, if ever, make the headlines. In many respects full back is an unglamorous position but good full backs are worth their weight in gold to a team. I remember once talking to George Best about Manchester United's successful European Cup side of 1968. George reckoned that the United full backs Tony Dunne and Shay Brennan were the most consistent performers in the United team that season and to this day have never received true recognition for their efforts. That was very much the case with the Tottenham pairing of Peter Baker and Ron Henry. Peter and Ron got on with their jobs quietly and efficiently. Week-in, week-out, they were consistently good but because they did their respective jobs without fuss or extravagance, their true worth to the team went unrecognised by many. Peter was a hard, uncompromising player whose style balanced perfectly the more skilled approach of his fellow full back Ron Henry. I can never recall a winger giving Peter the runaround. In common with most full backs of the time, Peter's first tackle on a winger was always a bloody belter, to the point of being brutal. 'He has to know I'm there,' Peter would say, and such was the ferocity of his first, perfectly timed tackle that the winger knew Peter was there all right. Peter may well have played football quietly and efficiently, but he also played the game as if someone had just hit his mother with a five iron.

I would rate Ron Henry amongst the best left backs I ever played with, a list that includes my England team-mate Ray Wilson and the great Cyril Knowles. Ron was a thinking player, one who read a game very well. He always used the ball intelligently and was a master of positional play. Sadly, Ron only won one cap for England, in Alf Ramsey's very first match as manager. We were given a 5-1 drubbing by France and on his international debut Ron was cited as being one of the players responsible for our heavy defeat. He was never to be recalled by Alf, which is a shame. Though not in the class of Ray Wilson, Ron deserved more than the solitary cap he won. He was very forthright in his views and on several occasions locked horns with Bill Nicholson on some point of play. Coaches and trainers were all subjected to Ron's view on tactics, training and the game in general. He was no fool and he didn't fool himself either. According to Ron, he knew the time had come for him to retire from football the day he was berating Bill Nich about a tactical point and Bill walked off the training pitch faster than Ron could keep up with him.

Our skipper Danny Blanchflower led by example both on and off the field. Danny was a very intelligent guy, articulate and sensitive to the needs and feelings of his team-mates. He was more of a captain than a footballer, but that does not mean to say Danny was not an outstanding player. He was, though the one person who believed that the most was Danny himself. Danny oozed confidence and that confidence carried over into his play where he would often bluff and double-bluff opponents. He was a beautiful passer of the ball, a visionary in the middle of the field, and he never knew when he was beaten. Danny was a very deceptive looking player. Physically, he didn't look up to the job, but he was one of those players who, whenever an opponent came near him, appeared to be all bone and elbow. He possessed tremendous stamina and to my mind bound that Spurs team together. Danny was the leader of the Spurs dressing-room culture, but a benevolent and objective one as befitted his style of play. He was, in fact, one of the most thoughtful players I ever encountered throughout my career.

Danny was an inspirational player, in many ways an artist. He had a tremendous way with words and, when the *Observer* gave him his own column, insisted on writing it himself. Though still a player at the time, he refused to compromise his views in order to conform with the football authorities, which made him unpopular among some who dwelt in the higher echelons of the game.

Danny was forever being quoted in newspapers, simply because just about everything he said was so eminently quotable.

Following a Spurs victory over Arsenal, the football writer Bill Holden asked Danny, in the light of the fact that sportsmanship was very important to him, how important it was to him to win games.

'Winning isn't everything,' replied Danny, 'but wanting to

win is.' Asked by Alan Williams of the *Daily Express* for his opinion of the Burnley chairman and president of the Football League, Bob Lord, who could often be bombastic and egotistical, Danny replied, 'He's a self-made man who worships his creator.'

On being asked by a reporter from the *Belfast Telegraph* what it was like for him to play alongside Dick Keith in the Northern Ireland team, Danny replied, 'Stimulating! Every pass from Dick is an adventure.'

In the course of interviews, you don't hear today's players coming out with answers like that.

Danny was the Oscar Wilde of Windsor Park. He would wax lyrical about football and its relation to life. Football and its relation to endeavour. Football and its relation to trouser turn-up fluff. To ask him anything about football would induce a reply as epic as any of Tennyson's poems. Straight out of the dressing room following a game for Northern Ireland, Danny was confronted by a reporter who asked for his opinion on George Best.

'George makes a greater appeal to the senses than Finney or Matthews did,' replied Danny with characteristic lyricism. 'His movements are quicker, lighter, more balletic. George offers grander surprises to the mind and the eye. He has ice in his veins, warmth in his heart and timing and balance in his feet.'

The reporter looked up from his notebook, somewhat agitated.

'Yeah, yeah,' said the reporter with disinterest, his pencil poised, 'but how do you rate George as a player, Danny?'

Following Bill Nicholson's pre-match talk to the players, Danny would then get up and give the real team talk. It was the same with Northern Ireland. Danny would talk tactics and assign players with specific roles, but he would also counsel the opinions of his Northern Ireland team-mates on such matters. Prior to one international, the Northern Ireland winger, Billy

Campbell of Dundee, whose work rate Danny believed left much to be desired, came up with an idea on tactics. Danny heard Billy out. When the winger had said his piece, Danny took the floor. 'Thank you for your idea, Billy,' said Danny. 'I feel you would do well to remember that ideas are very funny things. They never work unless you do.'

Danny's knowledgeable, forthright and witty articles for newspapers were a joy to read. Should a sub-editor strike out a column for fear that it would offend the sensibilities of the reader, Danny would storm into the dressing room brandishing a letter of resignation as thick as the 'Yellow Pages'. No doubt such a letter would be beautifully written. Danny wrote so beautifully and eloquently about anything and everything, I could imagine a letter from him to the Highways Department of his local council complaining about dog shit was a work of art. Should Danny ever have written such a letter, at some point he would have made mention of such laudable qualities as honesty, probity, self-restraint, devotion, magnanimity and, of course, the beautiful game. His beautiful game.

At centre half we had Maurice Norman, 'Big Mo' as we called him. Mo was as hard as a pine-knot, as dependable as the weather. He was big in build and big in heart, though oddly not that brilliant in the air. Mo was so big that he usually got on the end of a high cross before his opponent had started jumping. On those occasions when Bill Brown came out and flapped at a cross, there would be Big Mo, forehead hammered flat through contact with a thousand muddy case balls, to head the ball away from the danger area. With his chest hair protruding from his V-neck shirt like stuffing from a burst sofa and legs like bags of concrete, Mo cut a formidable and easily recognisable figure on the pitch. I played with more skilful centre halves than Mo, but none stronger. As I used to say, if King Kong went into a dark alley with Big Mo, only one would emerge. And it wouldn't be the monkey.

Dave Mackay is to my mind the greatest player ever to have worn a Tottenham shirt. He had everything – power, skill, drive, strength, stamina and, above all, infectious enthusiasm. He tore into opponents and he tore them apart. Playing against Dave must have been like walking through a lion's cage wearing a three-piece suit made of sirloin.

Dave was a mighty player, ferocious in the tackle but always very fair. When Bill Nicholson signed Dave from Hearts in 1959, his new Spurs team-mates were taken aback by his commitment and drive. According to Bill, the players took a step back and looked at one another as if to say, 'What's happening here?' When Danny Blanchflower retired, there was only one choice as captain. Dave. Not only did he make an enormous contribution on the field, his dynamic character was also a major influence in training, in the dressing room and everywhere he went and in everything he did. Leadership is action, not position, and Dave was a man of action, but, as I have said, scrupulously fair. There is that famous photograph of him holding Leeds United's fireball midfield player, Billy Bremner, two feet off the ground. Dave's teeth are gritted and Billy's elevation was due to the fact that Mackay had picked him up by the shirt front, most of which is concealed within a clenched fist that looks as big as a ham shank. Billy had been a naughty boy that day. He had gone over the top on me for a start. When he executed a similar tackle on Dave, Dave took exception to it. The story goes that Dave was so mad at Billy, he butted him in the face and the referee Norman Burtenshaw gave Dave his marching orders. Only for Dave to respond by saying to Norman, 'If you send me off, fifty thousand fans here will come on and lynch you!' Norman Burtenshaw is then supposed to have said, 'Er, okay, but any more of that and you'll be off.'

It makes for a good tale, but it isn't my recollection of events. I never saw Dave butt Billy, nor did Terry Venables or anyone else who played in the Spurs team that day. In fact I could never believe Dave capable of doing such a thing, no matter how angry he was. Dave adhered to a strict code of conduct. He put everything behind every tackle, but always played the ball and expected similar treatment himself. If any opponent went outside the rules, either written or unwritten, Dave took exception. On such occasions as the one with Billy Bremner, Dave would, quite literally, take matters in hand. He was a lawmaker rather than a lawbreaker.

That photograph of Dave lifting Billy off the ground is one of football's most famous photographs. If you look closely at it, you will notice that Dave is wearing not studded but moulded boots with rubber soles. You may find that surprising, but Dave, like me, always preferred rubbers to studs. We even played in rubbers when the pitches were heavy and thick with mud. Only when conditions were absolutely dreadful did Dave and I ever resort to wearing studded boots. The reason behind our preference for rubbers was simply one of comfort. The top players of today are paid a million pounds plus a season to wear the boots of a particular manufacturer. They often have half a dozen different types of boot in the dugout, each one supposedly more suited to a particular pitch condition. I was a Tottenham player for nigh on eleven years and in all that time only had four pairs of boots. When I found a comfortable pair of boots, I stuck with them. Every Spurs player was given two pairs of boots every season, one studded pair for when pitches were muddy, one moulded pair for when pitches were firm. If at the start of a new season I was happy with my existing pair of boots and they hadn't fallen to pieces, I never took up the club's option of new boots. At Tottenham, we were considered fortunate to be provided with two pairs of boots every season.

The fact that Dave Mackay courageously fought back from a twice-broken left leg was the mark of the man. The first time the damage was done was during a European Cup Winners' Cup tie against Manchester United at Old Trafford in December 1963. The match was only some ten minutes old when Dave hurtled into a fifty-fifty tackle with the United full back Noel Cantwell. Dave's leg was broken in two places and he spent sixteen weeks in plaster. When he finally had the plaster removed they discovered his left leg was four inches thinner than his right. Day after day he worked away in the Tottenham gym lifting twenty-pound weights (just over nine kilos) with his foot to strengthen the ailing leg. A year later he made his comeback for Spurs in a reserve team game against Shrewsbury Town in the Football Combination League. With characteristic gusto Dave went into a tackle against Shrewsbury's Peter Dolby which resulted in another fracture to the very same leg. The doctors said the bones had joined together too solidly the first time, which had affected the circulation of his blood. The extra weight put a burden on his left leg, effectively making it susceptible to a fracture. It says much of Dave's character, determination and application that as soon as he was able, he repeated the whole process of rehabilitation all over again.

Dave won three FA Cup winner's medals, a League Championship medal and a European Cup Winners' Cup medal with Spurs, though he missed the actual final through injury. He left Spurs in 1968 and joined Brian Clough at Derby County where he won a Second Division Championship medal and the following year was voted Footballer of the Year. He inspired and guided Spurs to some notable victories, but his greatest victory was over adversity. A devout Jock, you could almost hear the bagpipes playing when Dave went into action. He wasn't particularly tall but the minute he pulled on a football shirt he seemed to almost visibly grow and his trademark puffed-out chest would expand with pride. Whenever England beat Scotland, we England players would take the mickey out of the Scots who were our team-mates in club football, and vice versa. Following England's historic 9-3 victory over Scotland in 1961, I asked my soon to be Spurs team-mate Bobby Smith if he was going to rib Dave Mackay on their return to White Hart Lane about the drubbing we had handed out to Scotland. 'I don't think so,' said Bobby, who was a formidable man in his own right. 'I like my face the way it is.'

The two Terrys, Dyson and Medwin, appeared to play musical chairs with the number seven shirt. Both were better to have on your side than against you, but like most wingers both were subject to inconsistency. In terms of quality there was only a fag paper's width between them, though for me Dyson's gritty determination and work rate gave him the edge over Medwin. Terry Dyson was man enough to admit he didn't possess the skill of some of those tremendous players around him, but he more than made up for that with his work rate. Dyson was a busy little buzzing player who could handle corners better than a Ferrari, whereas Terry Medwin was studious and scholarly. That legend of French football, Just Fontaine, once said, 'In general terms, a football team is made up of piano shifters and those who can orchestrate a piano.' Terry Medwin was one of those who could play a tune. He was a very correct player, a student of the game who exercised care and accuracy in everything he did. Terry Medwin could go through the gears like Michael Schumacher and those quick changes of pace were always a problem to opposing defenders.

All these years on it still hurts me to talk of our inside right, John White. John was known as 'The Ghost', a title given to him by the press after he had played for Scotland in a World Cup qualifier against Czechoslovakia in 1961. His nickname was wholly appropriate. John moved smoothly and seemingly effortlessly through matches and his ability to glide unnoticed into telling positions really was ghost-like. John was the schemer in front of Danny Blanchflower, his tidy footballing brain launched countless attacks for Spurs and Scotland and his pinpoint accuracy laid on many a goal for me, Bobby Smith and Cliff Jones. It was one of the great sights of football in the early sixties to see John lean over then drift the ball effortlessly thirty yards through the air for Cliff Jones to leap at the far post like a Tweed salmon and head the ball into the net. Like the Australian spin bowler Shane Warne, John was a connoisseur's delight. For a time he would stand in space appearing to do nothing as the game unfolded about him. Then he would move into action, swiftly and sleekly. Having furtively moved into position and received the ball, the action would be one of sinuous movement and deft touches. He was an unselfish player and therein lay his greatness. With the ball at his feet, John would bring all his team-mates into the picture. That every Spurs player instinctively played up to John was no more surprising than an orchestra playing up to Sir Malcolm Sargeant. He preserved the balance and dictated the tempo in much the same way.

John was modest and unassuming, ever deprecating his own considerable talents. Surprisingly for someone who was ostensibly a quiet sort, John was the practical joker in the Spurs team. John originally roomed with Cliff Jones but following an incident after our European Cup match against Benfica, Bill Nicholson changed the room-mate roll call and placed John with me. When we played Benfica we stayed in a salubrious hotel in Estoril, the walls of which were decorated with ancient swords and shields. At two in the morning, Bill Nicholson was called from his bed by the hotel's night manager who told Bill some of his players had started a fight. Fearing the worst, Bill took off down a corridor to a landing at the top of a staircase where, instead of finding the fisticuffs he had expected, he found John and Cliff Jones each with a sword, re-enacting the fight between Basil Rathbone's Sheriff of Nottingham and

Errol Flynn's Robin Hood, from the old Hollywood movie of the same name. John was a real wind-up merchant. He convinced Bill that he and Cliff had been re-enacting the sword fight because he was very interested in the legend of Robin Hood.

'Did you know that when Robin Hood lay on his deathbed by an open window in the Blue Boar Inn, he asked for his bow and arrow to be brought to him,' John informed, Bill. 'He told Little John and Maid Marion he wanted to fire his bow one last time and wherever the arrow landed, that was where they should bury him.'

'Where did they bury him?' asked Bill, completely taken in by all this.

'In the ceiling,' said John.

John died in tragic circumstances on the afternoon of 21 July 1964. He was a good golfer with a handicap of fourteen and had gone to Crews Hill Golf Club to get some practice in on his own. A storm blew up, John took shelter under a tree which was then struck by lightning. If he had been in the open, in all probability he would still be alive to this day, as well we know, sheltering under a tree during an electric storm is not advisable. At the inquest the coroner said that if someone with medical training had been nearby, John's heart might have been revived. The coroner's verdict was one of misadventure.

I don't think the club did enough for his family. A fund was started and Spurs played a memorial match in November 1964 against a Scotland XI which raised in the region of £15,000. John was a top footballer, an international who had been a member of the team that had won the double. In his will he left £2,926. His widow Sandra was the daughter of Harry Evans who, for a time, had been Bill Nicholson's assistant at Spurs. John's tragic death devastated the family and had a profound effect on everyone at the club. His untimely death was a source of deep emotion to all who knew him and a matter of sad regret to those who didn't but appreciated football played at its most sporting and entertaining best.

Bobby Smith was a beer-barrel-chested centre forward whose rumbustious, barging performances made him the scourge of defences. Bobby was a battering ram, a goal getter, a brick outhouse in a number nine shirt. He was unmistakable on a football pitch with his flailing elbows and stabbing shoulders. Cheeks puffed out when he unleashed a stinging shot. Seething and snarling. Full of hell and damnation like some muddied Othello. With the promptings of Danny Blanchflower and Dave Mackay ringing in his ears, he would be driven like leaves before an autumn wind. Bobby never believed he had participated in a match until he had slammed into the opposing goalkeeper and made chips of him by sending him through the net. He liked to let every opposing defender know who was boss right from the word go. I saw continental defenders freeze at the sight of Bobby galloping towards them like some demented dray horse but he also deployed more subtle methods with which to gain the psychological advantage. I can recall one game in Czechoslovakia against Slovan Bratislava when the Slovan left half caught Bobby with a late tackle on a frozen pitch. Bobby stumbled as he attempted to remain upright and then he turned. I thought he was going to locate the back of that defender's head with his fist by putting it through his face, but he didn't. He fixed the defender with a stare that was as cold as the night itself and slowly raised a finger of one hand to indicate 'no more'. There was no more. Not from that defender at any rate.

Due to his considerable physical presence, a lot of people thought of Bobby as being a clumsy player. Far from it. For a man of his size his play possessed a lot of finesse and he was particularly deft and delicate when laying the ball off. On countless occasions he'd cushion the ball when receiving it before stroking it into my path. His lay-offs were always perfectly weighted, placid and precise. We dovetailed beautifully though I have never felt that Bobby has ever been given due credit for his part in my goal haul.

Sadly, Bobby had one great weakness and that was betting. He lost most of the money he earned to the bookies. I used to try and tell him, 'Bobby, whenever you first enter a bookies, there is a sign to tell you who's gonna come out on top. There are four windows for taking money and only one for paying out.' Bobby lost a lot of money. In the end he was forced to sell the medals he had won with Spurs and a good many of his England caps. At times he stretched our friendship to the limit by asking me to lend him money to pay off gambling debts, but we always did remain the best of pals. I know only too well about the perils of addiction and I would go as far as to say that Bobby was addicted to gambling.

For a time I roomed with Bobby and I can remember being in a hotel room having a nap one afternoon before we were due to play OFK Belgrade in a European Cup Winners' Cup tie. As I dozed I could hear Bobby on the telephone to a bookie in London. 'Is that you, Izzy? Yeah, it's ya best customer. Here we go. Twenty on the favourite in the first at Kempton. Tenner on Bell Boy in the second at Haydock. Twenty on London Gazette in the second at Kemp.' And so he would continue. When we were supposed to be resting, Bobby would spend the afternoon pacing up and down the room, constantly checking his watch. Eventually, he'd phone his bookie again to get the results. When his horses romped home, Bobby was the most generous guy on God's earth; unfortunately, his losses far outweighed his successes.

On one occasion in Holland, prior to Spurs playing a pre-season friendly against Feyenoord, Bill Nicholson called all the players to a meeting in our hotel. Bill was cross, he said someone had been running up a massive telephone bill on the club's account with the hotel. Suddenly Bobby jumped to his feet. 'Okay, okay, gaffer. Keep ya shirt on. I'll settle it up when we get home,' Bobby said. Up to that point, Bill didn't have the faintest idea who had been making all those calls. Should Bobby have kept mum he would, in all probability, have got away with it. Bill looked across to Bobby, knowing only too well the nature of his telephone calls. 'I will keep my shirt on,' said Bill, 'and I only hope you haven't lost yours.'

When in his pomp, I would go as far as to say that our left winger Cliff Jones was one of the best wingers in the world. In full flight, Cliff was a sight to behold. He was so fast we used to say that if Cliff played in his overcoat it wouldn't make one iota of difference. He'd still fly past his full back. The only way most full backs could stop him was to resort to shabby tactics, such as tripping him up. When that happened it was always a source of wry amusement to us all to see Cliff's momentum plunge him forward, so that his chin ploughed a furrow in the pitch. Cliff was only five feet nine inches tall but a terrific sense of timing enabled him to be a highly effective header of the ball, which was unusual for a winger. Many was the time Cliff rose at the far post to head vital goals for Spurs, and with the ball at his feet and his eyes fixed on an opening, he could also pack a terrific shot. Cliff was a superb footballer, though at times I felt frustration when playing alongside him because he would take off at top speed with the ball at his feet and take on defenders as if playing on his own, oblivious of the fact that I had run into a good position to receive the ball.

Those players formed the core of that Spurs team of the early sixties. There were others, such as Tony Marchi, Eddie Clayton, Frank Saul, Mel Hopkins and Les Allen who, though unable to hold down a regular place, would I am sure have walked into most First Division sides of that time. Les Allen was a particularly talented player who had played a vital role in the Spurs team that won the double. Les was a member of one of the game's most famous footballing families. His son Clive was a stylish centre forward who, in a career that spanned from 1978 to 1996, won five caps for England and was voted Footballer of the Year in 1987. Les's nephews were also top class pros.

The 1961–2 season began for me with the pain of a move to Milan that I did not want and ended in glory at Wembley as a member of a super Spurs side that won the FA Cup. But it is not entirely correct to say my football that season culminated in an appearance at Wembley. Following Spurs' success over Burnley, no sooner were our celebrations over than I was off to contest another trophy.

The World Cup, with England.

CHAPTER NINE

LET'S TWIST AGAIN

In 1961–2 I represented England at both full and Under 23 level. There is no doubt in my mind that while I was out in Milan, regarding my selection for the full England team it was a case of out of sight, out of mind. During that time England played four internationals and I wasn't chosen for any of them, which was more than a little disconcerting for me as I knew a World Cup was coming up and I wanted to be part of the England set-up. With my return to Spurs, my performances once again came to the attention of Walter Winterbottom and he called me up for what was England's most important match of the international calendar, against Scotland.

With the sombre memory of their 9-3 defeat at Wembley the previous season at the forefront of their minds, I knew the Scots would go all out to exact revenge. A victory for Scotland would erase that crushing defeat from the memory. Though the fixture was steeped in history and tradition, the last result was all that mattered to both sets of players and their respective supporters. Should the Scots win on this occasion, for them it would be as if that 9-3 drubbing had never happened. Should England be victorious, the morbidity of the Scots would be ingrained in their souls. The game was going to be some occasion; 147,000 tickets had been sold, all but a hundred or so snapped up by the Scots.

The England party stayed just outside the stately little town of Ayr and on the Thursday afternoon and Friday morning trained at Somerset Park, the home of Ayr United, before journeying up to Glasgow. Ayr is Burns country and no one is more synonymous with Scotland and all things Scottish than Robbie Burns. So England felt at home straightaway. The worship of Shakespeare in England is cold and academic, when it isn't downright lip service. But in Scotland Burns is a living force. He is part of daily life for there was Scotland spoke in every word he uttered. So why the English FA always chose to encamp in the heart of Burns country prior to a match at Hampden, I'll never know. It was as companionable as a cat and goldfish.

Following a training session at Ayr United's ground on the Friday morning, we travelled up to our hotel in Glasgow. I imagined Glasgow in the early sixties to have been much the same as it was in the thirties and forties. It was the Glasgow of Billy Connolly the shipyard apprentice, of the labour activist Jimmy Reid. A meeting of extremes. The splendour of the rich and the abjectness of poverty. Side by side so that they appeared to be in sharper contrast than in most other great cities.

The dominant feature of early sixties Glasgow was the Clyde. I'd passed shipyards when on my way to play games against Newcastle and Sunderland, but I never saw shipyards such as the Clyde boasted. From the heart of the city these yards ran shoulder to shoulder down to Greenock. They were a continuously ragged skyline of gaunt poles and battleship-grey electric cranes below which was ship after ship. Some near to completion in their cradles and almost ready for the smash of champagne, some just keels, like the skeleton of a whale in the British Museum. The sound of these yards could be heard even above the clamour of daily Glasgow life.

Hampden was hellish and harrowing for an England team.

Yet for all its vitriol and violent undercurrent, the fixture was also bound with much romanticism. I still have the match-day programme from this game. The romanticism is evident on the cover which shows a kilted piper aside a line drawing of a packed Hampden, proud and prominent on a tartan background. On the pages that detail the Scotland team, romanticism is to be found in the origins of just about every player. My Spurs team-mate Bill Brown 'first played for Carnoustie Primrose'. Alex Hamilton, for Westrigg Bluebell. Pat Crerand – Duntocher Hibs. Billy McNeill – Blantyre Victoria. Ian St John – Douglas Water Thistle. Names that could have leaped straight from the pages of Sir Walter Scott or John Buchan.

The programme carries numerous adverts for tipples. The whiskies of John Begg, Bell's and Teacher's. The beers of Drybrough's and William Younger. Those who sold the advertising space for the programme certainly knew their target market, the desires and likings of the vast majority of the 147,000 supporters who were to be present that day.

On arriving at Hampden I joined my England team-mates for a cursory inspection of the pitch. As the game was always played in April, one of two Hampden pitches would be available. Should there have been a lot of April showers, it was a mudbath. If, as on this occasion, the weather had been fair leading up to the match the winds of April dried out the barren pitch leaving it bone hard and bumpy.

I remember standing in the middle of the pitch with Bobby Charlton, Johnny Haynes and Bobby Smith chatting about the condition of the pitch when there was suddenly an almighty noise. It was if every supporter in the ground had thrown a tin tea tray down the terracing. The noise was so sudden and loud we nearly jumped out of our skins. We looked across towards a corner flag where the noise seemed to be coming from. At first we saw nothing within the cavity walls of the emergency exit, though it became apparent to all that the noise was that of drums. The drums suddenly went quieter to be replaced by the sound of bagpipes. In no time at all the drone of bagpipes wound up and hit the rhythm of their tune, 'Bonnie Dundee'. It was then that he emerged from the tunnel: the kilted leader of the Regimental Band of the Scots Guards, his shoulders lurching forward and back alternatively in time with the beat. His face betrayed no expression as he marched into the stadium, kilt flapping, all polish and precision. Behind him, they came. Row after row of pipers with no break in the uproar of 'Bonnie Dundee'.

On seeing the pipers emerge into daylight, the early supporters in the stadium roared their approval. It was as if the cheers went unheard. The pipers showed no reaction whatsoever. They simply carried on playing and marching as if they were the only ones present. The sight and the sound of these Scots Guards was awesome and filled me with admiration. In much the same way as those pipers did who led that solemn and sombre march through the streets of London on the occasion of the funeral of the Queen Mother. But the effect these pipers and their music had on me and my England team-mates was nothing compared to that it had on the Scottish supporters. Cries of 'Scotland for ever!' tumbled out of the terraces. Never in the history of football has there been a more moving and poignant pre-match spectacle than the sight and sound of massed pipers prior to a Scotland–England game at Hampden. Not ever.

What do I remember of the game itself? The unique, intimidating atmosphere of a Hampden packed to the rafters with balmy and boisterous Scots. Looking down at the sandy ground to avert my eyes from the erupting terraces after goals from Davie Wilson and Eric Caldow gave Scotland their first victory over England at Hampden in twenty-five years. 'The Hampden Roar', enough to turn English legs to jelly, a noise that was unbelievably topped when Scotland scored their goals. Being annoyed with the referee, Leo Horn from Holland, when he disallowed for offside what I believed to be a legitimate goal after I had run on to a through ball from Johnny Haynes. Being angry with Mr Horn when he disallowed another effort of mine. This really did get to me. During the second half I fired a shot at goal. The ball crashed against the underside of the bar and bounced behind the line before rebounding out and being cleared by Eric Caldow. Inside the actual goal there was a small hump in the ground covered with grass. When it came down off the bar, the ball hit the side of this hump and rebounded into play. I plainly saw the ball had gone behind the goal line, that it was a goal. The reaction of one or two Scottish players also told me that they too thought it was a goal. Unfortunately, Mr Horn didn't. I scored 357 goals in the First Division, 55 in FA Cup ties and 44 in 57 matches for England, but I feel as if I had as many disallowed for one reason or another. Why I had so many goals disallowed I'll never know. Perhaps I timed my runs so finely that linesmen were in a quandary and gave the defending team the benefit of the doubt. Maybe I did score a couple of hundred offside goals. Whatever, I felt I had scored two legitimate goals against Scotland at Hampden that day and, if not two, was bloody certain I'd scored one.

Following our defeat against Scotland, England embarked upon a two-match warm-up to the 1962 World Cup in Chile. Goals from Ron Flowers (Wolves), Gerry Hitchens (Inter Milan) and John Connelly (Burnley) gave us a 3-1 victory over Switzerland at Wembley. Following that game we flew out to Lima to face Peru. On my debut in international football in 1959, England had performed very poorly against Peru. This time, however, the story was very different, as was the composition of the England team. I managed to score in Lima again, not once but three times, and a penalty from Ron

Flowers gave us a comfortable 4-0 victory before we flew down to Chile for the real stuff.

At this point Irene, the children and I were living in our new home in Upminster. We had lived with Irene's parents in their council house on the Harold Hill Estate in Dagenham for four months before buying our own house. Number 22 The Fairway was a four-bedroom detached house that overlooked a common, while the rear looked out on the pitch and putt of the local golf course. We loved that house though financially it was a gamble. The house was out of our price range so I went to see Bill Nicholson to see if the club would help us out. The club did.

The arrangement was that the club would buy the house for Irene and me and that we would, over a period of time, buy it off the club. In addition to my basic wage of £60 a week, I was also paid a weekly bonus of £20. I had a three-year contract with the club which, in addition to the combined weekly wage of £80, paid me £1,000 twice a year. The arrangement was that Irene and I would live off the £20 weekly bonus and the club would keep the £60 as a mortgage repayment over three years, and that they would also keep the bi-annual £1,000 as payment against the mortgage. It was a hefty outgoing every week, but it meant we had the home of our dreams and that it would be ours within three years. The reality was that it took Irene and me a little longer than three years to pay off the club. As a member of England's successful 1966 World Cup squad, like every other player in the squad I received a £1,000 bonus less tax for winning the trophy. Once tax had been deducted every player received less than £400 for having helped win the World Cup. That figure was more or less the exact amount that we owed Spurs in 1966, so we used the World Cup bonus to pay off the 'mortgage'.

We moved into our new home in April 1962, but I didn't see much of the house because, after Spurs had played Burnley in the Cup Final in May, I went away to South America with England for the World Cup. The task of decorating and furnishing our new home fell to Irene who, of course, also had to look after Lynn and Mitzi.

Irene did a great job of turning our new house into a home. Whenever I have a job to do in the home I'm focused on that job and that job alone. Irene, like most women, is different. She has the ability to do two, sometimes, three things at the same time. A woman's ability to be multifunctional has, I am sure, much to do with bringing up children. While I was in South America with England, Irene was at home where she would be decorating a room, offering attention and support to Lynn and Mitzi as they played, and at the same time keeping an eye on a meal that was cooking.

I loved 22 The Fairway. Thanks to the efforts of Irene, in my absence she stamped our mark on that house. Over a period of time, little by little she erased all traces of the previous owners. Secure and comfortable in the notion that all about us was an extension of ourselves, our life as a family unfolded. When we first moved in I thought we were there to fulfil our dreams, but really we were there to make our memories.

Danny was born in January 1963, three years later, we had Andrew. It was in that home that we experienced the trials and tribulations, the happiness and joy and the ups and downs of family life. The tense atmosphere of when the kids were at each other over who should have a particular toy. The joy of seeing wonderfully innocent excitement build up in one of the children in the weeks preceding their birthday. Birthdays for kids are just so very, very special. As you get older your own becomes less important, but to a small child his or her birthday is fantastic. Christmas morning dropped into the middle of August. 'A new teddy. Wow! That's great!' you hear yourself saying, and it is. Giving love is different for every one of us and

I feel when we understand that, a husband and wife and a family understand how to live with and be with one another.

In that house on The Fairway in Upminster, birthdays and Christmases came and went to mark the passing of time. Time in which there were moments of great happiness amongst periods of happiness. Sudden arguments and explosions to mark lengthy periods of general contentment. Family life. When the children are finally tucked up in bed, when you let the toil of a common day slide from your body with a fag and a drink. Where any child who begs to be allowed to mow the lawn is too young to do it. Where for a small child washing plastic cups at the kitchen sink while standing on a stool is pure entertainment. A life in which even a child of four is capable of calculating that her coy appearance with a teddy at the living-room door when her parents have friends round for drinks will be enough to earn her twenty minutes out of bed and a biscuit. Where after throwing a party for your child's fifth birthday, your first reaction is the relief at having survived it. When after spending a good chunk of your wages on toys for a birthday, you feel you should have just given your child the things a toddler really wants to play with – leaves in a drain, a piece of electric flex, a paper clip.

Family life. Where even in the happiest and most relaxed of homes you never truly relax. Because you know that, should your small child ever walk across a desert where the only objects are an alphabet brick and a coffee table, in that vast emptiness she would come across that spot, fall over the brick and bang her head on the table. Our home. Where Irene is a goddess. Where Irene is an irritation. Where Irene is impossible. Where Irene does the impossible. Where Irene is. Where I never realised what the consequences of the cumulative effect of what I said and did would be. Where, fifteen years on, I would have given a king's ransom to be. Family life at 22 The Fairway. My life.

*

The one drawback to writing an autobiography is that you have to remember events you would rather forget. Like the 1962 World Cup.

In 1961 I firmly believed England had a team that was good enough to go on and win the 1962 World Cup. I would go as far as to say that I believe the England team of 1961 was actually better than the side that won the World Cup in 1966. Come 1962, however, the team that Walter Winterbottom created had received a series of cruel and telling blows. Up to our game against Switzerland in May, Sheffield Wednesday's Peter Swan had established himself as England's regular centre half. Peter was a man of rock and oak, a fine pivot, dominating in the air and a great ball winner on the ground. Unfortunately Peter picked up an injury against Switzerland that was so bad it ruled him out of the World Cup. His replacement was my Spurs team-mate Maurice Norman, a very good centre half but totally inexperienced at international level. Our warm-up match against Peru was Maurice's international debut and his second game was our World Cup opener against Hungary. Whereas Peter Swan had formed a great understanding with the other defenders, particularly our goalkeeper Ron Springett, who was a Sheffield Wednesday team-mate, it was all new to big Mo. Missing the World Cup in Chile was a big disappointment to Peter, but sadly worse was to follow. In 1964 the *Sunday People* disclosed that a number of top footballers had fixed the result of games to stage a betting coup. One of the games was Ipswich Town's defeat of Sheffield Wednesday in December 1962. The *People* alleged that Peter and team-mates David 'Bronco' Layne and Tony Kay, who had subsequently joined Everton, had each won £100 by betting on their team to lose. In effect, alleging they had thrown the match in question.

The allegations had come from Jimmy Gauld, a former player, who was the ringleader of the betting coup. Within weeks of the story in the *Sunday People* a number of other players, mostly in the lower divisions, were also implicated in the scandal. The story shook English football to the core. The players were charged with 'conspiracy to defraud' and all were eventually suspended from football for life by the FA. The court case took place at Nottingham in January 1965 and ten of the thirty-three players who appeared in court were given jail sentences. Jimmy Gauld received four years and was ordered to pay £5,000 costs. The other nine received sentences ranging from four to fifteen months. Peter Swan was one of those nine. He went to jail along with former team-mates Tony Kay and David Layne and the former Celtic, Portsmouth and Scotland Under 23 goalkeeper Dick Beattie. It was a scandalous and untimely end to Peter's career. He was in his prime and would, I am sure, have had many years of First Division football ahead of him.

For England to lose our regular centre half for the World Cup was a blow, but it wasn't the only setback we received. My Spurs team-mate Bobby Smith had established himself as England's regular centre forward. Bobby had spent a good part of the 1961–2 season struggling with an ankle injury. During England's 2-0 defeat at Hampden, Bobby took a knock on the ankle in question. He just couldn't shake off that injury and had to pull out of the World Cup squad. He was bitterly disappointed and sadly never really recovered from that ankle injury. He played another five games for England in 1963 but the old injury came back to haunt him. His form dipped, he never played for England again and he left Spurs for Brighton. After only a short period at the Goldstone Ground, he was forced to retire from football. In little over three years Bobby Smith went from a rampaging bull of a centre forward, the scourge of Europe, to a guy who couldn't get through a game for Brighton reserves because of the pain inflicted every time his ankle came into contact with the ball. It was a cruel and swift transformation.

Bobby Robson had been superb for England in midfield. Bobby really was a fine international player whose influence on the side and the way we played had been highly significant in England's run of successful results. Sadly, as with Peter Swan, Bobby also picked up a debilitating injury during our final warm-up match at Wembley against the Swiss and he too missed the World Cup. To lose the services of three key players when we were on the point of leaving for South America ripped the spine out of that fine England team. But out of darkness cometh light. Bobby Robson was replaced by Bobby Moore, but at the time Bobby Moore was only a kid. Like Maurice Norman, Bobby's international debut was in our final warm-up match in Peru, his second in our World Cup opener against what proved to be a very useful Hungarian team. When first I realised we were going to play in the World Cup with three totally inexperienced players in key positions, I re-evaluated my assessment of our chances. Though I never stopped trying, deep down inside I knew England weren't going to win it.

The FIFA posters and handbills promoted the 1962 World Cup as 'A World Cup To Remember'. It was, however, one to forget. Initially the choice of the host country had been between Argentina and Chile, with the former looking more likely to stage the tournament. Tragically, in 1960 Chile suffered a series of earthquakes and they were awarded the World Cup on a sympathy vote. Chile was a poor country and had only four venues suitable for staging World Cup matches. What's more, FIFA's ticket pricing proved way beyond most people's pockets, which resulted in some very poor attendances.

The 1962 World Cup was the first to really benefit from television. The vast majority of households in the UK now owned a television set and there was great interest in seeing a World Cup from another continent, even though many of the games were shown in the form of highlights. Sadly, what the British public witnessed on their grainy grey TV screens in the main did not meet with approval. The 1962 World Cup was dominated by the fear of failure. Many teams played ultra-defensively and the clash of the European and South American styles resulted in, at best, some very fractious games, at worst some that degenerated into brawls. What had been promised as a 'feast of football' turned out to have all the appeal of week-old leftovers.

Thanks to the sudden loss of three key players, England never settled down in Chile. There always appeared to be disruption of some sort, we were never comfortable in what we were doing, on or off the pitch. Hungary were no longer the superb footballing side they had been in the fifties in the time of Puskas, Hidegkuti and Kocsis. However, they proved too good for us in our first group match. With Bobby Moore, Mo Norman and Gerry Hitchens respectively replacing Bobby Robson, Peter Swan and Bobby Smith we were unable to find our usual rhythm. We had our moments but we stuttered and spluttered and Hungary ran out 2-1 winners. England's goal came from Ron Flowers from the penalty spot.

As everyone knows, it's important to win your first game in a World Cup and if you don't win it it's vitally important that you bloody well win the second. England's next match was against Argentina and no one outside the England dressing room fancied our chances. Gerry Hitchens had struggled to get to grips with international football and for the game against Argentina Walter Winterbottom replaced Gerry with Middlesbrough's Alan Peacock. I, of course, had formed a great understanding with Bobby Smith. Through no fault of our own, Gerry Hitchens and I had struggled to read one another. Now I had another partner up front in Alan Peacock who was making his international debut. That's another indication of how the game has changed. Can you imagine England of today giving international debuts to players in a World Cup? Not to mention that such a debut came in a side that already contained a couple of players who had only two caps each. Credit to Alan, he gave it his all. He was a lean centre forward far removed from bullish Bobby Smith, but he had some good touches and he could really get up and head a ball. It was Alan's header that was handled on the line by an Argentinian defender which led to Ron Flowers giving us the lead from the penalty spot. Further goals from Bobby Charlton and yours truly gave us what to many was a surprising 3-1 win over Argentina.

Our final group match, a 0-0 draw with Bulgaria, was best summed up by Frank Wilson of the *Daily Mirror* who said afterwards, 'I had six cups of coffee during that match, but that still didn't keep me awake.' The Bulgaria game was as lifeless as a string of dead fish, but the draw was good enough to take England through to the next stage where we met the World Cup holders, Brazil.

Walter Winterbottom recalled Gerry Hitchens at centre forward because Alan Peacock had picked up an injury. That apart, I think Walter believed Gerry's experience of Italian football would be better suited against Brazil than that of Alan Peacock who had played his football in the Second Division with Middlesbrough. No, I didn't see the logic in that either, though as it turned out I don't think it would have mattered who Walter had chosen to lead the line against Brazil. The Brazilians were just too good for us.

We played Brazil in Vina del Mar in what turned out to be a good game of open, attacking football that went some way to restoring pride in the tournament. Didi, Zito and Amarildo were always a source of danger to England but the guy who did the damage was their magnificent seven, Garrincha. Time and again the player everyone knew as 'The Little Bird' chirped his own sweet song. He fluttered up and down our left flank, only to then leave us in his wake with his explosive acceleration and amazing ball control. 'The Little Bird' was highly effective in the air and it was with a header that he gave Brazil the lead after half an hour following a corner from Zagalo.

When you go a goal down to Brazil, you feel you have a mountain to climb. For a time we chased shadows but when I flashed a header against a post, there was Gerry Hitchens to whack in the rebound. We went into the half-time interval in good shape, but minutes after the restart Brazil turned it on as only they can. There seemed to be little danger when we conceded a free kick some twenty-five yards from goal, but to a Brazilian, that's a golden opportunity to have a pot at goal. Garrincha sliced his right foot across the ball and it swerved wickedly through the air. Our goalkeeper Ron Springett moved one way, then the other, then back again as he attempted to follow the trajectory of the ball. Ron got his hands to the ball but it spun up in the air and there was Vava to leap and nod it home. On the hour, Garrincha produced his party piece, a shot from twenty-five yards that swerved, swung, looked as if it was going to knock the hands off the town hall clock, but then dipped over Ron's head before cutting a swathe across the back of the net. I felt there was no disgrace in England's 3-1 defeat at the hands of the Brazilians. Brazil were far and away the best team in that World Cup and justice was done when they retained the trophy by beating Czechoslovakia in the final, 3-1, a fine achievement considering they had been without the injured Pele.

An amusing incident occurred during England's game against Brazil. A little dog managed to get on the pitch and for all the efforts of officials and players proved as quick and elusive as Garrincha himself. The game was held up for some minutes as everyone tried to coerce the dog to come to them, but this little dog was having none of it, he was enjoying himself too much. I've always liked dogs, and I dropped to my knees to get on terms with the dog heightwise and patted the ground in front of me, inviting it to come and play. At first it was wary, but hearing what I hoped would appear to be a playful voice, the dog approached me. When it came up to me, I shot out a hand and grabbed it by the scruff of the neck before picking it up and giving it a cuddle. Officials were quickly on the scene and I handed the dog over to them.

That incident received global coverage on TV, the way that sort of story does. It was a light moment during a World Cup that had precious few. Fifty players were hospitalised and four of those sustained fractures. The game between Chile and Italy was a disgrace to football. That match was beamed back live to Great Britain and was shown just as kids were getting home from school. What they witnessed was far from family entertainment. Players from both sides rolled around on the ground feigning agony after just about every tackle. There was bad blood in the air and just before half-time there was the real stuff. Chile's Sanchez broke Maschio's nose with a left hook clearly seen by all who were watching on television but somehow missed by the match officials. Minutes later Sanchez was fouled by Mario David, only for Sanchez to get up and swing another left hook which floored the Italian. All hell broke loose, there were scuffles and fights and even the photographers and police got involved. The English referee Ken Aston did his best to sort it out but took no action. The game restarted only for David to kick Sanchez. Ken gave David his marching orders, but the Italian wouldn't leave the pitch, a cue for more scuffles, flailing fists and spitting. The Chile–Italy game was a disgraceful episode in the history of the World Cup. Ken Aston later said the only consolation was that such terrible goings-on only happened to a referee once in his career, if ever. Dear old Ken, he was the FIFA's touchline representative in charge of England's World Cup quarter-final against Argentina in 1966!

I'll always have a soft spot for Walter Winterbottom, the man who gave me my first international cap. He also has my sympathy for having had to do the job of England manager with his hands tied while being answerable to football club chairmen blinded by vested interest. The farcical situation throughout his sixteen-year reign as England manager was that Walter managed the team but didn't have the sole responsibility for selecting it.

In the first half of his reign, Walter had access to arguably the greatest English players of all time in the likes of Tom Finney, Stan Matthews, Raich Carter, Tommy Lawton, Nat Lofthouse, Wilf Mannion and Stan Mortensen. With players of that quality to call on, England should have cemented their traditionally held reputation as masters of world football. It is an indictment of the system Walter was subjected to, rather than his skill as a manager, that even with such wonderful talents to tap English football went into decline in this period. If decline is too strong a word, then it certainly stood still.

Following the 1962 World Cup, Walter set about trying to create a new England team capable of contesting the 1966 World Cup. In England's first game in October 1962, against France, he introduced four new players to the forward line, Mike Hellawell (Birmingham City), Chris Crowe (Wolves), Ray Charnley (Blackpool) and Alan Hinton (Wolves). I was the only forward from the 1962 World Cup to retain my place and it must have been a dickens of a job for Walter to persuade the FA selection committee to go along with so many changes. It wasn't a good game or an inspiring England performance; we drew with France 1-1 and Walter found himself the subject of headlines in the newspapers for the very first time. 'Winterbottom Must Go' said those headlines. In the following two internationals, a 3-1 win over Northern Ireland and 4-0 victory over Wales, Walter was working his notice. Walter was, of course, replaced by Alf Ramsey, though Alf wasn't the FA's first choice to succeed Winterbottom. That was the Burnley skipper Jimmy Adamson, who in terms of coaching was a protégé of Walter's. It was only when Jimmy declined the FA's offer that they then turned to dear old Alf and the rest is history, of the most glorious kind. Such golden history was, however, to involve much bad luck and heartache for me.

CHAPTER TEN

FROM ME TO YOU

Has there ever been a season like 1962–3? Has there ever been a period in history like 1962–3? I don't think so.

The 1962–3 season saw Tottenham Hotspur achieve European glory when winning the European Cup Winners' Cup. Spurs were the first British team to win a European trophy and our success was a watershed for British football. Our victory in the Cup Winners' Cup was evidence that British football, in particular English football, could once again not only compete with the best teams in Europe, but beat them. In many respects Spurs' success in Europe enabled British football to cast off the inferiority complex it had had since England's humiliating defeat to Hungary in 1953 and the failure of any team to win any of European club football's three major trophies. Spurs' victory over Atletico Madrid opened the door to the success of other British teams in European competitions. No longer did people feel that our football wasn't up to the mark when compared with that of the top continental sides. In 1962–3 we won the European Cup Winners' Cup but we did much more than that. Spurs gave British football hope and confidence and the realisation that the new methods of coaching, training and tactics that had come into the game since the late fifties had at last borne fruit.

And 1962–3 also saw 'The Big Freeze', one of the worst

winters on record in this country. The football fixture list was devastated by snow and ice that gripped some parts of the country in early December and did not clear until the end of March. I was a kid in 1947 and that too was an amazing year. Nineteen forty-seven saw the coldest winter and the hottest summer for centuries. Throughout my childhood and teens, every season was compared to that of 1947. As far as the winter weather was concerned, that of 1962–3 replaced 1947 as the benchmark for comparisons. The newspapers of the time justifiably dubbed the winter of 1962–3, 'The Big Freeze'. It was, and I remember it well.

This period also saw great changes in society and popular culture. A new decade always takes a few years to assume its own identity. The so called 'Swinging Sixties' really got underway in 1962–3 with the emergence of the Beatles, Mary Quant, Terence Conran's Habitat, the availability of the birth control pill and the deeds and doings of the first wave of young working-class people to have benefited from university education. John Osborne's 'angry young man' was still angry in the sixties, but in the 'white hot revolution of technology' they found ample opportunities for their new ideas.

Football reflects society and 1962–3 saw the end of innocence. The innocence that had prevailed in British society and the game of football for decades couldn't continue after the events that unfolded during 1962 and '63. October 1962 saw the Cuban missile crisis when we all feared the world was on the brink of nuclear war. The establishment was rocked by revelations of Russian spies operating within our own civil and secret services. The names Burgess, McLean and Philby became synonymous with treachery. Dr Beeching's report decimated our railway network. The Establishment was further rocked by the 'Profumo Affair' which played a significant role in bringing down the grouse-shooting establishment Tory government of Harold Macmillan and also 'liberated' the press. We had 'The Great Train Robbery' and President Kennedy was assassinated.

The Kim Philby Affair and in particular the Profumo Affair changed the attitude of the general public towards the Establishment. When we heard about the exploits of Christine Keeler and Mandy Rice-Davies in high society, including government circles, we suddenly saw the Establishment as being no purer than the rest of us. Respect, in all its forms, had begun to be diluted.

Harold Macmillan was a gift to the emerging satirists of 1963. Macmillan and the Establishment in general became the favourite target of a brand new programme on BBC television, *That Was The Week That Was*. This programme was broadcast on a Saturday night and launched David Frost, Willie Rushton, Millicent Martin, Lance Percival, Ned Sherrin and Bernard Levin on an unsuspecting public. Every aspect of the Establishment I had been told to respect and hold dear – government, royalty and the Church – came in for stinging criticism in the name of satire. The barriers were coming down and *That Was The Week That Was* was at the forefront of their dismantling. Every Monday morning at Spurs' training ground, *That Was The Week That Was* was the prime topic of conversation. 'Did you see that sketch about prostitutes? How do they get away with it?' someone would ask. They got away with it because we no longer saw the Establishment as being something we should look up to and respect. After decades of respecting Establishment figures because we believed them to be our betters and eminently more qualified to make major decisions on our behalf, we now saw them for what they were. No better, no purer and no wiser than us.

The age of innocence came to an end in 1963 in football as well. The roots of the money-ridden game we know today are to be found in the Champions of 1962–3, Everton.

Ipswich Town had won the First Division Championship

with a team comprising local lads and cheap signings. With the exception of Derby County in 1972 and 1975 and Blackburn Rovers in 1995, little did we know that no other 'town' team would ever lift the Championship. The English Championship was to be the preserve of the rich clubs of the cities. In winning the Premiership in 1995, Blackburn, though a town, did so thanks to the millions of pounds invested by their then owner, Jack Walker. Up until 1962–3 it was still possible for a provincial town club such as Ipswich or Burnley to win the Football League Championship. Following Everton's success in 1962–3 it became harder and harder.

Everton spent heavily to win the Championship in 1963. Having spent what was considered at the time to be an astronomical amount of money, £200,000, on five players, the Everton manager Harry Catterick then spent £60,000 on Tony Kay from Sheffield Wednesday and £45,000 on right winger Alex Scott from Rangers. In terms of transfer fees, £305,000 doesn't seem a lot of money these days but in 1963 it was an unprecedented amount for a club to spend, and the press responded by dubbing Everton 'The Cheque Book Champions'. You never see such a thing for what it is at the time. Only with the passing of the years did people realise the effect Everton's spending spree was to have on football. It gave birth to the notion that, while money is not a guarantee of success in football, a club will never achieve success without it. Everton's money-fuelled success was not the sole reason for the end of the age of innocence in football, but it was a major contributory factor. Money was now seen as a key player in the game.

Spurs, along with Burnley and Leicester City, gave Everton a good run for their money. I mentioned earlier that I believed Spurs were a better team than the Ipswich side that had won the Championship the previous season and this was borne out when the two clubs contested the Charity Shield at Portman

Road. We steamrollered Ipswich, eventually winning 5-1 with
goals from Terry Medwin, John White, Bobby Smith and a
couple from me. As the two teams left the pitch the Ipswich
centre forward Ray Crawford offered his congratulations to
Bobby Smith, saying, 'You killed us. You could have had
eight, not five.' Ray was right, with a bit more luck it would
have been eight. We went about that game with a point to
prove, that we were the better team, and to our minds we had
proved it.

The new season started well for Spurs. We kicked off with
a 3-0 home win over Birmingham City and though we lost our
next match, 2-1 at Aston Villa, we then posted four handsome
wins that included a 6-1 success at West Ham and 4–2 victories
over Aston Villa and Manchester City respectively. Come the
end of September when we were due to play Nottingham
Forest, we were handily placed amongst the pace setters.
Spurs' game against Nottingham Forest I remember
particularly well. When Forest arrived at White Hart Lane
they came with the reputation of having one of the meanest
defences in the First Division, having conceded only eleven
goals in ten matches to date. The game was only five minutes
old when Ron Henry uncharacteristically made a wayward pass
that was intercepted by Forest's Trevor Hockey. Hockey raced
clear and thumped the ball past Bill Brown to give his side first
blood. From the restart I got on the end of a pass from Terry
Medwin and as the Forest goalkeeper Peter Grummitt
advanced, slipped the ball wide of him to restore parity. Five
minutes later, following a similar move, I gave us the lead. Four
minutes after that, Danny Blanchflower sliced open the Forest
defence with a slide-rule pass, Cliff Jones got on the end of it
and we were 3-1 up.

Minutes later John White ghosted into space, Terry
Medwin fed him the ball and it was 4-1 with the game still less
than half an hour old. We continued the pressure on the Forest

defence. Les Allen was getting through a tremendous amount of work and using the ball particularly well and it was from passes from Les that Terry Medwin and myself added to our tally. 6-1 to Spurs at half-time. As I left the pitch for the half-time cuppa, I could imagine the reactions of crowds at the other games around the country when that scoreline was posted on their half-time scoreboards.

When a team has conceded so many goals in a first half they often come out full of determination in the second period. They know they aren't going to win the match, but the foremost thought in their minds is one of damage limitation. If they can get through the second half without conceding a goal, the events of the first half may be put down to an aberration. In such circumstances, a pro will feel that to get through the second half without conceding, or better still, scoring themselves, is in some way a moral victory. As the second period got under way, no doubt the Forest players were of a similar mind, but we had the bit between our teeth and were in no mood to ease up.

In the second half the Forest defence pushed up in an attempt to catch us offside, but our one-touch football, slick passing and movement off the ball in which we timed our runs almost to perfection rendered Forest's ploy obsolete. After fifty-one minutes Cliff Jones sprung the offside trap, and raced clear with the Forest wing half Calvin Palmer giving chase. Just inside the penalty box, Palmer stuck out a leg and the smiles swept across our faces as we saw Cliff pitch headlong before his chin cut a furrow in the ground. Up stepped Les Allen to make it seven. Two minutes later Ron Henry slipped a beautifully weighted pass through to Cliff and he sidestepped the spreadeagled Peter Grummitt to make it eight. No matter how much a team dominates a game, irrespective of how many goals they rattle up, the opposition will always have a ten-minute purple patch when they turn the screw. This proved to be the case with Forest. Following Cliff Jones' goal, Forest seized the initiative and it took three good saves from Bill Brown to keep them at bay. Having weathered this spell of Forest pressure we promptly went down to their end of the field and added to their angst. Dave Mackay stole the ball from John Winfield, sidestepped a challenge from Geoff Vowden, looked up and saw me making a run. Dave pushed the ball into my path and I ran on to stroke the ball past Grummitt. Nine.

In the last fifteen minutes only some terrific goalkeeping from Peter Grummitt prevented us reaching double figures. There's a good pro for you. Peter had conceded nine goals, but was determined not to suffer the ignominy of double figures. In that final period Peter twice denied me and made a spectacular one-handed save from a stinging shot from Ron Henry. Minutes from the end, Forest had the final word when Trevor Hockey swept home a cross from Geoff Vowden to make the final score 9-2.

My four-goal haul against Forest took my goals tally to thirteen in eleven league matches. I felt I was doing the job Spurs were paying me to do.

Following our epic victory against Nottingham Forest, the goals continued to flow. Our next game was a thrilling 4-4 draw in the north London derby against Arsenal and that was followed by a run of five successive victories which included a 6-2 win against Manchester United and another hat-trick for me, a 5-1 victory at Leyton Orient and a 4-0 success over fellow title challengers Leicester City. On Boxing Day we stuffed Ipswich Town 5-0 at White Hart Lane, a game in which I helped myself to yet another hat-trick courtesy of the good spadework of my Spurs' team-mates.

Following the Boxing day result, Spurs were second in the table and I had twenty-four goals to my name in as many league matches. We had found our rhythm, we were on a roll and enjoying consistency in our play and results. All was going to plan. Then the snow came.

Some areas of the country, particularly the North, had enjoyed a white Christmas. In the south east the snow began to fall on Boxing Day and it just kept on falling. Day after day, week after week. For the first couple of weeks, like every other home owner in The Fairway immediately following a fall of snow I'd be out there clearing the drive and the pavement outside our home. Only for more snow to fall later in the day or during the night. After a couple of weeks like all my neighbours I gave up this daily routine. The snow on the pavements would be packed hard by the feet of passers-by. Then snow would fall on top, making even the shortest journey on foot hazardous.

The snow that first fell on most of the country on Boxing Day stayed until late March and played havoc with the football fixture list. Between Boxing Day and early March Spurs only managed to play two league matches and one FA Cup tie. One of these league games was at Arsenal, the only club whose pitch had undersoil heating. Only three third round FA Cup ties out of thirty-two went ahead on the day they were scheduled. Fourteen of these ties were postponed ten or more times. Having drawn their third round tie 1-1 on 3 January, Blackburn Rovers and Middlesbrough had to wait until 11 March before replaying. On one Saturday in January only four Football League fixtures took place, and only five on 2 February. The following week there were seven games in England but the entire Scottish League programme was whited out. Following their 1-0 win over Spurs on 8 December, Bolton Wanderers did not play another match until 16 February.

For four successive Saturdays the football pools were declared void. It was then that the pools companies came up with the idea of the pools panel who would determine the likely outcome of matches. The weather was so bad, this panel of 'experts' sat in judgement on four consecutive Saturdays.

Clubs came up with all manner of whacky ideas in an attempt to beat the freeze. Flame-throwers were used on Blackpool's pitch at Bloomfield Road. A tar-burner drove up and down the pitch at Stamford Bridge. Leicester City hired a hot-air tent and when that didn't work, dotted braziers filled with burning coke all about their Filbert Street pitch. Birmingham City hired a snow-shifting tractor from Scandinavia, while Wrexham shovelled eight tons of sand onto the Racecourse Ground pitch. QPR moved to the appropriately named White City stadium in the hope that the pitch there would be more accommodating. The ice was so thick and semi-permanent at The Shay, the home of Halifax Town, that in a desperate attempt to generate income the club opened the pitch as an ice rink and people did actually come and skate on it.

When 'The Big Freeze' loosened its grip on Britain and more or less normal service was resumed in mid-March, the Football League decided that the season would be extended until the end of May, though I believe the last match of the season took place at Workington Town on 1 June! Spurs won the two league games we had managed to play in January and February, though we surrendered the FA Cup to Burnley, losing 3-0 at home on a pitch that was covered in snow and like Halifax Town's 'ice rink' underfoot.

When normal play resumed in March, Spurs picked up where they had left off. Following our enforced lay-off we enjoyed an unbeaten run of eleven league games which included eight victories and only came to an end in April when we lost 3-1 at Sheffield Wednesday. From there we hit a bad run of form in the league, though at the same time we were making great progress in the European Cup Winners' Cup. This run of poor results in which we won just three of our last eleven league matches was, I believe, due partly to our European commitments, and to injuries that at certain times denied Spurs the services of Peter Baker, Dave Mackay, Danny Blanchflower, Maurice Norman and Bobby Smith. The players who came into the side did a good job, but so many changes in such a short time knocked us out of kilter and disrupted our rhythm. Despite our run of poor results in the run-in to the end of the season we still managed to finish as runners-up to Everton and had the consolation of being the highest scoring team in the entire Football League with 111 goals. I managed thirty-seven of those in forty-one appearances, which made me the top goalscorer in the Football League. It was the third time I had been the leading goalscorer in the First Division and in my five years of professional football I had yet to finish a season not featuring amongst the leading goalscorers in the top flight. Oddly enough, some of the games that gave me most satisfaction were those in which I didn't score, such as Spurs' first match in the European Cup Winners' Cup.

In 1962–3 the European Cup Winners' Cup was in its third season. In terms of kudos it was secondary to the European Cup, but generally thought to be of greater importance than the Inter-Cities Fairs (UEFA) Cup. With the FA Cup having a higher standing than the Football League Championship, the European Cup Winners' Cup to some extent basked in the reflected glory of the FA Cup. The competition was seen as being very strong as the cup winners of the respective countries which had entered were in the main amongst the leading clubs in Europe – Glasgow Rangers, Sparta Rotterdam, Napoli, Vitoria Setabul, Rapid Vienna, Borussia Moenchengladbach, Seville and, by virtue of being the holders in 1962–3, Atletico Madrid. It was only much later, when the barriers of Europe came down and teams from newly established countries such as Latvia, Moldova and Lithuania and those of the new recruits to UEFA, such as the Faroe Islands and San Marino entered the European Cup Winners' Cup that its kudos and importance diminished. Democracy ultimately diluted the importance of the European Cup Winners' Cup in the eyes of both clubs and supporters, which led to its eventual demise in 1999. In 1962–3, however, the European Cup Winners' Cup was seen to be of vital importance, and nowhere more so than within the confines of White Hart Lane.

Spurs began their quest for European glory on the last day of October though there was precious little in the way of sophisticated continental football about the tie because we drew Glasgow Rangers. Or as the Tottenham programme for the tie quaintly referred to them on its front page – 'the Rangers Club of Glasgow'. Spurs had a bye in the preliminary round whereas Rangers had given ample evidence of their pedigree by defeating Seville. The Rangers side included a number of Scottish internationals in Bobby Shearer, Eric Caldow, Willie Henderson, Ralph Brand, Davie Wilson and the jewel in their crown, 'Slim' Jim Baxter. We knew Rangers would be tough opponents but we were confident of beating them.

I wasn't a member of the Spurs team that had won the double in 1961–2. Cliff Jones was and he reckons the team of 1962–3 was better than the double winning team, though in truth it had changed little, the only addition being myself. Whatever, we proved too strong for Rangers on the night. In front of a crowd of 59,000 in which there was a large contingent of Rangers' supporters, we turned on the style and goals from Mo Norman, John White (2), Les Allen, who was in the side for the injured Bobby Smith, and an own goal from Bobby Shearer gave us a handy 5–2 victory to take up to Scotland.

After the game I had mixed feelings. I was delighted we had won, but disappointed that although we had scored five goals I hadn't managed a single one. Bill Nicholson, however, made a point of telling me how pleased he had been with my role in the game. 'You set up four of our five goals, you played a team game. Well done, Jimmy,' he said. A number of newspapers the following day had me down as 'man of the match'. I couldn't agree, but it did make me think that although my job was to score goals there was also satisfaction to be had from playing a supporting role.

We had to wait six weeks for the second leg during which time the Scottish press stirred the Rangers players and supporters into a frenzy. The Scottish newspapers began by intimating that it was not impossible for Rangers to claw back the three-goal deficit. After a fortnight they were saying it would be done, that Rangers would nick it. After a month, they were saying Rangers would breeze through because, as one Glasgow paper put it, 'this Spurs side is easy pickings'. The Rangers players were on a bonus of £200 a man to beat us. Come the night I was left in no doubt that they were up for it, as were the 80,000 'Gers supporters crammed into Ibrox. When the teams took to the pitch the noise was deafening, the atmosphere intimidating in the extreme. People used to think I took every game in my stride, never feeling any anxiety or worry whatsoever. In fact I lived on my nerves as a player; deep inside I never felt I was the cool, calculating, assured guy that I appeared to be on the pitch. Until you have competed at the highest level, played in such a frenzied and intimidating atmosphere as there was at Ibrox that night, I don't think you can truly comprehend the anxiety, stress and pressure a footballer feels. I was never frightened on a pitch, but though my general demeanour suggested I was cool, inside I often experienced a plethora of emotions. In such circumstances as Spurs faced at Ibrox, you have to get your mental attitude right and be totally focused, because if you're not you become aware of the atmosphere and the baying crowd and you lose it. Because you're not concentrating, the game starts to pass you by, the more you're not involved, the more you become prey to the atmosphere and the crowd. That's why it was as important to me that I was mentally fit for a game as much as being physically fit.

What helps, of course, is if you get off to a good start. The game at Ibrox was only five minutes old when Dave Mackay put me through and I slipped the ball wide of Bill Ritchie to give us an early lead. As soon as I stroked that ball I knew it was going to end up in the net. What's more I also knew that for all the game was only five minutes old, the tie was effectively over.

When that ball kissed the back of the net you could have heard dust settle. It was as if somebody above had leaned forward, flicked a switch and turned off the sound of bedlam within Ibrox. It was eerie. There were 80,000 people in the ground yet I heard Bill Brown shout 'Yes' and clap his hands when that goal went in. It was that quiet.

We beat Rangers 3-2 on the night to progress to the next round on an aggregate score of 8-4. Due to the severe winter weather we had to wait another three months before we met our next opponents, Slovan Bratislava of Czechoslovakia. The Slovan team had a lot of quality about it. Their goalkeeper Villiam Schroiff, Josef Venglos, who in the 1990s had a spell as manager of Aston Villa, Jan Popluhar, Anton Moravcik, Pavol Molnar and Jozef Obert had all played for Czechoslovakia in the 1962 World Cup with all but Venglos having appeared in the final against Brazil. I felt it was going to be a tough one for Spurs. Little did I realise just how tough it would be.

At this stage of my life drinking was not a problem. I enjoyed a drink but could go a week without alcohol and never miss it. Prior to flying out to Czechoslovakia, however, I did indulge a little in the Heathrow bar simply because I was never comfortable when flying. I wasn't the only Spurs player who got very anxious about it. Cliff Jones also disliked being up in an aeroplane, and it was Cliff who joined me in that Heathrow bar before our flight to Bratislava.

'Flying doesn't frighten me really,' Cliff told me as we downed a couple of swift ones, 'it's the thought of crashing that puts the fear of God into me. Everything about flying and aeroplanes is unnatural. Different. Odd.'

'I know,' I said in agreement, 'everything is odd. Take aeroplane meals. When you have eaten everything, your tray has more on it than when you started.' When we arrived in Bratislava the weather was so cold the Danube had frozen over. However, a thaw was setting in which resulted in the Slovan pitch being an absolute nightmare. Parts of the pitch were still frozen, yet other parts which had been subjected to the watery sunshine had thawed and become a quagmire. Tony Marchi was Danny Blanchflower's replacement at right half. Tony was a good player but did not possess the guile and inspiration of Danny. For the Slovan game, Bill Nich gave a first game of the season at outside right to young Frank Saul. On paper, it was a very strong team that faced the Czechoslovakians, but we never got to grips with the tricky conditions in what turned out to be an ill-tempered and physical game.

Bobby Smith was back to partner me in attack, but the Slovan defence proved to be a difficult nut to crack. The bad feeling emerged in the opening minutes when Bobby challenged the Slovan goalkeeper Schroiff for a high ball and nearly embedded him in the perimeter wall. That did it. From that moment on it was all blood and thunder, disorderly conduct with the referee Leo Horn keeping score. Bobby Smith had a running battle with the Slovan centre half Jan Popluhar, in fact with any other Slovan player who came within five yards of him. It was gruesome stuff and but for some terrific goalkeeping from Bill Brown we could have lost by far more than the final scoreline of 2-0. As the teams left the field all manner of threats and counter-threats were exchanged. Bobby Smith walked up the tunnel alongside Schroiff and let him know exactly what he could expect in the second leg. 'Londres! Londres!' Bobby kept snarling, brandishing a huge fist.

That wasn't so much a threat from Bobby as a promise. When we played the second leg a little over a week later the game was only minutes old when, following a cross from Cliff Jones, Bobby made chips of Schroiff by sending him into the back of the net. Popluhar then decided to take Bobby in hand, but Bobby was having none of it. He caught Jan Popluhar a blow to the cheek with his elbow that could have floored an ox. Minutes later when contesting a high ball, Bobby launched himself through the air like some fridge freezer swinging from the jib of a crane. I think those three challenges put the wobblers into Slovan. Crosses were coming in from Frank Saul and Cliff Jones, Bobby was challenging for the ball and there was Dave Mackay, John White and myself ready to pick up the pieces. Dave and John got a goal apiece, I managed two and one each from Cliff Jones and Bobby Smith gave us a memorable 6–0 victory. I say memorable because after the initial naughty challenges from Bobby Smith, Slovan decided their best ploy was to play a bit of football which they were eminently capable of doing. That suited Spurs and me. When it came to a purely footballing contest, I fancied us against any team in the world.

I had found the second leg against Slovan a highly enjoyable experience, but the first leg of our semi-final against OFK Belgrade of Yugoslavia was anything but. We played OFK on a warm April evening but the reception we received from the capacity crowd of 45,000 and the OFK team was anything but warm. OFK had obviously decided that their best chance of taking a first leg lead to White Hart Lane was to employ tactics similar to those adopted by Slovan in Bratislava. To muscle us out of the game. This was to be the only game in which I was ever sent off, though I am claiming mitigating circumstances. I didn't hit anybody! OFK had reached the semi-finals with a reputation for having stopped other teams from playing their natural game. Most notably, their 2-0 victory over Napoli in a quarter final replay after the first two legs had ended in a 4-4 aggregate scoreline. The draw for the semi-finals was made before OFK's replayed tie against Napoli, so Bill Nicholson went to see both teams in action and what he saw of OFK didn't meet with his approval. OFK were ultra-defensive and nasty with it.

They carried that attitude into our game. Boots were flying, elbows were flailing and OFK deployed all manner of underhand tricks to stop us from playing. Tempers and nostrils flared, there were a number of set-tos and numerous late challenges. During the second half, Bobby Smith and the OFK centre back Blagomir Krivokuca went up for a high ball. Bobby caught Krivokuca with a blow to the abdomen with his elbow and the OFK defender crashed to the ground like a bag of hammers. Play continued as Krivokuca struggled to regain his wind. That done, he stood up as straight as a Corinthian column, looked about to see who he could exact revenge upon and came storming over to me. Krivokuca threw a punch at me. I ducked, he missed and when I bobbed back up, I took a swing at him and made contact with the same thing he had done. Fresh air.

John White and the OFK outside right Spasoje Samardzic, whose name was not so much that of a footballer as a bloody good hand at Scrabble, were quickly on the scene to pull us apart. Not that Krivokuca and I were actually in bodily contact with one another. Unfortunately for me the Hungarian referee had spotted my futile attempt as a southpaw, booked me and sent me off for violent conduct. For a moment I thought the referee was also going to give the OFK defender his marching orders as well, or at least caution him.

'Name?' asked the referee.

'Blagomir Srdjan Krivokuca,' he replied.

The referee's pencil hovered over his notebook for a moment, then he snapped the notebook shut. Why he seemingly changed his mind, I don't know.

As I walked off the pitch bottles and fruit rained down from the terraces. I was very upset at being sent off; in fact, I was fuming. On seeing my emotional state, Cliff Jones, who was sidelined through injury, came out and put a comforting arm around my shoulder. Nobody likes being sent off and I felt I had let the team down.

The Spurs trainer and kit man Cecil Poynton took to his feet and, sporting a grim look on his face, handed me the keys to the dressing room. In the changing room I pulled off my strip and would have had the obligatory early bath, except that the water had just been run and was like molten lead.

Goals from John White and Terry Dyson gave us a 2-1 lead to take back to White Hart Lane. It was a great result for Spurs, but I couldn't hide my disappointment at being sent off, especially as it meant I would be suspended for the return leg.

As my team-mates celebrated victory I sat drinking a cup of tea, feeling very down. 'It's ya own fault,' said Cecil Poynton, 'you ain't got no business being sent off. Ya shuddana reacted like that. You's a pro 'n' ya should act like a pro. Too right that ya feel disgraced with yaself. Ya the first Spurs player to be sent off in a game since 1928. You've blemished the good reputation of this fine club.'

I felt awful.

'Who was the last Spurs player to be sent off then, back in 1928?' I asked, for want of anything better to say.

'Me,' replied Cecil.

In front of a crowd of 60,000 my team-mates safely steered us through to the final of the European Cup Winners' Cup, winning 3-1 at White Hart Lane and 5-2 on aggregate.

Spurs' opponents in the final were Atletico Madrid, the holders of the Cup Winners' Cup following their success over Fiorentina the previous season. Danny Blanchflower had returned to the side for the second leg against OFK but had jarred his knee in the gym on the day of the match and only played after receiving a pain-killing injection. When we travelled to the Feyenoord stadium in Rotterdam for the final, Danny was still a doubt. But he knew that at thirty-seven, this would probably be the last big game of his career and he was desperate to play.

As a precautionary measure, the reserve team player John Smith was added to the squad but following another pain-killing injection from the club doctor Brian Curtin, Danny pronounced himself fit to face Atletico Madrid.

The Spurs party didn't stay in Rotterdam itself, instead we decamped to a very plush hotel in the seaside resort of Scheveningen, a suburb of The Hague. Bill Nich reckoned that was better for us, as we were removed from the clamour and build up to the match that was taking place in Rotterdam. 'You can relax here,' Bill told us and he was right.

In addition to being the Spurs captain, Danny Blanchflower was also Bill Nicholson's assistant and enjoyed a considerable say in tactics and matters regarding the team. Which was just as well, because what Danny had to say in the dressing room prior to the final won us the cup.

As part of his pre-match talk, Bill Nicholson went through the Atletico Madrid team and it was obvious to all that he appeared to be in awe of every one of their players. Bill began with the Atletico goalkeeper, Madinabeytia.

'Terrific goalkeeper. Bosses his area, great shot stopper,' said Bill.

The Atletico right back Rivilla was, according to Bill, 'a terrific player', as was their number three, Rodriguez.

'Then we come to Ramiro,' said Bill. 'We'll have to watch

this lad. He's a fantastic player, very good on the ball. Adelardo and Mendoza. Now those two really are a class act. Great distributors of the ball and lethal in front of goal when given the chance. So watch out for them. Chuzo, their centre forward, very mobile, very skilful, great in the air. If we're not careful he'll cause us real problems . . .'

At this point, Danny jumped to his feet.

'Hang on a minute, boss. What is all this? Can you imagine their team talk next door?'

Bill asked Danny what he was getting at and in no uncertain terms Danny told him.

'For heaven's sake, boss. You're making them sound like world beaters. They're not world beaters, but we are. I say forget them. Let's concentrate on our own strengths as a team, which by the way, boss, are far and away better than those of that lot next door. If their centre half is big and ugly, then ours is bigger and uglier. No disrespect intended, Mo. If this Chuzo fellow can cause problems in a penalty area, then Jimmy G here can cause ten times as many problems for them. Adelardo and Mendoza? I wouldn't swap Johnny White for the pair of them. We are strong. We are the stronger. More skilful. More devastating in attack. More uncompromising and creative in midfield. More impenetrable in defence. We are the team that is going to win this cup!'

That pumped us up. It was a tough call for Bill. He was the boss and he could have felt that his position as manager was being compromised by Danny bringing him into check. It was then that Bill gave evidence of being the great manager we all knew him to be. He held his hand up and fell into line with Danny. Never again did I ever hear Bill Nicholson pump up an opposing team. In fact he would later use the very same ploy Danny had used, during our FA Cup run in 1966–7 when one or two players were of the mind that Spurs faced tough opposition in the form of Birmingham City.

We were fired up when we took to the pitch to face Atletico Madrid and we went on to produce one of the all-time great performances by a Tottenham team. Holders of the Cup Winners' Cup, Atletico were also in second place in the Spanish Primera Division behind Real Madrid. In the previous two seasons they had finished in third and second place respectively. They were a very good team but on the night had no answer to Spurs.

It's a hard call, but Spurs against Atletico Madrid is to my mind the greatest game I ever played in. The game had everything. Silky skills, precise passing and movement off the ball. Fluid attacks, constructive defensive play and breathtaking midfield creativity. The game was passionate, entertaining, dramatic, colourful and, above all, peppered with goals.

After fifteen minutes, Cliff Jones cut in from the right and slipped the ball to a point in the Atletico penalty box where he knew I would be lurking. A yard from the penalty spot. All I had to do was steer the ball past Madinabeytia. Thank you very much: 1-0.

Terry Dyson was having the game of his life in the game of his life. Terry was twisting and turning Atletico's right back Rivilla so much I thought the Spaniard was going to collapse with spiral blood. Ten minutes before half-time, Terry chased what looked to be a lost cause. He not only kept the ball in play but managed to cross it into the penalty area to the feet of John White who made no mistake. Atletico were playing their part in what was turning out to be a great game of football. They were giving it a go as half-time approached and their pressure paid off as they won a penalty when Ron Henry handled a goalbound shot from Adelardo. Up stepped Atletico's left winger, Collar, to make it 2-1.

Atletico had the stuffing knocked out of them in the second half when we went 3-1 up courtesy of what I must describe as a very fortuitous goal from Terry Dyson. Yet again Terry turned Rivilla inside out and having gained a bit of space he drifted a cross just under the Atletico bar. The goalkeeper seemed to have it covered and I thought he would simply reach up, collect the ball and hold it into his body. Madinabeytia, however, punched the ball into his own net though the referee, Mr van Leeuwen from Holland, credited the goal to Terry who, I am sure, wouldn't have had it any other way.

That goal was a huge boost to us and a really bad psychological blow to the Spaniards. Following Terry's goal we upped the ante and ran rings round Atletico. I managed to get on the end of a cross from Terry to make it 4-1 and minutes from time Terry crowned what had been a superb personal performance when he sprinted twenty-five yards down the middle of the pitch with the ball glued to his boot before unleashing a twenty-five yard screamer into the roof of the net. A glorious climax to a glorious night for Tottenham Hotspur.

Our victory over Atletico, the manner and the margin of it was all the more commendable given that we had been denied the power play and talismanic presence of Dave Mackay who missed the final through injury. As we joyously paraded the European Cup Winners' Cup around the ground, I happened to see Dave and realised he was feeling somewhat detached from the celebrations. I went over to Dave, put a comforting arm around his shoulders and reminded him that his efforts in the previous rounds were largely responsible for us having reached the final. It was at this moment that I saw something I never thought I'd live to see. Dave Mackay cried.

Back in the dressing room with the cup, the celebrations continued and the champagne flowed. Every man had played his part in our victory. Like Terry Dyson, I too had scored twice, but there was no doubting the fact that Terry was the man of the match. Terry was a decent little player, in and out of the team, and with all due respect one who didn't possess the skills of some of the players around him. But this proved to be his game of games. It's funny how that happens in football. On the occasion of a really important game, it is often not the so-called big names who produce a scintillating match-winning performance, but a player who many consider to be a lesser light. That was very much the case when Manchester United won the European Cup in 1968. Every United player played his part, particularly George Best, Bobby Charlton, Nobby Stiles and Alex Stepney, but United's often unsung left winger John Aston produced the game of his life in the game of his life. Though John went on to play many more games for United and later Luton Town, he never truly repeated the superlative form he displayed on the night United won the European Cup. Likewise Terry Dyson at Spurs. Terry was incredible against Atletico Madrid. I had never seen him play so well and never did again, a point borne out by something Bobby Smith said to Terry as he sipped champagne from the cup his superb performance had helped win.

'Well done, Terry, fantastic performance tonight. Absolutely brilliant,' said Bobby. 'If I were you, I'd facking retire now.'

What's more, Bobby meant it.

Tottenham's success in the European Cup Winners' Cup was a great lift to the club and its supporters but it was also a great boost to British football. We had proved that British teams could not only compete with the best in Europe, but beat them and handsomely so. The benefits of this belief and optimism were not to be felt overnight, but in many respects the success of Spurs in Europe begat that of West Ham United in 1964, Celtic in 1967, Manchester United in 1968 and Newcastle United in the Inter-Cities Fairs Cup of 1969. British football was once again a force to be reckoned with.

CHAPTER ELEVEN

IT'S NOT UNUSUAL

One of the most important aspects of football management is the ability not only to see what lies ahead but to recognise and act on things close at hand. Bill Nicholson was well aware that a number of players who had formed that wonderful double-winning team were, in football terms, getting old. If Spurs were to have a successful team in the near future, Bill knew he had to break up the side and introduce new blood. What's more he knew that to make wholesale changes over a short period of time would be disastrous. The rebuilding of Tottenham had to be gradual and over time.

The seasons of 1963–4 and 1964–5 were ones of transience for Tottenham Hotspur as Bill and his new assistant Eddie Baily set to work dismantling what had been a great team and rebuilding another. It says much for Bill's timbre and quality as a manager that he saw the need to do this. Many has been the manager who has created a team that has brought success to a club, but has then made the mistake of allowing those players to get old together.

The break-up of the successful Spurs side of the early sixties was necessary, but it did affect our consistency. It says much for Bill's management, the players who remained and those who were introduced into the side in 1963–4 and 1964–5 that Spurs were always in contention for the First Division Championship in this period, although we were never to win it. We also enjoyed some good cup runs, but compared to what had gone before, a decent run in a cup was only relative success. Though Spurs were not to win a trophy during this period, and would not win one again until 1967, I thoroughly enjoyed my life and football at Spurs.

Spurs led the First Divison table for much of the first half of the 1963–4 season but the changes to personnel took their toll. In the later half of the season our form, though decent overall, was erratic. The players Bill Nich introduced were quality, but they needed time to settle in and become familiar with their new team-mates. The result of these changes was that we never found a consistent rhythm to our play over a concerted period. There were some outstanding performances and results, but there were also, at best, indifferent performances, at worst, some that were downright awful.

We lost the opening game of the 1963–4 season at newly promoted Stoke City. In front of a crowd of 40,638 at the Victoria Ground, a goal from Bobby Smith was not enough to give us even a share of the spoils. Two goals from the mercurial Jimmy McIlroy, who in the previous season had joined Stoke from Burnley, gave the Potters the ideal start to their new life in Division One.

We quickly put our opening day defeat behind us, winning our second match 4-1 at Wolves, a scoreline we repeated in our first home match against Nottingham Forest. Wolves were then beaten 4-3 before we went headlong into a disastrous result at Blackburn Rovers. Spurs were sitting at the top of the First Division table when we travelled to Ewood Park, but Blackburn gave us a right old mauling when they sensationally beat us 7-2. Andy McEvoy scored four of the Blackburn goals that day, the others coming from Bryan Douglas, Fred Pickering and Mike England. Though Andy McEvoy scored four, Blackburn's real match winner was my England colleague

Bryan Douglas, who pulled all the strings that day and gave Ron Henry a torrid time. Bryan was a lovely little player, a subtle playmaker who also had an eye for goal, as his 115 goals in 503 appearances for Blackburn testifies. Bryan grew up in the shadow of the Ewood Park floodlights and never wanted to play for any other club than his home town team. He had a great first touch and displayed a lot of skill on the ball. This skill, when combined with a sleight of foot, perfect balance and a terrific burst of speed, enabled him to mesmerise defenders with what is now an almost forgotten art in football: dribbling. When the 'Swinging Sixties' got underway and most players wore their hair longer, as was the fashion of the time, Bryan never changed. He still sported a short back and sides with the hair above his forehead swept up into a wavy quiff above his poker face. Bryan remained loyal to Blackburn throughout his career, spending seventeen years at Ewood Park. A rover in name only.

We quickly put the nightmare of Blackburn behind us in our very next match and reversed roles when we put Blackpool to the sword by beating the Seasiders 6-1 at White Hart Lane. I scored a hat-trick in this game and was amongst the goals again in our following match, scoring twice in a 4-2 victory over Aston Villa. This was the beginning of a purple patch for Spurs. We then proceeded to post 3-0 victories over Chelsea and West Ham respectively, only to then beat Birmingham City 6-1, a game in which I had the good fortune to score yet another hat-trick.

When Spurs played Leicester City in mid-October we were at the top of the First Division but it was very, very tight. We were only two points ahead of Burnley in ninth place. Spurs led the table on eighteen points but breathing down our necks were seven clubs on seventeen. The First Division was very competitive in 1963–4 and when Bill effected the changes to the team and we suffered a series of disappointing results in late February and March, our title pretensions were done for. Spurs finished the season in fourth place, behind Everton, Manchester United and the new Champions, Liverpool. What's more, we exited the FA Cup at the first hurdle. Having drawn 1-1 at home to Chelsea in the third round, my old club turned the tables on us at Stamford Bridge, winning 2-0 in front of a massive crowd of 70,123. We also suffered disappointment in our attempt to retain the European Cup Winners' Cup which we qualified for by virtue of being the holders. After receiving a bye in the first round we drew the English cup holders Manchester United. We took a two goal lead to Old Trafford but the second leg proved to be disastrous for Spurs. Not only did we lose 4-1 on the night to go out of the competition 4–3 on aggregate, but Dave Mackay broke a leg in a clash with Noel Cantwell.

The loss of Dave was a bitter blow to us as a team. Four weeks earlier, Danny Blanchflower had played his last game for Tottenham Hotspur, ironically at Old Trafford against Manchester United. For Spurs to lose the services of two such influential and talismanic players within the space of a month ripped not only the engine room but much of the creativity out of the side. Looking back, it was if a great Spurs team had died overnight. 'Super Spurs' had played to an audience of over three million. They had set new standards for English football and had restored pride and prestige to British football. Spurs had been the celestial fire that had changed the hard flint of English football into a bright, clear crystal. That fire had been touched with football genius and had illuminated all about them. Suddenly, that light went out.

Bill Nicholson had two players in mind to replace Danny Blanchflower: Mike Bailey of Charlton Athletic and Alan Mullery of Fulham. Bill was also looking around for a replacement for right back. Peter Baker had announced his retirement and planned to emigrate to South Africa. At one point Bill was considering signing Alan Mullery and playing him at right back. When he suggested that to Mullers, Alan wasn't keen. Alan's lack of enthusiasm for playing full back didn't deter Bill from signing him, however. Bill simply had a rethink about the right back position. Bill opted for Mullers rather than Mike Bailey because he thought Alan was a more consistent performer; also, Alan's record showed he hadn't missed many games through injury. Bill was never keen on players who took up residence in the treatment room and so he signed Alan Mullery in March 1964 for £72,500. This was a considerable fee for the day but Bill knew that, as manager of what many considered to be a rich football club, he had to pay above the market rate to get the player he wanted. Paying so much money for Alan never rested easy with Bill, but he knew he had to do it, as he had done with me, if he was going to do his best to strengthen the side. Alan Mullery was a strong, forceful, influential player. He was different from Danny Blanchflower in the way he exerted himself on games but was commanding nonetheless.

In 1964, following the tragic death of John White, Bill for a time played me at inside right, with Cliff Jones moving inside and Terry Dyson taking over from Cliff on the left wing. Nineteen sixty-four saw a lot of changes at White Hart Lane. In addition to those I have already mentioned, Tony Marchi, who had been a good utility player, left the club to take over as player-manager of non-league Cambridge City. Terry Medwin retired, Les Allen went to Queens Park Rangers and later Terry Dyson also moved on to pastures new when he signed for Fulham. Better than ability is the ability to spot ability and here Bill Nicholson had shown he had it by the bucketful. Bill went out and signed three players who were to enjoy significant roles in the future success of the club, two of whom no other top club appeared to have any interest in. Bill paid

Dundee £72,000 for Alan Gilzean who at the time was being chased by Liverpool, Everton and Sunderland, but he also brought in two relative unknowns: Pat Jennings, a young goalkeeper from Watford for whom Bill paid £27,000, and Cyril Knowles, a right back from Middlesbrough who cost £45,000. All three were to become legends at White Hart Lane.

Alan Gilzean was a replacement for Bobby Smith and Bill faced tough competition in order to get his man. Sunderland had actually offered Gilly more money than Spurs but he chose Spurs, basically because he believed we had the better team and he would enjoy his football more at White Hart Lane than at Roker Park. I wonder how many current Premiership players would turn down a club that was offering more money for one where they believed they would enjoy their football much more?

I was to form a great striking partnership with Alan Gilzean. Alan was an unorthodox player very different in style to Bobby Smith. Alan was more of a footballing centre forward with a great awareness of the play that was unfolding about him. Like Bobby, Alan was very good in the air, but again, their styles were different. Bobby used to get up and head the ball full-on with his forehead, whereas Alan preferred to glance it with a turn of his head. Alan's style of heading the ball was not one that was coached at the time, simply because the margin for error was so small. But Alan had this style of heading off to a tee. It suited Alan and Bill never tried to change him, though Bill would, on occasions, chide Gilly about his idiosyncratic style of play. 'Where did you learn your football. What were you trying to do out there?' Bill would ask.

Alan liked to play the ball up the wing into space and expected someone to tank up from midfield to get on the end of his pass.

'For heaven's sake, Alan. If we don't have a man running,

hold the ball up for us, or else play to feet. You're not playing against Partick Thistle now. With the quality we face every week, we need to keep possession,' Bill would tell Alan.

Alan would take all Bill's remarks in good spirit. Alan was easy to talk to and easy to get on with, a very amiable and amicable man. He never moaned and just got on with the job. You could be open and frank with him and he would never go away and sulk. He was very honest both as a player and a man but there was also something of the loner about him. Gilly would join the rest of us for a few beers but after that, we never knew what he did or what his interests were. He didn't talk much about his life outside football, and I took that as a sign that I shouldn't ask.

I enjoyed a great understanding with Gilly. As striking partners it was almost as if we had been made for each other. We had an almost telepathic understanding right from his very first game for Spurs in December 1964 when he helped me score our goals in a 2-2 draw with Everton. I don't think I was ever happier than when playing with Gilly at my side, he was a tremendously talented player and an unselfish one, too.

Bill Nicholson was trying to build another great Spurs side, but he never quite made it. Other players who were signed included Jimmy Robertson from St Mirren and Laurie Brown from Arsenal. Bill took a breather from his rebuilding but would later sign Terry Venables from Chelsea and Mike England from Blackburn Rovers. I had some great moments with this 'new' Tottenham team but we never did recapture the glory and success of the Blanchflower, White and Mackay era.

One player Bill had set his heart on signing but didn't get was Fulham's Johnny Haynes. I enjoyed a great understanding with Johnny in the England team. We could read each other like a book. Alan Mullery was a super player in midfield for Spurs, but I never truly felt as comfortable playing in front of Alan as I did Danny Blanchflower, or, when with England,

Johnny Haynes. In the early sixties, Johnny Haynes was just about the most famous man in the country. He captained Fulham and England and smiled at us in the barber's from Brylcreem ads. Prior to the abolition of the maximum wage, the Fulham chairman Tommy Trinder was forever telling Johnny that he would pay him £100 a week if only he were allowed to. When the maximum wage was lifted Johnny reminded Tommy of that fact. Tommy was between a rock and a hard place and had no option but to keep his word. Johnny Haynes thus became British football's first £100 a week player.

Johnny spent his entire career by the Thames with Fulham, which was odd because he was never a 'typical' Fulham player. He was far too good. In the days when the only automatic sprinkler for a pitch was the club cat and dope wasn't something you smoked but Fulham's latest recruit from Division Three, Johnny Haynes was the proverbial jewel in the crown of English football, a highly gifted player touched by football genius. His left foot was so sharp and precise it could have opened tin cans. It was said of Whistler, probably by himself, that he mixed his paints with brains. That was what Johnny did with his football. His style was graceful, colourful and he orchestrated every telling move. Chopin may well have written preludes, but Johnny Haynes created finales.

In 1961 Johnny turned down a lucrative move to AC Milan; two years later he rejected Bill Nicholson's offer to join Spurs. Why Johnny was content to stay at Fulham I can't say for certain, but I think it had much to do with Johnny's love of the colourful characters who were there at the time. There was a laugh waiting in my belly every time I went to Fulham because the club was just chock-a-block with colourful, funny characters – and, let it be said, one or two decent players as well as the genius of Johnny.

The Fulham chairman Tommy Trinder had made his name

and fortune as a comedian in the variety halls but had made the transition to television in a big way when he landed the job hosting ITV's popular variety programme *Sunday Night at the London Palladium*. Tommy was a very funny guy, passionate about football and Fulham in particular. When Johnny Haynes first got into the Fulham team as a seventeen-year-old he immediately demonstrated ample evidence of a genius of a footballer in the making. At the time Tommy Trinder was appearing in a show in Portsmouth. The president of Portsmouth Football Club was the famous Desert Rat, Viscount Montgomery of Alamein. Knowing Tommy was in town and aware that he was free on a Saturday afternoon, Viscount Montgomery invited him to be his guest at a Portsmouth home game.

Following the match, both were in the Portsmouth board room enjoying a drink, with Tommy straining to hear news of Fulham's game on a wireless that was babbling in the background. Eventually the news came through that Fulham had won 2-0 with both goals scored by young Johnny Haynes.

'Did you hear that, sir?' said Tommy. 'Another two goals for Haynes. He's some young player I can tell you. Mark my words, sir, he'll go on to become the England captain one day. He's got everything.'

'How old is he?' asked Montgomery.

'Seventeen,' replied Tommy.

'Seventeen? What are you doing about his National Service?' asked Monty.

'That's the only sad thing,' said Tommy, thinking on his feet, 'he's a cripple.'

Bill Nicholson continued to dismantle and reconstruct the Spurs team throughout the seasons, from 1963 to 1966. In addition to his big money signings, Bill also introduced a number of promising youngsters who had come through the ranks. Phil Beal, Derek Possee, Frank Saul, Keith Weller, Eddie Clayton, Roger Hoy and Tony Lowe all contributed to the first team during this period. They were all decent players, their contributions varied in terms of quality and effectiveness, but they were not of the stature of Blanchflower, Baker, White and co. In fairness to these players and a number of those Bill signed for decent fees, who was?

Spurs finished sixth in the First Division in 1964–5. Our tally of goals scored, eighty-seven, was laudable but the number of goals we conceded, seventy-one, told its own story. The Champions that season, Manchester United, conceded thirty-nine. Leeds and Chelsea who, finished second and third respectively, conceded just over fifty apiece. Even Sheffield United, who finished fourth from bottom, conceded fewer goals than Spurs, sixty-four.

Though Spurs failed to win any trophies in the mid-sixties I continued to enjoy my football and just being at the club. On a personal note I was doing all right. I scored thirty-five goals in forty-one League matches in 1963–4 to finish the season as the First Division's leading goalscorer once again, a feat I repeated the following season with twenty-nine goals. Due to illness and injury I played only twenty-nine games for Spurs in the 1965–6 season but managed fifteen goals. In addition, I was a regular member of Alf Ramsey's England team and scoring regularly for my country.

I can recall some super matches from this period of my career. In 1964–5 Spurs enjoyed a thrilling 7-4 victory over Wolves at White Hart Lane. Cliff Jones has never allowed me to forget this match, primarily because he scored a hat-trick and though we scored seven on the day, I didn't feature among the goalscorers. All I can say is, I had a hand in setting up four of them. The final match of the season saw Spurs entertain Leicester City in what turned out to be another extraordinary game. Although neither side was involved in the race for the

title or embroiled in a fight to avoid relegation, there was a
decent end of season crowd of 33,000 at White Hart Lane and
both teams saw the match as an opportunity to show off one or
two of their party pieces. It was a highly entertaining game of
football for the fans, played in great spirit with lots of open,
attacking play. Spurs were leading 5–2 with about ten minutes
of the match remaining when we were awarded a penalty. Cliff
Jones had already scored a hat-trick, I had one goal to my
name, fancied another, so I stepped up to take the spot kick. As
I did, I noticed the Leicester goalkeeper, my good pal and
England colleague Gordon Banks, had his back to me. Gordon
was by his left-hand post wiping the palms of his hands on the
grass inside his goal. As a bit of a lark, I stepped up and dinked
the ball with the toe end of my boot into the opposite corner
of Gordon's goal. The White Hart Lane crowd saw the joke in
this and as the ball crossed the line, offered an ironic cheer. To
everyone's amazement, however, the referee blew his whistle
and awarded the goal.

Peals of laugher swept down from the terraces and the
players of both teams fell about laughing. All but one that is.
Gordon. Banksy was furious. He didn't see the funny side. He
sprinted up the pitch in pursuit of the referee and it didn't take
long for Gordon to catch him.

'You can't give that. I had my back to the play. I wasn't ready.
It's a bloody ridiculous decision,' remonstrated Gordon.

'Goal!' said the referee.

'How can you give a goal?' asked Gordon.

'I played advantage,' explained the referee.

'Played advantage?' gasped Gordon. 'From a penalty?'

'Played advantage,' repeated the referee, 'best law there is.
Allows a referee to ignore all the other rules for the good of the
game!'

That Spurs were no longer the superlative force they once
had been was made clear by a trip to Torquay United in the FA

Cup in 1965. Torquay were in the Fourth Division but having sailed into the lead we took our foot off the gas and, in the end, were lucky to return to London with a draw.

The atmosphere prior to this game was one of the oddest I ever encountered in football. Talk about a dichotomy. The whole of Torquay was bedecked in blue and white and up for the Cup. The 20,000 tickets had sold out within a couple of days and the local newspaper carried reports of how the club could have sold three times as many, such was the interest in the tie. What began as a mild inflammation and then turned into an enjoyable malady had developed into a raging fever come the day of the match.

Set against this was the atmosphere of the Hotel Regal and the other genteel hotels in the area where the elderly came to winter. The palms and the manicured lawns of these hotels appeared to me more in keeping with the 1920s than a Cup-fevered town in the 'Swinging Sixties'. Inside the Hotel Regal, old ladies dozed in large armchairs, while elderly men with thin white hair, sagging skin, faltering lips and rusted clothes moved about their number looking to swap *The Times* for the *Telegraph*. These hotel residents appeared to be perpetually silent but their eyes missed nothing. It was as if even the sight of the laundry van pulling up on the forecourt held for them the possibility of catastrophe. Whereas the appearance of the Tottenham team seemed to them a quaint revolution, a signpost of the changing times.

It's not normal for Spurs to be in Torquay. Cup fever has gripped the place and the town isn't its normal self. There isn't anything normal about this. One of the reporters assigned to cover the game is Danny Blanchflower. As Spurs take to the pitch, the band of the Devonshire Regiment (First Rifle Volunteers) are there to meet us. The bandleader asks a club official, 'Shall we play it now?' The official replies, 'Yes. After all, we won't make Wembley. Play it now.' As we warm up the band plays 'Abide with Me'.

Nothing is normal. Torquay take the lead. Mo Norman equalises. In the second period two goals from Alan Gilzean give Spurs a 3-1 lead. Time was when we would have taken that as a cue to steamroller the opposition and rattle up five or six. But this ain't normal. We find ourselves on the back foot. We're pinned into our own half of the field. We can't break out. Robin Stubbs scores for Torquay. Four minutes from time, Stubbs scores again. The Torquay fans go wild and I'm aware of something abnormal within the Spurs team. We're rattled. A minute from time, Stubbs finds himself free at the far post with the ball at his feet. It's not at his feet for long, however. The ball is goal-bound and only the outstretched leg of Ron Henry keeps us in the Cup.

We comfortably accounted for Torquay in the replay, winning 5-1. The majority of my team-mates saw the first match, when we conceded a two goal lead and were fortunate in the end to make a draw, as 'just one of those things', 'one of those days'. I didn't see it that way. I saw the Torquay game as clear evidence that Spurs were no longer 'Super Spurs' and hadn't been for some time. In 1965-6 Spurs finished eighth in Division One. Since 1962-3 our decline in the First Division had been gradual, 2nd, 4th, 6th, 8th. Because the decline had been so gradual and with each new season for a time we could kid ourselves that we were in with a shout for the Championship, no alarm bells rang within the club. The perception was that Spurs were still a very big club, one that possessed all the qualities necessary to compete for major honours. We were kidding ourselves. In the mid-sixties Spurs were a better than average First Division side, but we were no longer a great side. Great sides don't go 5-1 up at home and end up not winning the game, as happened when Spurs faced Aston Villa in March 1966.

Spurs met Villa on the back of an eight-match run that dated back to 1 January in which we had won only two games. The game against Aston Villa was one of the most thrilling league matches ever to have been seen at White Hart Lane but it was not a great Spurs performance and served to further emphasise our frailty in midfield and defence.

That's the truth of it. Spurs were no longer the great team they had been when I joined them, but that did not detract from my enjoyment of playing for the club. Nor did it diminish the love I had for football. The football part of Jimmy Greaves was sated. I became a different Jimmy Greaves when I stepped across that white line. I gave it my all and the Aston Villa game was no exception.

At the time of the Villa game I felt I was just getting back to top form after a debilitating bout of hepatitis which sidelined me for nearly three months. When a footballer has had a lengthy spell out of the game as a result of injury or illness, it's not the first or second match that he finds hard, it's the third and fourth. Though lacking match fitness, his enthusiasm and adrenalin enables him to get through the first two games of his comeback without too much discomfort. Come the third and fourth, however, it's as if he hits a brick wall. Suddenly he realises he is not as sharp, that his first touch is not as precise as it was. Lacking the adrenalin pump he experienced during the first two games of his comeback, he struggles to come to terms with the pace and tempo of a game. Doubts creep in to his mind, his play becomes anxious.

You get through that. I had taken ill after Spurs' game against West Brom in October and returned to the side to face Blackburn at the end of January 1966. I got through that match okay and our following game against Blackpool, but had struggled in the next two matches against Fulham and Arsenal. I felt a lot better in Spurs' next match at Liverpool and got through the ninety minutes without any discomfort or anxiety whatsoever. When we met Aston Villa in March, I was raring to go. I knew I was over the illness and match fit once again.

From the kickoff I was hungry for the ball against Villa. In the second minute I won a corner and took the kick myself. I found Dave Mackay with the corner and his shot was turned into the Villa net by Alan Gilzean. Minutes later, Derek Possee and Eddie Clayton combined well to send me away. The Villa keeper Colin Withers blocked my first effort but my momentum carried me forward and I swept in the rebound. Two minutes later a bullet header from Frank Saul put Spurs 3-0 up. Minutes later, Villa's giant centre forward Tony Hateley rose above Laurie Brown for what would be far from the last time in the game to head Villa back into it. Just before half-time, Laurie Brown atoned for having let Hateley get above him when he fired through a thicket of legs. Less than a minute later Jimmy Robertson dived full length to get on the end of a cross from me to head us 5-1 in front.

At 5-1 to the good at half-time it should have been a case of 'game over'. But Spurs' propensity at the time to be a Jekyll and Hyde side came to the fore in the second half, as did our inability to cope with high crosses from the opposition. The Villa wingers Jimmy MacEwan and Allan Baker started to pump high balls into our penalty area. Alan Mullery was out of sorts at right back, a position in which he was never comfortable playing, and Laurie Brown simply couldn't cope with Hateley's prowess in the air. In the space of five minutes two goals from Tony Hateley and one from Alan Deakin spun the game on its head. Eleven minutes from time, Allan Baker got round Mullers, scooped the ball into the air and Tony Hateley got up so high I thought he'd pass out from a lack of oxygen: 5-5.

Bill Nicholson watched helpless from the directors' box as his team displayed a brand new formation – sixes and sevens. We were rattled and all over the place. Three minutes from time, Alan Deakin caught us square across the back and raced clear with only Pat Jennings to beat. Pat came rushing out to narrow the angle and spread himself, only for Deakin to dance round him. Alan Deakin side footed the ball towards goal and as he did so the horrible headlines flashed up in my mind. 'Spurs 5-1 Up, Lose 6-5', 'Spurs Surrender Four-Goal Lead'. Fortunately, Alan Mullery recovered sufficiently to get back and hook the ball off the line to save our blushes.

In many respects the Spurs–Villa match was a great game of football. There was drama, entertainment, a great comeback and ten great goals. But from Spurs point of view our performance had been far from that of a great team. The days of Spurs having a great team were over, though there proved to be one more glorious Cup run that was to end in success and an unforgettable day at Wembley.

While Spurs were in gradual decline, England, under Alf Ramsey, were very much in the ascendancy between 1963 and 1966. Alf's first game in charge of England was a disaster and provided him with ample evidence of the task that lay ahead if he was to achieve his aim of winning the World Cup in 1966.

That game was against France in February 1963 in the European Nations' Cup in Paris and we got stuffed 5-2. In truth it was a poor team performance but our goalkeeper Ron Springett, young Brian Labone of Everton, Chelsea's Bobby Tambling and Ron Henry, in his only appearance for England, carried the can. The next two England matches also brought little in the way of joy for Alf, a 2-1 defeat at Wembley against Scotland and a 1-1 draw with Brazil. In May 1963 Alf enjoyed his first success as England manager when goals from Bobby Smith, Bobby Charlton and two from yours truly gave England a 4-2 victory over Czechoslovakia. 'We're up and running,' said Alf after this game. How right he was.

In October 1963 England played a Rest of the World side at Wembley to celebrate the centenary of the Football

Association. Though it was only a friendly against a
representative side whose players were not familiar with one
another, England's game against the Rest of the World was
seen as being of great importance. A crowd of 100,000 turned
up at Wembley on a Wednesday afternoon to see England pit
their wits and skills against such wonderful footballers as
Puskas, Di Stefano, Raymond Kopa, Lev Yashin, Eusebio,
Djalma Santos, Denis Law and Jim Baxter. The result was a
football feast for everyone present. The game was goalless until
the seventieth minute when I took a pot shot at goal which was
blocked, and the Southampton winger Terry Paine cracked in
the rebound. Minutes later a series of seductive passes between
Uwe Seeler, Denis Law and Puskas ended with Denis Law
equalising. Even as I write this, I'm in awe of making mention
of a move involving Seeler, Law and Puskas in the same team.
As the play unfolded I would have given anything to score the
winner in this match. Three minutes from time, the dream
came true. Soskic of Yugoslavia (who had replaced Yashin)
parried a typical thunderbolt from Bobby Charlton and I was
there to stroke the rebound into the net.

Now this *was* a great game of football. Supporters and press
alike were all in agreement, but England's success in this
prestige match proved a great fillip to English football and Alf's
kudos as England manager. England's victory against a team
containing some of the best players in the world was further
evidence that the England team and English football in general
were making good progress after lying dormant in the fifties.
A month later in England's first international at Wembley
played entirely under floodlights, we beat Northern Ireland
8-3 in a game in which I scored four times and Terry Paine
helped himself to a hat-trick.

The mid-sixties were heady days for England, Alf and me.
Following England's defeat to Scotland in Alf's second match
in charge, we played thirty-six internationals between 1963 and

the World Cup of 1966, of which we lost only four. I played in twenty-four of those games and scored twenty-one goals for my country. I felt I was very much a part of the England set-up and Alf's plans for the World Cup of 1966. I was, but the fickle finger of fate was to ruin it all for me.

I had great times with England during this period, both on and off the pitch. My liking for a drink was well known to Alf, though at this stage of my life I could still take it or leave it.

Alf had me sussed and the first time I was aware of that was before an England game against Czechoslovakia in 1963. Alf had called the squad together and was in the process of giving us all the post-match itinerary when he made a veiled reference to my drinking.

'The team coach will be ready to leave forty-five minutes after the game, gentlemen,' Alf informed us. 'Irrespective of the result, we shall all journey back to the hotel, TOGETHER!'

There was a shuffling of feet and a little coughing on the part of Bobby Moore, Ray Wilson, Mo Norman and Bobby Smith which I took as my cue to act as their spokesman.

'All well and good, Alf,' I said, 'but a few of us were wondering whether it might be possible to nip out for a couple of hours after the game for a beer before returning to the hotel?'

Alf studied me for a moment.

'Gentlemen, if some of you want a facking beer you'll come back to the hotel to have it,' said Alf.

He didn't say it in a nasty way and there was a twinkle in his eye when he did say it, but the way those eyes fixed on to me, we all knew he was letting us know he was the gaffer. I scored two goals against Czechoslovakia and further goals from Bobby Smith and Bobby Charlton gave us a fine 4-2 win in Bratislava on what was Alf's first tour as England manager. Alf was delighted with the result and our overall performance but we still did our drinking back at the hotel that night. Though it has to be said that, once back in the hotel bar, the first person to put his hand in his pocket and buy a round was Alf.

Alf Ramsey and I got on very well with each other even though our attitudes to football and the way it should be played were different. Alf was very technically minded and believed in the importance of tactical variations and gameplans. On the other hand, I still more or less went out and played off the cuff. Alf's public image was of a taciturn and stoic man, but he was great company and a ready wit. He liked a drink and along with my England team-mates I had several long sessions with Alf after matches when he would drop the veneer a little and let himself go. When he dropped the mask, he was a different person altogether from the serious-minded manager the public knew. He had a good sense of humour and a lot of warmth and charm, though I must admit there were occasions when I stretched his charm and affability to the limit.

Having a few beers was very much a part of the culture of a footballer in the sixties. When playing for England I always roomed with Bobby Moore and though one of the most cultured players in the world, Bobby was never averse to joining me for a pint, often at his instigation.

I loved Bobby Moore as a player and a man. As a player he had no equal. He didn't so much run around a pitch as glide over its surface. Always comfortable on the ball, his superb vision and astute footballing brain enabled Bobby to spray beautifully weighted passes to all corners of a pitch. He was always available in space to his team-mates, a veritable magnet for the ball. And how Bobby would use that ball! He played football with all the art, intelligence, nous, craftsmanship and pride at his considerable command. Bobby was an intellectual, cerebral player who became a master of his craft. A lot of footballers, even internationals, play by instinct. Bobby was above all that. He was able to read a situation before it transpired and act accordingly, which is why he always appeared to be in the right place at the right time. He was a captain of calm authority whose very presence on a pitch was not only reassuring but an inspiration to his team-mates. Whenever I played alongside Bobby, I was always reminded of that phrase of George Orwell's about how some people are simply born more equal than others. Bobby had no equal on a football pitch. He was the master of the short pass, the king of the long pass. As he used to say, 'Long ball, short ball, it don't matter, Jimmy, as long as it's the right ball.' Invariably, a pass from Bobby was always the 'right' ball. That he delivered the right ball time and again when under great pressure from marauding opponents was the mark of the man. He played the game simply and sublimely. To many coaches football is a puzzle. It never was to Bobby, though many a time, when confronted with his presence, an opponent would do a passing impression of a jigsaw and go to pieces.

Bobby also had a great sense of humour and he loved a good time. After West Ham had won the European Cup Winners' Cup in 1965, the West Ham team simply returned to Upton Park and went home. Spotting his manager Ron Greenwood taking to his car, Bobby said, 'You know the trouble with this club, boss? We don't know how to celebrate and enjoy the good times.' I had many a good time with Bobby, and we did plenty of celebrating. Our liking for a lager got Bobby and me into several scrapes with Alf, so many that it reached a point where it was rumoured that Alf was about to relieve Bobby of the England captaincy before the 1966 World Cup triumph and hand it to Bobby Charlton. The first time we really upset Alf was on the eve of England's departure for a match against Portugal in May 1964. It had been a long hard domestic season and a few days earlier England had beaten Uruguay at Wembley courtesy of two goals from West Ham's Johnny Byrne. The England party had got together straight from their respective clubs and some of us were desperate for a few hours' leisure time.

We were staying in London's West End at the Lancaster Gate Hotel and, fed up at the prospect of another night of playing cards or watching TV in the hotel, Bobby and I called into a few rooms to ask if anyone fancied joining us for a swift beer in a pub down the road. Johnny Byrne, Gordon Banks, George Eastham, Bobby Charlton and Ray Wilson proved willing accomplices.

We took off to the local, had a few beers, then headed off to a favourite drinking haunt, the Beachcomber. It was just a social drink really; we took it steady and spent the evening putting the football world to right. It was nearly midnight when we returned to our hotel and each of us realised our absence-without-leave had annoyed Alf. There, on our pillows, were our respective passports, Alf's way of saying, 'Any more of this and you won't be travelling with England.'

Alf left it until the morning of the Portugal match before saying his piece. Following a training session he said: 'You may all go and get changed now, except that is, those players who I believe would like to stay and talk with me.'

Sheepishly, we stood gathered around Alf while the rest of the squad returned to the changing rooms with quizzical looks on their faces. Alf was short and to the point.

'You can count yourselves lucky to be standing here right now,' he said. 'If there had been enough players in this squad, I would have sent you all home when back in London. Gentlemen, may I for the first and last time remind you of your responsibilities as members of the England team. All I hope is that you have learned your lesson and will not behave in such an irrational and irresponsible manner again. Gentlemen, the matter is now closed.'

Alf named all of us in the team to play Portugal and we didn't let him down. We repaid his faith by beating one of the top teams in the world at that time 4-3, with two of the AWOL men, Johnny Byrne and Bobby Charlton, sharing the goals.

That night back at our hotel Alf said, 'Gentlemen, you may now partake of a beer if you are so inclined. Jimmy and Bobby [Moore], I'll have a gin and tonic, if you would be so kind.'

The number of post-war football managers who can be termed as being truly great is small: Sir Matt Busby, Bill Shankly, Jock Stein, Bill Nicholson, Sir Alf Ramsey, Bob Paisley, Brian Clough, Sir Alex Ferguson and Arsène Wenger. I consider myself very fortunate indeed to have played for two of that elite number. Alf was a great manager, one who possessed a profound knowledge of the game and whose style of man-management, though occasionally aloof, was highly effective. Alf knew the characters and idiosyncratic ways of every player under his charge and treated each and every one of us as an individual. I never responded to a good rollicking so Alf never gave me one. Whereas Alf knew he could get the best out of Alan Ball by rollicking him on those rare occasions when Alf believed Bally's performance left something to be desired. Alf also had a very detailed knowledge of opposing teams and players, though he always used such knowledge in a very positive way and never built up an opponent so that we thought we were going out to face someone who was a cross between Pele and Superman. On the contrary, no matter how big the name Alf would always highlight some aspect of a player's game that he perceived to be a weakness. The Dutch midfield player Fransen was a good ball winner but Alf felt his distribution was poor. 'Pass a ball? He'd have trouble passing wind,' remarked Alf. Alf's knowledge of football was profound, he was an intelligent man though not as well read as he would have people believe. Alf was a Dagenham boy but I always gained the impression that he was at pains to cover up his humble working-class roots. His father had owned a smallholding in Dagenham that supplied hay to the horses owned by cabbies and a nearby dairy. For some reason Alf always tried to keep that quiet. He also made a strenuous effort to rid himself of his

east London accent. It's common knowledge that Alf took
elocution lessons, something that it would never have entered
my head to do. I don't think Alf took elocution lessons to
ingratiate himself with the ex-public schoolboys in the FA
because he was above that. Moreover, I think his attempts to
plum up his accent had more to do with a fear of making a
social *faux pas* when in their company. It didn't always come off.
Hearing Alf order breakfast on a train could occasionally be
both mindbending and a little embarrassing. 'Hile half the
baycorn hand scrambold heg. No thank you, I don't want no
orange duce,' Alf would say, reminding me of Harold Steptoe
trying to rise above his station.

Alf could also trip himself up on occasions with his habit of
suggesting that he was well read. He did read many books but
I caught him out once. The England squad were having a get-
together at the Bank of England ground. After lunch Alf had
called us in to a lecture room to discuss a forthcoming match.
Having discussed this the conversation somehow got
sidetracked on to the subject of club chairmen and the
afternoon started to drag. Every player, particularly Jack
Charlton and Gordon Banks, had something to say on the
subject but I stayed mum simply because I wanted to get back
to my room. Eventually Alf remarked that I hadn't been
participating in the discussion about club chairmen.

'Haven't you anything to say on the subject, Jimmy?' asked
Alf.

'Not really,' I replied, 'there's little choice in rotten apples.'

Alf was a little taken aback at my response.

'Come, come, Jimmy. I would have thought you, of all
people, would have had something more poignant and
articulate to say on this subject,' said Alf. 'Little choice in
rotten apples? We are English, Jimmy. We speak English, the
language of Shakespeare.'

'That is Shakespeare, Alf,' I informed him.

Though at times he tried to be something he wasn't, the England players loved Alf. I wouldn't go as far as to say I loved him, but I certainly respected the man, held him in the highest regard and believed him to be a great manager, even before England won the World Cup. Alf always referred to us as being 'his players' and he didn't care about anything but 'his players'. We respected him because he showed us respect and our relationship with him was such that every player went out and gave his all for Alf. When Alf Ramsey died in 1999 the saddest people of all were we twenty-one surviving members of the 1966 World Cup squad.

Alf was not a man to talk in a complicated way about tactics. But he knew what he wanted in terms of a gameplan and within that gameplan there was always the freedom for individuals to express themselves on the field. You could say things to Alf and he wouldn't take them personally. England's final warm-up game before the 1966 World Cup was against Poland in Chorzhow. I was next to Alf as we disembarked from our plane and took in the scene that was laid before us. Chorzhow is in Katowice and in 1966 boasted a bleak skyline of grey flats, pitheads, steel foundries and chemical plants, the latter of which belched smoke and gas into a yellow fog that hung over the city. I took one look at this and turned to Alf. 'Okay, Alf,' I said, 'you've made your point. Now let's get back on the plane and piss off home.'

It's right that people should remember the glorious day when England won the World Cup in 1966. It was a great achievement and Alf Ramsey was the architect of that success but a lot of myths have grown up around that tournament. One in particular had a damaging and lasting effect on the reputation of Alf Ramsey. It is a commonly held belief that following England's fiery quarter-final success over Argentina, Alf called the Argentines 'animals'. That stuck with Alf for the rest of his life and made both him and successive England teams very unpopular abroad, particularly in South America. The truth is, Alf never did call the Argentinian team 'animals'. I could never recall Alf saying that at the time and in researching this book every newspaper and magazine of the time bears this out. Without exception, when referring to Alf's post-match comments when he was asked for his opinion on the World Cup at that stage, Alf is quoted as saying, 'I've been a little disappointed that the behaviour of some players in this competition reminded me of animals.'

At no point is there any reference whatsoever to Alf directly referring to the Argentines as being 'animals'. In the aftermath of England's quarter-final what Alf is widely quoted as saying may be taken as an oblique reference to Argentina, but he certainly did not refer to them directly as being 'animals', as so many people believe. The tournament of '66 had, up to the point of England's game against Argentina, been besmirched by some really roughhouse play. For example Pele had to all intents and purposes been kicked out of the competition by Portugal. Uruguay had also employed shabby tactics when dealing with opponents. In saying what he said, I think Alf was referring to the tournament in general rather than solely the behaviour of Argentine players against England. But he suffered from being misquoted for the rest of his life. Why he never chose to confront this and put the record straight, I don't know for sure. Maybe, being the gentleman he was, Alf believed an argument conducted in the media would be unbecoming of an England manager. Whatever, he suffered unduly for something he never said. Regarding the 1966 World Cup there is another myth I would like to explode. I've seen it written that Alf Ramsey was the man who denied me the opportunity of being a part of England's successful team. That's not strictly true. The man who did that was Joseph Bonnel.

CHAPTER TWELVE

OUT OF TIME

A series of questions.
i) How long was the Hundred Years War? ii) Which country makes Panama hats? iii) In which town do Grimsby Town play? iv) From which animal do we get catgut? v) Yes or no? Jimmy Greaves' slide into alcoholism was a result of his disappointment at missing out on England's World Cup success of '66. Here are the answers: i) 116 years, ii) Ecuador, iii) Cleethorpes, iv) horses and sheep, v) no.

The answers to some questions are not as obvious as they may seem. Many people believe, and I have seen it written, that I was so bitter and heartbroken not to have been a part of England's World Cup winning team that I immediately sought solace in drink and plunged into alcoholism. Of course I was disappointed. Of course I was upset. Who wouldn't be? But the truth of the matter is, my decline into alcoholism came not in the immediate aftermath of England's success of '66, but in the early seventies following my retirement from full-time professional football.

One well-known football writer recently wrote in one of the Sunday broadsheets, 'Greaves' omission from Ramsey's side had a damaging effect on his career and his life. Following the heartache of '66, Greaves went into immediate decline as a player.'

The truth is somewhat different. In the season immediately following England's World Cup triumph, I scored twenty-five goals in thirty-eight league matches for Spurs to finish as the First Division's third leading goalscorer. That season I was also the leading goalscorer in the FA Cup, won an FA Cup Winners' medal with Spurs and regained my place in the England team. The following season, 1967–8, I was once again Spurs' leading goalscorer with twenty-six goals, which put me amongst the top five goalscorers in Division One. In 1968–9, I scored thirty-six goals for Spurs which made me not only the club's leading goalscorer yet again, but the leading goalscorer in the entire Football League. Now that doesn't sound like a player 'in immediate decline' to me. I ask you; could a hopeless alcoholic get through an arduous season in top flight English football and score thirty-six goals in the process? Of course not. My decline into alcoholism came later.

Seven months before the 1966 World Cup I contracted hepatitis, an illness that affects the liver, but it was not brought on by anything to do with my consumption of alcohol. I spent fifteen weeks on the sidelines and the hepatitis drained me of energy, strength and stamina. I made my Spurs comeback in February '66 when Alf Ramsey was well ahead with his team-building programme for the World Cup. I have never worked harder in my life to recapture optimum fitness. I sweated out each training session and after 'official' training spent countless hours on my own lifting weights and working on my sharpness and speed off the mark. I hardly touched alcohol during this period. This was a time in my life when I could control myself and my desire to regain full fitness and my place in the England team far outweighed any desire I had for enjoying a beer. I was desperately keen to be a part of Alf's plans because I was convinced England were going to win the World Cup. Alf had a great squad of players, the majority of them good international-class players. Those who weren't in that category – Bobby Moore, Ray Wilson, Gordon Banks and Bobby Charlton – were world-class players and any team that wins a World Cup must contain two or three players who come into the category of 'world class'. England also had home advantage and the right mood running through the game at domestic level.

The hepatitis robbed me of a half of yard of pace but I knew I was good enough and sharp enough to produce the business for England better than any other striker Alf had at his disposal. That may sound a little conceited but any goalscorer who lacks confidence and belief in his own ability will not score goals. I had implicit self-belief and I know Alf thought I was the right man for the job because he told me so.

I finally clinched my place in Alf's team for the World Cup during the tour leading up to the Finals. I wasn't the only player to do so; the other player to make his mark on that tour and convince Alf he was the right man for the job was Bobby Moore. Prior to England's pre-World Cup tour, Alf had been toying with the idea of giving the number six shirt to Leeds United's Norman Hunter. But a succession of superlative performances from Bobby against Norway, Denmark and Poland convinced Alf that he should stick with the West Ham skipper. With all due respect to Norman, I think that decision was one of the main reasons for England triumphing in 1966, for Bobby emerged as the player of the tournament, never putting a foot wrong. I missed out on England's fine 1-0 victory over West Germany at Wembley in February '66 and also the next international, a thrilling 4-3 victory over Scotland at Hampden Park. Alf included me for England's next game a month later at home to Yugoslavia and I repaid his faith by scoring after just nine minutes. I was beginning to motor with some of my old enthusiasm and sharpness against Yugoslavia and felt, given a run of games in the England team, I could prove beyond doubt that I should have the leading striking role in the team. Alf rested me for England's first match of their tour, against Finland, but brought me back to face Norway in Oslo. With just about every player out to show Alf what he could do, England were on fire that day. Norway had no answer to us and we won 6-1 with me scoring four goals for England for the second time in my career. Though I was to play in the two remaining games of the tour against Denmark and Poland I'm convinced Alf decided after the Norway game to play me in attack for England's opening game of the World Cup against Uruguay. Alf shared the view of his players that England would win the World Cup and went on record as saying so. That caused a bit of a stir in the press because quite a number of football writers didn't agree.

The build-up to the tournament had an element of sensation and farce when the World Cup was stolen. The trophy had been on show at the National Stamp Exhibition at Central Hall. Why on earth the World Cup was included in a stamp exhibition I'm not sure. I assume it was there in support of the Post Office's special issue of World Cup stamps that had been produced to commemorate the occasion. News that the World Cup had been stolen reverberated around not only England but the world. The theft of the Jules Rimet trophy was a huge embarrassment to the Football Association and the country in general.

London's finest were on to the case straightaway. The unfolding story of the search for the World Cup made the headlines for days. Though the police left no stone unturned in their investigation they just couldn't get a lead on who had stolen the cup or why.

After seven days the police seemed to be no further on in tracking down the cup. Then a Londoner, Dave Corbett, quite literally stumbled across gold while out walking with his dog Pickles in Norwood, south London. Mr Corbett's dog disappeared into the front garden of a house and began rummaging around at the base of a hedge. The dog uncovered a brown paper parcel and when Mr Corbett arrived on the scene he was astonished to find the parcel contained the missing World Cup. The discovery of the cup made even bigger headlines in the newspapers. The press now had the added ingredient of human or, rather, canine interest, seeing as a dog had accomplished what the police had failed to do. If I remember rightly someone was eventually charged with stealing the cup, but that story was overshadowed at the time by Pickles, the dog whose discovery brought him worldwide fame.

The 1966 tournament was the first World Cup really to tap into its commercial potential. It was also the first World Cup to enjoy blanket coverage on television, though not all games were shown live simply because a number took place simultaneously. That, and the fact that admission prices were three times higher than those of a normal Football League match, resulted in poor attendances at some games. Of course, England games, and those featuring the other teams considered to be among the favourites to win the cup – Brazil, West Germany and Portugal – were invariably sell-outs. For people to see football on television was still something of a treat. BBC TV's *Match of the Day* was less than two years old and had still to establish itself on our screens. The first *Match of the Day* had been broadcast in 1965 and featured Liverpool at home to Arsenal. The BBC obviously didn't comprehend just how much of a pull televised football was for its viewers because the first programmes were broadcast on BBC 2, which at the time not every TV owner had access to. What's more, the first programmes went out at 7.45 on a Saturday evening. The viewing figures generated during the World Cup of '66 went a long way to persuading the BBC that there was a huge audience for televised football, even in the form of highlights.

Following the World Cup, *MOTD* settled into its new slot on BBC 1 on Saturday night just as the pubs were closing, though the programme still only broadcast highlights of one First Division game. ITV had paved the way for televised football. In the late fifties and early sixties ITV had been so desperate to televise football that they occasionally broadcast matches involving the Show Biz XI that included stars such as Tommy Steele and Dave King. The audiences for these Sunday charity games convinced ITV that the public had a great appetite for football on television but initially they couldn't strike a deal with the Football League. Negotiations continued and in 1962–3 ITV regional companies negotiated a deal to occasionally show highlights of a league match in their area. The following season the ITV companies finalised a deal with the Football League that enabled them to broadcast the highlights from a regional game every Sunday teatime. Come the 1966 World Cup both BBC and ITV were geared to showing football, and the innovation of satellites enabled England's opening game against Uruguay to be seen by an audience of five hundred million people around the globe, at the time the world's largest television audience.

What they saw was a paradox: Wembley in carnival atmosphere anticipating a feast of entertainment followed by an awful game of football. England began well but Uruguay's negative tactics soon choked the life out of the game. Uruguay became a clinging cobweb of shifting pale blue shirts, hell-bent on suffocation rather than inspiration. For the supporters it was not riveting stuff. It was more like watching riveting.

I flashed a shot just wide of the post. Bobby Charlton had a thunderbolt of a shot charged down by a knot of defenders and I think that was the total sum of our efforts at goal. Try as we did, we just couldn't find a way through Uruguay's blanket defence. When the final whistle blew, the referee, Istvan Zsolt from Hungary, signalled the end of the game with an almost apologetic spread of his hands. The Wembley crowd booed Uruguay off the field. I felt very down; it had been a very dull and uninspiring start to the World Cup, for both England and me.

Alf had not completely abandoned the idea of using wingers and for our next game against Mexico he brought in Southampton's Terry Paine in place of John Connelly of Manchester United, with Martin Peters of West Ham slotting into midfield in preference to Alan Ball. England finally opened their goal account in this game and what a goal it was. Bobby Charlton received a pass deep in our own half of the field and glided down the centre of the pitch before striking a thirty-yard thunderbolt up into the right hand corner of the Mexico net. When Roger Hunt added a second, England were home and dry with their first win of the tournament.

We were cock-a-hoop in the dressing room after the game. We had three points from two games and had yet to concede a goal. Every one was praising Bobby Charlton for his great run and thunderbolt goal, though big Jack was at pains to remind everyone of his part in his brother's fantastic goal.

'It's all very well you lot praising our kid,' said Jack, 'his goal was a cracker. But what you all forget is, it was me who hit that two yard pass that sent him on his way!'

The England dressing room was in jubilant mood, but not every member of the squad was gloriously happy. Alan Ball was very upset at being left out of the team. Alan can be quite an emotional character and his emotions were getting the better of him. He was talking about walking out and going home, but back at our hotel over a few lagers Bobby Moore, Gordon Banks, Bobby and Jack Charlton and myself talked Alan round and persuaded him to buckle down and stick it out. Fortunately Alan saw sense, stayed and went on to play a key role in England's progress in the tournament and, of course, the victory over West Germany in the final.

Though I didn't score against Mexico I felt satisfied with my overall performance and contribution. Alf was seemingly satisfied with my efforts as well because he named me in the team for our final group game, against France. Liverpool's Ian Callaghan became the third winger tried by Alf when he replaced Terry Paine. England reached the quarter-finals with a 2-0 victory over France courtesy of two smartly taken goals from Callaghan's club-mate, Roger Hunt. The game, however, proved a nightmare for me. Our defence played very well. Bobby Moore and Jack Charlton were the linchpins and Martin Peters the link in a system which expanded and contracted to strangle the French whose only answer on a pitch made slippery by teeming rain was a fallible offside trap. Bobby Charlton wasn't his usual self and I hadn't hit top form either when a crunching tackle from France's Joseph Bonnel poleaxed me. Bonnel had dragged his studs down my shin and my leg opened up like a red rose towards the end of its bloom. There were no substitutes so, after having a dressing applied by our trainer Harold Shepherdson, I simply carried on playing. At this point I wasn't aware of the true extent of the injury, though it was very uncomfortable. It was a wet night and the Wembley turf was sodden. Towards the end of the game I thought I'd got a hole in my boot because I was aware that my sock was soaking. It was only when I bent down to do some running repairs that I realised it was soaked with blood and that the entire sock was crimson.

After the game I had fourteen stitches inserted in the wound on my leg, the scar is still clearly visible to this day. Back in my room in the hotel I lay in bed and was consumed by the reality of my situation. It sent shivers down my body. I realised there and then that, should England reach the final, I wouldn't be playing. In the darkness of my room I realised my World Cup was over.

England were due to play their quarter-final against

Argentina in three days. There was no way I would be fit for that match. Should England beat Argentina their semi-final was scheduled three days later. Again there was no way my injury would heal sufficiently within six days to allow me to play in the semi-final, should we get there. I knew that if England beat Argentina and went on to win their semi-final, there was little likelihood of Alf Ramsey changing a winning team for the World Cup Final itself. Even if my injury healed sufficiently within the ten-day period between the France game and the World Cup Final, I realised I was going to be on the bench in civvies with the remainder of the squad. I was very disappointed and down, but at no point was I ever bitter or resentful. That ain't me. When England did progress to the final I was delighted for my team-mates and the country, though at the same time very disappointed to have missed out on the greatest day in the history of English football. But my disappointment had nothing to do with any decision on the part of Alf or the fact that my replacement, Geoff Hurst, did so remarkably well and created history himself by becoming the only player to score a hat-trick in a World Cup Final. My disappointment was all to do with Bonnel of France and the injury I sustained following one of his challenges, and for the record I don't hold a grudge against him either. Injury is part and parcel of the lot of a professional footballer. I could have sustained that injury in training, or in our final warm-up match in Poland before our World Cup began. I got to play in three of England's games in that glorious World Cup and count myself fortunate in that respect. There were 1,800 English pros who hadn't made it to the World Cup. I have been totally honest about this. So I have to say that while I was 99 per cent certain that Alf would not change a winning team for the final, the remaining 1 per cent harboured the hope that he would and include me. On the morning of the final Alf was very distant and I sensed that he had made up his mind to pick an unchanged team. After breakfast I went back to my room and started packing my bags. Bobby Moore asked me what on earth I was doing.

'It's all over for me, mate,' I told him. 'I'm just getting ready for a quick getaway once the final is over.'

'You can do that tomorrow morning,' Bobby said. 'We'll all enjoy a few bevvies tonight, together, to celebrate us winning the World Cup.'

Alf didn't say much to me. He just told me that he was going with an unchanged team and hoped I would understand his reasons for having done that.

'Sure, Alf,' I told him. 'They'll win it for you and England.'

'I think so,' he said, and then took off to talk to the other lads who would be joining me on the sidelines.

Alf couldn't have said a lot more to me. He knew I was choked and disappointed but he was doing what he thought was right for the good of the team. There were ten other players in the squad as unlucky as me so there was no reason why Alf should single me out for a special word of sympathy. Not that I was seeking sympathy. I was very, very disappointed that my dream of playing for England in a World Cup Final had not been realised. But I was not bitter against Alf or anyone else. Alf had a job to do. He did it.

It says much for the tremendous spirit within that squad that all eleven players who had been left out gave their total support to the eleven who played against West Germany. We were out there on the pitch with them in spirit and come the final whistle in extra-time, I felt totally exhausted. It was as if I had been out there playing on the pitch myself.

When that final whistle blew I didn't immediately jump up and celebrate and neither did Alf. The whistle sounded but the West Germany full back Karl-Heinz Schnellinger continued to run with the ball and I believe for a brief moment Alf, like me, thought the game was still in progress. When it became apparent to all that the whistle we had heard was indeed the final whistle I ran on to the pitch and grabbed the first player I came across. Nobby Stiles. I danced around the pitch with everybody else but even in this moment of triumph and great happiness, deep down I felt my sadness. Throughout my nine years as a professional footballer I had dreamed of playing in a World Cup Final. I had missed out on the match of a lifetime and it hurt.

As the celebrations got into full swing that night, I slipped away, returned to our hotel, packed my bag and took off home. I was later told by Bobby Moore that Alf thought I had snubbed him after the game, but that was never the case. I was delighted for Alf and didn't want to put a downer on the greatest moment of his career by letting him see the hurt in my eyes.

Had there been substitutes in 1966, in all probability I would have been on the bench and I am sure with the game going into extra-time Alf would have put me on. That's my belief – but since there were no substitutes it's irrelevant.

That night I did get drunk. The next morning, Irene, myself and the children took off on the family holiday we had had planned for some months. I read the *Sunday People* on the plane. One of the headlines read 'England Create Football History'. That's what the 1966 World Cup had suddenly become for me – history.

England's World Cup success was not the beginning of a new era for English football. It was the end of an era. Our World Cup success was the end-product of the modernisation, coaching and tactical innovations that had begun in the late fifties. The progress English football had made following our acceptance in the mid-fifties that our football had fallen behind that of other countries resulted in England winning the World Cup. That progress and development failed to continue apace

after the success of 1966. England qualified for the 1970 World
Cup by virtue of being the holders and went out in the quarter-
finals. It would be another twelve years before England were
to qualify for another World Cup Finals. In nobody's book can
that be called progress.

After the initial euphoria of winning the World Cup had
died down, though English football was to change it did not
embark upon a new, exciting era of development and success as
many hoped.

That triumph was a watershed. English football was never
to be the same again. 4-4-2 and 4-3-3 brought with it better
organisation and the days of high-scoring matches drew to a
close. In winning the First Division title in 1961, Spurs scored
115 goals, the fourth time in five seasons that the Champions
had scored more than a century of goals. In 1962-3, when
Spurs finished as runners-up to Everton, we scored 111 league
goals. When Leeds United won the Championship in 1969
their total of sixty-six goals was the second highest tally in the
First Division. In scoring seventy-seven that season, Everton
were not only far and away the highest scoring team in
Division One, but in the entire Football League. In Divison
Four, Halifax Town were promoted as runners-up having
scored just fifty-three goals all season. Just a single goal more
than Peterborough United's Terry Bly had himself scored in
the same division in 1961.

Tactics and the fact that teams were becoming better
organised put paid to the open attacking play we had seen prior
to 1966. People ape success and for a number of years
following Alf's 'wingless wonders' of '66, the sight of a winger
delighting and disappointing in turn as he dribbled his way
up some muddy touchline disappeared from our grounds. The
4-4-2 and 4-4-3 formations and a greater desire not to concede
goals rather than score them beset the English game, and even
filtered down to parks football. Perversely a World Cup Final

that produced a thrilling game of football and six goals spawned a game which produced far fewer goals than before. When I first established myself in the Chelsea team in 1957–8 there was a total of 1,721 goals scored in the First Division. In 1968–9 that number had fallen by 469 to 1,252 goals. The following season the number of goals scored in Division One fell again, to 1,123. Within a ten-year period nigh on six hundred goals per season had disappeared from First Division matches alone.

In 1957–8 Leicester City finished the season fifth from bottom in Division One, though they scored ninety-one goals. In 1960–61 Newcastle United were relegated from the First Divison having scored eighty-six goals. When Derby County were crowned Champions in 1972 they had sixty-nine goals to their name. Even the great Liverpool side that won successive Championships in 1976 and '77 only managed sixty-six and sixty-two goals respectively. In 1960–61 only three First Division teams scored less than Liverpool's total of sixty-two that brought them the Championship in 1977, and I don't have to tell you which end of the table those three clubs finished.

The Boxing Day fixtures of 1963 produced a goal glut that was extraordinary even by the standards of the time. Spurs were involved in a 4–4 draw at West Bromwich Albion, our goals coming from Bobby Smith, Cliff Jones and two from myself. Back in the dressing room after the game I listened to the wireless and was gobsmacked by the series of results I heard. Our match against West Brom had been a very open and entertaining game as the eight goals suggests. I thought such a game would make the headlines on *Sports Report* but it was overshadowed by the amazing events that had occurred elsewhere. The results from the First Division read as follows: Blackpool 1 Chelsea 5; Burnley 6 Manchester United 1; Fulham 10 Ipswich Town 1; Leicester City 2 Everton 0;

Liverpool 6 Stoke City 1; Nottingham Forest 3 Sheffield United 3; Sheffield Wednesday 3 Bolton Wanderers 0; West Bromwich Albion 4 Tottenham Hotspur 4; West Ham United 2 Blackburn Rovers 8; Wolves 3 Aston Villa 3.

I was as astounded as all my Spurs team-mates. A total of sixty-six goals had been scored in ten First Division matches. High scoring games were, however, not limited to the First Division. Elsewhere, Manchester City beat Scunthorpe United 8-1, Coventry beat Shrewsbury Town 8-1, Aldershot won 5-4 at home to Tranmere Rovers and Bradford City beat Barrow 7-1. In the newspapers the following morning the goalscorers appeared like lists of eleven-plus successes.

I'm not saying English football changed for the worse following 1966, only that it did change. For decades terrace songs had been part and parcel of a football match. When I played at West Ham United I'd hear the Hammers fans singing 'I'm Forever Blowing Bubbles'. At Newcastle United it was 'The Blaydon Races', at Charlton, 'When the Red Red Robin Comes Bob Bob Bobbing Along' and of course at Spurs it was 'Glory, Glory Hallelujah'. The nation got behind England for the 1966 World Cup. The English supporters at Wembley were united in their support of the team and wanted to display that support. Though the English supporters were united as one, they came from all manner of clubs and therefore did not have a uniform song to sing. So they simply chanted 'Eng-land, Eng-land' over and over again.

The 1966 World Cup tournament was the first to enjoy blanket coverage on TV. A number of supporters watching at home heard this chanting and when they returned to the terraces of their respective clubs they adopted the habit. Instead of 'Eng-land, Eng-land' they simply chanted the name of their club. I suppose such supporters were attempting to recreate the big-match atmosphere of Wembley during the World Cup at their own grounds. In addition to which, there was an element of reflected glory. As a result, following England's success in 1966 chanting on the terraces became commonplace at our football grounds. Football supporters no longer wanted 'community singing' at Wembley where both sets of supporters sung old favourites such as 'I'm A Lassie from Lancashire' or 'Underneath the Arches' while being conducted by Frank Rae. In the main, those who sung at football matches were young, and in the sixties the young wanted to do their own thing. Their 'own thing' had no place for the traditional old ways. Chanting took off in a big way after 1966 and in many respects changed the culture of the football terraces.

Young working people now had more disposable income and with the advent of motorways going to away games became easier. Where previously a club might enjoy the support of a couple of coach loads of fans at an away game, in the late sixties big clubs could enjoy the support of 1,000 and more. Such a number made their presence felt on a terrace and the constant chanting of the name of their team brought an element of friction to grounds.

It would be overly simplistic of me to suggest that this was the start of hooliganism in football. There are many other factors to be taken into consideration with regard to the growth of hooliganism in the seventies and eighties, but the seeds of such were planted post '66. Support at football matches appeared to change in the aftermath of the World Cup. The terraces lost much of the tolerance, conviviality and bonhomie that had previously existed.

During a television interview immediately after the World Cup Final, Kenneth Wolstenholme asked Alf what he felt about his team.

'Great pride,' said Alf, 'they have been magnificent throughout the tournament. They did a very professional job.'

Alf's reference to his players (of which I was one) having

done a 'very professional job' was to have a great influence on
the way managers, coaches, players and supporters were to
view football in the future, though I don't doubt for one
moment that Alf never realised the significance of what he had
said or envisaged what the consequences of his words would
be.

England's historic success was seen to be the result of
players being 'professional' and 'doing a professional job'. Alf
had had a gameplan and he picked the players to suit that
gameplan. What he didn't do was create a gameplan to suit the
styles of the players at his disposal.

Each player had a job to do within that gameplan. They did
it and England won the World Cup. Though players enjoyed
a degree of freedom within this gameplan, there was no place
for a player who might want to stamp his own idiosyncratic
style on the course of a game. No place for a maverick with a
penchant for playing to the crowd. Players had to be
professional and do the job they were being paid to do.

The modernisation of English football had picked up
momentum since the late fifties. Even before 1966 coaches
were having a bigger say in how the game should be played and
teams were better organised. By referring to the pride he felt
in his players having done 'a professional job', Alf unwittingly
tolled the death knell for players who were given to fully
expressing themselves in the course of a game. Being
'professional' seeped into the subconscious of the game and
any player who took it upon himself to play-act in the course
of a match, or play to the gallery, was deemed to be
'unprofessional'. As such an important element of British
football was lost. In the late sixties and the seventies gifted
individuals such as Rodney Marsh, Alan Hudson, Stan Bowles,
Tony Currie and Robin Friday (Reading) found themselves
branded as mavericks and unprofessional. The notion that you
had to be 'professional' at all times killed off footballers who

played to the gallery, but strengthened the role of others in the game.

The role of a coach grew in importance. In the sixties and seventies the play on the field was dictated by the likes of Bobby Charlton, Dave Mackay, Alan Mullery, Colin Bell, Rodney Marsh, Alan Hudson and George Best. After 1966 the influence of coaches grew and carried on growing, so that we have the situation today whereby coaches dictate proceedings from the sidelines and are loath to allow any player to express himself or take it upon himself to dictate a game. That is one of the biggest differences between football in the sixties and now. Ostensibly it is now coaches and not players who dictate games.

Of course coaches have a positive role to play in football today. One aspect of their role is to teach youngsters skills and technique, though in saying that I am mindful of what Stanley Matthews once said to me on the subject of coaches: 'You can coach a youngster and improve his skill, technique and awareness,' said Stan, 'but you can't put in what God left out.'

The World Cup of 1966 and the success of England touched every part of the game. It being a World Cup, the programmes that were issued for games were special issues. The tournament brochure on sale at all the group games was a lavish production containing photographs of every participating player. The programme for the final was also a special issue. Appropriately, it had sixty-six pages and contained not only pictures of every member of the England and West Germany squads, but numerous full page photographs featuring action shots from games leading up to the final itself. Once supporters saw these lavishly illustrated programmes, the eight-page programmes issued by their own clubs, many of which up to 1966 rarely carried more than a single photograph, appeared comparatively poor value for money. In the wake of the World Cup clubs started to produce more lavish match-day programmes to match the expectations of their supporters. Before 1966 some clubs did produce programmes that were very informative and contained a number of photographs. Chelsea, Spurs, Arsenal and West Ham are prime examples. Interestingly, the match-day programmes of Chelsea, Spurs, Arsenal and West Ham also stood out from the rest in that they didn't contain any advertisements. It was as if the clubs thought their good names would be besmirched by resorting to vulgar commercialism within the pages of their official organs. Again the influence of the 1966 World Cup would, in time, change that.

The 1966 tournament was the first World Cup really to exploit its commercial potential. Global television coverage proved fertile ground for such embryonic commercialism. The 1966 World Cup had its own corporate logo, World Cup Willie, a little lion bedecked in a Union Jack shirt. The Willie logo appeared on all manner of commercial products and World Cup souvenirs, from breakfast cereal and soft drinks, to ashtrays and T-shirts. There was even a 'World Cup Willie' record. Here the football authorities showed how out of touch they were with the youth culture of the day. The World Cup Willie song was what you would term a 'novelty song'. It was recorded by Lonnie Donegan, who was a hark back to the skiffle days of the fifties. Lonnie may have been a great artiste in his own right, but the target audience of the 'World Cup Willie' song – young kids – just didn't relate to him. They were interested in the Beatles and the Stones. Lonnie Donegan was someone their mums and dads had listened to. Though Lonnie Donegan's 'World Cup Willie' song received a lot of patriotic air play on BBC radio, it rarely featured on the pirate radio stations which the vast majority of youngsters listened to at the time, and didn't become a hit.

The 'World Cup Willie' song apart, the 1966 World Cup proved a tremendous success in more ways than one. Though attendances for some group matches were disappointing, generally attendances were good. Revenue from television rights and money generated from what was the first true commercial exploitation of a World Cup made healthy profits for both FIFA and the Football Association. It was reported that the FA had made a profit of nigh on £3 million from the World Cup. The FA told the press that a good chunk of this money would be used to create a network of regional coaching centres throughout the country with the aim of developing the game at grass-roots level. Whatever became of that idea? Winning the World Cup in 1966 remains a historic achievement in English football. A great honour was bestowed upon England, but great honours carry with them a heavy burden. To this day no England team has emulated the success of the side of '66 and the sense of expectation and failure has, over the years, weighed heavily on countless England teams and managers. England expects. English football has lived with expectation since 1966 and continues to do so.

Winning the World Cup in 1966 was not only a landmark in English football, it has proved to be a benchmark. Though the transition didn't happen overnight, English football was never to be the same again. The way the game was played changed. The attitude of managers and players changed. The role of the coach changed. The atmosphere on the terraces changed. Even match-day programmes changed. The commercial potential of football was seen to have set its roots in very fertile ground, all of it mainly as a result of the 1966 World Cup.

Around the same time, the Beatles released their *Sgt. Pepper* album. All pop music prior to the release of this album is now seen to have been leading up to *Sgt. Pepper*, and all pop music since in some ways, owes a debt to that groundbreaking album. The same can be said of English football and the 1966 World Cup. The modernisation of the English game which began in the late fifties resulted in winning the World Cup, and the game we know today has stemmed from the events of 1966. Winning the World Cup had a profound effect on some people. It changed the lives of Alf Ramsey and Geoff Hurst. But, contrary to common belief, it didn't change mine.

CHAPTER THIRTEEN

A WHITER SHADE OF PALE

Spurs' warm-up to the 1966–7 season involved pre-season friendlies against Dundee and a Polish Select XI. I was feeling fit and was raring to go. Against Dundee I scored two of our goals in a 3-2 win and scored again in our 2-1 victory over the Poles. There then followed a friendly 'behind closed doors' against Charlton Athletic where I managed to score four in Spurs' 6-2 victory.

Spurs opening match of the season was at home to Leeds United, considered at the time to be one of the very best sides in Europe. There were only five minutes on the clock when the cockerel that stands atop the press box high up in the main stand at White Hart Lane was crowing its head off. Alan Gilzean played me through, I cut the ball back into the path of Alan Mullery and we had the perfect start to a new season. Nine minutes later, Alan returned the compliment and I sallied forth before sliding the ball past the Leeds goalkeeper Gary Sprake to make it 2-0. The shirt sleeved crowd of 44,000 were treated to another Spurs goal courtesy of Alan Gilzean and we ended up beating Leeds by 3-1.

Spurs' next game was a disappointing 2-0 defeat at Stoke City after which we hit the form button losing just one of our following nine games and registering seven wins in the process. Come 1 October I had scored nine goals in ten league games as well as seven in three pre-season matches. To be honest I didn't feel like a player in 'immediate decline'.

I played a total of thirty-eight games in the First Division for Spurs in 1966–7 and ended with twenty-five goals to my name. Having been involved for most of the season in the race for the Championship title, Spurs eventually finished third on goal difference behind the runners-up, Nottingham Forest, with both teams trailing Manchester United by four points. It was disappointing not to have won the Championship, but the fact that we had been in with a shout until the last two games of the season, and enjoyed the added bonus of a great run in the FA Cup that took us to Wembley served to create a fantastic dressing-room atmosphere.

Bill Nicholson had created another stylish team. Though we would never scale the heights achieved by the 'Super Spurs' side of the early sixties, we proved that the glory days at White Hart Lane were not over. Spurs hadn't won a trophy for four years and we were mindful that in the eyes of the club and its supporters, that simply wasn't good enough. So we did something about it.

By 1966–7 the players Bill had brought to the club, such as Alan Mullery, Pat Jennings, Cyril Knowles, Alan Gilzean, Mike England and Terry Venables, had got over their growing pains and established themselves as top-quality players. I felt we had come through our period of transience and now had a settled team playing attractive, fluid football. Spurs were up and running again like a well-oiled machine. We had developed a great understanding with one another and, driven by the talismanic qualities and boundless enthusiasm of Dave Mackay, I fancied us to beat any team.

It was almost like the glory days of the early sixties again. Somewhere high above White Hart Lane a star danced and we produced some exhilarating performances and were involved in numerous games where the entertainment was top-drawer stuff.

Nottingham Forest had a very good team. We played Forest at White Hart Lane at the end of September and preserved our 100 per cent record in what turned out to be a classic game of football. Alan Mullery's goal in the fourth minute, driven with great power from the edge of the penalty area, was similar in execution to the one he had netted against Leeds United on the opening day of the season. When I coaxed the ball into the net in the seventeenth minute following a centre from Jimmy Robertson it seemed we were launched on a comfortable road to victory. However, Frank Wignall's goal, driven home low and hard following a raid down their left in the thirty-third minute, proved just the tonic Forest needed. They started to up the ante and as time wore on sensed they had the chance of taking at least a point.

The game ebbed and flowed. There were bouts of breathtaking one-touch football and the tempo of the game continued to quicken as both sides fought for ascendancy. In the second half we lost the firm grip we had exerted early in the game, though there were times when I felt we were unlucky not to add to our lead. A sublime Spurs move that involved a dozen passes ended with me crashing the ball against the Forest crossbar and Peter Grummitt produced a spectacular one-handed save to deny Jimmy Robertson from the rebound. Minutes from the end the Forest full-back John Winfield burst upfield to let fly a tremendous twenty-five yard shot that made our crossbar reverberate and hum like a tuning fork. When the final whistle sounded the 35,000 crowd stood to applaud both teams from the pitch.

Our next game at Fulham was another thrilling encounter. Alan Gilzean gave us the lead from a pass from Terry Venables after only two minutes. I felt we were totally in control of the game but it is one of the great attractions of football that a game can be turned on its head in a matter of minutes, as was the case in this match. On eleven minutes Steve Earle rose like a Bero cake to head in a free kick from Johnny Haynes. From the restart, Johnny won possession and threaded one of his perfectly weighted passes through our defence for Allan Clarke to run on to. Young 'Sniffer' belied his inexperience when confronted with the oncoming Pat Jennings and calmly passed the ball into our net. Having been a goal to the good in the space of a minute, we were now chasing the game. Chase it we did. Right from the word go. From the restart Gilly tapped the ball to me. I laid it back to Dave Mackay who hit a great crossfield ball into the path of Jimmy Robertson who was in full flight down our right wing. Jimmy cut inside and hit a sweet shot wide of the Fulham keeper Tony Macedo to put us back on level terms. Three goals in little over two minutes. A packed Craven Cottage was going wild.

I remember it going dark after Jimmy's equaliser. Clouds the colour of ebony gathered over the Cottage and someone up there opened the sluice gates. The rain came down in torrents and we soon found ourselves sloshing about on a pitch that was like molasses. The pace of the game inevitably slackened but when the storm passed over, both sides kick-started the tempo. Only some inspired goalkeeping from Tony Macedo kept us at bay but in the seventy-seventh minute Terry Venables got the better of him.

We won a corner on the right. Jimmy Robertson floated the ball into the Fulham penalty area, Gilly knocked the ball down to me and I tried my luck at goal. The shot came back from a maze of legs, Steve Earle swung one of his and the ball left the penalty area in an arc and dropped in the path of Terry Venables who promptly dispatched it into the Fulham net for what was Tel's first ever goal for Spurs.

Even at that stage the game had produced more drama than a season at the Old Vic, but this game still wasn't done. A minute later Gilly was on the end of a cross from Frank Saul to send the ball goalbound. Tony Macedo arced backwards and managed to push the ball up into the air; when it came back down I was there to make it 4-2. Three minutes later Steve Earle hit one of those crosses that's impossible to defend. The ball swung away from Pat Jennings and there was the Fulham winger Graham Leggat, whose header set up a grandstand finish.

Even Fulham supporters of many years standing were in agreement. The game had been one of the best they had witnessed down at the Cottage for years. The press had also enjoyed their afternoon out. Writing in the *Daily Express*, Norman Giller said, 'This was a game to warm the heart on what was a day of filthy weather. Exciting, dramatic, pulsating, thrilling. Those words do not do justice to the fayre served up by two teams bent on achieving victory by way of superbly entertaining football.'

I always enjoyed going down to the Cottage. Games against Fulham were keenly contested and the football invariably open and expansive. Probably too open for the liking of many Fulham supporters given that Spurs usually won there. After a game at Fulham there was always the treat of conversations with the many great characters connected with the club at the time. Fulham was an unconventional club. As well as Tommy Trinder, the bandleader Chappie D'Amato was also a director for a time, as was 'The Clown Prince of Soccer', the great Len Shackleton. Everything about Fulham appeared unconventional. Craven Cottage had once been the home of the writer Bulwer Lytton. Lytton wrote *The Last Days of Pompeii* there and I suppose there is more than a touch of irony in that. John Moynihan described the Fulham of the sixties as being 'a side of comic triers watched by garrulous actors who detest the thorough efficiency of other teams that are now highly organised'.

There was some truth in that, though the term 'comic triers' is harsh. Fulham contained a lot of players who were comical but the likes of Tosh Chamberlain, Maurice Cook and Bobby Keetch, all at the club in the early sixties, could also play. As could their team-mates, George Cohen, Bobby Robson and, of course, the peerless Johnny Haynes. Likewise those who came later, Allan Clarke, Steve Earle, John Dempsey and Les Barrett.

Following a game the Spurs players would join the Fulham lads and their hangers-on for a drink in the Cottage itself. Over a beer we'd swap football gossip and the latest tales of the escapades of Tommy Trinder, Bobby Keetch, Tosh Chamberlain or whoever.

One such tale in particular comes to mind. Bobby Keetch was a real 'Bobby Dazzler'. He was a tough-tackling defender whose blond hair, good looks and impressive physique made him very popular with what at the time were termed 'dolly birds'.

After a game Bobby could be seen driving up and down the Fulham High Road with some gorgeous young girl at his side. Saturday night would find him in Wheeler's club in Soho dressed in an Edwardian coat over a multicoloured shirt that looked as if it had been designed by Mary Quant when she was suffering from a migraine. Away from football Bobby would talk of Pop Art, Bob Dylan, Vietnam, the latest edition of the alternative newspaper *IT* and why the Stax label had more 'soul' than Tamla Motown, holding court with a bevy of beautiful young girls. To listen to Bobby you'd never think he was a tough, uncompromising footballer. That he was had as much to do with him being a product of the times as it did his own cosmopolitan character. With the emergence of George Best who had been dubbed 'The Fifth Beatle', the fame of some top footballers exceeded the game itself, something that had been recognised by the actor Richard Harris, who on being asked if he had been a star in rugby league, replied, 'There are no stars in rugby league. That's soccer.'

Bobby was a well-known footballer but not one who enjoyed so-called star status. At the end of a season Bobby was called into the office of the Fulham manager Vic Buckingham to discuss a new contract. When Bobby sat down, Vic drew his attention to two contracts that were on his desk.

'I'm going to give you the choice of two options,' Buckingham informed Bobby. 'The first contract is for two years and will pay you £25 a week, win, lose or draw. So no matter how well or how badly the team does in the next two seasons, you will be paid £25. No more, no less.'

Bobby wasn't enamoured with that and asked Buckingham about the other contract on offer.

'This contract can earn you the sort of money you would receive if you were at Spurs, Arsenal or Manchester United,' said Buckingham. Bobby immediately sat up, keen to hear more.

'This contract will pay you only a basic of £17 a week,' said Buckingham, 'but the attraction is the bonuses. Should we lose, you will just pick up the seventeen pounds. But for a home draw you'll receive an extra £3 and for a home win, an extra £8. For a draw away from home you'll receive an extra £10 which will give you £27. For an away win, there's a bonus of £15, making your wage £32. But that's not all. Should this club achieve a top four finish to the season, you'll receive a lump-sum bonus of £350. Should we reach the FA Cup Final, your bonus will be £500 and should we win the Cup, you'll receive a £1,000 bonus in your hand!'

For a moment Bobby said nothing as he mulled over what was on offer, then reached for the pen on Buckingham's desk.

'I'll take the twenty-five quid,' said Bobby.

Following a 3-0 defeat at West Bromwich Albion on Boxing Day, Spurs lost only once in twenty-eight league and cup matches that formed the second half of the 1966–7 season. It was a great run. Though it didn't clinch us the League title there was to be the considerable consolation of another glorious success at Wembley in the FA Cup.

Our single defeat was at Old Trafford against our fellow title contenders Manchester United. It was a game in which I was looking to continue my quest to create a new club record of scoring in nine consecutive matches, one I had set back in 1961–2. I had netted in seven consecutive games for Spurs and though I wasn't really bothered about the record, the newspapers made much of the fact that I was two goals light of a new record. It was not to be. Our game at United was featured on *Match of the Day* and viewers saw an enthralling game of entertaining cut-and-thrust football which, unbelievably, produced only a single goal. Unfortunately that goal was scored by United in the dying embers of the game; though we produced a spirited late rally, it was to no avail. I'm not saying that defeat at United cost us the title because the game took place in mid-February and we still had sixteen league games to play. We were undefeated in those sixteen matches, registering eleven victories, but even that super run proved in the end not enough to enable Spurs to overhaul Best, Law, Charlton and co. Our undoing was a sequence of poor results back in the autumn when we failed to win a single game in six. It says much for the character and spirit of the players that we put that run of poor form behind us to launch a concerted challenge for the title, but though we never thought as much at the time, the damage had been done.

It's an indication of the type of football that we were playing that Spurs featured regularly on *Match of the Day* during this season. One such game was our 4-0 home victory over Newcastle United. I scored twice in this game and one of the goals still pops up on television from time to time. I picked the ball up just inside the Newcastle half and simply started running. Tackles came in but somehow I managed to avoid them and skip past the Newcastle defenders to find myself in their penalty area with only their goalkeeper Gordon Marshall to beat. As Marshall came out I simply upped a gear, swerved away to my right and passed the ball into the empty net. Oddly, I had scored a carbon-copy goal the previous season in a 4-0 home win over Blackpool and that was also captured by *Match of the Day* cameras.

Though denied the Championship by Manchester United, Spurs sated the appetite of our supporters for success by winning the FA Cup. The third round pitched us in a London derby away to Millwall. Once again the *Match of the Day* cameras were there to record the event but what they recorded was ninety gruelling and goalless minutes of football. The pace of the game scarcely slackened from first to final whistle, and if we had taken our chances there would have been no need for a replay. But Millwall's defence put up a heroic performance and when their goalkeeper Lawrie Leslie wasn't putting paid to our efforts on goal, it was his fellow defenders Brian Snowdon, Harry Cripps, Tom Wilson, John Gilchrist and Ken Jones who were.

A crowd of 41,260 saw the first game at The Den and an even larger crowd of 58,189 turned up at White Hart Lane for the replay. We pounded the Millwall defence but yet again their defenders displayed considerable resolve and mettle. Millwall lived up to their nickname of 'Lions' that night and only a well-taken goal from Alan Gilzean eventually broke the deadlock.

In our game against Portsmouth in round four, Pompey showed similar resolve. We camped in the Portsmouth half of the field in the first half but simply couldn't break down a defence well marshalled by my old Chelsea team-mate Ron Tindall. In the second half, however, it was a different story. Seven minutes after the break Alan Gilzean gave us the lead with a spectacular diving header following a free kick for a foul on Cliff Jones. Minutes later, Alan did it again, coolly finishing after Jimmy Robertson and I had exchanged a series of passes. Alan's second was hotly contested by the Portsmouth players who believed he was offside when I played the ball to him. The referee, Mr Mitchell from Lancashire, however, waved away their protests and, hand on heart, I think he got it right. In the sixty-sixth minute I fastened on to a midfield pass from Gilly and accelerated away before putting the tie beyond Portsmouth's reach. Pompey did score late in the game when a shot from the former Burnley centre forward Ray Pointer smacked against a post and Ron Tindall pounced to score what I later told him must have been his first goal since 1909!

You need a bit of luck in the Cup and we were getting it. When the draw was made for round five Spurs came out first, followed by Bristol City, who at the time were struggling in Division Two. (Then as now, each team was allocated a number, but try as I might, I could never make sense of the logic behind the sequence of numbers. In terms of alphabetical order, Torquay United preceded Tottenham. Should Torquay come out in the draw before us and have the number twenty-six, I naturally assumed Tottenham would be number twenty-seven, but that was never the case. Answers on a postcard please.) Such was the appeal of the FA Cup in this period, even the draw attracted a massive audience when broadcast live on the radio. The draw for each round of the FA Cup was broadcast on a Monday lunchtime on what was then called the Light Programme, now Radio Two. Some things lend themselves more to radio than television and this is very much the case with a live FA Cup draw.

In the sixties television ignored the draw completely, simply because there was no daytime TV other than a lunchtime news bulletin and programmes for schools. When it did move to television, the draw lost its drama and mystery. One of those minor though important rituals in football, one that separated the fanatic from the passive supporter, had gone, handed over to the unforgiving cameras of television by programme makers determined to 'create an atmosphere'. Little did they appreciate that radio did exactly that.

In 2003 the draw returned to radio after an absence of some years, but it still goes out live on TV. Where television coverage of the Cup draw really overeggs the pudding is the draw for the semi-finals. Once the first two clubs have been drawn the show is over, but not for television. We now have to endure the irrelevancy of the second part of the semi-final draw knowing full well who will play who. The semi-final draw has much in keeping with bad sex. Much anticipation and excitement, followed by an event that's over in seconds that leaves you deeply dissatisfied. Television and hyperbole has robbed the Cup draw of its sense of drama and I can't help feeling it's all the poorer for that.

Though Bristol City put up a doughty fight at White Hart Lane, Spurs were always in command of the game and comfortable winners in the end. I scored both our goals in a 2-0 victory that took us into the quarter-finals where our opponents were Birmingham City.

An all-ticket crowd of 51,500 turned up at St Andrews to see a very tense, dull game of football. We missed our best chance of the game just before half-time when Frank Saul turned Jimmy Robertson's centre wide of Jim Herriot, but also wide of the Birmingham goal. The nearest Birmingham came to breaking the deadlock came in the seventy-fifth minute when Pat Jennings saved at the second attempt an effort from my old Chelsea buddy, Bert Murray. Apart from those incidents much of the play was confined to a battle in midfield. Typical cup-tie action it was not.

The replay was totally different. I think Birmingham believed their chance of beating us had gone with the draw at

their place, because in the replay we swept them aside. Terry
Venables and I got a couple of goals apiece and further goals
from Frank Saul and Alan Gilzean gave us a very comfortable
6-0 win, which seemed to make a nonsense of that very tight
first encounter.

The semi-finals pitched Spurs against Nottingham Forest
and Chelsea against Leeds United. We played Forest at
Hillsborough in front of 55,000 fans. Spurs' seven cup ties had
been watched by a total of 377,773 spectators, an average of
53,967 per game. That was the magic and the draw of the FA
Cup in the sixties. In 1966-7 just under four million people
attended FA Cup matches from round one to the final. The
following season that number was 3,586,824. In 2001-2 the
total number of fans attending FA Cup matches was 1,809,093.
Although many grounds do not boast the capacities they did in
the sixties, the fall in attendances for FA Cup matches in recent
years has nonethelesss been alarming. What have FA officials
and marketing johnnies done to the Cup? In 2002-3 only
5,436 turned up at Burnley to see their third round replay
against Grimsby Town. A meagre crowd of 14,500 were
present at the Stadium of Light to witness Sunderland's replay
against fellow Premiership side Bolton Wanderers. After that
tie the then Sunderland manager Howard Wilkinson told the
press that his club's priority was to stay in the Premiership.
Said Wilkinson, 'To finish the season seventeenth in the
Premiership would be like winning the FA Cup for this club.'

Once the FA Cup had much to do with giant killing, now it
seems that many people in the game are intent on killing the
Cup. The desire to retain a place in the Premiership at all costs
and the pursuit of money has reduced the importance of the
FA Cup in the eyes of supporters. If managers don't believe the
Cup to be important, why should supporters? I have always
believed that football, in particular the FA Cup, is about the
pursuit of glory and sporting distinction, not the pursuit of

In action for England against the Rest of the World in a match played in October 1963 to celebrate the Centenary of the Football Association. Goals from Terry Paine and yours truly helped England to a 2-1 victory over a star-studded World XI. *(EMPICS/S&G/Alpha)*

168 MOOR LANE, CRANHAM, ESSEX.

UPMINSTER 7373

I check in the wing mirror that my 'cheese-cutter' cap is on straight. It's 1963 and the lorry is part of a haulage business I started while a Spurs player. By 1970, the various businesses I ran with my brother-in-law Tom had a turnover of over £1 million. *(Daily Mail)*

September 1964: I score my 100th goal for Spurs against West Bromwich Albion. *(Daily Mail)*

With my dad Jim at White Hart Lane, 1964–5 season. Dad was treasurer of Fanshaw Old Boys and the players of that team were my childhood heroes. *(Jimmy Greaves)*

Visiting Henry Cooper as he prepares for his fight against
Muhammad Ali in 1966. From left to right, Jack Charlton,
Ray Wilson, Bobby Moore, me and Bobby Charlton.
(Daily Mirror/Monte Fresco)

I try my luck in England's third match of the 1966 World Cup against
France. A little later, French defender Joseph Bonnel caught me with a
late challenge and my World Cup was over. *(Popperfoto)*

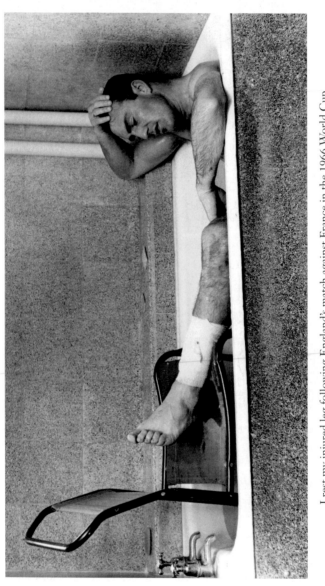

I rest my injured leg following England's match against France in the 1966 World Cup. The gash required fourteen stitches and the scar is still prominent today. *(Topham Picturepoint)*

The pre-match kick-about on my debut for West Ham United at Maine Road, 1970. West Ham beat Manchester City 5-1 and once again I scored on my debut. The pitch is like molasses – and this was before the game! *(Sporting Pictures)*

My Testimonial match at Spurs against Feyenoord in 1972. A crowd of 45,799 turned up to see what was a very competitive match and a great night for me. Spurs won 2-1 and here I am opening the scoring (despite the Feyenoord players' justified appeals for offside).
(Daily Mail/E. Sampson)

With two footballing greats, Eusebio and Gordon Banks, prior to an exhibition match in the USA. *(Daily Mirror/ H. Prosser)*

A low point: the sad, soulless eyes say it all. *(News of the World)*

With my good pal Ian St John during *Saint and Greavsie* in 1985. A few years later, with *S&G* still high in the ratings, we were on our way out – our informed and entertaining approach to football considered out of step with 'the serious business of football'. *(London Weekend Television)*

Lining up with the *Sporting Triangles* team at Central TV in 1987. Left to right, me, Bryan Robson, Nick Owen, Seb Coe, Tessa Sanderson, Dennis Taylor and Lloyd Honeyghan. *(Central Independent Television)*

With my good pal Les Scott, who collaborated with me on the writing of this book.

At home with Irene and six of our ten grandchildren. Irene and I love visits from the grandchildren we call 'The Kling-ons'. When they visit Irene is given to saying, 'It's life, Jim, but not as we know it.'
(*News of the World*)

money. When Spurs reached the FA Cup Final in 1967 our supporters had a great day out at Wembley and we were fortunate enough to create a golden moment that would live forever in the memories of those who were present. I think some of today's managers should think about that before fielding weakened teams in the FA Cup in the belief that they must 'get their priorities right'. These days it would appear that the needs of shareholders have priority over the needs of supporters. I can't help but believe that's wrong.

In our semi-final against Nottingham Forest I produced something that was unusual for me. I scored from twenty-five yards. We were attacking the Leppings Lane End when the ball was half cleared from the Forest penalty area. I was in what you could term the old inside left position some seven yards outside the box and the ball came to me as if I'd beckoned it. I got my head over the ball and simply rifled it back towards goal. We were in the lead.

Many semi-finals tend to be dull, unenterprising games because there is so much tension to the play with both sides knowing they are just one step away from Wembley. Our game against Forest was an exception to this rule. It was an enthralling game with both teams intent on giving it a go. In the end a second Spurs goal from Frank Saul gave us a narrow 2-1 victory. I think we just about deserved it and with Chelsea also enjoying a narrow 1-0 win over Leeds in the other semi-final the press boys scribbled 'Cockney Cup Final' in their notebooks for the first time in the twentieth century.

Spurs' inspired form in the league and our great FA Cup run created a superb dressing-room atmosphere. It was a joy to turn up every day at our training ground in Cheshunt because, though there would be a tough morning of training ahead, it was fun. There was a great team spirit among the players and we were forever playing tricks on one another and having a lark. Here the miscreants were usually Dave Mackay, Terry

Venables, Gilly and yours truly. One trick we perpetrated on several occasions was at the expense of Spurs' assistant manager Eddie Baily. As we were leaving the training field we'd call over one of the young apprentices and inform him a message had arrived for Eddie, then ask the apprentice to run over and deliver it.

The apprentice would run over to Eddie and we would fall about laughing when he delivered the message – 'Mr Baily, your brother, Bill, has telephoned to say he won't be coming home.' The more we played that prank on Eddie the more irritated he became. The more irritated Eddie became, the more we did it, and the more we laughed.

After training there would be more larks in the showers. One popular prank was to squeeze shampoo on someone's head as he was in the process of rinsing his hair of the shampoo he had already applied. Again we'd be in fits watching Frank Saul or Cyril Knowles frantically trying to rinse their hair wondering why on earth there was still so much shampoo. Occasionally someone would start singing, which was the cue for us all to join in and put silly lyrics to the song. We'd take it in turns to sing a verse, each trying to outdo the other in producing an alternative lyric that was both funny and clever. I can't remember exactly what was sung, but a vague recollection tells me it would go something like this. Dave Mackay would kick it off by singing the first verse of 'Amore' and the rest of us would pick it up from there:

Dave:	When the moon hits your eye
	Like a big pizza pie
	That's amore!
Terry Venables:	When we're down at West Ham
	There's a hell of a man
	It's Bobby Moore, eh?
Gilly:	When you're down on the course

> And you're feeding some horse
> That's some more hay!

Alan Mullery: When you have no left peg
> 'Cos an eel ate your leg
> That's a moray

Greaves: When Othello says 'By heck'
> Who has my wife by the neck
> It's a Moor, eh?

Cliff Jones: When a stone with a hole
> Is said to have soul
> It's Henry Moore, eh?

At which point Dave Mackay would put an end to the nonsense by singing,

> I've had quite enough
> Of this bloody silly stuff
> So, no more, eh?

Although Tottenham versus Chelsea was the first all-London Cup Final of the century, there was a big difference between the two clubs and the respective teams. Spurs were a mixture of seasoned players such as myself, Alan Mullery, Mike England, Terry Venables, Jimmy Robertson, Dave Mackay and Cliff Jones. The 'kids' were Cyril Knowles, twenty-three, Pat Jennings, twenty-two, and right back Joe Kinnear, at twenty the youngest member of the team. I was confident about our chances of winning the Cup because we played enterprising, thoughtful football and had enough experience in the side for us not to be overawed by the big occasion.

Chelsea, on the other hand, were the bright young things, London's glamour team. In 1967 London was the creative heart of world fashion and pop music. The epicentre was the King's Road, just around the corner from Stamford Bridge. It boasted trendy, go-getting young people who were at the forefront of fashion and fad, and the Chelsea team reflected that image.

Chelsea were watched by the stars of film and TV. They even had Richard Attenborough on their board. Celebrities such as Michael Caine, Michael Crawford, Jane Seymour, Lance Percival, Richard O'Sullivan, Vidal Sassoon, Ronnie Corbett, Honor Blackman, Richard Harris and Peter O'Toole were regular supporters and were occasionally joined by Hollywood stars such as Raquel Welch and Steve McQueen. A lot of Chelsea supporters came out of the fashionable watering holes dotted along the King's Road, whereas Spurs fans appeared happy in the snugs and smoke rooms of the pubs around White Hart Lane.

Chelsea were the team that epitomised 'Swinging London'. They played the game with style, swagger and flamboyance. Chelsea were professional in their approach, but I sensed their players were wrapped up in the occasion of Wembley. It was as if they saw the Cup Final as being *the* socialite party of the year. I knew we were going to play them off the park.

The press billed the game as 'The Final of Finals'. Endless column inches were devoted to how both teams had 'met and maintained a high standard of football on their way to Wembley'. As the *Daily Mail* put it, 'A Final to savour is in prospect as both teams are bristling with skill in midfield, power in attack and strength in defence.'

Spurs' build-up to the final was no different from that of a normal league game. We trained as usual at Cheshunt and only spent one night away from home, which was on the eve of the final. The mood in the dressing room was very upbeat. We had arrived at Wembley having lost just once since Boxing Day. We had a very happy dressing room, as I have intimated, one full of fun and high spirits. But when it came to playing a match, we were all focused and I think I can best describe our collective attitude towards a game as being one of studied professionalism.

I heard it was different over at Chelsea. Stories were getting back to me that the Chelsea dressing room was far from a happy one. The Chelsea manager Tommy Docherty had promised his players a hefty bonus if they beat us in the final. However, the Chelsea board were not in agreement with Tommy and the players were naturally rather upset about that. The grumblings of the Chelsea players intensified with the allocation of Cup Final tickets. The players believed they had received a meagre allocation from the club and again voiced their dissatisfaction. When you hear stories like that coming out of your opponent's camp, there is only one thing a player can do. Believe them.

Only two of the Spurs team had graduated through the ranks at the club, right back Joe Kinnear and left winger Frank Saul. The rest of us had been bought by Bill Nicholson and most had experience of playing at Wembley either in a Cup Final or at international level. Chelsea didn't have that experience. They were making a trip into the unknown and I could almost smell their fear and trepidation. The final had a touch of the first and last about it. It was the first FA Cup Final where substitutes were to be allowed. It was also the last time the nation would watch a Cup Final in black and white on TV. Though some parts of the country had colour television, the vast majority of places were still watching in monochrome, on 625 lines.

Spurs had appeared in four FA Cup finals and won every time. To beat Chelsea would be the club's third FA Cup success in seven seasons. Our pedigree was good but that, of course, counts for nothing on the day. And what a day it turned out to be.

Chelsea were without the services of the talented Peter Osgood who had broken his leg in a league game some weeks earlier, but in Bobby Tambling, a pal from my days as a youth team player at Stamford Bridge, Charlie Cooke, Tony Hateley and Tommy Baldwin, they still had players who could produce something special that could change the course of a game.

There wasn't a clash of strips as such, but to accommodate black and white television, both teams sported a variation of their normal kit. We didn't wear our normal dark blue shorts and blue and white stockings. Instead we took to the pitch in a strip of all white. Chelsea, who normally played in blue shirts and shorts with white socks, walked out wearing an all blue strip.

The press had predicted that Chelsea's energy and method would cancel out what they believed to be our natural skills as a team. However, we seized the initiative from the start and never really let it go. The Chelsea centre forward Tony Hateley was six feet two inches tall. Many thought his height and prowess in the air would be a problem for us, but they never were. You get some centre forwards who are six feet two but only jump five feet ten. That didn't apply to Tony. He was masterful in the air but his aerial prowess was never really a threat, partly because he was well shackled by our centre half Mike England and partly because Dave Mackay and Alan Mullery worked hard to snuff out Chelsea's attempts to play a high ball up to him. You can be the best header of the ball in the world, but if you don't receive the service, a team might as well have Ronnie Corbett up front.

The duel between Mike England and Tony Hateley proved fascinating from beginning to end. They were never more than a couple of feet from one another in either penalty area. Mike won the battle in our box with Tony Hateley doing a similar job on Mike in the Chelsea penalty area.

This was a day when Alan Gilzean was superb. Gilly had this marvellous capacity to get into great positions, receive the ball and lay it off beautifully to the rest of us. In this final he did that time and time again, proving what we already knew – that he was a great team player. Gilly was clever, astute and no mean scorer of goals himself. Whenever Bill Nicholson complimented him on a goal, Gilly would play it down, saying it was a simple tap-in that anyone could have scored, or a free header that his grandmother would have put away. The only time Gilly didn't take that line was when he had to sit down with Bill to renegotiate his contract and talk money. Then, suddenly, Gilly would change his mind about the goals he'd scored.

Every member of the Spurs team produced a great performance in the final. Alan Mullery got through a tremendous amount of work in both midfield and defence and I can't recall him hitting a single wayward pass throughout the entire ninety minutes. My room-mate Jimmy Robertson was a constant threat to Chelsea with his direct and penetrating runs, while on the other flank Frank Saul was also proving to be a headache for Chelsea.

Chelsea adopted man-to-man marking. This suited us. Marvin Hinton was given the unenviable job of marking Gilly. Hinton played out of his usual position as an orthodox centre half and it quickly became apparent to me that it didn't suit him. We found a lot of space in midfield which allowed us to dictate the game. This resulted in Chelsea resorting to the long ball, or putting too much reliance on Charlie Cooke's ability to take on defenders. Charlie was a great winger, one who could really motor, but on the day he seemed obsessed by the thought of proving what everyone knew. That he was one of the best dribblers in football at that time. This again suited us because the more Charlie held on to the ball, the less open we were to a quick break. With Chelsea having the younger legs that could have caused us problems.

Our dominance in the first half eventually paid dividends. Alan Mullery had a shot which cannoned off the legs of the

Chelsea skipper Ron Harris. The ball could have gone
anywhere, but it fell at the feet of Jimmy Robertson who half-
volleyed it into the net from eight yards. With our noses in
front, I knew there was no way we wouldn't go on to win the
Cup.

When we came out for the second half, we started as we had
left off. We were all over Chelsea but it took us twenty minutes
to put the final beyond doubt. Our second goal followed a rare
spell of pressure from Chelsea. Frank Saul beat two Chelsea
defenders in the space the size of a hearth rug but found no
way past John Hollins who put the ball out of play for a throw-
in on our left. Dave Mackay's long throw floated into the
Chelsea penalty area, Jimmy Robertson flicked the ball on to
Frank Saul who turned on a shirt button to lash the ball past
Peter Bonetti. Goodnight Vienna!

Chelsea did pull a goal back, four minutes from time. Pat
Jennings failed to get his banana-like fingers to a cross from
John Boyle and Bobby Tambling ghosted in at the far post to
head the ball into the net. It ruffled our feathers, but not
unduly. We played 'keepy ball' for the remaining four minutes
and when the referee blew for time, I think even the most
ardent Chelsea fans were of the mind that Spurs were worthy
winners.

When Dave Mackay led us up what he called 'John Buchan
Way', so-called because there were thirty-nine steps leading up
to the Royal Box, it was a very sweet moment for me. I was a
winner again at Wembley.

Being totally honest, I didn't give my disappointment over
the previous year's World Cup one moment of thought. I was
too wrapped up in the glory of winning the FA Cup for a
second time. I hadn't managed to score in the final but that
didn't bother me. Spurs had won the FA Cup and that was the
main thing. Besides, I'd finished the season as the club's leading
goalscorer for a sixth successive season and was the top

goalscorer in the FA Cup that season. I felt I'd contributed.

Spurs' post-final banquet was a great night. Bill Nicholson sat at the head of the top table with the FA Cup always within his reach. Bill wasn't often given to wit, but he was that night. It is always the custom on such nights for just about everyone connected with a club to say something about winning the FA Cup. Everyone was waiting to hear what Bill had to say and he didn't let us down.

'An after-dinner speech is an odd thing,' said Bill. 'You eat a meal you don't want so you can get up and tell a load of stories you can't remember to people who have already heard them. My father gave me the best advice on after-dinner speaking. Be sincere. Be brief. Be seated. That in mind, ladies and gentlemen, I give you the FA Cup!'

He brought the house down.

CHAPTER FOURTEEN

MY WAY

Spurs' success in the FA Cup meant we were once again on the trail of the European Cup Winners' Cup in 1967–8. Though we were not to be on that trail for long. Following a 6-3 aggregate win over the Yugoslav side Hajduk Split, we went out of the competition in the following round to Olympique Lyonnais on the away goals rule. We lost the first leg 1-0 in France which, on the face of it, we believed to be a decent enough result as we were very confident of pulling back the one-goal deficit at White Hart Lane. I felt confident we could score goals against Lyonnais at home and my confidence was not misplaced. I netted two on the night and there were further goals from Gilly and Cliff Jones. The trouble was, Lyonnais scored three themselves. Though we won 4-3 on the night that levelled the aggregate score at 4-4 and Lyonnais progressed to the next round by virtue of having scored away from home.

The domestic season of 1967–8 was one of the unhappiest I ever experienced in football. The tremendous team spirit Spurs had shown in the previous season deserted us. We never really hit a good vein of form and inconsistent performances saw us finish the season seventh in Division One, well adrift of the Champions Manchester City. In the FA Cup we enjoyed a super win over Manchester United after a replay, comfortably accounted for Preston in round four but could find no way past Liverpool in the fifth. I scored Spurs' goal in our 1-1 draw with Liverpool at White Hart Lane, but we went down at Anfield in the replay by the odd goal in three.

I played thirty-nine league games that season and finished with twenty-three goals, plus three in the FA Cup, but I was concerned about my overall form and believed I wasn't getting the best out of my game. I often felt tired and jaded but, most worrying of all, I realised my appetite for football wasn't the same. For a time during that season I actually contemplated retiring from the game. I found I had lost my snap. I wasn't enjoying my football as I had previously done. The fact I was not enjoying my football as much caused me to have occasional bouts of depression. I think Bill Nicholson had noticed my lack of verve because he went out and bought Martin Chivers from Southampton for what was then a club record fee of £125,000. Perhaps Bill believed that competition from Martin would motivate me and that I would produce my old snap and sharpness. When Martin arrived he took over from Gilly up front with Alan dropping back into a deeper role behind Chivers and myself. It wasn't an unsuccessful partnership, but there wasn't the fire of old. But that was true of the team as a whole. Bill sold Dave Mackay to Derby County and Cliff Jones to Fulham. I found it increasingly difficult to adjust to the changes in the team and my tally of goals that year was one of the lowest of my career.

Following the 1966 World Cup I regained my place in the England team when Alf picked me in the side to play Scotland at Wembley in April 1967. As luck would have it this was to be the first defeat for England since winning the World Cup. England did not get off to the best of starts against the Scots. Jack Charlton picked up an injury in the early stages of the game and, as there were no substitutes allowed, big Jack spent the rest of the game hobbling about up front. Minutes after

Jack's injury, Billy Bremner caught Ray Wilson with a tackle that was later than a south-east commuter train. Scotland defeated England 3-2, and for the benefit of any Scots reading this let me say that Scotland fully deserved their victory – against a nine-man England team. As far as the Scottish players were concerned this game was their 'World Cup Final' and after the match they were full of themselves. When the England team joined the Scottish players for the post-match buffet Denis Law called Gordon Banks over to where he was standing with Jim Baxter, Jim McCalliog, Billy Bremner and Ron McKinnon.

'Gordon, we need your help over here,' said Denis. 'Can you answer a question that's stumped us?'

Gordon said he'd try.

'England are World Champions,' said Denis. 'But we have just beaten you, so does that mean Scotland are the World Champions now?'

The Scottish lads roared with laughter. There was a large bowl of mayonnaise next to Gordon and how he resisted the temptation, I'll never know.

I played in England's next game, scoring once in a 2-0 victory over Spain, and three days later played against Austria in Vienna. A goal from Alan Ball gave England a deserved victory but little did I know when I left the field that it would be the last time I would do so as an England player. Though Alf picked me for every England squad for the remaining three internationals of 1967 and the first two of 1968, I never got to play. Alf seemed happy to carry on naming me in his England squad but I wasn't happy being a 'squaddie'. In 1968 I signed an extension to my contract with Tottenham and made my mind up to concentrate my efforts on Spurs. I had been in two minds whether to retire or have another couple of seasons but decided to have another crack with Spurs to see if I could recapture my old snap and zest.

I informed Alf that, though I still considered it an honour to be named in the England squad, I felt my contribution to the cause was little more than an extra body at the training camp. I told him that I would rather not be a part of the England training set-up unless I was going to be selected in the starting eleven. Effectively, I said I was retiring from international football. The press made a big hullabaloo about it, but I'd made up my mind. I wanted to concentrate on rejuvenating myself physically and channelling all my efforts into my commitment to Spurs. It seemed the logical thing to do. I certainly didn't intend it as a snub to England or to Alf, though the word came back to me that he took it that way.

I was aware that the edge to my game had been dulled. With the benefit of hindsight, I now think that was the result of a number of things. Though it had been two years since I had contracted hepatitis, following the illness I had worked my socks off to regain the strength, fitness and form that would enable me to make the England team for the World Cup. Following the World Cup, Spurs' super form in the league and our successful FA Cup run enabled me to get through the 1966–7 season on enthusiasm and adrenalin. In 1967–8 I think the after-effects of hepatitis caught up with me. Old mates such as Dave Mackay, Cliff Jones and Bill Brown left the club. Our form went wobbly and, without the stimulus of consistent victories and good team performances to pump my adrenalin and keep me focused and at optimum fitness, mentally I felt jaded. Where before I would be enjoying a match so much that when the referee blew the final whistle I was disappointed because I wanted it to carry on, that feeling was missing in 1967–8. Not being a regular in the England team didn't help either. I had to do something to rekindle the fire. That's why I knocked England on the head and devoted my efforts to Spurs.

The combination of an extended contract, a break from

being a makeweight at England training sessions and a more
than decent season for Spurs in 1968–9 proved the antidote.
Spurs finished in sixth place in Division One and reached the
semi-finals of the League Cup. My contribution was twenty-
seven goals in the league which made me not only the First
Division's leading goalscorer but the top goalscorer in the
entire Football League. I also scored nine goals in cup
competitions to finish with a grand total of thirty-six goals for
the season, way ahead of George Best of Manchester United
and Southampton's Ron Davies.

I had managed to shake off the occasional bouts of
depression and the fact that I was once again relaxed and
content enabled me to hit a good vein of form. The snap and
the zest had returned, the ball was hitting the back of the net
and I found it a joy to play football again.

The League Cup had come a long way since 1960–61 when
the first draw was made and those little wooden balls rattled
around a velvet bag without any sense of history or tradition.
It came of age in 1966–7 when the Football League decided for
the first time to stage the final at Wembley and offer the
winners a place in Europe via the Inter-Cities Fairs Cup. The
first Wembley winners were Queens Park Rangers who beat
West Brom 3-2 in a thrilling final played before a packed
Wembley. Unfortunately for QPR their success didn't lead to
them playing in Europe because the ruling at the time was that
such entrants had to come from the First Division. QPR were
actually a Third Division team when they won the League
Cup.

A Wembley final and the promise of a place in Europe was
a considerable attraction to First Division clubs and Spurs were
no exception. Prior to 1968–9, Spurs had only entered the
League Cup once, in 1966–7, when we went out of the
competition at the first time of asking when beaten 1-0 at West
Ham. Cliff Jones was on the point of leaving Spurs when we

played Aston Villa in round two, having been given a bye in the first round. That September night at Villa Park, Cliff created a little bit of club history when he gave us the lead. Though the League Cup was in its eighth season Cliff became the first Spurs player to score in the competition. His goal was followed by a hat-trick from Martin Chivers and we ended up winning the tie 4-1.

In the next round it was my turn to bag a hat-trick. Further goals from Jimmy Pearce (2) and Terry Venables gave us a comfortable 6-3 win over Exeter City. In the following two rounds we accounted for Peterborough United and Southampton respectively and when the draw was made for the semi-finals we got a plum – our near neighbours, Arsenal.

Arsenal were up there challenging for the First Division title along with Leeds, Liverpool and Everton. They were managed by Bertie Mee and their coach was Don Howe. At the time Arsenal were just getting it together as a team. They were very well organised, particularly in defence, and their knack of shoe horning single-goal victories from games had earned them the nickname 'Boring Arsenal'. I remember Gilly once mentioned how, in the Arsenal pre-season photograph, Don Howe, not known for joviality, appeared to be smiling broadly. I told Gilly the reason for that was because Don knew all the Arsenal players were behind the ball.

They got behind the ball all right when we played Arsenal at Highbury. Talk to the old Arsenal lads now and they deny they played a cautious game in the hope of nicking a goal then shutting up shop. All I can say is that the *Daily Express* report of Spurs' first leg semi-final at Highbury shows that we had eleven efforts at goal whereas Arsenal had three. The final score? Arsenal won 1-0. Don, Bob Wilson, Frank McLintock, Bobby Gould, George Graham et al? I rest my case.

Alf Ramsey would have been really proud of Arsenal when they came to White Hart Lane for the return leg. They did a 'real professional job'. They nicked a goal and though I pulled one back for Spurs, every attack we mounted floundered on an impenetrable wall of red and white shirts. Spurs went out of the League Cup to our north London neighbours 2-1 on aggregate. It was one hell of an anticlimax to what had been an exhilarating run in the League Cup. After the game we were all as flat as pancakes. It was as if we had been invited to a swinging party, only to end the night dancing with our mothers.

For me the 1968–9 season was very enjoyable. I had recaptured my enthusiasm and my touch for goals. I scored four hat-tricks, including a four-goal haul in our 5-1 win at home to Sunderland. When I scored against Stoke City in November it was my two-hundredth goal for Spurs. At the end of the season I joined my team-mates on a club tour of the USA and Canada where Spurs participated in the Toronto Cup competition.

I returned to England to find the newspapers had embarked on a campaign to have me reinstated in the England team. Reflecting on my thirty-six-goal haul of the previous season, Dick Railton wrote in the *Evening News*, 'How much longer can England afford to ignore the claims of Britain's top hot-shot?' In the *Daily Sketch* Brian Scovell wrote, 'Greaves is still only twenty-nine. Still a great player. Still capable of making an indelible mark on international football. Still this country's best scorer of goals. What other country would ignore their leading top-flight goalscorer when selecting their national team?'

All in all, there was quite a press campaign for my reinstatement in the England team. Alf is on record as saying, 'I am being crucified because I am not selecting Greaves, yet he told me he does not want to play for England.' That wasn't strictly true. Alf had misunderstood me. What I had actually told him was that I would rather not be called up unless I was

going to play. Away from football I had a number of business
interests at this time, including a growing haulage company.
What I didn't want to do was spend my time on a pitch at
England's Roehampton training ground as a pawn while Alf
explained a set piece to the eleven he was intending to play.

Deep down I knew there was little chance of Alf giving me
a telephone call. The press continued their campaign for my
reinstatement to the England team but I knew that in 1969–70
all my efforts would be channelled towards Spurs.

Spurs were once again in transience. In 1969–70, Bill
Nicholson introduced several youngsters to the side. The days
of him spending big fees on big-name players or rising stars
appeared to be over. Players such as Phil Beal, John Pratt, Tony
Want, Ray Evans, Dennis Bond, Peter Collins and Steve
Perryman were all decent players, but they were young and
inexperienced players are inconsistent. Spurs' form in
1969–70 was very patchy. We started the season with a 3-1
defeat at Leeds. We then beat Burnley 4-0 only to then lose at
home to Liverpool. There followed two successive victories on
the road, at Burnley and Crystal Palace. We drew at home to
Chelsea then beat Ipswich Town and West Ham. It appeared
that we were getting our act together but then came a 3-0
defeat at Manchester City. We bounced back to win 3-2 against
Arsenal in a thrilling game at Highbury but were then played
off the park at Derby where we lost 5-0.

Our next match was at home to Sunderland, who at the time
were struggling at the bottom of Division One having won just
one game all season. Supporters of whatever hue will tell you
that there is always a club that their team always seem to get a
result against. Conversely, there is always a team they never
seem to beat. It's one of the curiosities of the game that, though
players change over the years, this rule seems to hold true.
Since World War Two, Tottenham had almost always beaten
Sunderland at White Hart Lane. Even to this day that remains

the case. I think I am right in saying that, up to 2003, Sunderland have only beaten Spurs three times at White Hart Lane since 1945.

A struggling Sunderland side at home presented Spurs with a great opportunity to bounce back from our mauling at the Baseball Ground. Unbelievably, we lost. Sunderland were a mixture of seasoned pros such as Joe Baker, Cecil Irwin and Len Ashurst, and kids such as Dennis Tueart, Bobby Kerr, Billy Hughes, Mick McGiven and Colin Todd. The only goal of the game came when Joe Baker challenged for a high ball with Mike England and Peter Collins. Somehow the ball became wedged between all three bodies before squirting out and past Pat Jennings. The referee was in a quandary as to who had actually applied the final touch. No one was sure, though of course Joe Baker was adamant that it had been him. In the end, the referee put it down as a Mike England own goal. Not that it mattered to us.

Spurs were dreadful that day and Sunderland were not even that good, but they held out to snatch a rare win. Unlike Chelsea, Spurs had only a few celebrity supporters. The comic actor Leslie Phillips and the satirist Peter Cook were genuine supporters at the time. After the game, on *Sports Report*, Peter Cook was asked for his comments on the match. 'I'm still in a state of shock,' said Peter. 'I have just witnessed the worst game of football I have ever seen at White Hart Lane. I can't believe the result or the Spurs performance. I would have had more entertainment if I'd stayed at home this afternoon and watched a fish finger defrost.'

Such performances were alien to Spurs and their supporters, who had been brought up on a diet of Blanchflower, Mackay, Jones, Smith, White, Mullery and Venables. They were used to seeing Alan Gilzean and me hitting it off up front as a result of consistently good service. Following the debacles against Derby and Sunderland, Spurs won just five of the next seventeen league games and dropped into the bottom half of Division One. It was unthinkable that a Spurs team would ever do that. The nadir was reached in a fourth-round FA Cup tie against Crystal Palace.

Palace were embroiled in a fight to avoid relegation along with Sunderland, Sheffield Wednesday and Southampton. Spurs were drawn at home and Palace looked like they would be easy pickings. They weren't. At White Hart Lane we huffed and puffed, then just got in a huff because we couldn't break them down. The press believed Palace would have to play a more open game at home which would suit Spurs. Nothing suited us at Selhurst Park. Nothing went right for us, least of all the result. Crystal Palace beat us 1-0.

The press went to town, criticising every player and our performance as a team. Bill Nicholson was urged to 'clear out the dead wood in the side'. For Spurs' next game, at home to lowly Southampton, Bill dropped Gilly, Cyril Knowles, Joe Kinnear and me. Spurs produced another woeful performance, losing 1-0. I thought for our next game, Wolves at Molineux, Bill would recall me to the side. But he didn't. In fact he never picked me for Spurs again. I spent the remainder of the season in the reserves or kicking my heels on the sidelines. After the Palace game the press had called for changes to the team, one of those changes being me. However, as the weeks passed and Spurs continued to produce indifferent form and performances, the press began to call for my return to the first team. Bill Nicholson took no notice. I played out the remainder of the 1969–70 season in the Football Combination.

What goes around comes around. I had played my very first game for Spurs in their reserve team against Plymouth Argyle in December 1961. My last appearance as a Spurs player was in March 1970, in a rearranged reserve team fixture against Plymouth.

My continued absence from the first team alerted a number

of clubs to my possible availability. I didn't want to leave Spurs.
I wanted to stay and regain my place in the team. I still
believed I could do the business. My appetite for football had
been diminished by my stint in the Tottenham reserves, but I
believed it would be immediately rekindled by a return to duty
with the first team. I was after all scoring goals in the reserves,
helping Spurs to top the Football Combination, and the
newspapers of the day were continually highlighting Spurs'
dearth of goals in the First Division. While I was playing
reserve team football, Spurs had won just two of their seven
First Division matches. It was at this time that I accepted an
invitation to participate in the *Daily Mirror* London to Mexico
Rally. For several weeks my football career came to a standstill
as I spent more and more time on a motor rally trial run,
learning the art of navigation and rally driving from my co-
driver Tony Fall and the rest of the Ford team.

I took the rally driving so seriously that Bill Nicholson read
it as a sign that I was losing my appetite for football and had
resigned myself to winding down my career and concentrating
on my business interests. I was becoming somewhat of a
millstone to Bill. It was none of my doing really, but as Spurs
were having a hard time of it, every time he announced a team
without my name in it, the press took him up on it. Eventually
I got fed up with kicking my heels in the reserves and asked Bill
about my future.

The memories of that conversation are a bit woolly. I think
both of us believed the best thing would be for me to move on,
but we were reluctant to commit ourselves to the break. As
with marriages and long-term relationships, the decision to
split is often easier than the actual mechanics of breaking up.
So it was with Bill and myself. Our meeting ended with Bill
deciding we both needed thinking time in which to mull over
the situation.

Bill talked to the Tottenham board in 'confidence' about my

future. In football six people can keep a secret as long as five of them are dead. Word soon got out that I could be moving on from Spurs and one of the first to pick up the trail was Brian Clough, then manager of Derby County. Brian let me know through a third party that he would be very interested in signing me and linking me once again with Dave Mackay who was doing a great job for him in the Derby team. Clough was making a name for himself as one of the game's up-and-coming managers who had not only kick started the career of Dave but the fortunes of Derby as a club.

However, my mind was much taken with the idea of competing in the London to Mexico Rally and when not involved with the training that entailed, I was devoting much time to my business interests, which were flourishing. It is only when I now look back to this period in my life that I realise that Brian Clough would have been just the man to get hold of me and motivate me into reproducing something of my old form.

On transfer deadline day, 16 March 1970, Irene and I were moving house once again. We had left 22 The Fairway, Upminster, and had been living in Greenway Cottages, Hulton Moat, in Essex. However, we now decided to move back to Upminster and The Fairway, though this time not to number 22, but number 7. The house was full of cardboard boxes and tea chests, as any house is on the day of a move. Little did I realise that moving house was not to be the only move I would make that day.

The telephone rang. It was Bill Nicholson. Bill informed me that he was at the club and that he had Martin Peters with him, who had agreed to join Spurs from West Ham United. Bill went on to say that he was selling me to West Ham as a makeweight in the deal for Martin.

I was taken aback and I was angry. I was so annoyed with Bill for wanting to bring my Spurs career to an end I simply

said, 'Okay. If you don't want me at Spurs, I'll go.' I didn't have
to go, not if I didn't want to. I still had eighteen months of a
contract to run. I could have told Bill I was staying at Spurs and
there was little he could have done about it. But I was so
peeved that he appeared so willing to get rid of me, I went
along with it. What's the point of staying at a club that doesn't
want you?

Looking back on that day, I wish I had told Bill I wasn't
interested in moving. He could still have signed Martin Peters
because, as the makeweight, I had been valued at £90,000 in a
deal worth £220,000 to West Ham. Spurs could have paid the
full fee for Martin and kept me. But I had been switched off
football and my thinking was not objective, so I agreed to go
and see Ron Greenwood down at West Ham. It seemed such
a convenient move at the time. A transfer to Derby would have
involved another move of house, or me staying up there in
rented accommodation with Irene and the children in our new
home in Upminster. I could have done a lot better financially
because I had received a number of illegal approaches from
clubs while playing for Spurs reserves. But I didn't want to
uproot and move away from London. I never did make a
fortune from football. You may be surprised to learn that
throughout my entire career I never earned a basic wage of
more than £100 a week. I am ever mindful that that wage was
far in excess of what an ordinary working person earned, but
in terms of what some other players were earning at the time,
it wasn't top money, believe me.

The wage I was offered by West Ham United was nothing
to write home about either. However, the thought of playing
alongside Bobby Moore and players such as Geoff Hurst, Billy
Bonds, John Sissons and Frank Lampard was appealing. As was
the fact the West Ham training ground was only a fifteen-
minute drive from my home and businesses. All this helped
convince me to sign for West Ham. It was, however, a move

that was to benefit neither the club nor myself. It is also one that I have regretted ever since.

These days one often hears people talk favourably of what was at the time known as the West Ham 'Academy'. West Ham had a very good youth policy and legend has it that every player was brought up to play purist football in a sporting manner. That Upton Park was where the very best training and coaching took place. Where superb skills and technique were passed on to produce great players such as Bobby Moore, Geoff Hurst and Martin Peters. The West Ham Academy, it is believed, was an example to all other clubs of how training and coaching should be. I have to be honest and say it never struck me as being that way. Compared to what I had been used to at Spurs under Bill Nicholson and Eddie Baily, I found training at West Ham and the general running of team affairs to be lax, at times disorganised and occasionally shambolic. Fertile ground for a disenchanted footballer who had begun to drink more heavily than was good for him.

When I joined West Ham they were a bottom-six First Division club, in real danger of being embroiled in the dogfight to avoid relegation that was taking place between Sunderland, Sheffield Wednesday, Southampton and now Crystal Palace. Prior to me signing they had won just one of their eight First Division matches. They were not a club reaping the rewards of having English football's first academy. My debut took place at Maine Road against Manchester City. March had come in like a lion and was going out like a tiger. Forty-eight hours of incessant rain had turned the Maine Road pitch into a quagmire and I was covered in mud just running on to the field for the pre-match kickabout. It turned out to be a game in which I would continue my record for scoring on my debut for every team I had played for. City had a good side at the time, but we ran them ragged. I scored twice, Geoff Hurst scored a couple and Ronnie Boyce

chipped in with one to give West Ham a stunning 5-1 win over
City and upset the form books. In a way I did myself no favours
by scoring those two goals on my debut. I had set myself a
standard that, in my heart of hearts, I knew I couldn't maintain.

In the following three games West Ham achieved two
things they hadn't done all season. They remained unbeaten
and didn't concede a goal. A goalless draw at Crystal Palace
was followed by a highly creditable 1-0 win over Liverpool,
then Wolverhampton Wanderers were soundly beaten 3-0
with me amongst the goals again. We rounded off the season
with a 2-2 home draw against Leeds United, which ended their
hopes of overhauling Everton at the top of Division One, then
achieved a good 2-2 draw at Arsenal. In my six games for West
Ham we had remained unbeaten but come the end of the
1969–70 season I was far from being happy and contented.

Though not a part of Alf's England plans for the 1970 World
Cup, there was no way I was going to miss out on Mexico. So
I drove there. In the London to Mexico Rally. There was a pub
near the Ford works at Dagenham that I would occasionally
visit, a popular watering hole for a lot of the Ford lads who I
got to know well. Unbeknown to me, Ford were looking for a
high-profile driver to partner Tony Fall, who in the previous
year had won the Rally of the Incas. One of the Ford lads asked
me if I would be up for it. I was in my cups, so to speak, and
found myself saying 'Yes'. I never gave the matter any thought
in the days that followed. I didn't believe anyone would have
taken my reply seriously. But they did. The wheels were set in
motion and I found myself committed to driving in the
London to Mexico Rally. I suppose I could have got out of it,
but as the preparations advanced, I found myself actually
looking forward to what I knew would be a thrilling and
unique experience.

My carrot was a fortnight's, all-expenses paid holiday in the

Caribbean with Irene once the Rally was over. So I set to work with Tony Fall, learning the art of rally driving. My training period involved a drive with Tony to Yugoslavia to see if we could get on with one another in the confined space of a car for a long period of time. We did get on and I enjoyed every minute of this new experience. With training underway, my interest in the Rally was heightened by my frustration at playing reserve team football at Spurs. My football career was at a standstill and I found myself spending more and more time on motor rally runs than I did on football matters. Bill Nicholson was somewhat alarmed by my enthusiasm for rallying and in an effort to rekindle my interest in football, and to allow me more time for my business interests, suggested reducing my training with Spurs. But the damage had already been done by me playing half a season in Spurs reserves.

My training for the rally was inadvertently my first step towards retirement from football. Though I still loved football, at the time I felt it didn't love me. Playing football was pushed down my list of priorities and I began to have my first thoughts of making a complete break from the game. A return to the Spurs first team would have squashed those thoughts and rejuvenated my enthusiasm for playing, but that never happened. Come the day the rally started, I was a West Ham United player. On 19 April, on a shooting green spring day at Wembley, Alf Ramsey waved a Union Jack to signal the start of the *Daily Mirror* London to Mexico Rally. Bobby Moore had already cut the tape and as Alf did his wafting the engines of ninety-six cars roared like tigers. In car number 26, a black and white Ford Escort, I sat next to Tony Fall. Bobby Moore came running up to our car just as we were about to speed off.

'Good luck, Jim,' said Bobby.

'Cheers mate,' I said. 'See you in Mexico!'

The car sped away. In front of Tony and me was a 16,245-mile drive across two continents and twenty-five countries. It was estimated that it would take eight weeks to reach Mexico City. If, that is, we were going to make it at all. In fact, Tony and I finished the rally in sixth place which I considered to be some achievement. Of the ninety-six cars that had started the rally, only twenty-three made it to Mexico. Sadly, a driver, a rally official and a cyclist had lost their lives along the way.

Tony and I celebrated our achievement by jumping fully clothed into a swimming pool. There was a chair in the pool and for the next couple of hours I had glue bum. I took up residence in that chair and bobbed about in the pool and drank bottle after bottle of Mexican lager. The only alcohol I'd consumed during the rally was on the voyage from Lisbon and during our short break in Rio. I had a raging thirst and I set about quenching it.

We had arrived in Mexico City just twenty-four hours after Bobby Moore had flown in from Bogotá following his infamous arrest on a trumped-up charge of shoplifting a bracelet. Bobby had been hidden away from the world's press in an embassy house on the outskirts of Mexico City. I'd had my fill of driving, so I persuaded Tony Fall, the football writer Norman Giller and an old pal, Lou Wade, to join me in a taxi bound for the 'safe' house where Bobby was staying.

When we arrived there was an army of press lads encamped outside. I asked the BBC commentator David Coleman what the situation was and David informed me that Bobby was indeed inside but that nobody was allowed to see him. Lou Wade was a business associate of Bobby's and, at six feet seven, looked as if he'd once fallen asleep in a greenhouse. I asked him to pretend he was going to storm the gates in order to create a diversion at the front of the embassy house while I sneaked around the back with Tony and Norman.

As I recall I was wearing bright red trousers, a yellow and green checked jacket, a frilly yellow shirt and a kipper tie. I was hardly inconspicuous but only in danger of being arrested by the fashion police because, once around the back of the house, there were no embassy security staff or local police to be seen. Tony and Norman helped me shin over the embassy house wall and I dropped down into the garden. I could see a couple of guards some yards away but bided my time before sprinting across the lawn to the house itself.

I found myself by a set of French windows through which I could see Bobby sitting reading a magazine and sipping what looked like a lager. I carefully turned the handle on the French windows and, to my great delight, they opened and I walked into the room where Bobby was sitting.

'Come on then, Mooro, what you done with that bracelet?' I asked.

Bobby was so startled he nearly dropped his beer.

'I told you outside Wembley that I'd see you in Mexico. Well, here I am,' I said.

We only exchanged a few words and didn't even get around to giving one another a hug before an embassy official arrived and I was escorted off the premises. Bobby, however, said that he wanted to see me so I had to go through the pantomime of leaving by the front door, ringing the bell and asking to be readmitted before being officially invited on to the premises, this time in the company of Lou Wade. Bobby told me about the trumped-up charge and the three of us whiled away the time catching up on what we'd all been up to, while getting some of our tax back courtesy of the embassy's cocktail cabinet.

Irene and I took Ford up on their offer of a Caribbean holiday after the rally. When we returned to England it was time for me to buckle down to pre-season training with West Ham United. I had always looked forward to the start of a new season. On the first day of training I'd be hopeful as the break of day, ready and raring to go. But this time I felt so very different. I trained with my West Ham team-mates at Chadwell Heath, but found myself going through the motions.

In the first weeks when we were working on our strength and stamina I found myself doing something I'd never done in training. Cheating. When running I'd do so at less than three-quarter pace but move my arms quickly so it appeared as if I was putting plenty of effort in.

To strengthen our thigh and stomach muscles we had an exercise whereby we would lie on our backs with our legs straight, then raise our heels six inches off the ground and hold them there until told otherwise by Ron Greenwood. When Ron's back was turned, I'd have a little rest and drop my heels to the ground. When the season began I had worked hard enough to get through a First Division game, but that was about it. I was nowhere near as fit as I had been two years previously. What's more, I realised that one aspect of my play that was crucial to my game was not what it had been. My sharpness and speed off the mark.

At the beginning of the 1970–71 season a lot of people were re-examining English football. When Gerd Muller volleyed an extra-time goal for West Germany on a June Sunday in Leon, he not only put England out of the World Cup but set a lot of people thinking.

Some of the results of this thinking were ungrateful and irrelevant. Alf Ramsey had been pilloried by press and supporters alike, in the main for the substitutions he had made during the game with West Germany, particularly that of Bobby Charlton who had given way to Colin Bell of Manchester City. Bobby wasn't having the best of games but his presence on the field had cancelled out that of West Germany's Franz Beckenbauer. With Bobby out of the picture, Beckenbauer exerted his influence on a game in which England conceded a two-goal advantage.

England had failed in Mexico and those managers who had organised their own team's pattern of play on what they believed were England lines began to re-evalute in the aftermath of the 1970 World Cup. For four years managers and coaches had reasoned: 'You can't do better than copy the World Champions.' Now that England were no longer World Champions, managers and coaches looked at different tactics and patterns of play.

'Getting it right at the back' became an article of faith, one which ignored the fact that unless a coach had good midfield providers and sharp strikers with an eye for goal, defensive security wasn't going to yield many goals or be the key to success. In the early seventies those clubs who were well organised in defence but also boasted good service from midfield and strikers who could score goals were Derby County, Leeds United, Liverpool, Ipswich Town and Arsenal. It is no coincidence that it was these teams who were contesting the honours as the seventies got under way.

Just about every First Division team at this time was well organised at the back. In 1970–71, before their renaissance that was to take place in the following seasons, Ipswich Town narrowly avoided relegation but only conceded forty-eight goals. The following season Huddersfield Town were glued to the foot of the First Division for much of the season and were subsequently relegated. Yet Huddersfield only conceded fifty-nine goals in their forty-two league matches.

The early seventies saw teams placing more emphasis on defence, but as with the examples of Ipswich Town and Huddersfield Town that was no guarantee of success or survival if a team did not have the creativity in midfield and the striking power up front to breach the rearguards of opponents employing similar tactics. It was a vicious circle. One unmovable force met another and, in comparison to the open, fluid football of the late fifties and early sixties, in the early seventies goals were at a premium. When a team did score goals rarely was the emphasis on how well they had played in attack. The emphasis was placed on the opposing defence who had conceded the goal and it was always negative. The words 'We gave away cheap goals' entered the vocabulary of coaches, managers and, eventually, the supporters.

The supporters endured this because coaches, managers and even players had convinced them that this was the modern way to success. Four years on from Alf's quote in the aftermath of 1966, the word 'professional' had become the excuse for a multitude of sins.

It was amazing really because in the 1970 World Cup, Pele, Jairzhino and Rivelino had demonstrated that even the most carefully constructed defence could be overcome by individual and collective flair. English football did not possess at the time a player of Pele's stature. No country did. However, for all English football managers and coaches had been in awe of Brazil's style of play, they never adopted it, or even adapted a version of it. Having copied the style and method of the World Champions of 1966, English football turned its back on the style of the World Champions of 1970. Brazil had demonstrated that in four years the game had moved on. English football once again found itself out of step with current developments. That's one of the reasons why it would be twelve years before England were to qualify for the World Cup Finals again. English football had its share of flair players in the seventies. Those mavericks Alan Hudson, Tony Currie, Frank Worthington, Stan Bowles, Charlie George, Rodney Marsh and Peter Osgood were very popular with supporters but not with successive England managers, and mustered only a handful of caps between them. It wasn't Alf's fault that a bunch of slavish imitators distorted the system he had evolved. Just as it was not the fault of the Huddersfield Town centre forward of 1970–71, Jimmy Lawson, that he could not play like Pele and ended the season as the club's leading scorer in the First Division with just nine goals. The way Brazil had played in the World Cup should have put English football on another train of thought, but it didn't. Having seen Brazil firmly plant their flag on football's aesthetic summit, supporters were expecting something a little more creative and a little less destructive from their teams.

However, as the new decade unfolded the reverse occurred. The 1970–71 season saw minimum admission prices increased to 6/– (30p), an increase of 25 per cent on the previous season. In 1974, in post-decimalisation Britain, the minimum cost of attending a match had increased to 60p. The lack of open, attacking football that resulted in goals and the hike in admission prices affected attendances. In 1957–8, when I established myself as a Chelsea player, the total number of people attending Football League matches was 33,610,985. In 1970–71 that figure had fallen by five million. Come 1985–6 the total number of people attending League matches was 16,488,577, less than half that of 1957–8.

The formation of the Premier League, improved stadia in the wake of the Hillsborough disaster and the subsequent Taylor Report and a concerted effort on the part of clubs and the authorities to rid football of a criminal element, often erroneously referred to as being 'football hooligans', has in recent years arrested the decline in attendances. The number of supporters attending matches has enjoyed a year-on-year rise since 1992. In 2002 the total number of people attending football matches in the Premiership and Nationwide Leagues was 27,756,977. Eleven million more than 1986 but still well short of the number that attended matches in the fifties and sixties.

Of course, people have so much choice regarding leisure pursuits these days, but there were no home computers, DVD players or satellite TV in the early seventies. That attendances in the early seventies were much lower than they had been in the early sixties was, in the main, down to the type of football that was on offer.

CHAPTER FIFTEEN

WHAT MADE MILWAUKEE FAMOUS . . .

As fate would have it West Ham's opening game of the 1970–71 season was away at Tottenham Hotspur. It was the first time I had been back to White Hart Lane following my transfer to West Ham and I wondered what sort of reaction I would get from the Spurs supporters. I need not have worried. When I took to the pitch with my West Ham team-mates a crowd of 53,640 gave me a rousing welcome and my first touch of the ball was greeted by warm applause. West Ham flattered to deceive that day. We came away from Spurs with a 2–2 draw, our goals coming from Peter Bennett and yours truly, with both Spurs goals scored by Alan Gilzean.

West Ham's next two games were also London derbies, at home to Arsenal and Chelsea respectively. We drew both games but then contrived to win only one of our next eleven league matches and went out of the League Cup in the third round at Coventry City. Come New Year, West Ham were down at the basement of Division One with only Nottingham Forest, Burnley and Blackpool beneath us. Another dogfight relegation battle was on the cards.

By now I was drinking heavily, though there were times when I could go without alcohol for days and not feel the urge to drink. When I did drink, however, I really tucked it away. I found a number of my West Ham team-mates to be willing partners in these drinking sessions. Bobby Moore, Brian Dear, John Cushley, Frank Lampard, Harry Redknapp and John Charles often helped me prop up a bar. Occasionally we would also be joined by Geoff Hurst. The difference between that West Ham team and the Spurs players I had left behind was that Tottenham could really play good football. With the obvious exceptions of Bobby Moore, Geoff Hurst, Billy Bonds, and later, the much underestimated Bryan 'Pop' Robson, West Ham was heavily populated with journeymen First Division players. And, being honest, I was one of those journeyman players.

I had always promised myself that the day I realised I was no longer enjoying my football would be the day I hung up my boots. As the 1970–71 season unfolded I became increasingly downcast about West Ham's game and thoroughly miserable about my own. West Ham were struggling and there seemed no end to that struggle. That's how I saw it and it appeared Ron Greenwood saw it that way too, because he told Bobby Moore and me he was thinking of resigning.

We were flying over the Atlantic in a Jumbo jet on our way to play a friendly against the Brazilian team Santos in New York. Bobby Moore, a business associate of his, Freddie Harrison, and I had taken up residence in the bar in the upper deck of the Jumbo. Presently Ron Greenwood joined us. We asked Ron what he was drinking and he asked for a Coke. Freddie, however, laced Ron's Coke with Bacardi. In the hour that followed Ron must have drunk five Cokes at least, each one laced with Bacardi by the mischievous Freddie. It was a terrible thing to do and my only defence is that, like Bobby, I was merely an onlooker.

The Bacardi served to loosen Ron's tongue. People talk a lot of rubbish when they are drunk, but alcohol can also induce people to tell the truth. Ron confessed to Bobby and me that he felt responsible for West Ham's plight in Division One and was thinking of 'doing the decent thing' and resigning. I felt choked. Ron had been manager of West Ham for ten years in which time he had guided them to the FA Cup and European Cup Winners' Cup. He was in fact only West Ham's fourth manager since 1902 and had always done his level best for the club and had given them a reputation for playing quality football. What West Ham were not doing at this time was playing quality football. Ron had momentarily lost his way as a manager and I felt a sense of shame because I had done absolutely nothing to help him get back on track.

As our Jumbo touched down in New York, I vowed that if Ron quit West Ham I would get out of football for good. But he never mentioned resigning again and I stayed on at Upton Park until the end of that miserable season. Ron had realised that Freddie Harrison had been doctoring his drinks but to his credit he never took umbrage. He simply laughed it off, or, rather, slept it off.

And it was a miserable season. In November, following a run of three games without a win, we came unstuck again when Coventry City beat us 2-1 at Upton Park. In his report of the match in the *News of the World* Terry McNeill said, 'West Ham touched the depths in the first half, when they conceded two sloppy goals.' In the *Daily Express* Norman Giller wrote, 'West Ham plummeted to new depths of inadequacy against Coventry City. West Ham lost their tempers. Now perhaps they can get down to the all-important business of winning matches.'

Though we bounced back in our next game, winning 4-2 at Derby, where I scored what was only my fourth goal of the season, it did not erase from the memory our horror show against Coventry. For our next game at home to Liverpool, even the West Ham United programme put the knife in. 'The home defeat at the hands of the Sky Blues brought a chilling prospect for the future,' read the programme, 'and it is somewhat unnecessary to dwell upon a dreadful match that brought a lot of recrimination. The second-half rally was scant consolation for a first half in which the Hammers had really plumbed the depths, and the day ended on an unhappy note.'

When you read that in your own programme, you know you're in trouble. West Ham's game at Derby County was my five-hundredth appearance in the Football League and the goal I scored was my 351st in league football. I had always believed I had been born to score goals. It came so naturally to me. I had honed what I believed was a natural talent at Chelsea and Spurs, but now that talent had deserted me and I wasn't working to get it back. I've always believed that everyone has a natural talent for something, but that you have to work at it in order to develop natural talent to its optimum. I was always a big fan of Morecambe and Wise who I believe were naturally funny guys. Eric Morecambe was a big fan of football, an avid Luton Town supporter and for a number of years was on the board at Kenilworth Road. I once had a conversation with Eric in which I told him how naturally talented and funny I believed he and Ernie to be. Eric told me that from an early age he believed he and Ernie had a talent for comedy, but that they had had to hone their skills and learn their trade in the variety halls before ever getting an opportunity to appear on television. In short, they too worked at their natural talent.

'What would you and Ernie have become if you hadn't been comedians?' I asked, as a matter of interest.

'Mike and Bernie Winters,' said Eric.

See what I mean? Eric Morecambe was funny on and off screen because he had a natural talent for comedy.

At West Ham the natural talent I believed I had for scoring goals had deserted me, and I was so demotivated and miserable about my football that I didn't possess the will to work hard in an attempt to rediscover my touch for goals.

My West Ham career reached its nadir on New Year's night

in Blackpool where West Ham were due to play an FA Cup tie the following day. The West Ham squad were staying at the Imperial Hotel where, on the eve of the game, I enjoyed a couple of lagers with Bobby Moore before deciding to call it a night and go to bed. As Bobby and I were walking through the hotel lobby we fell into conversation with some BBC cameramen who were in town to record the game for *Match of the Day*. They were waiting for a taxi to take them to the 007 nightclub, owned by the former heavyweight boxer Brian London.

The camera boys told Bobby and me that there was little chance of our game with Blackpool taking place as the pitch was frozen and outside there was another very sharp frost.

'We're all wasting our time up here,' one cameraman told us. 'There's going to be a pitch inspection tomorrow, but it'll be academic. There's no way it will be fit for football.'

We were then interrupted by a member of the hotel staff who told the cameramen that their two taxis had arrived.

'We only ordered one,' said one of the Beeb men.

'Don't worry. We'll take the other one,' I said, on an impulse.

Bobby and I walked towards the hotel door and collected the thirsty Brian Dear and the casually interested Clyde Best on the way. 'We're just nipping down to Brian London's place for a quick nightcap. The game's going to be called off,' we told them. Brian came along for the drink. Clyde was not a drinker, but came along for the ride.

I consumed about a dozen lagers in the club. It says much about my alcohol consumption at the time that I wasn't drunk. Bobby and Brian Dear drunk about five each, while Clyde Best had spent the entire evening with a single Coke. We arrived back at the Imperial at around 1.45 a.m. and ordered coffee and sandwiches before retiring to bed with no one any the wiser as to what we had been up to.

I slept until around ten in the morning, then showered, had some toast and tea and joined my team-mates for the short trip to Bloomfield Road. When we arrived at Blackpool's ground there was a shock waiting for me. The match referee had deemed the skating rink of a pitch fit for play. We then committed the real 'crime'. We lost 4-0 to Blackpool. We lost not because four of us went out for a late-night drink, not because of a frozen pitch, simply because the team wasn't good enough. We had no rhythm to our play, we lacked cohesion and were not collectively strong. The balloon went up on Monday morning when a so-called West Ham supporter telephoned the club and a national newspaper and said he had seen us drunk in Brian London's nightclub in the early hours of the morning of our cup tie with Blackpool. In all probability he did see us, but what he didn't see was four drunken West Ham players.

Following those two telephone calls, the proverbial brown stuff came into close proximity with rudimentary air-conditioning. You always know when football is in trouble – it makes the front page. The story of our visit to Brian London's club screamed from the front page of every newspaper. It was as if we had perpetrated a heinous crime. All these years later I still feel anger and resentment at the way the West Ham board, in particular Ron Greenwood, handled the situation. We were out of order, me more than anyone. Disciplinary action had to be taken but I feel the matter could have been dealt with internally. Instead they fined us and dropped us and did it in the full glare of publicity by calling a press conference. The disciplinary action could have been dealt with in private. When players step out of line, a good manager will face the press, protect his players and play the matter down, then give those concerned a rollicking behind closed doors and implement whatever fine he believes suitable. Ron never did that; he said his piece to the press, which I found very sad.

When a manager protects players in the glare of unfavourable publicity, he wins their respect. The players want to go out on to the pitch and give their all for him. I didn't feel that way for Ron in light of the way he handled the situation. What little collective spirit existed amongst the West Ham players at the time evaporated. I was particularly nauseated by the treatment Bobby Moore received. Bobby had been at the club as both man and boy. He first signed for West Ham as an amateur, then signed as a pro in 1958. All told, he had been at the club for nigh on fifteen years in which time he had given nothing but loyal and top-quality service to West Ham. Bobby was shattered by the way he was treated by the club. Just one step out of line in fifteen years and they crucified him for it. I saw Bobby in the car park after the press had been told of the disciplinary action that was being taken. He was drooping; he looked as if he'd been stuffed by an incompetent taxidermist working at breakneck speed.

In those final few months at West Ham I was as happy as the day is long. The day in question being one in mid-January somewhere in Antarctica. I started to use drink as a crutch. Because I was not enjoying my football I was becoming anxious, agitated and downcast, but I found that once I had a few drinks inside me my anxieties and worries floated off into the ether.

In my last few months at West Ham United I began to consume beer in larger quantities than ever. Drinking had not been a problem when I was at Spurs. I did it because I liked it and I could take it or leave it. At West Ham I was in the early stages of alcoholism. I drank because I needed to. I knew every pub from the east of Aldgate Pump to Southend. If anyone asked directions from Stratford East to Southend I could tell them how to get there by way of pubs.

'Come up past the Two Puddings on to the A11, past the Charleston, the Thatched House, the Bell and Red Lion before getting on to the A12 at the Green Man in Leytonstone. From the Green Man follow the road past the George on the corner of the crossroads in Wanstead High Street, past the Redhouse, Redbridge, Oscars, Newbury Park and just after the Moby Dick in Chadwell Heath, you take the flyover at Gallows Corner on to the A127. From there it's a straight run down to Southend past the Fairlane Motel, the Halfway House, the Brighton Run, the Fortune of War and finally the Weir in Rayleigh. Bob's your uncle, you're then in Southend!'

After training at Chadwell Heath, if I didn't patronise any of the pubs on the Southend route I would go to the Slater's Arms opposite Romford greyhound stadium and stay there until Jack said 'Time gentlemen, please!' If not there, I would head home only to prop up any number of bars in the Upminster area. All I was interested in was drinking. Football didn't matter to me anymore. Once I had consumed half a dozen lagers the world suddenly didn't seem such a bad place after all.

Huddersfield Town at home. They're down and so am I. I have finished the season as West Ham's second leading goalscorer, behind Geoff Hurst. As Disraeli said, however, there are lies, damned lies and statistics. In finishing the season as West Ham's second top scorer I have just nine goals from thirty league matches. The same tally as Jimmy Lawson, Huddersfield's leading goalscorer. Where have all the goals gone? Where's the excitement, the buzz, the thrill from stepping over that white line? Look at them, up there on the terraces, picking over the bones of we players who have gone over the top. Merciless men in grubby overcoats. Trendy youths with their long hair sitting on their shoulders and the collars of their brightly coloured shirts nearly down to their nipples. They think we're their property. To be discovered, lauded, feted, giggled at, scorned at, vilified and then rejected.

Off we go, for the last time. What's that song on my lips? As usual, can't get rid of it. That ain't changed. 'Bout the only thing that hasn't.

Huh, huh, huh, huh, is the evening of the day-hey, hey hey . . .

Huh sit and watch the chil'drun play-hey, hey, hey . . .

Huh smiling faces I can see-ee . . .

Huh but not for me-ee . . .

Hi sit an' watch as . . . go by-huh huh hi . . .

'Frank! Feet! Feet! Facking hell, Frank! . . . Nah, nah, play it to me feet, Frank. Fack's sake! . . . Nice, Geoff. Nice! . . . Not that way, John, you'll turn on to Roy Ellam . . . John! . . . Bloody hell! . . . No, no, John, I was there waiting for it . . . only you . . . I ran ten yards to get there, John . . . if you ain't gonna lay it . . . No, you're trying to do too much, John . . . Bobby! Bobby! . . . McGill! . . . pick him up . . . pick him . . . forget him, he's Frank's . . . watch McGill . . . Well done, Bonzo . . . Hey, Bobby? Well done, mate . . . Tommy! Tommy! . . . Yes, yes! . . . Fackin' hell Tommy . . . not a fackin' greyhound . . . pointless knocking it down there . . . into feet, will ya? . . . oh, fack you 'n' all . . . Listen Tommy, son . . . Tommy? . . . Tom! . . . Tom! . . . See that, Roy? Dunner listen . . . Wazzat Roy? . . . You got more o' them than us? Dunno 'bout that . . . Look at him, Roy . . . head down, ain't looking . . . straight into trouble . . . piece of cake for your lad . . . see what I mean, Roy? . . . What we fackin' doing here, Roy? . . . Yes, Clyde . . . Yes! . . . Clyde? . . . No! Ain't no good . . . play it into feet! . . . Into me feet, Clyde! . . . Fack me, how many times? . . . Hey, c'mon, ref? . . . Well done, ref . . . Should think so 'n' all . . . well late that was . . . Take your time, John . . . John, no! . . . Take your time with the kick! . . . Bloody hell! . . . You're putting us under pressure, John . . . you shudda taken your time . . . don't rush it . . . He's yours, Tom!

Yours! . . . Don't foul! . . . Don't foul him there, Tom! . . .
Tom! . . . Bloody hell, Tom! . . . What a place to give away a
free . . . Stand over it, John! . . . Don't run off, John . . . Stand
over . . . Stand! . . . No, I won't John . . . I'm telling ya you
shudda stood over it . . . John? John? Think, mate . . . Just listen
will ya? . . . Fack him! He's Bobby's . . . ah, fack it! . . . fack the
fackin' lot . . . don't need this . . . How long, liner? Bloody hell,
ref . . . blow ya fackin' whistle . . . put an end to it . . .'

Up to now, my friend, in telling my story we've hopefully had
a few laughs along the way. Let me warn you now: there are no
laughs to be had from this next stage of my life. None at all. It
was to be a long time before I was to laugh again.

I left West Ham United in May 1971. I not only left
football, I departed from life and family living. In writing my
autobiography I have, up to this point, occasionally asked
friends and former team-mates for the benefit of their
memories. In so doing, a number of them filled in gaps or
reminded me of events and instances I had forgotten. A lot of
what is to follow has been pieced together from those who
witnessed my decline into alcoholism. Simply because much of
it is just a blur in my memory. All I can recall of this period is
that in five years I managed to wreck my marriage to Irene, my
family and my life. This was a very, very dark period in the life
of Jimmy Greaves. I'm a very, very lucky man. Because
eventually I turned my life around. When I retired from
full-time professional football at the age of thirty-one, I was
suddenly free of the daily discipline I had known for sixteen
years. Some people can't handle too much freedom. They
abuse it or else just don't know how to use it to best effect.
That was me.

For two years after leaving West Ham I didn't touch a
football or attend a single game. In no time at all I put on
nearly two stone. Some of the excess weight was due to a lack

of exercise, but most of it was the result of drinking throughout the day. Every day.

My regular routine was to call in at my businesses for a couple of hours every morning, then take off to a pub as soon as licensing hours allowed. As a footballer I had more or less stuck to drinking beer, but at this point in my life I adopted an 'anything goes' approach to alcohol. I'd go into a pub at lunchtime, down half a dozen pints of lager and follow that with a similar number of large shorts. To soak up the alcohol I'd have a sandwich or a ploughman's. When last orders were called, I'd down a couple of large ones before going home for a kip. I'd have some tea with Irene and the children and would then be clockwatching, kicking my heels until evening opening time in the pubs of Upminster where I would be first in and last out. In the course of a day I would have consumed sixteen pints and anything up to eight large shorts.

The drink made me blind to the heartache and angst I had brought to Irene, the children, other family members and friends. Irene was appalled by the way I let my physical appearance deteriorate and by the way I had let myself go in general. She was first to recognise I had a serious drinking problem. Me? I could stop drinking whenever I chose to do so, or so I believed.

At this stage of my life I had no money worries. The packing business I had started with my brother-in-law Tom with a £1,000 bank loan when I signed for Spurs had flourished into a sizeable concern with a turnover in excess of £1 million. Our other business interests involved sports shops, a country club, a haulage company, ladies and menswear shops and insurance and travel agencies. I was chairman of the parent company and, when sober, conducted that role to the best of my ability. As chairman of the parent company I often had the job of taking existing or prospective clients to lunch. They had lunch, I simply consumed more drink.

I managed to hold it all together, albeit tenuously, for two years. Then the real drinking started.

For all he or she lives in an alcoholic haze, an alcoholic is both cunning and calculating. An alcoholic will find ways of having a drink available at any time of the day or night. In my early days of hard drinking, I rarely took a drink at home. It was the atmosphere of pubs that appealed to me as much as the contents of my glass. At first I drank to be sociable. When I became unsociable, I drank even more. A little over two years after leaving West Ham I just couldn't get through a waking hour without a drink of some sort. I started to smuggle bottles of vodka into our home and hide them from Irene so that she would never know how much I was really consuming in the course of a day. She would see me taking the occasional drink from the drinks cupboard and have a go at me for drinking too much. I'd tell her it was 'just the one'. When Irene left the room, I would then fill my glass from a bottle I had secreted. When the bottle in the drinks cupboard had only a couple of centimetres of vodka left in it, I'd top it up with water to try and make Irene think I'd only had the occasional snifter.

Irene put my heavy drinking down to the fact that I was upset because I had retired from football too early. She was right. But I just couldn't find it within me to admit to anyone that I was pining for the beautiful game. As long as I had a drink inside me my sadness and anxiety left me and I was happy. However, between the fleeting moments of deluded happiness, I found myself moody and morose and subject to dark depression. My answer to that was to drink even more. Some nights I'd stagger through the door with no knowledge at all as to where I had been for the past several hours. During these terrible times, I put my lovely Irene and our beautiful children through a living hell. All my frustration at knowing what I was doing to myself and what I had become would manifest itself in sudden outbursts of temper. I tried to control these temper tantrums. I wanted everything to be like it had been, and when my drinking made that impossible I'd lose it. In frustration I'd smash my hand into a door, or swipe some food off a plate and hurl it across the room. I was ill and I was seeking no help for my illness.

Irene learned to judge my moods and knew when to give me a wide berth. It must have been terrifying for her. A living hell. For the next two years I drank heavily knowing I was an alcoholic. Deep down I didn't want to drink, but I needed to drink. It was like feeding a monster with an insatiable appetite for alcohol. On occasions I would drink up to twenty pints of beer in the course of a day, go home, then drink a whole bottle of vodka before going to bed. I couldn't go without a drink. I used to put a bottle of vodka by my bed so that I could have a few drinks as soon as I woke up. That stopped my hands shaking, steadied my nerves and set me up for another day of binge drinking. In time a couple of drinks first thing turned into four, then five. In the end I'd consume an entire bottle of vodka before getting out of bed. As I have said, there is never one reason for something happening; it is the combined effect of a number of things happening simultaneously. It would be overly simplistic of me to suggest my decline into alcoholism was all down to me having given up football. That was a major factor, but it wasn't the sole reason for my alcoholism. The football culture of the sixties played a part. Footballers have a lot of time on their hands after training. Today a top footballer will use that time to pursue his commercial, promotional and marketing interests. The players of the sixties had few such commitments. When training finished most went home to their families and their gardens. Some holed up in a betting shop. Others, like me, headed for a pub.

Social drinking amongst players was actually encouraged in the sixties. It was thought that such 'get-togethers' fostered team spirit. As long as drinking didn't affect a player's performance on a Saturday afternoon, managers ignored it. It was simply not an issue to them.

The relatively lax drink-driving laws of the time also played a part in my drinking. Drink-driving is now a social stigma and quite rightly frowned upon by any reasonable person. That wasn't the case in the sixties and early seventies. People knew it was wrong to drink and drive, but few realised how wrong it was. After training with West Ham I'd consume five or six lagers at the Slater's Arms then get behind the wheel of my car and drive home. Irresponsible madness, I know. But that's how it was back then.

I also drank to blot out very bad memories. The tragic death of our beautiful Jimmy junior most prominently of all. There were other 'reasons', too. Though now I see them not so much as reasons as excuses. That said, I have no excuse for what I became, and for the hell I put Irene and our children through.

Irene and I sat down to talk. We came to the conclusion that a return to football could be the answer to my problem. Any former pro will tell you that a footballer never loses his skill. It's the legs that go. I'm in my sixties now but put me in a garden, throw me a ball and I can still do the things I could do at the age of twenty-four. What I can't do is the running.

Irene and I decided that if I was to play at a lower standard than league football, my skills and technique would see me through a game. I wouldn't be as fast and sharp, but in a lower standard of football where the players are not as fit I wouldn't have to be.

I made a comeback of sorts with my local Brentwood team and when the news got about that I was playing again, a semi-pro team playing a much higher standard of football than Brentwood gave me a ring. That club was Chelmsford City. I signed for Chelmsford and, though I had an enjoyable enough time of it at their then ground of New Whittle Street, it was a half-hearted effort on my part.

The highlight of my spell at Chelmsford City was our participation in an Anglo-Italian Cup tournament. The English teams that entered this competition were, like Chelmsford City, all part-time professional clubs such as Northwich Victoria and Redditch United. We found ourselves up against the likes of Sampdoria, Udinese and Cremonese. If I remember rightly, Chelmsford won their opening game, as did Northwich Victoria, thereafter each game was a matter of damage limitation. Especially over in Italy where Chelmsford City, who were used to playing in front of 1,500 spectators suddenly found themselves playing before a crowd of 24,000. After a few months at Chelmsford City, I once again hung up my boots to concentrate on my sole interest in life. Drinking.

When I ran out of booze at home, I'd take myself off to the local supermarket. I would pick up a basket and buy a pound of carrots and a loaf of bread on the pretence that I was getting a few odds and ends in for Irene, then walk over to the drinks section and pick up a couple of bottles of vodka. That done, I would pay for my purchases, drive home and down a bottle of vodka in less than forty-five minutes. The last person who wants to confront alcoholism is the alcoholic. For two years I kidded myself that I would give up the drink 'tomorrow'. That 'tomorrow' never came. I knew I had to do something to keep myself basically fit, so I took up golf, tennis, squash and played in the occasional charity football match. My general fitness did improve, but that only meant I had a faster recovery rate after my heavy drinking sessions than most alcoholics. People who saw me running around a tennis court, or playing at the home of some local amateur football club, would never believe that in the previous twenty-four hours I had consumed twenty pints of lager and a couple of bottles of vodka. Mr Hyde was momentarily Mr Jekyll again.

They say you become an alcoholic when your drinking costs you more than money. I had now reached that stage. My drinking was costing me the love of Irene, the respect of my children and my reputation as a businessman of some note. I knew I had to do something to arrest my decline and put my family life back on track, so I agreed to go into a private nursing home for treatment and supervision.

The care and treatment I received gradually reduced my craving for alcohol. I left that nursing home in fine fettle and feeling pretty damned pleased with myself. I knew I could give up the booze if I really wanted.

For several weeks I never touched as much as a drop of alcohol. I could beat the booze at any time and I felt I had proved that. So two months after my release from the nursing home, I decided that from now on I would only drink in moderation and confine myself to two social pints a day and no more.

Within weeks those 'two social pints' had escalated to ten a day. In no time at all I was back to drinking up to twenty pints a day and more than the occasional bottle of vodka. I returned to the nursing home, after which I returned to the drink. This is how I lived for the next three years. Boozing. Nursing home. Boozing. Nursing home. Boozing. Nursing home. They didn't have a revolving door in that nursing home but it appeared to me as if they did. I saw doctor after doctor. Psychiatrist after psychiatrist. I parted with a fortune in consultation fees. I received nothing but the very best advice and ignored every word. I was a hopeless and helpless alcoholic. People close to me knew of my illness but it was not common knowledge in the football world. Simply because on those odd occasions when I had returned to football for a testimonial game or an exhibition match I managed to get through such games okay and no one detected I had a serious problem.

I played for Spurs in a testimonial game for Pat Jennings at

White Hart Lane and displayed enough of my old skill in and around the penalty box that Bill Nicholson and Keith Burkinshaw took me aside and tried to talk me into making a comeback at Spurs. They would have been flabbergasted if they had been able to see the state I was in just forty-eight hours earlier following a particularly vicious bender.

I went as far as discussing the possibility of a comeback with Spurs with the chairman of the Professional Footballers' Association, Derek Dougan. Derek was very helpful and made all the right noises but I scotched the idea – not because I didn't want to play football again, but because I didn't want to let down Tottenham and their supporters.

For Pat Jennings to be granted a testimonial at Spurs was a relatively recent departure from normal club policy. For years Spurs had allowed a loyal player of some years standing to leave the club on a free transfer as a gesture of their gratitude. This enabled the player to negotiate a better deal for himself with his new club as that club did not have to pay Spurs a fee for his services. That policy changed following the departure of Dave Mackay to Derby County.

Just about every player who left Spurs joined a club in a lower division or, if they joined another First Division club, one that was not a threat to Spurs' title aspirations. When Dave joined Derby they were a mid-table Second Division team. However, under Brian Clough and Peter Taylor, Derby enjoyed a meteoric rise. With the team benefiting from Dave's leadership on the pitch, Derby not only won promotion but emerged as genuine contenders for the First Division Championship, a title they won in 1972.

Bill Nicholson and the Spurs board were determined there would be no repeat of the Mackay situation, so they changed club policy and began to grant testimonials in the early seventies. The first to benefit from this change of policy was yours truly. Tottenham had paid Milan £99,999 for my services in 1961. When I left the club for West Ham, my value in the Martin Peters deal was put at £90,000. So after nine years' service at White Hart Lane you could say the club had had their money's worth out of me.

It was a group of loyal Spurs fans who approached the club and asked if they could organise a testimonial on my behalf. The club said 'Yes' and those supporters formed themselves into an organising committee. Those lads were Peter Spall, who owned Spall Sports; Maurice Keston, a lifelong Spurs supporter; and John Bairstow, who was chairman of a hotel chain. Other Spurs supporters joined their number and preparations for my testimonial got under way.

I had played in numerous testimonials myself, most notably that of Stanley Matthews in 1965. What a night that was! The pre-match entertainment was a game between two sides billed as post-war favourites, one skippered by Stan's old Blackpool captain Harry Johnson and the other by the former Arsenal player Wally Barnes. I played in the main match of the evening which contained a galaxy of top-drawer names such as Johnny Haynes, Denis Law, Jim Baxter, Puskas, Lev Yashin, Di Stefano, Eusebio, Uwe Seeler, Karl-Heinz Schnellinger and two of my Spurs team-mates of the time, Cliff Jones and Alan Gilzean, as well as Stan himself.

My testimonial took place on the evening of 17 October 1972 and the opposition were the Dutch giants Feyenoord. I was staggered by the response of the Spurs fans. A crowd of 45,799 turned up on what for me was a great night. I had the honour of leading Spurs out on to the pitch; ironically, right behind me was Martin Peters. My memory isn't playing tricks on me this time. As I led Spurs on to the field, Feyenoord walked out alongside and I was gobsmacked to see that one of their players was wearing glasses! Closer inspection revealed them to be made of some sort of soft plastic, similar to those worn by the contemporary Dutch international Edgar Davids.

It was, however, the referee who needed glasses. After only three minutes I latched on to a through ball when in an offside position but was allowed to carry on and slide the ball past the Feyenoord goalkeeper with my left foot. As opposed to the many legitimate goals I had disallowed during the course of my career, this one was definitely offside. But what the heck. It was my testimonial.

Though it was only a testimonial it turned out to be a very keenly contested affair. Another Spurs goal from Ray Evans gave us a 2-1 victory on what was a fantastic return to White Hart Lane for me. After all the expenses had been paid I was presented with a cheque for £22,000. To this day I thank everyone involved in organising and participating in my testimonial, particularly those marvellous Spurs fans who came to give me their support. Hand on heart, I can say that not one penny of the money I received did I fritter away on drink. I used some of the money to become a Lloyd's underwriter and gave the rest to Irene to spend on home improvements. In addition to playing in the occasional testimonial or charity game, I also turned out in a number of exhibition tournaments. One such tournament led to me coming face to face with the Mafia.

One morning at our Upminster home I opened my mail to find a cheque for one thousand Canadian dollars. The accompanying letter informed me that I would be able to cash the cheque in Toronto should I agree to play in an indoor cup competition that was being organised by the former Sunderland player Ken Chisholm. The letter had come from a Canadian football nut, who I will simply call Joe, for reasons that will soon become apparent.

Later that day I received a telephone call from Bobby Moore who told me that he too had received a cheque for $1,000 in the post. It transpired that other recipients of this windfall were Jack Charlton and Gordon Banks. The idea was that we would form a team of England Old Stars and would compete in this indoor tournament against similar old pros from other countries.

The indoor tournament proved a great success, what's more, we won it. A crowd of 22,000 turned up for the finals which made the backer, Joe, feel there was a market for this type of football in other countries.

I wasn't sure, but Joe was so enthused that he organised similar indoor tournaments in a number of other countries, such as Germany and France. At the time one of my business interests was a travel agency, Greaves Travel on Marylebone High Street, which, though I have no connection with it now, still trades under the same name. Joe persuaded me that the subsequent tournaments were going to be real money-spinners, so my travel agency organised all the flights and hotel accommodation for every participating player. The players came from all around the world and the next thing I knew my travel agency had stood £30,000 up front.

Joe had no concerns. He believed each tournament would be as successful as the one he had staged in Toronto and that I would have my money back in no time. He was wrong. The Toronto tournament proved an exception. Every subsequent tournament played to sparse attendances and the debts mounted. Joe was unperturbed and told me not to worry. He owned a number of bars in Toronto which were doing well and informed me that he himself would pay me the £30,000 I was owed 'in a matter of days'.

I flew back home from Germany. The days turned into weeks and the weeks into months, but there was still no word from Joe; more importantly, no cheque in the post for £30,000. As you can imagine I was somewhat peeved at this. I attempted to get in touch with Joe in Toronto but every telephone number I had for him had been disconnected. I was at a loss as to what to do next. One of the players who had participated in the original tournament in Toronto was a former Yugoslav international whom I had played against when I was at Spurs and he was at Hadjuk Split. This guy had emigrated to Canada, settled in Toronto and become a policeman. He had played for Yugoslavia Old Stars in the Toronto tournament and we'd had a few drinks together, talking about the old days. He wasn't a close buddy or anything like that, but I knew him well enough to get on the telephone to him. I explained my dilemma, told him I would be most grateful if he could spare some time to get a contact number for Joe and left it at that. A couple of days later, he rang me back with a telephone number where Joe could be contacted. The telephone number was for one of Joe's bars. I rang it up and asked to speak to Joe.

'Who wants to know?' a gruff Canadian voice asked.

I told the voice on the other end of the line who I was and why I wanted to speak to Joe.

'You telling me, buddy, Joe owes you thirty thousand pounds?'

I confirmed it and once again explained why the debt had been incurred.

'Then you better fly over here, buddy. Sounds like we got some talking to do with Joe,' said the gruff voice ominously.

'Gruff Voice' gave me the name of a bar in Toronto where we were to meet and I flew to Canada from Heathrow.

On arrival in Toronto I immediately took a taxi to the bar in question and presented myself before the manager. I told him I had been summoned to a meeting involving Joe. The manager disappeared into a back room, only to re-emerge and ask me to go through.

When I stepped into the back room of this bar my legs nearly failed me. Seated behind a desk was a gorilla of a guy in his fifties with a neck that looked like it could dent an axe. He was very smartly dressed in a dark blue wool suit and white shirt. The tie he was wearing looked as if it would have cost for a little longer than we first anticipated,' said Gruff Voice.

Again, Joe nodded sheepishly.

Gruff Voice turned to the bespectacled man.

'This is Mike, our accountant. Mike will sort you out, Mr Greaves. Won't you, Mike?'

Mike nodded nervously.

'Now, Mike. If ya'd be so good,' said Gruff Voice.

'But the bank's closed,' said Mike timidly.

'Then go down and open it,' Gruff Voice ordered.

Mike hurriedly left the room.

I spent a very nervous half an hour sitting in that room in silence while Gruff Voice attended to paperwork. It was the most uncomfortable half-hour of my life. I was so nervous and edgy, sweat was running down my back in rivulets. By the time Mike reappeared my shirt was wringing wet.

Mike produced a bag containing £30,000 in Canadian dollars. I thanked Gruff Voice for his time and understanding and beat a very hasty retreat from that room. I went straight to the airport and caught the next flight home.

When I arrived at Heathrow I was a nervous wreck as I approached customs. The limit for bringing currency into the UK at the time was £2,000 and I had £30,000 in a holdall. Fortunately the customs lads on duty that day were football fans and recognised me. They were more interested in talking about Spurs and getting my autograph than looking in my holdall and I passed through the gate without any bother. Needless to say, I never accepted an invitation to play in an overseas exhibition tournament again.

My doctor, a former Olympic competitor, put me in touch with Alcoholics Anonymous. I attended a few of their meetings but what they had to say went in one ear and out the other. I looked around at the other people attending these meetings and convinced myself that they had a real problem with drink little less than the price of my return flight to London. Behind him stood two guys who wouldn't have been out of place in a *Rocky* movie. Both were wearing expensive suits. One was a hatchet-faced man wearing sunglasses. The other had a face like a collapsed lung and was wearing a black felt hat with the brim pulled down to reveal just a glimpse of shark-like eyes. At one side of the desk sat a bespectacled man in his forties, whose face was a glummer version of Clement Freud's. On the other side of the desk sat a very nervous Joe.

'Joe don't own his bars no more,' the man behind the desk informed me, in so doing revealing himself to be Gruff Voice. 'You see, it's like this, Mr Greaves. Joe opened up his bars thanks to us. We loaned him the dough. Only Joe here, he ain't played ball. Joe fell behind with the payments. Now we don't allow that, do we, Joe? No. So we have taken over all of Joe's bars, until such time as they have earned enough money to pay us back what he owes us. Plus interest, as this is purely a business arrangement. Now, Mr Greaves, you tell me that our friend Joe here, he also owes you dough?'

I was bricking it. It was obvious to me that these guys were the local Mafia and, to be honest, I didn't feel very comfortable about that. But I had come all the way from London for this meeting so summoned up the courage to say my piece. I told Gruff Voice the whole story of how Joe had come to owe me £30,000. They listened to what I had to say without interrupting me and when I finished my tale, Gruff Voice turned to Joe.

'This here guy correct in what he says?'

Joe nodded.

'Okay,' said Gruff Voice, 'this is what we'll do. We're going to pay you the thirty-thousand pounds you are owed, Mr Greaves. Today.'

Gruff Voice turned once more to Joe.

'Seems to me, Joe, like we gonna be holding on to your bars

or a little longer than we first anticipated,' said Gruff Voice.

Again, Joe nodded sheepishly.

Gruff Voice turned to the bespectacled man.

'This is Mike, our accountant. Mike will sort you out, Mr Greaves. Won't you, Mike?'

Mike nodded nervously.

'Now, Mike. If ya'd be so good,' said Gruff Voice.

'But the bank's closed,' said Mike timidly.

'Then go down and open it,' Gruff Voice ordered.

Mike hurriedly left the room.

I spent a very nervous half an hour sitting in that room in silence while Gruff Voice attended to paperwork. It was the most uncomfortable half-hour of my life. I was so nervous and edgy, sweat was running down my back in rivulets. By the time Mike reappeared my shirt was wringing wet.

Mike produced a bag containing £30,000 in Canadian dollars. I thanked Gruff Voice for his time and understanding and beat a very hasty retreat from that room. I went straight to the airport and caught the next flight home.

When I arrived at Heathrow I was a nervous wreck as I approached customs. The limit for bringing currency into the UK at the time was £2,000 and I had £30,000 in a holdall. Fortunately the customs lads on duty that day were football fans and recognised me. They were more interested in talking about Spurs and getting my autograph than looking in my holdall and I passed through the gate without any bother. Needless to say, I never accepted an invitation to play in an overseas exhibition tournament again.

My doctor, a former Olympic competitor, put me in touch with Alcoholics Anonymous. I attended a few of their meetings but what they had to say went in one ear and out the other. I looked around at the other people attending these meetings and convinced myself that they had a real problem with drink

that we would form a team of England Old Stars and would compete in this indoor tournament against similar old pros from other countries.

The indoor tournament proved a great success, what's more, we won it. A crowd of 22,000 turned up for the finals which made the backer, Joe, feel there was a market for this type of football in other countries.

I wasn't sure, but Joe was so enthused that he organised similar indoor tournaments in a number of other countries, such as Germany and France. At the time one of my business interests was a travel agency, Greaves Travel on Marylebone High Street, which, though I have no connection with it now, still trades under the same name. Joe persuaded me that the subsequent tournaments were going to be real money-spinners, so my travel agency organised all the flights and hotel accommodation for every participating player. The players came from all around the world and the next thing I knew my travel agency had stood £30,000 up front.

Joe had no concerns. He believed each tournament would be as successful as the one he had staged in Toronto and that I would have my money back in no time. He was wrong. The Toronto tournament proved an exception. Every subsequent tournament played to sparse attendances and the debts mounted. Joe was unperturbed and told me not to worry. He owned a number of bars in Toronto which were doing well and informed me that he himself would pay me the £30,000 I was owed 'in a matter of days'.

I flew back home from Germany. The days turned into weeks and the weeks into months, but there was still no word from Joe; more importantly, no cheque in the post for £30,000. As you can imagine I was somewhat peeved at this. I attempted to get in touch with Joe in Toronto but every telephone number I had for him had been disconnected. I was at a loss as to what to do next. One of the players who had participated in the original tournament in Toronto was a former Yugoslav international whom I had played against when I was at Spurs and he was at Hadjuk Split. This guy had emigrated to Canada, settled in Toronto and become a policeman. He had played for Yugoslavia Old Stars in the Toronto tournament and we'd had a few drinks together, talking about the old days. He wasn't a close buddy or anything like that, but I knew him well enough to get on the telephone to him. I explained my dilemma, told him I would be most grateful if he could spare some time to get a contact number for Joe and left it at that. A couple of days later, he rang me back with a telephone number where Joe could be contacted. The telephone number was for one of Joe's bars. I rang it up and asked to speak to Joe.

'Who wants to know?' a gruff Canadian voice asked.

I told the voice on the other end of the line who I was and why I wanted to speak to Joe.

'You telling me, buddy, Joe owes you thirty thousand pounds?'

I confirmed it and once again explained why the debt had been incurred.

'Then you better fly over here, buddy. Sounds like we got some talking to do with Joe,' said the gruff voice ominously.

'Gruff Voice' gave me the name of a bar in Toronto where we were to meet and I flew to Canada from Heathrow.

On arrival in Toronto I immediately took a taxi to the bar in question and presented myself before the manager. I told him I had been summoned to a meeting involving Joe. The manager disappeared into a back room, only to re-emerge and ask me to go through.

When I stepped into the back room of this bar my legs nearly failed me. Seated behind a desk was a gorilla of a guy in his fifties with a neck that looked like it could dent an axe. He was very smartly dressed in a dark blue wool suit and white shirt. The tie he was wearing looked as if it would have cost

little less than the price of my return flight to London. him stood two guys who wouldn't have been out of pl Rocky movie. Both were wearing expensive suits. On hatchet-faced man wearing sunglasses. The other had like a collapsed lung and was wearing a black felt hat w brim pulled down to reveal just a glimpse of shark-like ey one side of the desk sat a bespectacled man in his forties, face was a glummer version of Clement Freud's. On the side of the desk sat a very nervous Joe.

'Joe don't own his bars no more,' the man behind the informed me, in so doing revealing himself to be Gruff Vo 'You see, it's like this, Mr Greaves. Joe opened up his thanks to us. We loaned him the dough. Only Joe here, he a played ball. Joe fell behind with the payments. Now we do allow that, do we, Joe? No. So we have taken over all of Jo bars, until such time as they have earned enough money to p us back what he owes us. Plus interest, as this is purely a business arrangement. Now, Mr Greaves, you tell me that our friend Joe here, he also owes you dough?'

I was bricking it. It was obvious to me that these guys were the local Mafia and, to be honest, I didn't feel very comfortable about that. But I had come all the way from London for this meeting so summoned up the courage to say my piece. I told Gruff Voice the whole story of how Joe had come to owe me £30,000. They listened to what I had to say without interrupting me and when I finished my tale, Gruff Voice turned to Joe.

'This here guy correct in what he says?'

Joe nodded.

'Okay,' said Gruff Voice, 'this is what we'll do. We're going to pay you the thirty-thousand pounds you are owed, Mr Greaves. Today.'

Gruff Voice turned once more to Joe.

'Seems to me, Joe, like we gonna be holding on to your bars

but not me. I remember thinking, 'I'll never sink so low as this lot. No chance!'

There was no stopping me. I drank myself into oblivion on a daily basis. Irene, who had lovingly nursed me for two years, had by now reached breaking point. She just couldn't take any more. I left home and for a time lived with my parents, only going back home on visits to see Irene and the children.

Irene's brother Tom was also my business partner. Tom had seen the strain and the agony I was putting Irene through and was also aware that I now had only a passing interest in our business affairs. We started to have our differences and I now accept that it was all of my doing. Tom was being responsible and I wasn't. I wasn't up for a business life any more, so sold my interest in the company that Tom and I had so proudly and conscientiously built up over the years. I was left with the travel agency and a couple of menswear shops. Eventually the menswear shops went to the wall, mainly because of market forces but also due in part to my drinking which had impaired my judgement and acumen as a businessman.

There was no way that my marriage could survive the pressures I put on it. I can recall very little of this dark period in my life but have been assured that I turned into a monster. There is a scene in David Lean's 1953 film version of Harold Brighouse's *Hobson's Choice* where Hobson, played by Charles Laughton, has become an alcoholic and suffers from the DTs. It's a comic scene in which Hobson sees giant fluffy rabbits walking about at the end of his bed. There is nothing comic about having the DTs. I experienced them and it was as if the worst excesses of a Stephen King novel had become a reality before me. I can recall lying on my back shaking uncontrollably as nightmare visions unfolded all about me. Walls moved and came crashing towards me, ornaments and furniture took on life and walked around the room and demon faces gazed at me from the ceiling. I was in Hell.

I would stumble about with a three-day growth of stubble on my face, not knowing if it was nine o'clock in the morning or nine at night. When I became impossible to handle, friends would book me into the alcoholic ward of Warley Psychiatric Hospital.

On release I would manage to go without alcohol for a few weeks, only to binge drink, become incapable of looking after myself and be returned to Warley. Incredibly, people still wanted me to play football. The American team, St Antonio, made me an offer. I spoke to their representative for ten minutes on the telephone before convincing him that there was no way I wanted to play soccer in the United States. Little did he know it, but while he was talking to me I was lying flat on my back in Warley hospital barely able to hold the telephone because my hands were shaking so much.

The *Sunday People* learned of my alcoholism and informed me they were going to run with the story. I didn't want the *People* to run with the story as they saw it, I wanted them to get it right. In order for them to do that, I decided to co-operate. The story made front-page news, as such stories tend to. I hadn't welcomed the publicity but once my plight became public knowledge I made the decision to use it to my advantage. With everybody knowing of my chronic alcoholism I hoped what remaining pride I had might help me defeat the illness. I was now divorced. As Irene said, she didn't divorce me. She divorced the stranger I had become. I desperately wanted to defeat my alcoholism, but I knew I couldn't do it alone. I needed help. So I summoned the strength and courage to telephone Alcoholics Anonymous.

CHAPTER SIXTEEN

MY FIRST, MY LAST, MY EVERYTHING

I faced my demons. I was a helpless alcoholic peering over the precipice of life. I sought the help and guidance of Alcoholics Anonymous and at last started to take their words seriously. I knew it was going to be a rugged and rocky road to recovery, so I at first made the journey by taking very small steps.

Alcoholics Anonymous had a shock in store for me right from the start. I was told an alcoholic never truly conquers his alcoholism. It is a cunning illness that can creep up and hit you the moment you lower your guard. AA ingrained in me the knowledge that being sober today is no guarantee of being sober tomorrow. Yesterdays and tomorrows have no place in the life of an alcoholic, I was told. You live only for today.

The first steps I took were minute. I was encouraged to set myself the task of getting through an hour without a drink. When I managed that single hour, my goal was to get through another hour without alcohol, to make it two hours without booze. Slowly but surely I managed to maintain these hourly goals, so that in the first instance they combined to enable me to get through a whole day without alcohol. That done, I awoke the next morning and started the process all over again. Hour by hour, day by day until a week passed and I hadn't touched a drop of drink.

Of course it wasn't as simple as it seems. It was very tough. I craved alcohol, but this time I really did want to give it up. So I fought my desire for drink not on an hourly basis, but in each minute that passed. Alcoholics Anonymous didn't make me feel ashamed, embarrassed or weak about my problem. On the contrary, they instilled in me strength of character, resolve and the willpower to beat my illness. Qualities I was told that existed within me as they do in every human being. What I had to do was reach inside myself and discover those inner qualities and bring them to the fore.

I attended a series of meetings at AA where a volunteer chairperson introduced a subject for discussion relating to different problems of alcoholism. Those present would talk about their own experiences and exchange points of view. These shared experiences helped me understand the nature of my illness and made me realise that many of the things I had done were common to others, because our actions were prompted by the illness. One of the key elements to recovery was self-discipline and to help me achieve that I adhered to a set of guidelines known as 'The Twelve Steps to Recovery'. In these steps I had to do the following:

i) Admit I was powerless over alcohol – that my life had become unmanageable.

ii) Believe that a power greater than myself could restore me to sanity.

iii) Make a decision to turn my will and my life over to the care of God as I understood Him to be.

iv) Make a searching and fearless inventory of myself.

v) Admit to God, to myself and to another person the exact nature of my wrongs.

vi) Be entirely ready to have God remove all my defects of character.

vii) Humbly ask Him to remove my shortcomings.

viii) Make a list of all the people I had harmed and be willing to make amends with them all.

ix) Make amends with such people wherever possible, except when to do so would injure them or others.

x) Continue to take a personal inventory and, when wrong, promptly admit it.

xi) Seek through the power of prayer and meditation to improve my conscious contact with God as I understood Him, praying only for knowledge of His will for me as a person and the power to carry it out.

xii) Having had a spiritual experience as a result of these steps, to try to carry this message to other alcoholics and to practise these principles in all our affairs.

Those steps are the copyright of Alcoholics Anonymous World Services Incorporated and they formed the way forward and the guidelines to my future life.

I am not a religious person. I respect, even envy, those who find strength and faith through the workings of the Church. When with England it may surprise you to learn that I would occasionally accompany Nobby Stiles to church on a Sunday morning. Nobby could be a little terror on the pitch but off it he was a very religious, responsible and serious young guy. Alf would ask where Nobby and I were, and be told by Bobby Moore or Bobby Charlton that we had gone to church. All Alf would say was, 'Oh, right. Okay'. When Nobby and I returned to the England hotel, no one ever made mention of our churchgoing. No one ever asked us about our beliefs. It was considered to be a private matter, which suited me fine. To this day I keep my religious beliefs to myself. I follow my religion not in a church but carry it around with me in my heart, my soul and in my head.

After a number of weeks under the supervision and care of Alcoholics Anonymous I became much more aware of my spiritual, physical and mental wellbeing, stronger willed and more purposeful because of it. I was now living alone in a small bedsit in Wanstead. I had managed to go without drink, but I was still a chronic alcoholic. The difference was that I was not now hopeless or helpless. The weeks turned into months. A year went by but I was still only taking small steps on a daily basis in an attempt to defeat the drink. Alcohol, of course, existed, but as time passed, I was simply of the mind that it did not exist in my world. Nor would I allow it to.

I was living alone in the bedsit, though I would often visit Irene and the children, sometimes three or four times a week. Irene and I were divorced, but my frequent visits served to instil in me the belief that we had never truly parted. I still loved her dearly. We still communicated and had a relationship of sorts. Certainly a better relationship than when I had been drinking myself into oblivion. Though Irene and I were not living under the same roof, the fact that I saw a lot of her and the children further encouraged me. Prior to joining Alcoholics Anonymous I had lived in despair; now I lived in hope. Slender hope, maybe, but hope nonetheless.

Instead of living in pubs, I lived in my little flat in Wanstead and tried to pick up the pieces of my life. At night I fought the temptation to visit a pub. I either read books or newspapers, or watched television. Only an alcoholic seeking a cure could tell you just how many adverts there are on television for booze. When I did go out at night it was with fellow members of AA. It was good to hear people discussing the problems of drink in a language I understood as my own. I discovered my new friends had gone through similar, sometimes identical, experiences to me. We had empathy with one another and when we attended AA meetings together, we were not criticised or patronised but understood.

I rediscovered the feeling of love, compassion and companionship through the AA. We came from all walks of life and from every race, creed and colour and we met together in fellowship and were bound together by one common bond. We were all in various stages of rehabilitation and we helped each other along the difficult road to recovery. We had a human failing of which we were all aware and our goal was to overcome it together. As a footballer I had played in some great teams. But I had never been a member of such a team as this.

I even made a return to football with non-league Barnet. I was helping a fund-raising organisation called The Gold Diggers, which raised money for worthy causes by organising football matches and pro-celebrity golf days. 'The Gold Diggers' included in their number Eric Morecambe, Jimmy Hill and the former QPR, Liverpool, Fulham and Watford goalkeeper Dave Underwood. At the time Dave was chairman of Barnet and it was he who persuaded me to turn out for 'The Bees'.

I'd known Dave for some years. In 1972 he put together a team of 'Golden Oldies' which played a number of exhibition matches in the Middle East. I was a member of that team as was Stanley Matthews. We played a match in Kuwait which was only the second time I had ever played alongside Stan.

In addition to Stan and me, our team also included the likes of Johnny Haynes, Ron Springett, George Cohen, Jimmy Hill and that legend of Welsh football, the imperious John Charles. We were all getting on in terms of football, but could still play and give a younger team more than a run for their money. The problem we encountered in Kuwait was the heat. The temperature was a stamina sapping 110 degrees Fahrenheit on the day of the game and we soon found ourselves wilting in the heat and losing 4-1.

Stan was knocking on fifty-eight years and had exhausted himself by repeatedly weaving his own particular brand of magic up and down the dusty touchline. Dave could see that

Stan was suffering, so he came to the side of the pitch to indicate he was going to substitute the maestro. As soon as Stan caught sight of Dave he realised what was happening and moved across to the other wing. Dave walked all the way round the perimeter of the pitch to the left wing with the intention of beckoning to Stan. Stan's pride, however, wouldn't allow him to be substituted. As soon as Stan saw Dave on the left touchline, he moved back to his normal berth on the right. So it went on. Dave running from one side of the pitch to the other in an attempt to collar Stan, Stan continually switching wings.

Eventually Dave cupped his hands to his mouth and shouted at the top of his voice, 'Gentlemen, it is my privilege to accompany the great Sir Stanley Matthews off the pitch. Please accord him the ovation his display today so richly deserves!' The Kuwaiti players stopped in their tracks and started to applaud, and then the capacity crowd took it up and cheered Stan as the great man made a reluctant though character-istically dignified exit.

Stan had never played his professional football in an era of substitutes. It was the only time in his life that he was ever substituted. My old Spurs team-mate Cliff Jones replaced Stan and, with his fresh legs, we managed to get back in the game and eventually forced a 4-4 draw.

No player likes to be substituted, especially when his team then turns the game around and achieves a result in his absence. Our comeback was largely due to Cliff, who ran the Kuwaiti full back ragged. Stan was a gentleman and great sportsman. After the game he made a point of going up to Cliff and complimenting him on his efforts. Cliff didn't want Stan to feel downhearted about being substituted, so proceeded to butter him up.

'Thanks, Stan,' said Cliff, 'but I should be thanking you. My job was easy because you had run rings around that full back and by the time I came on for you, he was knackered. It was down to your efforts that we managed to come back and get the draw.'

For a moment Stan was silent. 'As long as you realise that, then it's okay,' he said, before turning to me and winking.

When Dave invited me to play for Barnet they had just won promotion to the Southern League Premier Division. The standard of football was nowhere near what I had been used to, but it wasn't bad. When Denis Law retired from football he once went along to watch non-league Witton Albion of the Cheshire League in action. Denis only went the once. He felt he couldn't watch part-time professional football where the skill and technique of the players was not that of full-time pros. It just left him frustrated.

My attitude was different. I jumped at the chance of playing in part-time professional football because it complimented my recovery programme. Playing for Barnet would help my physical fitness, provide me with a discipline of sorts and give me another focus. I was of the mind that the more interests I had, the less chance there was of my mind dwelling on booze. When I signed for Barnet in 1977 I still had a major problem with alcohol and was surviving from day to day. But thankfully, I was resisting the temptation to drink.

The Barnet manager was Billy Meadows. Bill had rebuilt the side that had been relegated two seasons before and had done so by creating a team around former Football League players such as Bob McNab, the former Huddersfield Town and Arsenal full back, and Terry Mancini, who had given sterling service to numerous London clubs including Stringfellow's. In addition to us old pros, Barnet also boasted a number of players who had made a mark in non-league football, such as Les Eason and John Fairbrother.

While playing for Barnet I saw parts of the world I never thought I'd see, such as the fleshpots of Kettering, Nuneaton

and Minehead. I made my debut in August 1977 in a 3-2
victory over Atherstone Town. A few days later I was on the
goals trail again when netting in our 2-2 draw at Worcester
City. Our next game was at home to Minehead who in the
previous season had finished runners-up in the league to
Wimbledon. We beat Minehead which was a significant result
for the club. Having only just won promotion to the Southern
League Premier Division our unbeaten start to the season, in
particular the victory over Minehead, provided ample
evidence that Barnet were more than capable of competing
with the best at this standard of football. The attendance for
our game against Minehead was 886. I scored our winning goal
and in so doing turned towards the crowd, only to look up at
the terracing and find there was no crowd in that part of the
ground, so I had to run over to where the crowd was! It was a
far cry from the glorious European nights at White Hart Lane
with Spurs but that mattered not one iota to me. I was back
playing football and enjoying it.

At first I played up front for Barnet, but Billy Meadows then
switched me into midfield. That suited me because I no longer
had the legs to run around up front and chase a lot of lost
causes. I still had my football brain and skill, however, and was
still fairly mobile. Of course, I no longer had the sharpness and
speed off the mark I enjoyed in my younger days, but that was
not to my detriment either because I found I had more time on
the ball. After a few weeks of playing for Barnet I felt in good
shape. I was still very nimble and made my mark on games by
using my brain, rather than trying to depend on the speed I no
longer possessed.

In their first season back in the Southern Premier League
Barnet finished a creditable seventh. We were some points
adrift of Champions Bath City, but all told we felt pretty
pleased at our efforts. We were involved in some belting
games. I particularly recall a 5-0 home win over Kettering, a

4-2 victory over Redditch United and a thrilling 5-4 away victory at Atherstone Town.

Certain aspects of playing semi-professional football came as a culture shock to me. I remember being told that we were playing Camberley Town one particular Saturday in August. Camberley weren't in our league, so I asked what competition we were involved in and was somewhat taken aback to hear it was the preliminary round of the FA Cup. For me the FA Cup had always started in January with the Third Round proper. It was odd to embark on the 'Wembley Trail' in August with the sun on our backs.

Barnet battled through all the preliminary rounds of the FA Cup to reach the first round proper. I also found it strange when observing the reactions of my team-mates in the days leading up to the first round draw. They were bubbling with excitement at the prospect of being handed a plum tie with a 'big club' – such as Brentford or Reading.

When the draw was made, it came as something of an anticlimax to everyone when we were pitched against fellow non-leaguers Woking.

Our tie against Woking was only fifteen minutes old when we won a free kick just outside their penalty area. As the Woking players were busy organising themselves into a wall, I stepped up and curled the ball around them and into the top corner of the net. My team-mates ran up to me to offer their congratulations on my goal, but I was peeved to see the referee indicating he wanted the free kick to be retaken. I was furious and asked him why. The official informed me that neither he nor the Woking players was ready.

'If they ain't ready, that's their lookout. As for you, you awarded us the free kick and now you're penalising us for taking it quickly. Which, by the way, I'm allowed to do,' I informed the official.

The argument became more and more heated and I became

more aggressive. Eventually the referee decided he had had enough of my protestations and booked me. Which left me feeling very aggrieved and not a little annoyed with myself.

My fight against alcoholism came at a price. I was drying out and occasionally this left me in such a state that I simply stayed in my flat and roughed it out. I missed several training sessions at Barnet and the occasional game as a result of the drying out. The club were very understanding. When I did reappear at Underhill, no one ever thought fit to ask where I had been and I simply picked up from where I had left off.

Only a few months into my second season with Barnet I came to the conclusion that I had to leave the club. In 1978–9 Barry Fry had taken over from Billy Meadows as the Barnet manager and I asked Barry for a meeting. During that meeting I told Barry that I couldn't give him or the club the commitment they were looking for. My battle against alcoholism had resulted in me becoming increasingly absent from training and matches. I also wanted to devote more time to my remaining business interests. I informed Barry I felt it better for me to leave the club than let them down. Barry tried to dissuade me. I had scored twenty-five goals for Barnet from midfield in the previous season and he felt I could still 'do a job' for them.

'I can do a job for this club,' I told him, 'but not the job I want to do. I don't want to let anyone down. I'm sad about it, but it's best that I leave and concentrate all my efforts and energies on getting my life back together.'

Barry was very understanding and I think he appreciated my honesty. I was sad to leave Barnet because they were a great bunch of people, but it had to be done. I had a great time at the club and still have nothing but fond memories of my time there. We had a lot of laughs and it had been some years since I had laughed. I turned out alongside some decent part-time players such as Steve Oliver, Terry Tappin, Les Eason and John

Fairbrother, and enjoyed their friendship and camaraderie, but I had to go. If I was going to get the better of alcoholism and get my life back on track, I knew I had to commit myself totally to that cause.

In 1979 I could see light at the end of the tunnel and for once it wasn't a train coming. The reasons I had given to Barry Fry for leaving Barnet were all true, but there was another reason why I felt I had to give up football. The most important reason of all. I was living in the flat in Wanstead and the weekend was the main time for me to see Irene and our children. Playing football for Barnet ate into that precious time. I wanted to spend more time with my family. I wanted to spend my weekends with them, in fact, I wanted to spend all my time with them, but at this stage of my life circumstances did not allow that. I had hurt Irene so very badly. I prayed that, in time, that hurt could be healed. Irene had been granted a divorce but in 1979 we hadn't got as far as the decree absolute. I felt there was hope for us as a couple and weekends afforded me the opportunity to demonstrate to her I had changed for the good.

In the spring of 1979 I received a telephone call from London Weekend Television asking if I would appear as a guest on the *Russell Harty Plus* show and talk about my battle against alcoholism. My initial reaction was to say 'No' but I managed to shame myself sufficiently into facing up to the fact that I had to do this interview. I knew that if I didn't it would mean I was running away from my problem and running away would lead me in only one direction: back to the booze. So I accepted.

As Russell Harty introduced me in the programme I stood at the side of the studio wanting to get the hell out of there, but I knew it was best that I saw it through. It was a brutally honest interview. I heard myself telling Russell that I would always be an alcoholic. 'Though the important thing for me,' I told him, 'is that I must be a non-drinking alcoholic. The only way I can do that is not to have a drink today. That's the simple rule I must follow for the rest of my life.'

When Russell dug deeper into my history as a drinker I trotted out the stock AA doctrine, because I could not – and still can't – think of a better way of tackling the illness.

I felt like a prisoner suddenly released from jail when the interview was at an end. My mouth was dry and I couldn't wait to get back to the hospitality room for a drink. I felt everybody's eyes boring into me as I went up to the bar. When the barman asked what I'd like to drink, I felt really good about myself when I told him, 'Perrier water, please'.

At the time of my appearance on *Russell Harty Plus* I was going around with two pennies in my pocket hoping they'd mate. My financial situation was dire and to clear the debts I had incurred at the depth of my alcoholism I was selling sweaters around the markets and to small shops. The one luxury I had allowed myself was my car. I was driving a yellow Jaguar XJ6 and was determined to hang on to it even though some days I was pushed to come up with petrol money.

I was living in the flat but home is where the heart is and my heart was in a house on The Fairway in Upminster where Irene was living with our children, Lynn (21), Mitzi (18), Danny (17) and Andrew (13). I had made a real mess of everyone's lives and my inability to provide adequate financial support for my family forced Irene to sell our home on The Fairway. Irene bought a smaller, much more modest house half a mile away. For all that move had been the result of my drinking and behaviour I was still welcome in the family's new home at weekends on the strict understanding that I behaved myself and continued with my recovery programme.

Irene had found an escape from the misery that I had made her life. She demonstrated her strength of character by qualifying as a State Registered Nurse and by working at a local hospital was able to focus her mind on something other than my self-inflicted problems. To add to her burden, Irene had to get power of attorney over my remaining business affairs to prevent me sliding into bankruptcy.

I now found I had two objectives in life, both of which would involve a lot of time and effort on my part, and not a little luck, to achieve. They were both long shots but to achieve them was the only thing I wanted in life: to stay off the drink and win back the woman I loved.

The opportunity for me to demonstrate that I had at least started to beat my alcoholism came when Lynn announced that she was going to be married. Irene and the children wanted what Lynn wanted – for her to walk down the aisle with the family united behind her. As the plans for Lynn's wedding gathered apace, I found myself spending more and more time at home with Irene and the children. I was genuine in my behaviour and gradually I started to win Irene's confidence. For a number of years I had lost Irene's trust, but I knew deep down I had not lost her love. For a time Irene's love for me had been stretched fag-paper thin, but somehow the loving bond between us held together. That love was now very fragile, but it was love nonetheless. Irene and I started to see each other regularly. Gradually we rebuilt the bridges between us and I was able to show Irene that I was determined never to touch alcohol again. The only thing that had come between us was alcohol and now that no longer existed in my life.

Three months after our divorce became absolute, Irene sat me down. She told me she had been giving matters a great deal of thought and had reached a decision. She said she was willing to have another go and that I should give up the flat in Wanstead and move back in with her and the children. That night as I made my way back to my flat for the very last time I had tears of joy in my eyes. I looked up to the heavens and prayed that God would accept my thanks, and instil in me the strength and fortitude to carry on as I had been doing. So that I might may make Irene and the children happy again in the future.

'. . . I'm heading into Wanstead, there's Sylvan Road on my left, the park on my right. I'm coming up to the crossroads, there's the Conservative Club on my left, the George on the corner. There's Cliffie Jones taking the corner . . . Bobby Smith's up, he heads the ball back to Dave Mackay . . . Dave to Danny . . . Danny slides the ball across the turf . . . I'm on to it . . . the goalkeeper's coming out . . . there are only seconds left . . . there won't be another chance . . . I drop my left shoulder . . . the goalkeeper goes down to my left . . . I'm away to his right . . . Stay calm, Jim . . . stay calm . . . side-foot it in . . . Yes! It's there! . . . Yes! Yes! Yes! . . . Come on all you people . . . that's it . . . shout . . . it's the best feeling in the world . . . the best I've ever felt . . . I'm going home! Going home to my Irene . . . to my beautiful children . . . *this* is what it's all about . . . nothing else matters . . . Home! Home! . . . Home to my beautiful Irene . . . Oh, God in heaven, thank you!'

CHAPTER SEVENTEEN

I WILL SURVIVE

Irene and I celebrated our reunion by taking off on a second honeymoon. In actual fact it was our first honeymoon because when we were married my commitment to Chelsea had prevented us taking a honeymoon. We went to France and had the most joyous time. When we returned, I faced the 'all-eyes-on-Jim' test of giving Lynn away at her wedding and helping Irene host the reception afterwards.

A lot of people at the wedding had seen me in a desperate and disgusting state while I was in the depths of my alcoholism. No doubt some expected me to use Lynn's wedding as an excuse to start drinking again 'in moderation'. I never did that, nor would I have ever contemplated such a thing. I had too much to lose. This was Lynn's big day and I was never going to do anything to tarnish it.

I was a very proud daddy indeed in June 1979 when I walked Lynn up the aisle. She looked like her mum – beautiful. Mitzi was a gorgeous bridesmaid and I can recall being somewhat taken aback at how Danny and Andy appeared to be so grown up in their roles as ushers.

I was very proud that day for all sorts of reasons. Above all I took great pride, satisfaction and happiness from the fact that we were together as a loving family once again. And the person responsible for that was my lovely Irene.

At the reception, as the father of the bride I was in charge of the toasts. People were celebrating Lynn's wedding and there was enough booze around to have launched a liner. But I never touched a drop. I filled my champagne glass with Perrier water. When the time came for me to make a speech, it came from the heart and owed nothing to alcohol.

Sadly, Lynn's marriage was not to work out. Lynn and her husband parted after three years and for the record the failure of the marriage had nothing to do with Lynn. Lynn's marriage produced a beautiful daughter, Victoria. Just as I had been delighted to give Lynn away on the day of her marriage, I was happy to take my daughter and grandaughter back when the marriage ran aground, as any loving dad would. No one has a rainbow until they've had the rain. I hadn't had just some rainfall in my life – I'd subjected myself to a raging tempest – but the stormy period of my life was nigh on over. Colour shone once more to exorcise what had been a very dark period of my life.

I was back at home with Irene and the children and off the booze. The resumption of my loving relationship with my family was the bedrock on which I intended to build a new future. I wasn't sure what I was going to do in life. I adopted the Micawber philosophy of 'something will turn up'. Eventually, something did.

I received a telephone call from Frank Nicklin, the sports editor of the *Sun*. Frank offered me the opportunity of writing a weekly column for his newspaper whereby I would simply offer my views on current events in football. To this day I still write that column for the *Sun* and to this day I am still grateful to Frank Nicklin, who had faith in me when many others were closing doors to me.

Having been reunited with Irene and the family, the prospect of regular, gainful employment with the *Sun* restored in me a lot of my old confidence and bounce. I knew my life had purpose once again and I felt a buzz from starting to get my life back on to a sensible course.

During my meeting with Frank Nicklin, he asked if I played cricket. I told him I did. Frank told me that the *Sun* had a cricket team that played games to raise money for charity. The team had a game that very Sunday in Ilkeston: would I be available to play? I had arranged to play golf that Sunday morning but felt it would be ungracious of me to decline Frank's invitation to play cricket for the *Sun* as he had just given me a job with his newspaper. I told Frank about my golf commitment and informed him that, rather than travel up to Ilkeston with the *Sun* team, I would drive up to Derbyshire after my round of golf and meet the lads at the cricket ground.

I set off from the golf course in good time, but hit bumper-to-bumper traffic on the M1. There had been an accident and the tailback was so long it took me two hours to cover five miles. Once I had passed the scene of the accident the remainder of my journey to Derbyshire was done at snail's pace. This was a time before mobile phones so I had no way of letting Frank know I was going to be late. Eventually I arrived at Ilkeston cricket ground just as the *Sun* team were leaving the pitch having put the home side in to bat first. Frank had heard about the congestion on the motorway and figured that was the reason I hadn't turned up on time. 'Never mind, you're here now,' said Frank, 'get padded up. You can open the batting.'

I donned pads and gloves, borrowed a bat, walked out to the wicket and was bowled first ball. That was my debut for the *Sun* cricket team. After a four-hour drive, it was all over in thirty seconds. All that remained for me, was the long drive back to Essex.

I was to play only two more games of football. One was a testimonial match for my old Chelsea adversary, Ron Harris, at Stamford Bridge. It proved to be my very last appearance at a Football League ground, which was appropriate given that the first of my career as a footballer had been for the Chelsea youth team at Stamford Bridge. My partner up front in Ron's testimonial was not a footballer as such. He was the cricketer, Ian Botham. Playing alongside Both, it was almost as if I was back partnering Bobby Smith. Like Bobby, Both boasted a tremendous physique and such enormous strength that defenders just bounced off him. If Both had not concentrated his efforts on his unique talent for cricket I am sure he could have made the grade as a footballer. He was a very useful centre forward and played a handful of games for Scunthorpe United.

My very last appearance as a player was in a charity game for the *Sun* football team. For a number of years I had felt a twinge in my back when playing football, perhaps something to do with the abnormal knitting of bones that had nearly prevented my move to AC Milan – if only. Whatever, following these two matches the pain in my back was more pronounced and I decided that, at the age of thirty-nine, the time had come to hang up my shooting boots for good. I didn't turn my back on football for good. Far from it. My column with the *Sun* meant I had to keep abreast of current developments in the game, and I followed the progress of my two sons, Danny and Andy as they tried to make their mark in football at Southend United. Inadvertently, however, I was a millstone around both their necks, particularly that of Danny's. Every report I read on Danny began with, 'Danny Greaves, the son of . . .' It proved too big a burden. It was unfair of football writers constantly to compare Danny with somebody who had been very fortunate to have been born with the knack of scoring goals. Eventually both boys moved into non-league football and, as they were no longer in the spotlight, derived great pleasure from being involved in football at that level.

My regular income from the *Sun* enabled me to return my

stock of sweaters to my supplier, Geoffrey Green, who had helped me keep life and limb together when I was just clambering out of the pit of alcoholism. At this period of my life I was looking for something else to do other than my weekly column. Then, out of the blue, I received a telephone call from a producer/director called Bernie Stringle. Bernie was the man behind the famous PG Tips chimps commercials but, rather than wanting to make a monkey out of me, he told me he wanted to make a documentary. The vehicle for my appearance on *Russell Harty Plus* was that I had collaborated with Norman Giller on a book, *This One's on Me*, which, as the title suggests, told the story of my slide into alcoholism and what was at the time my on-going battle to overcome the illness.

Bernie told me he wanted to make a documentary based on *This One's on Me* but that he wanted to call it *Just for Today*. He asked me how much I wanted to be paid. I had no idea whatsoever, so plucked from the air the figure of £500. 'You must be joking,' Bernie told me. 'I haven't got the budget to pay you £500.' I asked him how much he did have. When he told me I knew I wasn't going to be flown off to exotic locations and his documentary wasn't going to have a cast of half a dozen, never mind dozens of people. We talked. Bernie came over as a decent sort of guy so I agreed to do it and we also agreed on a fee. The fee in question was so low that if Bernie had offered me no money at all for doing the documentary I wouldn't have noticed the difference.

Just for Today lasted fifty minutes but to enable Bernie to produce fifty minutes of usable film I had to spend hours doing unscripted, direct to camera talking which, unknown to me at the time, was going to launch me on a new career – in television. In August 1980, Tony Flanagan, the producer of ATV's *Star Soccer* was looking for a former footballer to work as an analyst on his programme that featured highlights of matches involving Midlands' teams. Several names had been put forward and, for various reasons, rejected. During a production meeting Tony surprised his colleagues when he came up with my name. There were objections, in the main because I had no connections with football in the Midlands. Apparently someone also said, 'What do we want Jimmy Greaves for? That would be asking for trouble, he's a piss-head.' 'Not any more,' said Tony, throwing a copy of the *Sun* across the desk. 'He's sober enough to write excellent articles in this newspaper. He's objective and not afraid to speak his mind. What's more, he proved in that documentary *Just for Today* that he can work to camera.'

I was about to embark upon a new career in television, one that would last longer than my career as a professional footballer and one from which I would derive a great deal of pride and satisfaction.

The *Star Soccer* editor Trevor East and his sports editor Gary Newbon contacted Norman Giller who at the time was acting as my representative. I was flattered by the approach from ATV. I wanted to take them up on their offer but had all manner of reservations about being up to the job. I talked the matter over with my old England skipper and Wolves' adversary, Billy Wright, who was an executive at ATV but was still undecided. So I turned to the one person whose advice I knew I could trust. Irene.

Irene believed I was up to the job and was very positive in guiding me in a new direction in life. 'Jim,' she said, 'don't dither. Get off your backside, in your car, and up to Birmingham!'

Which was exactly what I did.

The first person I was introduced to by Gary Newbon on arriving at ATV was a young football reporter who I was informed I would be working with on the programme. The reporter was fresh from Leeds University where he had gained a BA in Classics and he told me his name was Nick Owen. The second person I met was a female news presenter. Her name was Anne Diamond. The three of us had no idea that we were destined one day to work together with an as yet unborn television company that would be broadcasting from the crack of dawn on a daily basis.

My first appearances as a pundit on *Star Soccer* did not make for good television. For all I had managed to talk to camera for the documentary *Just for Today* those early appearances for ATV showed me to be a greenhorn in a television studio. If there was a wrong camera to look at, I looked at it. When I shouldn't have been speaking, I spoke. I was forever tripping over words and repeating myself. I was in awe of the way Gary Newbon and Nick Owen conducted themselves on camera. They read the Autocue effortlessly, and in such a way that you never would have believed they were reading aloud. It made me realise I had a lot to learn about television and presentation.

The cardinal sin I committed in those early programmes was trying to be a clever dick when asked about tactics and technique. Football is a simple game. I had always played the game simply and there I was trying to complicate it. What I was saying went over my head, let alone that of the viewer. After about four programmes I found myself more relaxed in front of a camera and I also changed tack when talking about matches. I came to the conclusion that it would be best for all if I just talked about the game as I would if I was standing on the terraces. If a game had been exciting I'd say so. If it had been rubbish I told the viewers it was rubbish. My delivery became more natural because I was being my natural self. I found myself talking humorously about certain aspects of a game as I had always done. A particularly poor game involving Leicester City I described as being 'as entertaining as watching a tea towel dry on a radiator'. On being asked if Bryan Robson had any weaknesses, I replied, 'Well, he can't cook for a start.' Asked for my impressions of a Coventry City midfield player who had run his socks off in a game but achieved very little, I replied, 'He floats like a bee and stings like a butterfly.'

Such comments came out naturally. Gary Newbon would laugh, as would the studio technicians, and the feedback from viewers was that they were laughing too. Of course, the fact that I had brought an element of humour to the game didn't please everyone. One leading sportswriter was obviously of the mind that I was treating football with less reverence than it deserved because he wrote: 'Why doesn't Jimmy Greaves go the whole way and put on a clown's suit? He was one of the all-time great footballers, but now all he can do is poke fun at the game to which he owes so much.'

That football writer was one of the 'old school' and I won't mention him by name because he still writes on football today for one of the broadsheets. (It wasn't my old pal Brian Glanville.) I thought he was a snob and resentful of the success of others. I simply dismissed his comment as characteristic of the man. The casual and humorous manner in which I talked about football was in fact characteristic of me. In my playing days I used to send up the game and the people in it who I thought were taking it too seriously. My occasional irreverence to football used to drive theorists like Walter Winterbottom, Alf Ramsey and Ron Greenwood to distraction. I will always maintain that football should be fun, and if the coaches who now dictate games and tactics would only forgo their influence and let players express themselves on the field, football would be all the better for that.

In those early days on *Star Soccer* Gary Newbon protected me like a mother hen. He encouraged me to be funny and told me that was what the viewers liked and that I should ignore those who said or wrote anything different. Looking back I have Gary to thank for steering me through those early appearances on *Star Soccer* and ATV's Friday evening preview programmes. In time Gary and I were to have our differences but that doesn't detract from the fact that I owe him much. I learned a great deal from Gary and I shall always be grateful to him for the way he guided me through the embryonic stages of my career in television.

I received a lot of help and good advice from people at ATV. One problem I had on air was knowing when to be funny and when to be serious. A director by the name of Syd Kilby recognised this and took me aside.

'You're a funny guy, Jim,' said Syd, 'and you're also able to talk seriously about certain matters. What you must do is know when to be funny and when to be serious.'

Syd then went on to offer me two pieces of advice that I have never forgotten, advice that was to stand me in good stead throughout the next sixteen years in television.

'Don't forget when you go on TV, people are inviting you into their homes. Respect that and conduct yourself accordingly,' said Syd. 'Second. You're funny and I don't want you to lose that. But always remember this. When a funny man talks seriously on a topic, people will listen. Don't mix the two.'

Syd Kilby was a great TV director, though a bit of a maverick who often found himself at loggerheads with the 'grey suits upstairs'. He knew television inside out, what's more, he knew what the public enjoyed watching. They eventually sacked him.

My first season with *Star Soccer* was so successful I was given the opportunity of contributing to a regular feature which they called *The Greaves Report*, in which I took an off-beat look at various aspects of sport. I played tennis against John McEnroe where I even managed to return his service. I faced Bob Willis bowling flat out, wrestled with Kendo Nagasaki, did a few laps with Barry Sheene, played squash against Jonah Barrington and managed to get off the court without suffering a heart attack, played bowls, croquet and even went fishing. I also sparred with an up-and-coming young heavyweight by the name of Frank Bruno.

Syd Kilby directed my sparring session with Frank Bruno. The idea was for me to 'fight' my way inside Frank's considerable reach and put a question to him each time I got to close quarters. Frank was six inches taller than me and one hell of a lot fitter and stronger. Syd didn't realise just how much effort and energy it took for me to get anywhere near Frank. Each time I fought my way close enough to ask a question, my lungs were panting like a forge bellows.

Breathless, I would put a question to Frank only for the soundman to interrupt and say, 'We have to cut. All I can hear is Jimmy's heavy breathing.' After half a dozen takes I suggested to Syd that we forget the sparring. 'Just have Frank on the ropes in the corner and I'll interview him there,' I said. That interview went well and a year later Frank and I had a rematch. By then I was doing a regular slot on the *Saturday Show*, a programme for young people hosted by Isla St Clair and Tommy Boyd. The idea for this interview was that I would ask Frank a question and then lightly hit him with three pulled punches. Bang, bang, bang. Frank would reply to my question then hit me with three pulled punches. Bang. bang, bang.

Unbeknown to me, in the twelve months that had passed since my first interview with Frank he had become a boxer of instinct. His instincts told him that whenever he was hit, he should hit back. Normally a boxer will control his instinct to respond to a punch, providing his brain operates at speed. I think you may be ahead of me on this one.

I asked my first question and hit Frank with three playful punches. Frank replied then landed three gossamer light punches on me. By my fifth question Frank's concentration lapsed and he obviously forgot what he was supposed to be doing. I asked my question – bang, bang, bang – at which point

Frank's instinct took over and he responded to my playful punches with two of his own that put the lights out for me. My legs buckled and I tumbled forward. Frank suddenly realised what he'd done and he reached out to prevent me hitting the canvas. I fell forward into his arms, my head spinning like a top, tears streaming from my eyes and a terrible feeling of sickness in my stomach.

Frank was full of apologies and felt very bad about what he had unwittingly done to me. The studio crew, however, were helpless with laughter and I have no doubts whatsoever that that particular interview ended up being shown at countless studio Christmas parties.

My first breakthrough on to network television came during the 1982 World Cup Finals when I was invited to be a member of the ITV panel under the chairmanship of Brian Moore. The World Cup panels had first been introduced during the 1970 World Cup when the likes of Malcolm Allison, Derek Dougan, Bob McNab and Pat Crerand had become household names by offering their opinions on games and players. I thus joined a new breed of football broadcasters, known in television circles as 'opinionators'.

I voiced my opinions on the 1982 World Cup under the calming influence and conscientious control of Brian Moore, an out-and-out perfectionist who was a credit to his profession. As chairman of ITV's World Cup panel Brian had the job of reigning in a posse of forthright opinionators such as Jack Charlton, Denis Law, George Best, Ian St John, Mike Channon, Brian Clough and yours truly. Brian accomplished that task with aplomb and the minimum of effort. When the debate became heated he'd glide into the verbal affray and restore order with a few well-chosen words and a smile on his face. We responded to him immediately because we all respected Brian as a consummate professional and as a man. You couldn't have exchanged heated words with Brian even if you wanted to. He had a face like a Benedictine and his voice sounded like Walt Disney's idea of how a grandfather should sound.

It was like a game of musical chairs in the studio, with opinionators coming and going, each one primed to condemn, crucify, compliment and, occasionally, cheer the managers and players who were doing their level best in what was England's first World Cup Finals for twelve years. Scotland and Northern Ireland had also qualified for Spain. All three teams gave it their all. They didn't play particularly badly, they just weren't good enough. Of the three Home Countries, it was Northern Ireland who covered themselves in the most glory. They surprised everybody – including themselves – by topping their group in which they enjoyed a fantastic victory over the hosts Spain with a goal from Gerry Armstrong, and despite having Mal Donaghy harshly sent off half an hour from the end.

The 1982 World Cup adopted a different format from previous competitions. There were six groups of four, with two going through from each. To complicate matters, Scotland, having finished on level points with the USSR in their respective group, then had to play the Russians in a play-off. The second phase of the tournament also took the form of groups rather than a straight knockout competition. This format proved unpopular prior to the finals and those of us who had believed it to be too cumbersome were seen to be correct in our assumption. There were too many games, too many demands on the players and too little entertainment in the 1982 World Cup. The top-heavy format of two group stages proved England's undoing, as did their inability to score goals. England played five matches, remained unbeaten and only conceded one goal, but they still went out of the competition. In their second group phase, England, though they did not concede a goal, didn't score one either. They played out goalless draws with both West Germany and Spain to finish as runners-up in their group which earned them a flight home. France burst the Northern Ireland bubble, beating them 4-1 after the Irish lads had gained a creditable 2-2 draw against Austria.

George Best was a fellow opinionator on the ITV panel and at the time I felt he shouldn't have been there. George should have been playing for Northern Ireland in what would have been his only World Cup Finals. He was looking trim and fit following two seasons in the USA. The Northern Ireland manager Billy Bingham should have taken George to Spain. Even if he had been only half fit, he would have been worth his place in the Northern Ireland squad. His brilliance as a footballer and his talismanic qualities would have been an invaluable asset to the Irish and it was beyond my comprehension that Billy Bingham had chosen to ignore George. I enjoyed many a good 'behind the scenes' conversation with George during that World Cup. We were of the mind that Glenn Hoddle of Spurs and Bryan Robson of Manchester United were the only contemporary players who would rate in the class of the great players of our era. We also found ourselves in agreement on several other matters, most notably that all coaches should be locked in a room during games where they could bore each other to death spouting their theories on tactics. I was given the last word on the 1982 World Cup. From the start I had chosen Italy as the eventual winners and, following Italy's 3-1 success over West Germany in the final, Brian Moore said it would be appropriate for me to sum up the 1982 World Cup.

'These finals have all been about long balls, short balls, square balls, reverse balls, high balls and low balls,' I said, 'and having been given the final word, I would just like to say being a member of this panel . . . has been a pleasure.'

My performances on ITV's World Cup panel came as a

surprise to the majority of people who were not aware I had been serving an apprenticeship in TV presentation with Central. I received a favourable press nationwide and also made an impression on the chiefs of ITV Sport. Following my appearance as an opinionator on the World Cup panel, I was rewarded with a regular slot on *World of Sport*, linking up live with Ian St John in *On the Ball* from my base in the Central studios. The seeds of what was to become *Saint and Greavsie* had been sown in what proved to be very fertile ground.

My initial appearances on *On the Ball* also coincided with ideas others were having to reunite me with Nick Owen and Anne Diamond where, rather than at Tiffany's, we would be having breakfast at Camden Lock.

TV-am was dying on its feet in 1983. It had been launched amidst much publicity, most of which centred around the programme's 'Famous Five'. In 1980 the Independent Broadcasting Authority awarded TV-am the lucrative breakfast television franchise. Peter Jay was the chairman and chief executive of a star-studded team that included Michael Parkinson, David Frost, Anna Ford, Angela Rippon, Robert Kee and Esther Rantzen. Esther later dropped out to have a baby, leaving behind the others whom the press dubbed 'The Famous Five'.

From the start, nothing had gone right for The Famous Five. The story was that when the contracts were sent out to the Five they were placed in the wrong envelopes. You can imagine the annoyance felt when Robert Kee discovered he was being paid less than Anna Ford, and by Angela Rippon when she learned her pay was far less than the others. So even before they took to the air there were ructions in the camp. When TV-am did take to the air its story was one of continual dissent and ultimately descent. Disagreements raged about the content, or rather the style of the programmes. Just about every item was too heavy and formal and viewers began to turn over to the BBC *Breakfast Time* programme where Frank Bough and Selina Scott were making great headway with a more friendly approach to breakfast news.

Within a month The Famous Five had an audience that had dwindled to 300,000 and a few weeks later they had so few viewers that the programme was officially zero-rated while the BBC were enjoying breakfast-time viewing figures of 1.6 million.

Advertisers became reluctant to spend money on commercials on TV-am and suddenly the franchise started to head towards a serious financial crisis. Peter Jay resigned and in April 1983 Angela Rippon and Anna Ford left. TV-am appointed a new editor-in-chief, a thirty-seven-year-old whizzkid called Greg Dyke, and this is where I entered the scene.

My pal Norman Giller told Greg Dyke that I would be the ideal person to present a hard-hitting sports strand on TV-am. Greg had just arrived from London Weekend Television with the simple brief to save TV-am from folding and he telephoned to ask if I would call into TV-am's headquarters in Camden Lock for a chat. 'What do you know about television?' was the first question Greg put to me. 'Well, I know which camera to look at when the red light comes on,' I informed him.

'No, not the studio side of television,' said Greg, 'I mean the important side. What the viewers watch. What do you know about that? What do *you* watch on television?'

Since giving up alcohol I had watched a lot of television. I told Greg I had catholic tastes, and watched everything from *Panorama* and costume dramas to *Coronation Street* and *The Clangers*.

'What do you find is the most moving thing about *Crossroads*?' asked Greg.

'The scenery,' I informed him.

'As a viewer, what disadvantage is there in watching a three-part serial?'

'You'll always miss one part.'

'What about commercial breaks?'

'They're never long enough for you to make a pot of tea.'

'What do you think is the easiest job in television?'

'Cameraman on *Points of View*.'

'What do you find fascinating about *Blake's Seven*?'

'There's only six of them.'

'What about *Star Trek*? Do you think that could be improved?'

'Yes. Particularly the beginning.'

'How do you mean?'

'When the opening credits are rolling, the voice-over says, "Captain James T. Kirk and the crew of the starship *Enterprise* boldly go where no one has gone before." Yet wherever they land, they always meet somebody.'

'If you received a preview tape of a programme described as an "offbeat sitcom", what do you think that would mean?'

'No sofa.'

'Classic sitcom?'

'A repeat.'

'How about a drama, "Based on a bestseller?"'

'The author ain't going to recognise it.'

Greg's eyes were filled with enthusiasm.

'I am going to give you a job on TV-am,' he informed me. 'You're going to be our television previewer. It will be a five-minute slot and I want you to tell the viewers what they should and should not watch. All I ask of you is that you do it with a bit of humour, like your answers to the questions I've just asked you. No over-the-head highbrow stuff. We're looking to attract a different audience to TV-am by dumbing down. You'll be ideal.'

'Well, thanks very much,' I said.

'No, no. I didn't mean that as an insult, Jimmy,' said Greg. 'You're an intelligent guy, but you're capable of communicating to people on different levels. I want us to become the *Sun* of breakfast television, not the *Daily Telegraph* like the other lot tried to make it. By saying you'd be ideal, I wasn't implying you were . . . what I mean is . . . you can . . . you're able to . . .'

'Greg, you're digging a hole for yourself.' I said. 'Shut up. I'll give it my best for you.'

At this juncture, Michael Parkinson, one of the survivors of 'the other lot', walked into the office. Greg told Parky that I was going to join the team.

'Marvellous,' said Parky. 'Our football coverage could do with Jim's knowledge and forthright views.'

When Greg Dyke explained I was to be the television previewer on TV-am, Parky's face fell like a cookbook cake.

'Oh, I see,' said Parky. 'That's, uh, interesting. Very interesting.'

Parky's response was understandable. He wasn't against me being the television previewer on TV-am. It just struck him as being an odd call on the part of Greg Dyke. It was 'an odd call' and no one saw it as more odd than I did, but I was determined to rise, not only at the crack of dawn but also to my new challenge. I mirrored Parky's reaction to my appointment as television previewer when Greg Dyke announced I would be sharing air-time with a small felt puppet called Roland Rat. Roland was brought in to entertain the younger viewers and a guy called Dave Claridge had a hand in his rise to fame. Thanks largely to Greg Dyke's shift in policy to 'popular' television, the viewing figures for TV-am began to rise. We started to close the gap on BBC TV's *Breakfast Time* and within twelve months had overhauled them in the ratings. As one BBC executive put it when referring to the success of TV-am and the appeal of our puppet friend, 'It's the first time that a rat has ever saved a sinking ship.'

I really enjoyed my time at TV-am and though the financial position of the company was, for a time, perilous, there were always plenty of laughs to be had.

During one programme, Anne Diamond and Nick Owen interviewed an Irish comedian called Mick McCarthy who earned a living working the cruise ships. Anne and Nick asked Mick about his work, in particular how he managed to keep coming up with fresh material when he was playing to the same audience week after week. Mick was followed on to 'the beige sofa' by the Spanish singer Julio Iglesias, who it turned out had once been a goalkeeper with Real Madrid. At one point during the interview he answered a question put to him by Anne by saying, 'That's *mañana*.'

Ever the consummate professional and mindful of the popular audience of TV-am, Anne said, 'For the benefit of our viewers who may be unfamiliar with the term, Julio, could you just explain what the Spanish mean by "*mañana*"?'

'*Mañana* – it means maybe this will be done, tomorrow,' replied Julio. 'Maybe the day after. Maybe it will be done next week. Perhaps next month. Who cares?'

Mindful of the fact that Mick McCarthy had been sitting on the sofa for some time and had not contributed to the conversation, Anne saw this as a good time to get him involved.

'Do the Irish have a word that is equivalent to "*mañana*", Mick?' asked Anne.

'No,' replied Mick, quick as a flash, 'in Ireland we don't have a word to describe that degree of urgency.'

My new career wasn't all plain sailing, however. I had my fair share of ructions and rumbles with people even in the early days. I was once embroiled in a particularly heated argument with Andy Allan, an executive at Central TV. The argument was over money; in short, I didn't think what Andy was offering was good enough. I really liked Andy and for us to be arguing over money was just crazy.

'Jimmy, why the hell are we shouting at each other?' Andy asked midway through our slanging match. 'You're the only star with whom I have this sort of verbal punch-up. Do you know why that is?'

'Because I'm an intransigent bastard?' I said.

'That is true,' said Andy. 'But the real reason is that it's because you're doing all the business negotiating yourself. For heaven's sake, do us all and yourself a favour. Get yourself an agent, like all the others. That way you and I won't have to fall out.'

Andy Allan had offered me some sound advice. I signed up with a theatrical agent called Barry Brown and let him handle the contract and money side of things. Having Barry representing my television interests took the heat out of my relationships with TV bosses, and I found they started to warm to me all the more for that. We had a very good business relationship though Barry never knew quite what to make of me. Barry used to say that he represented seventy actors and actresses and one novelty act, which was me. I can't fault Barry for the way he looked after my interests. I liked him as a man, though his constant dealings with producers who seldom told him the truth about the money they had available made him deeply suspicious of just about everybody. Barry was the only person I ever met who believed the Winslow Boy stole that postal order.

Life was once again sweet for me. I was back with Irene and in the bosom of my family. I was off the booze, and my new career in the media was going well. I had my weekly column with the *Sun*. I was getting up at the sparrow's fart to do my spot as a television previewer on TV-am. I had my job as an opinionator with Central TV on a Friday evening and a Sunday afternoon, and I was linking up with Ian St John from

Central studios in Birmingham to do an insert for *On the Ball* on a Saturday lunchtime. I didn't think things could get any better for me, but they were just about to.

My link-ups with Ian St John became very popular with viewers. Ian and I had a chemistry and it was a good one. In 1982 ITV were killing off *World of Sport*, though they still wanted some sort of presence for football in their schedules on a Saturday. To fill the void an executive of ITV Sport, John Bromley, came up with the idea of giving Ian and me our own programme to be broadcast from the LWT studios on a Saturday lunchtime. John even came up with a title. *Saint and Greavsie*.

CHAPTER EIGHTEEN

I SHOULD BE SO LUCKY

Saint and Greavsie first saw the light of day in 1982. I have always seen football as a celebration of life and that was what *Saint and Greavsie* was all about: a celebration of football at every level, in all its forms.

What Saint and I didn't want to do was to sit and pontificate on football, talk tactics and make the game out to be more complicated than it really is. We had seventy-eight international caps between us and collectively had played in well over a thousand first-class matches, but to us football had always been fun. We didn't want viewers to see football the way the so-called experts saw it, as a very serious game in which there was no place for fun and humour. We wanted to emphasise the fun element of football and we wanted to do that by speaking the same language as the supporters. In so doing, we won their trust.

Saint and Greavsie was an intelligent programme. We didn't 'dumb down' football; we told it the way it was. The way Saint and I worked the show was exactly how I used to play football. I left Saint to do all the hard graft – reading the Autocue and setting up all the insert items – while I slipped in and out of the action with one-liners and telling comment on the main items.

Saint and I set out to entertain and explain, in that order. We were lucky to have inspirational and imaginative editors in

Bob Patience and Richard Worth and excellent input into the show from such contributors as Martin Tyler, Alan Parry and Jim Rosenthal, who cast off the restrictive shackles of normal football reporting and threw themselves into the character of the programme.

We cast our net far and wide in our search for colourful characters in football and, to our great delight, discovered the game was full of them. We featured a group of Sheffield Wednesday supporters who attended every away match in a different fancy-dress costume, one week Arab sheikhs, the next deep sea-divers complete with helmets in which they had to open the little window in order to see the game.

There was the longest game in the history of football in 1984. Two teams of American students, the North Palm Beach Golden Bears and the Palm Beach Piranhas, set out to create a world record for the longest game. They did it too. The game lasted for sixty-eight hours and eleven minutes. One player, Ernie Schultz, played continuously for fifty-one hours thirty minutes to give a whole new meaning to the phrase, 'If he played 'til next Wednesday, he still wouldn't score.' We featured the chairman of Cowdenbeath, who, immediately after a game at their Central Park ground, got on a tractor to which was hitched a large rake. The chairman then proceeded to drive the tractor around the perimeter track to smooth the gravel so that it was suitable for the greyhound racing taking place later that evening. As I said at the time, 'I can never imagine Ken Bates doing that.' We brought to the screens the Stoke City fanatic who had seats from an old stand at the Victoria Ground in his living room, entry to which was gained through a turnstile.

We also featured some of football's most bizarre incidents, one of them in a cup match between two non-league teams played at Brunton Park, the home of Carlisle United. A player taking a penalty stubbed his toe on the ground, then fell over the ball which then bobbled two yards before the opposing goalkeeper dived on it, while every other player on the pitch collapsed with laughter.

Amazing own goals, incredible celebrations of goals, fantastic goals, jaw-dropping blunders and eccentric supporters. We featured them all on *Saint and Greavsie*. When someone in the game made a verbal *faux pas* to camera, we were on to it like a shot.

'I'm a firm believer that if you score one goal, the other team have to score two to win' – Howard Wilkinson.

'Stan Mortensen even had an FA Cup Final named after him. The Matthews Final' – Lawrie McMenemy.

'Hoddle hasn't been the Hoddle we know and neither has Bryan Robson' – Ron Greenwood.

We weren't above featuring 'Colemanballs' uttered by our own crew either.

'Oh, he had an eternity to play that ball, but he took too long over it' – Martin Tyler.

'And there'll be more football in a moment, but first we've got highlights from the Scottish League Cup Final' – Gary Newbon.

'With the very last kick of the game, Bobby McDonald scored with a header' – Alan Parry.

Neither were we above featuring ourselves.

Saint: 'Is he speaking to you yet, Jim?'

Me: 'No, but I hope to be incommunicado with him shortly.'

We had fun when looking at the minutiae of football. Such as a sign on the side of the main stand at Fulham when the club were strapped for cash and their manager had been told no money was available for new players. The sign read, 'No Transfers'. The notice in Barnsley Supporters Club – 'Happy Hour, 6.30 until 7 p.m.' The sign on a snack bar at Stoke City's Victoria Ground – 'Try Our Home Made Pies, You'll Never

Get Better'. The one in the bar at Worksop Town that read –
'The Lowenbrau Labelled Bottles In This Bar Have All Been
Tasted And Passed By A Panel Of German Beer Experts'. And
so it went on.

The programme also provided me with an opportunity to
offer my opinions on the game and here I was encouraged to
be as forthright as ever. I realised, of course, that not everybody
would agree with what I said, but football is a game of
opinions. I quickly learned, however, that I had to be careful
about what I said, because the country was becoming
increasingly litigious. I got into hot water following one match
in which I said the referee had dismissed a player just to get
himself into history before he retired. The referee in question
saw the programme and issued me with a writ for libel. I was
forced to apologise in the High Court for my unwise remark,
pick up the bill for his legal costs and make a payment to the
Referees' Association Benevolent Fund.

Following that incident I was taken aside by LWT's legal
advisers and given some advice. They told me that before
'shooting from the lip' I should make sure I began with the
phrase 'In my opinion'. That way nobody could issue a writ
against me for having an opinion. The lawyer went on to say,
'You get into trouble when you make an opinion sound like a
statement of fact.' I was learning my trade in television and
coming to terms with the fact that it wasn't easy being an
opinionator.

Saint and Greavsie projected the human side of football and
because we did that with humour we attracted a lot of people
to the show who normally wouldn't have watched a football
magazine-type programme. I believe *Saint and Greavsie* was
instrumental in introducing a lot more women to football. We
received countless letters from women and young girls saying
they had taken up following football simply because of our
programme, which they found 'entertaining and fun'.

Bill Shankly uttered one of the most famous quotes in football when he said, 'Some people think football is a matter of life and death, but it's much more important than that.' In saying that, Bill inflicted lasting damage on the game. It was a terrible thing for him to say. Football is not more important than life or death. Rather than being one of the best, as many believe it to be, I think what Bill Shankly said is the worst quote about football. When Bill uttered those words, football began to lose track of what it is all about – the pursuit of sporting excellence, entertainment and fun – all of which we tried to portray in the programme.

Having taken Bill Shankly to task, there is no doubt that he was one of the all-time great managers, a fact that his successor at Liverpool, Bob Paisley, recognised when he took over the reigns at Anfield from his long-time pal.

When Bob Paisley sat down in the manager's office on his first day in charge of Liverpool, he found a note left by Bill Shankly. The note was intended by Bill to be a confidence booster for Bob and simply read: 'Bill Shankly says Bob Paisley is the best football manager in the country.'

Bob read the note from his friend and predecessor, added two commas, stuck it in an envelope and posted it back to Bill. It read: 'Bill Shankly, says Bob Paisley, is the best football manager in the country.'

Saint and Greavsie was based on honesty and humour and finding the characters and personalities in the game, wherever they might be. What we also did, albeit unwittingly, was to introduce football supporters to one another again. For a number of years rival supporters had been segregated at matches. Hence there was an element of distrust between rival supporters basically because they had been denied the opportunity to communicate with one another. By featuring numerous, colourful supporters from many different clubs, *Saint and Greavsie* demonstrated that all supporters have the same needs, hopes, dreams and thoughts as well as sharing the same feelings of disappointment, despair and occasional anger. I think the programme fostered a better understanding between supporters who realised 'the other lot across the fence' were, in fact, just the same except they followed a different team and wore different colours. For me this was one of the most satisfying aspects about *Saint and Greavsie*. Since the late sixties, there had been a strong feeling that the 'social glue' of football had become increasingly unstuck. I feel *Saint and Greavsie* went some way to re-establishing in the minds of supporters that they were all part of the 'family of football'. That 'family' was wide and deep and through *Saint and Greavsie* I met many of its members and derived great delight from doing so. One programme involved Ian St John showing me around Anfield. As we stood outside the 'Bill Shankly Gates', the Saint read aloud the message on those gates.

'You'll never walk alone,' said the Saint.

'Unless you're a Hamilton Academical supporter,' I replied.

That quip resulted in me receiving an invitation to travel up to the home of Hamilton Academical where, I was assured, I would be given a warm reception not by a solitary supporter but by the many fans who did support the Accies.

That trip was one of the most enjoyable I ever undertook under the banner of *Saint and Greavsie*. In Hamilton Academical I discovered one of the friendliest clubs in the land. The hospitality shown to me was first class and made me feel rather small at having made a crack at the expense of their club. What I loved about Hamilton, their directors and their supporters was their humour and irreverence. On being shown into the club I was informed that the main entrance was styled after the marble halls of Highbury.

'See how the plywood on the walls has been given the effect of marble,' said one director, 'and underfoot, how the lino that's been laid is almost identical to the marbled floor you walk across when entering the home of Arsenal. No expense has been spared. Arsenal are one of the biggest clubs in the world, so what better can we do here at Hamilton than copy them.'

I loved the tongue-in-cheek tour I was given of the club by the Hamilton directors. Their attitude made for great television and served to reaffirm for me the belief that there were indeed many people who were in the game not for money but for fun and because they loved football.

My stock in television continued to rise and in 1987 Central gave me my own chat show in the Midlands. The series was run on a shoestring budget and involved me interviewing ordinary people who had done extraordinary things. Each show was rich and diverse. In one I interviewed two members of the Official Monster Raving Loony Party about their political manifesto, talked to the captain of the QE2 about his work, then interviewed a transvestite who was a respectable pillar of society.

It was all low-key but interesting and, above all, entertaining. We had a super production team under the guidance of a very talented young producer, Nick Rowan, and a top quality director, Tim Moores. Roving reporter John Swallow added even more colour to the series by contributing very humorous off-beat Alan Whicker-type inserts from around the Midlands.

I had a lot of fun doing this chat show. I never worked to a script as such, just bullet points. I had learned from watching Nick Owen and Anne Diamond that it was no good having a dozen or so questions preprepared for an interview. The secret to being a good interviewer is to be a good listener. It is much better to go into an interview with only three questions in mind and to have the second and third only as back-up. So when interviewing people I simply asked my first question and based my next question on something they had said during their answer, so that the interview came across as natural conversation between two people.

My chat show went down well with both viewers and Central TV executives. Central were so enthusiastic they took the idea to the network and the rest of the ITV companies agreed to give it the green light.

For the network show, Central chose to bring in an outside producer rather than trust the team that had been integral to the success of my Midlands-only show. The man they turned to was Roy Bottomley, an experienced producer and writer who had a string of credits to his name and was the number one writer on *This Is Your Life*. I met Roy for lunch at a Heathrow hotel where he outlined his ideas for the show. Roy had the idea that the show should take place in the setting of a kitchen with celebrities dropping in for a cup of tea and a chat. He also suggested I would have a 'handyman', who would act as the regular straight man.

I picked up on the word 'celebrities' and asked Roy if this meant I would no longer be interviewing ordinary people who had done extraordinary things. 'By just talking to ordinary people you cannot help but have an ordinary show and that won't wash with the network,' Roy told me. 'We need star names to make the show "sexy" and appealing.'

I told Roy I didn't want the series to become a plugger's paradise whereby celebrities only came on to talk about their latest TV series or book. Roy assured me that wouldn't be the case. We produced three programmes for the eyes of Midlands' viewers only before we went on the national network and the omens were not good. I was working to a script and it just wasn't me. I had been comfortable and at ease when chatting off-the-cuff to guests in the Central show, but the demands of Roy's script called on me to be an actor as well as a chat show host. I immediately realised that I was being asked to do a job that was beyond my capabilities. Roy wouldn't budge on the issue of working to his script and we began to have arguments. I had Joe Steeples working with me as programme associate. Joe and I had worked together on TV-am where my success as a television previewer owed a lot to him as he selected the clips and mapped out each format. Joe must have thought he had become invisible during my chat show because every idea he came up with to improve the show was ignored.

I had too many guests on the set at the same time and I found myself unable to afford any of them the attention they deserved. On one show Freddie Trueman was just one of seven guests. Freddie is a fantastic raconteur. No one has more funny stories to tell than Freddie; his one-man theatre tours play to sell-out audiences but I only had time to ask him one question and there was only enough time for a two-minute answer on his part. It was a complete waste of a great talent. Freddie spent most of the programme sitting on a stool while I had brief chats with the other guests knowing I was sitting on an unexplored goldmine.

The TV critics in the press slated me but it was nothing less than I had expected. By the fourth show we cut the number of guests to a maximum of four but the arguments continued to rage. I wasn't enamoured with some of the guests Roy came up with, nor was I happy still to be working to a script. What annoyed me about the guests was that Roy had booked too many leggy girls purely for decoration on the show and to make it 'sexy' in the literal sense. I had an enjoyable and worthwhile interview with Linda Lusardi about the problem she was having losing her Page 3 image and being taken seriously as an actress, but the majority of the girls who called into the kitchen had little to contribute other than their looks. I became frustrated by the giggles and monosyllabic answers to questions and on occasions found myself being flippant. When a researcher came up with an interesting fact about the life of one young model she giggled, 'That's supposed to be between you, me and the doorpost.' 'Well, it's an easy mistake to make,' I replied.

It was all cringe-making stuff. What it all boiled down to was that Roy wanted sexy glamour while I wanted guests with interest and depth to them. Our arguments continued to rage and eventually I boiled over. We were in the bar of a hotel near the studios. I was drinking my usual Perrier water but that didn't stop me losing my rag. Our words became very heated. I saw the red mist and grabbed Roy by his tie. I had lost my temper but luckily the programme director David Millard was also there. David pulled me off Roy and took me aside to cool down. I have to give Roy full marks for the way he responded to my outburst of temper.

'Don't mince your words,' said Roy, calmly straightening his tie. 'Why don't you say what you really mean.'

It was stupid of me to react the way I did and I regret it. There's a lot of stress in working in television. Everyone is always up against deadlines, your nerves are always on edge because you're forever performing live and there is no job security. It's a potentially explosive cocktail and I fell foul of it.

Hindsight is a wonderful thing. Roy's original idea for a kitchen-and-cuppa chat show was a great idea for someone, but not for me. Looking back now, I know I should have been up front with Roy from the start and told him I wasn't the right man for the job. I was comfortable with my original chat show when I didn't have the constrictions of working to a script. What Roy wanted me to do just wasn't me.

For some years ITV had been eyeing BBC's *A Question of Sport* with envy. ITV bosses wanted their own sports quiz but didn't want to air a series that was simply a version of the BBC show that consistently appeared in the Top 20 ratings. When the Birmingham-based comedian Don McLean came up with the idea of *Sporting Triangles*, Central were convinced they had a rival to *A Question of Sport*. There were enough differences in the format Don devised to give *Sporting Triangles* an identity and standing of its own, so it was given the go-ahead. *Sporting Triangles*, as the title suggests, involved three teams. I was asked if I would like to be involved and of course I did. I hoped I would be given the job of question-master but my boss at Central Sport, Gary Newbon, believed I would make a better team captain – so a captain I became. I was very happy to be involved in the show. I have always been a keen sports fan, and pride myself on a reasonable knowledge of most sports, so *Sporting Triangles* seemed right up my street. The former Wolves and Aston Villa striker, now turned SkySports presenter, Andy Gray was selected as one of my rivals and after several experiments, the role of the third captain was given to the 1984 Olympic javelin gold medallist, Tessa Sanderson.

One of the main differences between our show and *A Question of Sport* was that *Sporting Triangles* relied heavily on new technology. Nick Owen was given the job of question-master and, to our delight, Central received news that the series was going on the network.

Of all the television programmes I was ever involved in, *Saint and Greavsie* and *Sporting Triangles* gave me the most pride and satisfaction. Both shows were very successful and great fun to do, though I have to say *Sporting Triangles* could have been even better. The show suffered somewhat from its reliance on computer technology which at times proved so complicated that it put the pace of the show out of kilter. Nick Owen is one of the best presenters on television but he had his head and hands so full of complicated instructions that he was never his usual relaxed self in the first series. In my opinion, Nick also played the role of question-master with too straight a bat. He came across as being headmasterish when really he should have been treating the show as fun and allowing the captains and guests to spout throwaway lines and one-liners. The pace of the show suffered because of the time it took the computerised dice to move around the triangle board to decide which questions we would be asked, and there was no banter to fill the quieter moments.

Another mistake concerned the nature of the questions which were pitched at sporting mastermind level rather than with the target audience in mind. I was once asked, 'Which boxer was born in Slidell, Louisiana, in 1908, became the New York-recognised world featherweight champion in 1927, undisputed world featherweight champion in 1928, world lightweight champion in 1930 and world junior welterweight champion in 1931–2?' I have a decent general knowledge of boxing but I feel only a boxing expert would be able to come up with Tony Canzoneri as the answer to that one. I couldn't come up with an answer and I felt that if I couldn't the vast majority of our viewers wouldn't be able to either. Not every question was like that, but there were enough of them to make me believe we were alienating the family audience, making it hard for them to compete at home. *A Question of Sport* never made the mistake of asking obscure questions, and that was one of the reasons for its success.

Sporting Triangles limped into a second series by which time a lot of the mistakes had been rectified. Nick Owen loosened up, got into the spirit of the show and gave Andy, Tessa and me more freedom to come up with funny lines and entertaining banter. We were not challenging the ratings supremacy of *A Question of Sport* but our viewing figures grew by the week and in 1989 we were given a third series. Nick Owen had committed himself to another quiz show, so his role of question-master was given to a popular presenter in the Midlands, Andy Craig. That was not the only surprise. A press conference was called to reveal Tessa Sanderson was being replaced as a team captain by Emlyn Hughes. Emlyn was synonymous with *A Question of Sport* and for Central to lure him to *Sporting Triangles* was a real coup. Emlyn's switch surprised everyone, not least the BBC and a company that manufactured board games who together had just produced thousands of *A Question of Sport* games showing Emlyn and Bill Beaumont smiling from the box lid.

Emlyn Hughes had an immediate impact on the show in more ways than one. His happy-go-lucky demeanour and good general knowledge of sport had a very positive effect. There was, however, also a negative. In the winter of 1989 I was having lunch in the Central canteen when our producer Jeff Farmer sat down next to me.

'You'll never guess what Gary Newbon has done,' said Jeff. 'He's agreed a deal to allow Emlyn Hughes to wear his own sponsored sweaters on the show.'

I didn't think too much of this but a few days later when we all received new sweaters on the show, I smelled a rat. I phoned Jeff Farmer at home.

'Jeff,' I said, 'these new sweaters we have been asked to wear. They're not by any chance Emlyn Hughes-endorsed sweaters, are they?'

I knew from the silence on the other end of the line that they were. 'Yes, they are,' Jeff finally admitted. I informed Jeff that I wasn't going to wear an Emlyn Hughes-endorsed sweater, whether they had distinguishing logos on them or not, and so precipitated an argument that raged for days.

Gary Newbon came on the telephone and we had a real set-to.

'You *will* wear these sweaters,' said Gary. 'If you don't you'll regret it. You'll be sued for breach of contract.'

'Where does it say in my contract that I've got to wear a sponsored sweater?' I said. 'Pardon the pun, but don't try and pull the wool over my eyes.'

Our conversation ended with Gary slamming down the telephone on me. A friendship and working relationship that had been good for eight years was close to fragmenting. The idea of the sponsored sweaters, I believe, was not the brainchild of Emlyn but his agent, Bev Walker. Eventually, after weeks of this silliness, there came an equally silly finale to the saga of the sweaters. Jeff Farmer rang me up to say I didn't have to wear an Emlyn Hughes-sponsored sweater on *Sporting Triangles*. I felt I had made my point, and for the sake of fostering good relations I then agreed to wear an Emlyn Hughes sweater on the show. That's typical of me. I won't do something if I feel I am being forced to do it. Should the choice be up to me, however, invariably I end up doing what people would like me to do.

Sporting Triangles had a good run. Emlyn Hughes was good for the show and we had a lot of fun working together, but every TV series has a shelf life and eventually *Sporting Triangles* had had its day. After the creases of the first series had been ironed out, the show adopted a good pace and became more fun to do, more fun to watch. As I intimated previously, of all the TV shows I was involved with, *Sporting Triangles* was one of the very best. Looking back, I still take a great deal of pride and satisfaction from my involvement in that programme.

Throughout the eighties *Saint and Greavsie* continued to present football as fun, though it wasn't always football that we featured. We liked to diversify and feature other sports occasionally. I joined Ian Botham on a leg of one of his John o' Groats to Land's End charity walks and was rewarded with a revealing insight to the man himself and why he was so keen to help those less fortunate than he. Just one day on the road with Both tired me out. Both had been walking for days and when our walk came to an end I would have given a king's ransom just to sit down on the most uncomfortable of chairs. Both, however, completed his walk for the day then took off for a meeting to discuss his next charity venture: to walk in Hannibal's footsteps across the Alps in the company of elephants. I am such a fan of Ian Botham that when Irene and I bought two rabbits for the grandchildren we called them Mr Botham and Mr Gooch. A couple of weeks after we had got them, our grandchildren visited the hutch one morning and discovered there was a litter of rabbits. Mr Botham turned out to be more of an all-rounder than we thought and was rechristened Mrs Botham.

Another sporting giant to be featured on *Saint and Greavsie* was the boxer Mike Tyson. When our director Ted Ayling told me he had been granted permission for me to interview Mike Tyson for the show I was excited though somewhat circumspect. It was 1989, Tyson was the world heavyweight boxing champion and he didn't give too many interviews, so for Ted to get him on the show was a real coup. I had never met Mike Tyson but had been led to believe that he could be a trifle difficult to interview. Given the sheer size of the man it was not without trepidation on my part that we set off for Tyson's training camp in a small, remote town in the Catskill Mountains in New York State.

Ted Ayling, a cameraman, a soundman, and I journeyed through New York State in a 4x4 with me at the wheel. We drove to the Catskills past salubrious hotels then up into the mountains where there were no longer hotels to be seen. The terrain became more rugged and remote the higher we journeyed and it seemed unlikely that a town would exist at such an altitude, but Ted had the map on his knees and assured us that we were on the right track. Eventually we came across a small hillbilly town. It was a 'one horse' town, so small you got the feeling that the mayor and the village idiot would be one and the same person, and the local fire brigade would be a four-year-old bed wetter. It seemed a very unlikely setting for the training camp of the heavyweight champion of the world with a reputation for brutality in the ring. The town comprised only a handful of wooden buildings, none of which looked like a gymnasium, so I decided to ask for directions. The first person I confronted looked at me as if I was an alien from outer space. The name Mike Tyson meant nothing to him, so I walked a little further down the street to a barber's shop in the hope of being given directions.

There were two customers and the barber in the shop; not only did they look like one another, they looked just like the man I had stopped on the street. After this trio had got over their initial surprise at seeing a stranger in their town, I was given directions to a gymnasium situated a mile or so down the road. I returned to the lads in the 4x4, told them where we could find Tyson and off we headed.

'This is a bloody weird place,' remarked Ted.

'You can say that again,' I said, 'they all look interbred.'

'What d'ya mean?' asked the soundman. 'They're all bakers?'

Tyson's gym turned out to be above the local police station; he was there to prepare for his world title defence against Michael Spinks. We ascended a flight of rickety wooden steps, presented ourselves at the door of the gym and told an aide we were there to interview Mike Tyson. The aide left us standing at the door and when he returned a couple of minutes later he had a shock for us. He told us that Mr Tyson had no knowledge whatsoever of this interview and neither had anyone else in his camp.

That presented us with a real dilemma. I explained everything to the aide and begged him to return to Tyson with our most respectful wish that, seeing as we had travelled all the way from England, he might grant us just a few minutes of his precious time for an interview. The aide once again left us standing at the door. Ten minutes later, he returned.

'Five minutes. No more,' said the aide.

We were ushered into the gymnasium where Mike Tyson was belting a giant of a sparring partner around the ring as if he were a rag doll. I got the feeling that I wouldn't like to tango with Tyson let alone tangle with him. I had met Muhammad Ali and, though he too is a giant of a man, I'd felt comfortable with him because Ali exuded humanity, generosity of spirit and a warmth that brought a smile to my face. Tyson brought a chill to my heart.

The five-minute limit for the interview posed another dilemma. To get five minutes of usable footage you have to shoot much more than that. The time restriction was a real problem. I had to think, and quick, because I didn't fancy arguing with the aides, let alone Tyson himself.

I climbed into the ring to chat with Mike Tyson in front of the cameraman and soundman. Tyson's physique was awesome. His face had all the qualities of a fireside poker except its occasional warmth. He looked at me as if I was a side dish that he hadn't ordered and when he walked across the ring to greet me it was if he was trudging through deep snow. I felt as if I was standing next to an unexploded bomb. We chatted for three minutes then he demonstrated for the camera how he went about mounting a body attack. 'The main target areas,' he said as he pushed me into a corner under a playful attack, 'are the liver, the kidneys, the heart, the floating rib, and the abdomen.'

He brought a fist the size of a ham shank up into my soft underbelly. 'Not forgetting the solar plexus,' he said. 'The solar plexus punch was invented by that great English boxer of yours, Bob Fitzsimmons, when he knocked out James J. Corbett in Carson City, Nevada, on St Patrick's Day 1897, to become the world heavyweight champion.'

On hearing this I immediately saw an answer to our problem of only having a five-minute interview.

'Which was some victory,' I said, summoning my general knowledge of boxing, 'because Fitzsimmons was sixteen pounds lighter than Corbett and no more than a middleweight.'

Tyson then did something I never thought he'd do. He smiled.

'That's right, man,' he said, 'and Fitzsimmons was also four years older than Corbett.'

'And, oddly, Fitzsimmons then defended his title against another boxer whose Christian name was James J. – James J. Jeffries, that is.'

'That's right, man. In Coney Island, New York, 9 June 1899,' said Tyson.

The ice was broken. I had managed to steer our conversation on to Mike Tyson's favourite subject, the history of boxing. When an aide came to the side of the ring and pointed to his watch, Mike waved him away. He was happy to talk and we were more than happy to keep the camera rolling.

Tyson is a walking encyclopaedia of boxing. I have never spoken to anyone quite like him. He is an uneducated guy from the poor side of Brooklyn, yet get him on the history of boxing and he will talk articulately and knowledgeably about the subject. When it comes to boxing history, he could be a contestant on *Mastermind*.

I asked Mike about the influence that Cus D'Amato had had on him. D'Amato had managed former world champion Floyd Patterson and had taken Mike under his wing at the age of fourteen. I had opened the floodgates.

'This was like Cus's home, you know,' said Mike, waving an arm to indicate the gym. 'It's as if I can see him and hear him just by walking into the place. I can still feel his presence here. I can remember standing right here where I am talking to you now when he lectured me about discipline. Cus was the wisest man I ever met. He was like a father to me. I loved the man and there ain't ever a day goes by when I don't think of him.'

Come the end of our chat, our five-minute interview had expanded to over an hour. When I left that gym my attitude towards Mike Tyson had changed. When I first arrived I thought him to be a cold, brutal man. When I left, I considered him one of the most interesting and magnetic characters I had ever met. We left the gym with Mike asking us to convey his best wishes to Frank Bruno. 'Tell Frank to look after himself,' he said, 'tell him I want him after Spinks. I like Frank, he's a Christian and I admire that in him, but you'd better warn him, I'll be full of bad intentions when I meet him in the ring.'

Mike Tyson had given us some great material for *Saint and Greavsie* and when the interview was broadcast it went down very well with the viewers. My interview with 'Iron Mike' had turned out better than I could ever have hoped. But we didn't hang about in the Catskill Mountains. It was indeed 'a bloody weird place', so we drove back to New York without stopping and caught the first flight back to London.

Throughout the eighties *Saint and Greavsie* gained in popularity because of the way we emphasised the humorous and fun elements of football. At times that was no easy task because there were programmes in which Saint and I had to be very solemn indeed because football had become tragedy.

In 1985 there was the fire that swept through the main stand at Bradford City's ground which resulted in more than fifty people losing their lives. A fortnight later there was the tragedy of Heysel when more than forty people were killed – many of them trampled to death – when a wall and safety fence collapsed during rioting by Liverpool and Juventus fans before the European Cup Final in Brussels.

In 1989 ninety-four Liverpool supporters, including several children, were killed and more than 150 seriously injured when hundreds of fans poured into the Leppings Lane End at Hillsborough as Liverpool's FA Cup semi-final with Nottingham Forest was just kicking off. Following these three major tragedies I knew football could never be the same again.

Out of darkness cometh light. In 1990 Lord Justice Taylor produced his report on the Hillsborough disaster. In many respects, Bradford begat Heysel and Heysel begat Hillsborough. As Lord Justice Taylor said at the time, 'The years of patching up grounds, of having periodic disasters and narrowly avoiding many others by muddling through on a wing and a prayer, must be over.'

The Taylor Report offered an ultimatum to football to improve the 'squalid' conditions of Football League grounds and clean up the tarnished image of the game. The report said crowd behaviour could be linked to the poor standard of accommodation at grounds, and the country's national sport was blighted by poor facilities, poor leadership, hooliganism and fans caged and penned so that they appeared to be 'prisoners of war' rather than customers of a multi million-pound industry.

The Taylor Report recommended that terracing be banned from all First and Second Division grounds by August 1994 and from all Football League grounds by 1999.

What was chastening about the Taylor Report was that it was the ninth official report covering safety and control at football grounds. Previous reports had been compiled in the wake of tragedies at Bolton, Ibrox, Bradford and even the very first FA Cup Final at Wembley in 1923, but all had been virtually ignored by successive football governing bodies. Following three major tragedies in the eighties, however, there was no way those who ran football in this country were going to be allowed to ignore the Taylor Report.

The report submitted seventy-six recommendations which, in time, played a significant part in moulding the game we know today. Lord Justice Taylor's recommendations included the removal of 'prison-type' perimeter fencing; more clearly marked gates which should be unlocked at all times; a review of police operations at all grounds and better communications between police and emergency services; the recognition as offences of missile throwing, obscene chanting, racial abuse and encroachment on to the pitch by fans without 'a reasonable excuse'. The report also recommended it be an offence to sell tickets on a match day without the club's authority and that in the future all Football League designated grounds should be all-seater and provide a much higher standard of catering, refreshment and lavatory facilities.

The government stressed that the football industry had to be responsible for adhering to these recommendations and that the bulk of the cost of switching to all-seater stadiums would have to be raised by the clubs. The Football Trust would play a key role in helping clubs create all-seater stadiums, but the game had to look at other ways of raising the money and the direction in which they looked was television.

The Taylor Report was very damning of football and those who ran the game. Under pressure from government and public alike to clean up its act, football had no alternative but to change. As the Taylor Report had said, there was to be no more 'muddling through'. In April 1990 under the guidance of the then FA chief executive Graham Kelly, the Football Association issued its 'Blueprint for the Future of Football' which was set to revolutionise the game in England. Ten months later, in February 1991, the FA Council gave their approval to most of the proposals laid down in the 'Blueprint'.

The 'Blueprint' not only supported the recommendations of the Taylor Report, it also proposed that the whole structure of English football would have to change. The most radical change was the break-up of the 104-year-old Football League. The FA council gave their approval to the formation of a new

FA Premier League, to start in August 1992. John Quinton, a former chairman of Barclays Bank, was appointed as the unpaid, non-executive chairman and Rick Parry, an accountant, as its chief executive.

The initial idea was for the Premier League to have twenty-two clubs, to be reduced to twenty by the end of the 1994–5 season. It was to be linked by three-up/three down promotion and relegation to what would be the First Division of the Football League, that is, the Second Division as was. The Premier League was to have a whole new look to it. Every club had to adhere to the recommendations of the Taylor Report and provide facilities for its customers more in keeping with a multimillion-pound industry in the late twentieth century. There were also to be a number of cosmetic changes. Referees officiating Premiership games would wear green uniforms. There was to be a fifteen-minute half-time interval and three substitutes, including a goalkeeper, were to be permitted on the bench, any two of which could be used.

It all sounded very laudable. Football was to have a new, bright future. The only problem was, most clubs didn't have the money to implement the recommendations of the Taylor Report. Around the same time as the FA's 'Blueprint for the Future of Football' was issued another report saw the light of day. This report was called 'The Bankrupting of English Football' and was compiled by Dr Simon Pitt, an independent sports consultant.

According to Dr Pitt's report, Football League clubs were collectively up to £130 million in debt and were 'not capable of either managerially or financially facing that challenge'. Dr Pitt warned that unless football received a considerable injection of finance more than a dozen clubs faced extinction, while the majority of the rest would find it nigh on impossible to carry out the recommendations of the Taylor Report and adhere to the FA's 'Blueprint' for a bright new future for English football.

Pitt's report blamed the crisis in English football on the spiralling cost of players' wages, transfers, signing on fees and policing, which when allied to the fall in attendances and revenue in the previous decade, had left more than three-quarters of the clubs in the red. Dr Pitt said that English football had become 'undercapitalised and over-borrowed' and recommended that football's governing bodies explore every avenue open to them in their quest to 'inject considerable capital into the English game'.

It was a case of 'right time, right place' for the FA's 'Blueprint' which outlined a bright, brave new world for English football, one in which grounds were to be replaced by stadiums offering improved facilities, seating for all and hospitality suites for corporate entertaining. Where CCTV and better working relationships with the police and authorities would all but eradicate hooliganism. All of which made football an attractive proposition for a hungry TV company such as Rupert Murdoch's BSkyB.

Sky were out to wrestle football away from ITV and BBC. Sky had money and, if the terrestrial TV companies were to have any football at all, they were going to have to pay a much higher price for it than in the past. The new dawn for English football that was on the horizon was exactly what Sky were looking for. In particular, the formation of a new league, the Premiership. Sky outbid BBC and ITV, who had to settle for highlights of matches and selected live games, though both had to pay considerably more for that than before. Sky paid a lot of money to broadcast Premiership games but that came at a price to football. Seemingly overnight Sky now exerted a great influence over football, particularly on the scheduling of fixtures. In spring 1992 Sky revealed their plans for the following season, the first for the newly formed Premiership. There would be live telecasts of regular Sunday afternoon and Monday evening fixtures, the tradition of Saturday being 'football day' was coming to an end. On Sundays, Sky's live coverage of a Premiership game would be competing with a regional First Division match (the old Second Division) on ITV. Sky was not the only competition regional ITV companies would be up against. Channel Four were to broadcast a live match from Serie A in Italy. It is doubtful whether Sky would have pursued football with such vigour and so much money had there not been ample evidence that English football was about to clean up its act. English football in the eighties was unappealing to Sky, but the FA's 'Blueprint', as I previously intimated, was a case of 'the right time at the right place'. Sky saw in the plans the FA had for English football a marketable product. That was what football was to become, a product. One with distinctive and appealing branding, just like any other commercial product.

It was as if the FA were adhering to the words of my old director at Central TV, Syd Kilby: 'When you are on television, remember, people are inviting you into their homes. So conduct yourself accordingly.' Football was about to enjoy saturation coverage on television and the game would have to change if it was to 'conduct itself accordingly'.

I was sitting enjoying a pot of tea and a plate of sandwiches with Ian St John in a hotel a short distance from LWT studios. It was early in 1992 and we had been discussing the forthcoming Premier League, Sky and the changes that were planned for English football.

Saint and I agreed that Sky's live broadcasting of Premiership matches on a Sunday afternoon and Monday night would be just the tip of the iceberg.

'If the Premiership takes off, and football cleans up both its act and its image I can see us having even more live games on our screens,' I ventured.

'Aye,' agreed Saint, 'I can see a time when there will be a televised game every day of the week.'

'Me too,' I said, 'and as football grows in popularity, it won't limit itself to one televised game a day. There'll be two or three.'

'Aye, football's going to be dancing to TV's tune,' said Saint. 'We'll have expert analysts and pundits coming out of our ears. The game'll become a science as well as a product. A product has to be continually sold and marketed, Jim. The clubs will have more marketing johnnies than Saatchi and Saatchi. It'll be the end of the game as we know it.'

'Yes,' I said, 'and I think it'll mean the end of something else as well.'

'What?' asked Saint.

'*Saint and Greavsie*,' I informed him.

Saint and Greavsie was still attracting very good audience figures. Our irreverent attitude to football went down well with viewers, but I knew it was not in keeping with how TV bosses now wanted to project football. In much the same way as the respected former BBC commentator Eddie Waring had fallen from grace and seemed to have been chastised for not adopting a very serious approach to rugby league, I felt TV bosses believed the light-hearted way that Saint and I viewed football was at odds with what, we had been told, was now 'the very serious business of football'.

As the weeks passed by in 1992, Saint and I picked up on the body language of the TV executives who were our bosses. People became increasingly distant. If we entered a room in which a humorous conversation was taking place, the atmosphere would immediately change when people became aware of our presence. In earlier days the presence of Saint and myself had only served to add to the air of joviality. No one ever said as much, but Saint and I had the distinct feeling that our days at LWT were numbered.

At the end of the 1991–2 season the two of us travelled to Sweden for a series of *Saint and Greavsie* specials from the

European Championship Finals. Euro '92 was responsible for a question that has since been asked in countless pub quizzes: 'Who won the European Championships but failed to qualify for the finals?' The answer is Denmark who came into Euro '92 after UEFA decided that Yugoslavia, torn by civil war, could not take part. Having finished as runners-up to Yugoslavia in their qualifying group, Denmark were invited to play in the European Championships in Sweden at just eleven days' notice. When the Danish team heard of their 'last-minute' qualification most were sunning themselves on Spanish beaches.

With their squad hastily assembled and seemingly underprepared, Denmark kicked off with a match against England. Lucky them. The game ended in a goalless bore draw. England were woeful but the draw was a satisfactory start for the Danes. After their game against England, Denmark lost to Sweden when Tomas Brolin scored the only goal of the game. With one match to play, Denmark were bottom of their group. Denmark, however, then triumphed over France. Having drawn 0-0 with France, England then lost 2-1 to Sweden. Denmark progressed to the semi-finals and England caught the next plane home. It was depressing stuff. England's game against the Swedes was only memorable for Graham Taylor's controversial decision to substitute skipper Gary Lineker for Arsenal's Alan Smith. Gary had fired his final salvo for England after eighty caps and was still a single goal short of Bobby Charlton's all-time record of forty-nine goals. Gary was not happy about his substitution and showed as much when he came off the field. It was a tearful and bitter end to his international career and England's sojourn in Euro '92. I, of course, felt for Gary and England but that didn't stop me making a quip about the situation, 'After that, no doubt Walker's will be producing a new crisp flavour. Tears and Onion,' I said. The Saint immediately picked up on this,

'Seeing as England have played with more brawn than brains, perhaps we'll also see Brawn Cocktail-flavoured crisps in the shops'.

The fact that Saint and I were not seen to be paying due reverence to Lineker's situation and that of the England team in general must have gone down badly with TV bosses.

Saint and I conducted ourselves at Euro '92 as we had always done on *Saint and Greavsie*. We talked seriously and objectively about certain aspects of the Championships but we also had some fun. England's performances were far from entertaining, so we attempted to inject some entertainment of our own. Which is exactly what our bosses didn't want from us.

England v Denmark – 'That game had all the sophisticated allure of a leftover kebab.'

'David Batty is capable of playing really well in midfield for England. It leaves you wondering why he's never done it.'

Saint: 'Have you got Sky, Jim?' Greaves: 'No. But the neighbours think I have because I nailed the wok to the gable end.'

Saint: 'Graham Taylor is hoping England will fit together like a jigsaw.' Greaves: 'Well, against France they certainly went to pieces in the box.'

Saint: 'They prepared for these Championships out in Israel and they even took time out to take in some of the sights.' Greaves: 'But they couldn't get anywhere near the Wailing Wall because of England supporters.'

We were just being ourselves, but this was no longer what TV bosses wanted. The attitude and behaviour of TV executives present in Sweden towards us sent out a message to Saint and me. The very last insert to our last programme from Sweden called for us to ride off into the distance on bicycles. As we began to pedal away from the camera, I started to sing.

'I've told you once, and I've told you twice . . .'

Saint immediately joined in.

'But you won't listen to my advice . . .'

The pair of us then proceeded to sing the Rolling Stones' 'The Last Time'. For *Saint and Greavsie* it was the last time.

I was sitting at home one sunny Saturday morning in the summer of 1992 when the newspapers fell on to the mat. The front page of one of them was devoted to a story of more fighting in Sarajevo. I then looked at the front page of the *Sun* and the headline screamed at me: 'Saint and Greavsie Axed'.

Minutes later my telephone rang. It was Richard Worth, the director of *Saint and Greavsie*.

'Have you seen the front page of the *Sun* today?' Richard asked.

'I'm just looking at it now,' I informed him.

'Is it true?' he asked.

'I dunno,' I replied, 'no one has said anything to me. I haven't received a call or a letter from the bosses. Not a thing.'

Minutes after my conversation with Richard, the telephone rang again. It was our producer Bob Patience. Bob asked me the same question as Richard. Was the story of our sacking in the *Sun* true?

'Well, I haven't received official notification of it,' I informed Bob, 'but I work for the *Sun* and I know they only run with a story when they know it's true, or have been led to believe that it's true.'

Neither Saint nor I ever did receive official notification. No one wrote to me or telephoned. After ten years of *Saint and Greavsie* I learned I had been sacked by reading the newspaper I worked for. Saint and I knew the story of our sacking was true, but as we'd had no official notification that *Saint and Greavsie* had come to an end I suggested we turn up at the studios on the first day of the 1992–3 season just to see what reaction that provoked. We never did do that, simply because we didn't want to embarrass those former colleagues we still believed to be friends. I had seen it coming, but the *Sun* headline was still a shock to me. As I have said, every TV programme has a limited shelf life. Our attitude to football was not in keeping with the way football now saw itself going. Neither was it complementary to the way television wanted to project the game. We had had our day, but it had been a good day, one in which we had enjoyed a lot of fun. I wasn't bitter that *Saint and Greavsie* had come to an end, but I did feel sadness. My sadness had not so much to do with the fact that I would no longer be the co-presenter of a network TV programme. More, it was to do with how certain other people now saw the game that I loved – as a 'very serious business'. My career in television was to continue for another four years at Central. As an opinionator I gave my opinions on matches in the Midlands and the changing face of the game. In so doing, injecting as much fun as I possibly could.

In 1996 Ron Atkinson became a frequent visitor to the Central TV studios and I took that as a sign that I wouldn't be commuting to Birmingham every weekend for much longer. In television you know you are on your way out when they no longer provide a car to ferry you about between the studios and outside locations. I was at St Andrews on the final day of the 1995–6 season working as a summariser for Central on a Birmingham City match. When my work was done I stood outside the main entrance at St Andrews waiting for a car to take me back to the studios. The technical crew who had been working that day were packing away their gear. One of them asked me what I was doing and I told him I was waiting for a car to take me back to the studios.

'I think you might be in for a very long wait, Jim,' he said.

I ended up helping the technical lads load their equipment in return for a lift back to the studios in their van. Back at Central just about everyone had gone home. I threw my briefcase in the boot of my car and drove home. I never heard from Central again.

I had worked for Central for seventeen years and to this day I'm grateful for the opportunity and employment they gave me. But yet again I had been sacked, though no one thought fit to tell me. It was indicative of the way television was going. I simply slipped away from Central not knowing if I had actually been sacked or not. Central's subsequent failure to contact me convinced me that my career in television presentation was at an end. I wasn't bitter about it; how could I be? I had enjoyed a career in television that had lasted longer than my career as a professional footballer. Television had provided me and my family with a good income and a good quality of life. I had a lot to be grateful to television for. I had the knowledge and the wit but no longer the image that television desired. A good knowledge of football and the ability to talk objectively and humorously about the game were no longer prerequisites for a career in televised sport. Television wanted presenters who looked stylish and sexy on camera, and opinionators who talked seriously about what was now 'the very serious business of football'.

CHAPTER NINETEEN

IN MY PLACE

In the seven years that have passed until my writing this autobiography I've been kept busy. I write my column for the *Sun*, do the occasional after-dinner speech and promotional event, have embarked on theatre tours with Ron Harris and George Best respectively, and appear on television and radio now and again. I turn down much more television work than I accept. Regarding television I 'cherry pick' because I don't need to appear on TV to earn a living. Researchers ring me up and are invariably flabbergasted when I decline their invitation to appear on a certain programme. 'But it's television,' they say, 'everybody wants to be on television.' 'I don't,' I tell them. Usually I accept an invitation to appear on television because I like the programme in question, or the presenter. I have frequently appeared on *The Johnny Vaughan Show*, simply because I like Johnny as a person and his show is fun to do.

I am just as selective about after-dinner speaking and promotional events. My good friend Stanley Jackson, whose company F4 Group looks after some of my interests, would have me out every day of the week. But as I keep telling Stanley, 'I'm a family man with ten grandchildren. If you want us to earn serious money, start acting as my agent for babysitting.'

Looking back on my life, there are obvious regrets. I am still angry with myself for the pain I caused Irene and our family during my slide into alcoholism. I can never reverse that, but hopefully the love and care I have devoted to my family since 1979 have gone some way to healing that pain. Certainly now we are one big happy family. My life revolves around my family; they are everything to me.

When I was twenty-one if I could have looked into the future and seen society as it is now I don't think I could have got my head around that. I remember once as a Spurs player joining my team-mates in the White Hart pub. Over a couple of pints we discussed our hopes for society in the future. We hoped for a world in which there were no wars. A society in which people enjoyed more freedom, where there were no homeless people and it was safe for anyone to walk abroad at night on any city street. We hoped for relatively little poverty and a society in which there were no social, religious or racial tensions. We wanted a world for our children and grandchildren whereby people were tolerant and respectful of one another, where we could live and let live. Where we could leave the front door unlocked while our children played outside on the street in safety.

We were idealistic young footballers, who in the sixties believed such a future society was possible. I look at society now and there are times when I think it is just the opposite of the one we envisaged.

I'm in my early sixties now, but I don't feel old. If a young guy challenged me to a running race across a car park, I wouldn't be able to beat him. Should he challenge me to a car race around the M25, I'd win. I'm very active and still reasonably fit. I know my mind is sharp and mentally fit. Sir Matt Busby once said, 'In his twenties a man has the enthusiasm. In his thirties, the wit. After forty, comes the wisdom.' I go along with Matt on that one.

I was born in 1940. It was a time before television,

penicillin, polio shots, Viagra, contact lenses, the pill, hormone treatment and face-lifts. The only things that a girl wore that was see-through were her glasses, and the only thing in a kitchen that could stir, whisk and blend was a spoon. The only fast food was stewed prunes and the only thing that came ready to serve was tennis balls. In my childhood the only way of transferring money from one account to another was by marriage. There were no dishwashers, tumble-dryers, electric blankets, credit cards, air-conditioners or laser beams. When we rode our bikes we wore no helmets. We drank water from a drinking fountain in the park not a plastic bottle. We would spend hours building a go-cart out of pieces of wood, pram wheels and string, then go riding down a hill not giving a jot that we had no brakes.

We ate bread and dripping, chips, doorsteps of bread and butter and drank fizzy pop, but we were never overweight because we ran it off when playing. We had fights and occasionally came home with bruises the size of saucers, but simply got over it. At school not every lad made the football or cricket team. Those who didn't coped with their disappoint-ment and won our respect because of that. Some pupils weren't as bright as others. They failed exams, but no one was to blame. We didn't have DVDs, videos, PlayStations, PCs, picture-text mobiles, Internet chatrooms or hang-ups. We had friends. If we moved to a new neighbourhood we went out, walked around the streets and made new friends. If there were no kids on the street, we walked into gardens or knocked on doors and talked to them. We never sought permission from our parents to do this, we didn't have to. We were out there in the big, wide world without a parent by our side and yet, though it's unthinkable today, we survived.

In my teens it was a girl in a tight sweater that brought me out in a sweat, and not Tandoori chicken. We got married first then lived together. A Big Mac was a size sixteen raincoat. A chip was something you ate. Hardware meant a hammer and nails, and software was a cotton vest. 'Going all the way' meant staying on the bus until the terminus. Cigarette smoking was fashionable. Grass was something to be mown, a joint was either beef or lamb, and coke was an alternative to coal. The only swinging couples were trapeze artistes. There were no super-markets, so if you ever went into a grocery shop having bought something at another shop, you always tried to hide the bag. The only hairdryer for women was a chair near an open oven door. They were the days when I had fun from trying to be mad in a sane world, whereas I now often find myself trying to be sane in what appears to me to be an increasingly mad world.

Football reflects society. Football is a simple game, but coaches have made it complicated. In order to explain what is going on, television now employs countless former players to act as pundits, most of whom played their football in the late eighties and early nineties. Television employs this generation of player because they are still young enough to appear fashionable and as such, look good on screen. TV executives talk about a 'target audience', yet want television to appeal to a multicultural Britain. They fall over themselves in their quest for political correctness, which is why we had the situation that ITV's *Premiership* found itself in in February 2003. That programme was broadcast on a Monday night when Spurs had played at home to Fulham. The programme looked back on the Premiership action of the previous weekend, but the first item was highlights and discussion of that night's match at White Hart Lane. The panel consisted of not one but four pundits: Andy Townsend (Irish), Barry Venison (English), Ally McCoist (Scottish) and Robbie Earle (Jamaican), a panel seemingly chosen to adhere to the edict of reflecting multicultural Britain. TV executives don't realise viewers would be quite happy listening to just Robbie Earle or Ally

McCoist as long as what was being said was objective, informative and entertaining. We know we live in a multicultural society, and I'm glad to say most are happy to do so, but for television to attempt to reflect that in everything it does, including the composition of a panel on a football highlights programme, is just ridiculous. With regard to the programme in question, because there were four panellists, once the first person had made the telling points about the Spurs–Fulham game, there was little for others to add. But they felt they had to say something to justify their presence there, so the discussion drifted on to inconsequential incidents in the game, with everyone trying to explain why such and such a thing had happened. The discussion became pointless. Often a player will do something in a match purely instinctively. Yet to listen to pundits now, nothing a player does is off the cuff. They analyse everything to death and suggest reasons for everything that happens in the course of a game. Coaches and managers have complicated what is a simple game and TV pundits have followed suit.

They also try and blind you with science. Sky's Richard Keys is a good pal of mine, as is Andy Gray. I like both of them, but to hear them talk about a match on Sky you'd think football was rocket science. Following a game involving Manchester United, for example, Andy will refer to diagrams with arrows and circles which are meant to illustrate the pattern of play United have deployed. It all comes across as being very complicated stuff. However, when you hear David Beckham in a post-match interview, you are left with the feeling that there is no way in the world he could carry out to the letter such a set and complex pattern of play as previously suggested.

I was never in the army but when I now look back on my career as a footballer it is almost as if I was. Simply because of the fantastic camaraderie and collective spirit that existed amongst us as team-mates. When we took to the pitch we were willing to give everything for one another. If one person made a mistake, it was considered to be every player's mistake. We rallied round to cover that mistake. We looked to each other to bring out our own strengths and creativity. We were a strong unit that needed to succeed. It was instilled in us that, though we could display individual flair, we had to give our all for each other as a team. I'm not convinced such an attitude is as strong in football today. Neither am I of the mind that every player is devoted and loyal to his team-mates and his respective club. In 2002, the former Portsmouth, Stoke City and Sheffield United defender Lee Sandford gave an interview for the Midlands newspaper *Sentinel Sunday*. Having sung the praises of such overseas players as Gianfranco Zola and Thierry Henry, Sandford went on to say, 'Unfortunately, there are simply too many overseas players who are only here for the money and have no sense of loyalty to their club or team-mates. When I was at Sheffield United, we had a number of overseas players whose attitude to the club and their team-mates was dreadful. All they were interested in was how much money they were being paid.'

I am of the mind that it is not just some overseas players who maintain that attitude in football today. I can recall a conversation I had with the former West Ham United and Ipswich Town manager John Lyall.

'A player may have produced some indifferent performances in games. He hasn't been pulling his weight for the team. But then he goes and scores two goals in a match. I would immediately have his agent on the telephone demanding we give the player in question a rise,' said John. 'I look at some of the players nowadays and the money they are earning and I think, "No. Years ago they wouldn't have got through the gate at Upton Park."'

There is no doubt whatsoever that overseas players have contributed much and added greatly to the spectacle of English football. But not every overseas player is a Zola or an Henry or a Patrick Vieira. I think there are now too many mediocre overseas players in our game. On the first day of the 2002–3 football season, for the first time ever there were more foreign players on display in the Premiership than English – 117 to 103 to be exact. That can't be good for the future of English football.

The contributions of such players as Ruud van Nistelrooy and Dennis Bergkamp are not in question. But what of expensive imports like Igor Biscan and Tomas Repka? In 2002–3 both were on the books of Premiership clubs, and I find it hard to believe, in their cases and in those of others, that their respective clubs couldn't find their equal, or even better, within these shores. What frightens me about English football in the twenty-first century is that for every Henry or Vieira there are half a dozen or more Lilian Laslandes and Titi Camaras.

More and more Premiership clubs are also recruiting youngsters from abroad for their academies. Chelsea and Arsenal are just two examples, but Nationwide League clubs are following this trend. Ipswich Town have a number of overseas youngsters at their academy. It begs the question: is this country so devoid of young footballing talent that clubs have to recruit youngsters from overseas? Of course not.

Too many managers have become too dependent on agents bringing players to their notice. It makes life easier for them. They and their scouts don't have to go out and unearth gems; they can simply sit at home and watch videos. Of course there are managers and scouts who still comb the lower leagues and non-league football in search of talent, but their number appears to be dwindling.

When Chris Turner was manager of Hartlepool United in

2001, he was reported as saying he attended a midweek match at York City where, apart from him, there was just one other scout present, from Barnsley. 'Six or seven years ago there might have been a dozen or so representatives from other clubs at such a midweek game,' said Chris.

Another recent and disturbing trend has emerged regarding overseas players. Before the start of the 2002–3 Premiership season, Everton made a statement to the press in which they said 'New signing Li Tie is in line to be called up for a swift debut by manager David Moyes. Tie is the second signing from China as part of the club's new sponsorship with communications giant Keijan.'

Surely Everton are not so greedy for money that they agreed to sign a number of players from China as part of a sponsorship deal? The Everton statement seemed to indicate that was the case, which to my mind serves as further evidence that football has sold its soul and laid itself bare before the great altar to money making.

Such a trend is indicative of the many marketing and PR people who are now part and parcel of the game. In my experience many such people have little or no knowledge of the history of the game or concern for its wellbeing. Moreover, many don't seem to have an empathy with, or understanding of, supporters, something which was exemplified by a letter sent by a Derby County supporter to a friend of mine who is a football writer.

The letter was written by Peter Murgatroyd, a Derby supporter, in 2002, during the season in which Derby County were relegated from the Premiership. In his letter Mr Murgatroyd said that he attended a Derby County home game when they had lost 5-0 against Leeds United. He wrote, 'At the next Derby home match, the voice over the Tannoy said, "Following our last home game, no doubt you went home thinking about the many benefits I had mentioned available from Derby County Financial Services."' As Mr Murgatroyd stated in his letter, 'There was only one thing that any Derby supporter remembered about the previous home game!' In many respects the statement made by that Tannoy announcer crystallises the game today. No doubt the announcer in question was reading from a script. Whatever, the statement was indicative of those in the game who have no understanding of the feelings and needs of ordinary supporters. Such people ride roughshod over the emotions and feelings of genuine supporters in their quest to use club loyalty as a means of selling all manner of products. Which to me is crass.

When English football got into bed with television in 1992, Ian St John and I told each other that the game was about to change irrevocably. It has. Football is still a great game, it still boasts great players, but it is a different game. Just as governments and big business seem to want to encourage conformity, a one-size-fits-all culture, so this attitude has found its way into football.

To ensure football meets the demands of television, which wants the game to be attractive to a family audience, football's administrators seem hell-bent on turning the game into something it is not and never has been.

In an earlier chapter I expressed my regret about modern football's administrators' attitude to the physical aspects of the game, on their apparent desire to eradicate a certain robustness in order to make football more palatable for a television audience. I also wrote about the woolly charges of bringing the game into disrepute, and of misconduct. The fines meted out to players who have fallen foul of these two charges are often grossly out of proportion to the alleged offence, a prime example of this being the case concerning Roy Keane. Irrespective of your opinion of Roy Keane, the five-match ban and £150,000 fine he received in 2002 had no bearing on the actual offence he was said to have committed.

Following Roy Keane's appearance before what the FA described as an 'independent disciplinary committee' the chairman of that committee, Harry Bright, told the waiting press that Keane had been 'found guilty on both counts of misconduct'. The very terminology used gives me cause for concern. Roy Keane may have been foolhardy, reckless, silly and vindictive. But the phrase 'found guilty' implied he was some sort of criminal.

I think it's important to note that it was not Roy Keane's reckless challenge on Alfie Haaland during a Manchester derby that had resulted in him appearing before the disciplinary committee. Rather, it was because he had claimed in his autobiography that the challenge had been intentional. The size of the fine imposed on Roy Keane for admitting in his book that his challenge on Haaland was intentional is another disturbing trend, as was the £30,000 fine imposed on Tim Sherwood by Tottenham in 2002 for telling a reporter he did not consider Spurs good enough to win the Premiership. Both were out of all proportion to the supposed offence.

Following Roy Keane's appearance before the disciplinary committee it was widely reported in the media that the £150,000 fine was of little consequence to him. As one broadsheet newspaper put it, 'a fine of £150,000 will scarcely trouble a player paid a reported £90,000 a week'. The newspaper in question prides itself on its liberalism and sense of fair play. That newspaper should be ashamed for the line it took over Keane's £150,000 fine.

When Keane's disciplinary hearing at the Reebok Stadium was over, an FA spokesperson was reported to have said, 'Justice has been done'. It hadn't. It had been seen to be done and that is not the same thing, nor is it right. The extraordinary fines imposed on footballers for what are usually minor indiscretions have little to do with justice, or the punishment fitting the 'crime'. In my opinion, it has much to do with the desire of clubs and football's governing bodies to sanitise the game for the consumption of television.

If you were to ask me if I thought any footballer was worth a wage of £90,000 a week I'd have to say 'No'. But I don't blame footballers for accepting astronomical wages. A lot of people believe the salaries paid to the likes of David Beckham, Roy Keane and Thierry Henry are largely responsible for many clubs being in dire financial straits. I don't go along with that. Manchester United and Arsenal can afford the wages they pay. David Beckham's worth to Manchester United far exceeded his worth as a player. His image is estimated to have been worth at least £30 million to United. The number seven shirt worn by Beckham was United's bestselling replica shirt and it is estimated that 16.6 million in Asia followed the club because of David Beckham. When the news broke of him being hit in the face by a boot kicked across the room by Sir Alex Ferguson, United's share price fell 2 per cent to 117p, apparently because the market feared the incident would result in Beckham leaving the club. A lot of people believe that United paid David Beckham an obscene amount of money. I can understand that point of view, but Beckham's salary had to be weighed against how much his image earned the club. A player such as David Beckham is not paid simply for his talent as a footballer anymore. That's the way it is in top-flight football today.

At the other end of the scale, many clubs are struggling financially. Strapped for cash in the wake of the collapse of ITV Digital, denied the transfer fees they once received from bigger clubs and with mounting debts, many clubs are now facing severe financial hardship.

This dilemma prompted Manchester United's then Chief Executive Peter Kenyon to suggest that in a few years English football will have only around forty full-time professional clubs. According to Mr Kenyon this, and the return to regionalised leagues, is the solution to the financial crises that many clubs face in the twenty-first century. Mr Kenyon's view is one shared by many, but I am not one of them. Rather than fewer full-time professional clubs, what English football needs is more professional clubs which are more professionally run.

The collapse of ITV Digital has been quoted by certain chief executives and club chairmen as the prime reason for football's financial crisis. The collapse of ITV Digital, although it is relevant, is being used by many as an excuse for what is in effect bad business by some clubs.

You never miss what you never had. While there may be a case for clubs budgeting for money promised by ITV Digital, there can be no excuse for spending it before it had been received, as a number of clubs now in dire straits financially appear to have done. In 2003 we heard a number of chief executives and chairmen calling for a cap on wages. By calling on both the FA and Football League to introduce a cap on wages, I feel such people are hoping to hide behind that. Quite simply, a chief executive or chairman could then tell a player or his agent they can't meet the wage demand because they aren't allowed to.

It is no coincidence those smaller clubs who are not facing financial ruin have a ceiling on wages and stick to it, among them Crewe Alexandra, Walsall and Hartlepool United. A ceiling on wages makes for a rougher ride for those negotiating salaries and it may even result in a club missing out on a player. But it's better for a club to work within the parameters they have set out for themselves than to slide into considerable debt. Problems occur when a club's expectations exceed their realistic ambitions. In all probability Crewe Alexandra and Walsall will never make the Premiership, though that is their ultimate goal. But with prudent housekeeping and realistic ambitions such clubs can enjoy relative success. More than half the clubs in the Conference League have a full-time playing staff. The majority exist on relatively meagre attendances, but have cut their cloth accordingly. In my opinion English football needs more clubs to be run like Crewe, Walsall and Hartlepool.

Supporters love the Premiership and there has been a year-on-year increase in attendances since it began in 1992. This is good for the game, but I feel too many supporters are mistaking excitement for quality. Right through the divisions, too many supporters appear not to care too much how a game is played, as long as their team wins.

The Premiership can boast not only some top-quality players but it also contains some great players. A great player would be able to play in any era of football. But great players such as Gianfranco Zola and Alan Shearer apart, I believe the general standard of football and individual skill throughout the English game is nowhere near as high as it used to be.

In 1963 Bill Nicholson gave an interview for BBC TV's midweek sports programme *Sportsview*. Bill was asked to talk about his Tottenham team. He talked about the ability of Danny Blanchflower to control matches; John White's ability to ghost into space and always be available to his team-mates. He mentioned my ability to score goals, and Dave Mackay's ability to win the ball and make slide-rule passes that launched another Spurs attack. The next morning at training we ribbed Bill about his interview. 'I didn't think you had the "ability" to come across so well on television, boss,' quipped Danny Blanchflower. Bill's appearance on *Sportsview* was dubbed 'the ability interview'.

Forty years on Sunderland suffered a torrid season in the Premiership. Their manager Howard Wilkinson had to face the TV cameras as one defeat followed another. Wilkinson put on a brave face. Time and again I heard him praising the 'effort and commitment' shown by his players. Not once did he make reference to the ability of his players. Likewise, in a post-match interview following a game between West Bromwich Albion and West Ham United, the Baggies' manager Gary Megson said, 'I don't think you can fault the effort and commitment of the players today.' My point being, you could pick eleven devoted Baggies' supporters out of the crowd, put them in West Brom shirts and send them out to play. They wouldn't have the ability to play Premiership football, but I bet you couldn't fault their effort and commitment.

In the sixties, skill and ability were prerequisites for playing professional football, especially at Tottenham. Now, because of the frenzied pace at which football is played, effort and commitment have become substitutes for skill.

I'm not one to digest the myriad pointless statistics that are now issued after every game. I will, however, occasionally read such data. In 2002 I read statistics compiled for West Ham's game against Bolton Wanderers. According to the statistics, both teams gave away possession of the ball more than seventy times. My response to that is, you can't play football if you haven't got the ball.

The pace of the game today is beyond all but the most gifted of players and rather than skill being intrinsic to the game it has become a bonus. That skill was so evident in the game in my time as a player is all the more to the credit of those who played football at that time given the weight of the ball and the general state of pitches. In 2003 Charlton Athletic lodged a complaint about the state of the pitch at Stamford Bridge following their defeat against Chelsea. I saw that game. On hearing Charlton's complaint I was left thinking, 'What was wrong with the pitch? We used to play on pitches like that every week.'

Football has made great strides in recent years to rid the game of hooligans. The new infrastructure of family-friendly stadiums is a credit to the clubs, the game's administrators and the authorities. One should never underestimate what football has achieved. The improvement in stadiums has filtered down right through the game. Even part-time professional clubs now boast smart and tidy grounds that are a credit to English football. What football has achieved in recent years in this respect is remarkable. Football has shown other areas of society just what can be achieved when people are proactive and totally committed to a sensible plan. Imagine how society would be today if the same vivacity, imagination and respective level of investment had been committed to the redevelopment of public transport or our health service. When England played Australia in 2003 at Upton Park, the game had to be delayed because many supporters had not arrived at the ground. A spokesperson for Transport for London said, 'The problem occurred because too many supporters were journeying to the ground at the same time and it placed too great a burden on the system.' If the transport system and infrastructure of the capital city of what is the fourth strongest economy in the world can't cope with a football crowd of thirty-odd thousand, heaven help us.

There has always been rivalry between supporters. In the fifties and for the best part of the sixties it was a healthy rivalry. Though football has done much in recent years to eradicate the criminal element who infiltrated the game under the guise of being supporters, there remains an unhealthy attitude to rival clubs and their respective fans. At best this takes the form of disrespect. Opposing teams are booed when they take to the field. At worst it takes the form of moronic tribal rivalry whereby some supporters seem to hate a certain club and its fans, in so doing professing their undying loyalty to their own club. Such people delude themselves. In my day as a player I never came across a supporter who believed a seat should be ripped from its bolts and hurled at opposing fans for the sake of his club. It would never occur to supporters to shout or do anything that would besmirch the name of their club, or football in general. They loved their team and football too much to do that. There was rivalry between respective sets of supporters, but it was a healthy rivalry and people had respect for opponents. In 1965 I played for Spurs at Sunderland. As we made our way down the tunnel I heard a voice on the Tannoy say, 'Ladies and gentlemen, please give a warm Wearside welcome to our opponents today . . . Tottenham Hotspur!' Spurs ran out to warm applause.

In my days as a West Ham player we played Everton at Goodison Park. I had picked up an injury and my name wasn't in the West Ham line-up printed in the match-day programme. The injury, however, healed sufficiently for Ron Greenwood to include me in the team that day. As West Ham made their way from the dressing room to the pitch, I heard a Tannoy announcement: 'Ladies and gentlemen, there is a change to the West Ham team as printed in your programme,' said the announcer. 'At number eleven for West Ham today will be our old friend, Jimmy Greaves!'

A big cheer went up around Goodison Park and I took to the pitch to generous applause. When the game eventually got underway and I touched the ball for the first time, I was treated to another round of applause from those Everton supporters. Supporters had respect for other teams and their respective fans. Sadly, I don't see much evidence of that in football today. David Beckham is often vilified when playing at an opponent's ground. Good-hearted banter and mickey taking is fine, part and parcel of the game, but some of the things I hear supporters hurl at opposing players these days chills my blood.

The way football is projected on television nowadays leaves much to be desired. There is simply too much football on our screens. European games spread over three nights, league matches shoehorned into every gap in the schedules, inter-national matches, the Worthington Cup and FA Cup rounds now so much of a four-day event one half expects to see a tie coming from Badminton. It's all too much for even the most ardent supporter of the game. The pudding has been grossly overegged, but it is our minds that have become scrambled. One game merges into the next. Competitions lose their individual identities and unique appeal. An FA Cup tie is just another match, as is the final itself. Televised football has become chewing gum for the eyes. Like chewing gum, it quickly loses its flavour. That's why they put six sticks of gum in a pack. Television's answer to football losing its flavour on the bedpost overnight is hyperbole.

Every match is hyped to the limit. Not even a fixture between Tranmere and Barnsley is run-of-the-mill. The trailer extols such a fixture as having all the importance of an FA Cup Final of old. Such trailers are sharply edited showing players flying in to tackles, spectacular goals and acrobatic saves. Action follows action as the trailer promises even more heart-stopping action in store.

Ironically for an industry largely dependent on advertising revenue, television appears unaware of an old phrase in advertising: 'Never promise anything that the product cannot deliver.' Invariably games cannot live up to television's pre-match hype, which leaves the viewer feeling cheated and unfulfilled. During the course of my work as a footballer, TV presenter and now occasional after-dinner speaker, I've had cause to stay at numerous hotels. One thing that has struck me is that the quality of the hotel is usually in inverse proportion to the length of its name. The Holiday Inn Crowne Plaza Midland Hotel Manchester, for example, though fine in its own right, doesn't quite come up to the standard of the Savoy or the Ritz. Likewise, the less genuinely interesting a televised football match is the more outrageous the pre-match hyperbole. Thus Derby County v Wimbledon is billed as 'The Dons take on Derby County in the hope of taking the Rams by the horns and the pride out of Pride Park. Sizzling Nationwide League action, live on Monday night on Skysports One.' Underscoring the trailer is a music soundtrack that wouldn't be out of place in the finale scene of the film *Speed*.

I recall Spurs playing a game at Aston Villa in 1967. It was a thrilling game that ended in a 3-3 draw. It was a marvellous game to play in, and seemingly a great one to watch because the Villa Park crowd gave both teams a standing ovation as we left the pitch. There were no pre-match firework displays on the pitch. No media hyperbole. No musical fanfare as the teams took to the pitch. I mention this game not only because it was a cracking game of football, but because of the music that was playing over the Tannoy as Spurs ran down the tunnel. It was Bernard Cribbins singing 'Gossip Calypso'. For anyone not familiar with the song, it contains the lines 'Oh, Mrs Ware I do like your hair, please tell me, where did you have it done?' To which the reply is, 'At Madame Pom-Pom's down by the gasworks.'

'Gossip Calypso' is a novelty song, one as far removed from the *Rocky*–'Eye of the Tiger'-type music used by television to promote live matches as it's possible to be. Yet within two minutes of the Bernard Cribbins song ending, Spurs kicked off that game to a torrent of noise sweeping down from the Villa Park stands and terraces. Genuine football supporters are discerning folk. They don't need to be sold a football match. They don't respond to an incessant bombardment of insipid superlatives that promise every game will be a humdinger. Simply because experience has taught them football isn't like that. Neither are the passion, emotions and interest of genuine supporters for a game aroused by a thumping rock soundtrack. Television patronises football supporters. Genuine fans will watch a game on television, even when it does not involve the team they support, because they want to. They resent television's hyping of every single game that is broadcast, because TV does not do what the game has done since organised football began: recognise that supporters have a mind of their own and will discern which games they will and will not watch.

It was inevitable that 'pay per view' matches would eventually come to our TV screens and equally inevitable they would not find favour with supporters. In order to watch a 'pay per view' match a supporter will need three things: a TV licence, a subscription to satellite or cable TV and a one-off fee to watch the game in question. That TV executives believed supporters would go for 'pay per view' is indicative of how little they know about football and its genuine supporters. No genuine fan would pay three times for something they can pay for once by turning up at their local club. Television can hype a 'pay per view' match to the hilt, but it will never overcome that simple, undeniable fact.

I hear people say that football's boom period of the late nineties has turned to bust. Football hasn't gone bust, it has merely settled down to the reality of its situation. It was unrealistic of ITV Digital to expect the nation to be on the edge of their armchairs at the prospect of watching Bradford City v Grimsby Town. Any substantial and sustainable interest in such a fixture would only come from the respective supporters of the two teams in question, half of whom would be attending the match. It was also unrealistic of the clubs to expect ITV Digital to be forthcoming with oodles of money when their 'product' wasn't selling. Football didn't go bust in 2002; it simply suffered a reality check.

Football is truly global. FIFA and UEFA like to believe every nation is part of 'the family of football', a laudable notion and one that I fully subscribe to. But this has gone too far. With so many substandard national and international teams now participating, the international fixture list and the two major

European club competitions now read like menus offering spam rather than lobster.

When Spurs won the European Cup Winners' Cup in 1963 our seven matches were watched by a total of 377,099 spectators, an average of 53,871 per game. Our game in Bratislava was watched by 32,000, our tie in Belgrade by 45,000 and the final in Rotterdam attracted 40,000. Though smaller in number compared to the attendances at the other ties, those three matches attracted capacity gates to the respective grounds. It was hard work winning the European Cup Winners' Cup. Every team Spurs came up against was a quality side. The competition overall was one of a very high quality, as reflected by those huge attendances.

The quality of the European Cup Winners' Cup was gradually diluted over the years as the barriers came down in Europe and democracy made its mark. Eventually qualification for the Cup Winners' Cup entered the realms of the ridiculous. One team qualified in 1998 because it had won its country's respective cup competition in which it was one of only two teams to enter. In 1998 a tie between HB Torshavn and Apoel Nicosia attracted an attendance officially put at one hundred. In the same round 433 watched Sadam play Belshina. The names of such teams carried no weight, the attendances at their matches were no more than those who watch games in the lower reaches of part-time professional football in this country. I'm all for democracy in Europe, but it wasn't for the European Cup Winners' Cup.

Democracy has also affected international competitions. The two-year battle for qualification for the European Championships and World Cup has become mostly a slog, a duty to be endured, a forced march over rough territory. For England, victory over the smaller football nations, who often set their sights on nothing more than a face-saving draw, is taken for granted. The real issues are decided by head-to-heads between the pack leaders, more often than not simply two countries. The team that does not win automatic qualification from its group is then subjected to a play-off equation containing more 'ifs' than Kipling ever dreamed of. The carrot, of course, is a month's beano at the European Championships, or, better still, the World Cup. Both are parties worth attending, and non-attendance, as England and the other Home Countries know, is a stigma of the hairiest kind. That old tsar of the Football League, Alan Hardaker, once said non-qualification is 'a terrible thing for about six weeks and then everybody forgets it'. That's not how it is nowadays. The FA don't forget non-qualification in a hurry because it means millions of pounds less for their kitty. Football agents don't forget it either. The finals of a major international competition are a 'shop window' for the players they represent. Neither does television forget non-qualification in a hurry. Major finals without England mean a major drop in TV advertising revenue. Should the manager of a Home Countries team, especially England, fail to guide his side to the Finals of the European Championships or World Cup, he has more to contend with nowadays than just the disappointment and grumbles of supporters. Those who have seen the promise of millions of pounds evaporate into thin air do their worst.

On the subject of international football, I feel it appropriate here for me to convey my impressions of England under Sven Göran Eriksson. The 5-1 victory over Germany in 2001 apart, I settle down to watch every England game at eight o'clock. An hour and a half later, I look at my watch and it says a quarter past eight.

Football is a still a great game. It still boasts some great players. But football today is far different from the game I knew. I've outlined what I believe to be some of the negatives and positives to contemporary football. I find much I don't approve of but there is also much that I admire.

Gianfranco Zola and Alan Shearer are not only great players but wonderful role models for young people. And if any club wishes to develop a highly successful youth policy whereby young players learn good habits, they should look no further than my favourite role models, Crewe Alexandra. Sack-happy boards of directors should also take a long hard look at the way the Crewe board conducts itself and runs the affairs of the club. In 2003 Dario Gradi celebrated twenty years as manager at Crewe. Carlisle and Darlington are two places of similar size and population to Crewe. In the time Dario Gradi has been in charge of the Alex, Carlisle have had fourteen managers and Darlington fifteen. No further comment is necessary.

My old England team-mate Sir Bobby Robson is a credit to the game and has been for more than fifty years. Bobby was a super player and has since proved himself to be a great manager. To simply say that Bobby loves football doesn't come anywhere near describing his passion for the game. One might as well say Romeo was a little taken with Juliet, or that Madame Butterfly quite liked Pinkerton. Sir Bobby is now in his seventies yet manages one of the youngest teams in the Premiership. That he relates to his young players and they to him speaks volumes of the man and his style of management. I believe age is a quality of mind. If you've left your dreams behind and all your ambitious fire has been quenched, then you are old. Bobby's dreams and ambitions are as alive today as they ever were. That is why it matters not one iota that he is a man in his seventies managing a team several members of whom are in their late teens and early twenties. They share the same dreams and have the same burning ambition to succeed.

Bobby is active in thought and always ready to adopt new ideas. Age has brought him satisfaction, yet he is always dissatisfied. He's settled, yet ever unsettled. He always enjoys the best of what is, and is the first to recognise the best of what will be. He is a man who is generous with his time, sometimes too much so. Though he has suffered some appalling and unwarranted treatment in the press, he always conducts himself with grace and dignity when confronted with the media. His knighthood was wholly merited.

Sir Alex Ferguson is also a great manager. Like Sir Bobby Robson, Sir Alex has had just cause to feel aggrieved by some of the press he has received. But Sir Alex doesn't exude the dignity and grace of Sir Bobby when dealing with the media. On occasions he is given to swearing and behaving in a boorish manner with the press. What sort of example is that to set to his players? If a player sees his manager swearing at the media and behaving badly, how is he going to react when facing the press himself about a certain issue?

Any Nationwide League club that wants to know how to survive and flourish in the Premiership should study Charlton Athletic. The way the club is run, the type of football Alan Curbishley's team play and the way The Valley has been redeveloped is a lesson to all. As is the way Addicks' fans conduct themselves at matches, whereby opposing supporters actually feel welcome at the Valley.

I firmly believe the vast majority of genuine fans do welcome opposing supporters. I have seen opposing fans chatting happily with one another outside stadiums prior to matches. The family atmosphere that has returned to football in recent years is wonderful to see. However, this harmony is besmirched by the small minority who immerse their empty heads in moronic tribal rivalries and thus spoil football as a family spectacle for the majority.

The attitude of players has also changed considerably over the years. In 1965 Spurs drew 2-2 with Burnley. In the dressing room after the game I can remember Cliff Jones sitting down and taking off his boots. 'I really enjoyed that,' said Cliff. 'Yeah,' said Terry Dyson, 'it was a really good game.' Following a drawn game in the Premiership, I wonder how many players' first reaction would be to say, 'I really enjoyed that.'

I mourn the passing of some aspects of the game, but not others. In reflecting on some of the sights that were once common to football but are now no longer to be glimpsed, an opportunity for a little levity, I think:

Quagmire pitches – we trained on them, the reserves and often the junior teams played on the main pitch as well. Come January they resembled either Passchendaele or Wembley ice rink.

Players with moustaches – in the sixties and seventies no self-respecting Bulgarian or Romanian player was without one. In the early seventies even I sported one. In the late seventies and eighties Peter Shilton, Mick Mills and Ian Rush continued this trend which has since been replaced by the goatee, a.k.a. Rio Ferdinand.

Very good British goalkeepers – lest we forget that in Gordon Banks, Pat Jennings, Peter Shilton and Ray Clemence British football boasted world-class goalkeepers, who in their respective time were head and shoulders above Ron Springett, Gordon West, Tony Waiters, Peter Grummitt, Peter Bonetti, Jim Montgomery, Joe Corrigan, Jimmy Rimmer, Paul Cooper and Phil Parkes – who by comparison were merely very good goalkeepers.

Dads wrapping a scarf around a crush barrier – to enable their sons to sit in comfort on reinforced concrete and enjoy a royal view of the game.

The walking midfield player – when I played against Brazil or Uruguay, their midfield players strolled up and down the pitch, only then to suddenly burst into life when on the attack. The walking midfield was a common sight in Mexico '70, Germany '74, Argentina '78 and Spain '82, where players such as Ademir, Paulo Cesar and Socrates never broke sweat irrespective of the heat.

Australian football results that were like cricket scores – in the sixties results such as Sydney Olympic 21 Manley 4 reinforced the notion in British supporters that Australian football was for summer pools only.

Managers in hats – from the bowlers of Herbert Chapman and Tom Whittaker, through Bill Nicholson, Bill Shankly and Matt Busby's trilbies to Malcolm Allison's fedora. Who wouldn't pay good money to see Claudio Ranieri strutting around his technical area wearing a trilby?

The magic sponge – superseded by sprays and ultrasonic treatment. The magic sponge was at its best for getting an injured player back on his feet on a freezing day when the trainer had to break a layer of ice that had formed on the water in his bucket. Applied to any part of the body, pain would give way to shock and the injured player would take to his toes like a greyhound.

'Run it off!' – in the days before substitutes, the advice shouted from the dugout intended as a cure-all for any injury from a bleeding ankle or a twisted knee, to torn ligaments or a broken leg.

Rattles and rosettes – the latter sported only for cup ties, made of tissue paper in the club colours, the centrepiece of which was a cheap tin cup whose only resemblance to the FA Cup was that it had handles.

Match programmes that fitted in your pocket – as opposed to today where programmes are the size of a woman's magazine. A late injury apart, the team line-ups in the programmes of yesteryear were deemed to be the team that would play. These days line-ups consist of squads of up to eighty players in total. Useless.

The opening tackle – every full back's first tackle on his opposing winger was a humdinger. It was known in football circles as the 'let-him-know-you're-there tackle'. How a winger responded to it largely determined what sort of game he would have.

Sports Report's Personal View – at around five-thirty on a Saturday, BBC radio's *Sports Report* would give air time to a sports journalist to offer a personal view on some topic of sport. Journalists such as Don Davies, Bill Bothwell, Larry Canning, Bryon Butler, Maurice Edelston, Brian Glanville, John Arlott, Geoffrey Green and Peter Jones offered erudite, objective and knowledgeable vignettes on some aspect of sporting topicality. Often in prose, they were a pleasure to listen to. Mini-works of audio art that left the listener thinking.

Half-time scoreboards – the boards with alphabet letters that denoted specific matches, the key to which could be found in the match-day programme. These boards were the only way supporters knew what was happening elsewhere in the country. Situated in the corners of terracing or along perimeter walls, the crowd would gasp when seeing a sensational half-time scoreline posted on the board.

Being able to recognise a ground in a photograph from a tiny clue – modern stadiums are marvellous but tend to look the same and have few identifiable characteristics. In the past, even if one was to place a hand over the players featured in a photograph, a supporter would be able to indentify the ground by way of some tiny but telling feature.

The hooped railings of the perimeter fencing at White Hart Lane. The Archibald Leitch crisscross wrought-iron design on the main stands at Goodison Park and Roker Park. The bulbous design of the main stand at Villa Park. The 'chicken run' at Upton Park. The advertisements in large letters on the roof of the smaller stand at Bloomfield Road. The modernistic undulating roof at Coventry's Highfield Road. The cavernous space behind either goal at Stamford Bridge with the dog-track lights ringing the pitch. The clean straight lines of the front of the upper tier of the main stand at Highbury. The advertisement for the 'Pack Horse Hotel' that was always to be seen on the main stand at Bolton's Burnden Park.

The rows of small windows in the rear of the main stand at Craven Cottage which made supporters seated on the back row appear in silhouette. The double-barrel stand at Southend United. Archibald Leitch's gable, finial and clock, the centrepiece on the top of the main stand at Hillsborough. The rows of poplars visible behind the east terrace at Newcastle's St James Park, commonly referred to as the 'poplar side'. The 'chocolate boxes' of the oddly stepped Milton Road end at the Dell, the only uncovered upper tiers of terracing I ever came across at a British ground. Wolves' highly distinctive multispan roof, stepped in triangular sections along the east side of Molineux.

The distinctive distinguishing marks of English football grounds, most of them now gone.

The game is now very popular with television. The history, traditions, great games, players and characters of football are a godsend to documentary makers. There have been numerous football documentaries on our screens in recent years, but most represent an opportunity missed when they are not being downright crass about the game. There has been the occasional informative and entertaining TV documentary, such as *Kicking and Screaming*, Rogan Taylor and Andrew Ward's oral history of the game in England, but these are oases in a desert of documentary making. The vast majority of football documentaries that reach our screens appear to be aimed at people with only the briefest knowledge of the game. They scratch at the surface. Rarely do they make telling points or insightful revelations. Far too often they simply state the obvious. 'Bobby Moore was a great player, for both West Ham

United and England' informed one documentary, not adding
to that. Really?

I am often asked to contribute to football documentaries,
but more often than not will decline the invitation. Given the
style and content of the documentary outlined, I'm usually of
the mind that it isn't the type of programme I want to be
involved with.

I did, however, agree to appear on one TV football
documentary. This was a documentary purportedly celebrating
the life and times of Bobby Moore. I was happy to give my
thoughts and recollections of Bobby but when the
documentary was aired it was billed as *When Bobby Met Jimmy*,
a documentary about Bobby Moore and myself.

The makers of the programme informed me that while they
were in the process of putting Bobby's documentary together,
they learned that another TV company had also made a
documentary about him. Not wanting to duplicate, these
people changed tack and produced a documentary based on
the friendship between Bobby and me. I understood the
programme makers reasoning, but was still annoyed. Initially
I had agreed to take part in their documentary on the
understanding that my contribution would be just one of a
number of inserts from a range of people who knew Bobby. I
wasn't expecting a documentary based on Bobby and myself. At
least it turned out to be a worthwhile documentary.

In 2002 there was a documentary based on the careers of
three top-flight players, one of whom was Peter Shilton. Prior
to it being aired on television I met Peter at a charity golf day.
He'd heard about the documentary and as one of its main
subjects was puzzled as to why he had not been asked to
contribute. When the programme was broadcast, Peter found
out why. It was a disgrace of a documentary that simply made
snide comments at the expense of Peter and former England
team-mates such as Kevin Keegan. The opening line about

Peter was inaccurate, and it set the tone for the rest of the programme which did little more than belittle a player who had given his all for his country and was, in his time, the best goalkeeper in the world.

The Finals of a major international championship usually herald a plethora of football documentaries on TV. Most are neither entertaining nor educational and rarely, if ever, give the genuine supporter a reward for watching by telling viewers something they did not already know.

Most of these programmes are not only notable for the absence of former players, but for the lack of knowledgeable football broadcasters and journalists. Comedians, along with insert recollections from B and C category celebrities, appear to be the order of the day.

The likes of Bob Mortimer and Paul Whitehouse have replaced the David Colemans and Hugh McIlvanneys of this world. Bob Mortimer and Paul Whitehouse are funny guys, but you don't see Barry Davies or Brian Glanville on their comedy shows because they would have nothing to contribute. The same goes for comedians presenting football documentaries. The comments made by comedians and B and C category celebs on these programmes offer no sense of time and place. One TV documentary about the history of the World Cup broadcast during the 2002 tournament simply said of the 1970 final between Brazil and Italy, 'It was a cracking match.' It was. It was also the game when Brazil firmly planted their flag on the aesthetic summit of football for all other teams to strive to emulate. As Bob Paisley said at the time, 'At least we all now know what can be done in the name of football.'

During the 2002 tournament, Channel Four devoted the best part of three hours to their 100 Most Memorable World Cup Moments. Given that this programme was aired to a British audience, one would think the most memorable moment of a World Cup would be for one of the Home

Countries to win it. Not so, according to this programme. England's success of 1966 was ranked number four. Apparently better than England winning the World Cup was Michael Owen's goal in the defeat against Argentina in '98, and David Beckham's goal against Greece in the qualifying stages of the 2002 tournament. The comedian Jenny Eclair was called upon to offer her considered analysis of Owen's goal: 'I didn't believe it even when it was happening,' said Jenny. We were all the wiser for that.

Such programmes make me appreciate John Motson, Barry Davies, Alan Parry and Arthur Montford all the more. They put things into true perspective without going overboard. They were objective and knowledgeable in their analysis of football. Genuine supporters, only in warmer coats.

I suppose placing Michael Owen and David Beckham's goals above England winning the World Cup in a programme deemed to be about the tournament's most memorable moments (number one was Maradona's second goal against England in '86) says much about the age of the people who made the programme. I assume they weren't born in 1966. But age, or lack of it, is no excuse for people being unable to place things in true perspective. One didn't have to see George Best play in the sixties to know he was a genius of a player.

Having enjoyed a seventeen-year career in television I feel justified in commenting about that medium. I've watched several documentaries about the sixties, and rarely, if ever, do they truly capture what that decade was really like. Most of the celebrities asked to comment on the sixties never lived in that decade.

There's nothing wrong with having celebrities such as Bob Mills or Lorraine Kelly talking about what life was like in the sixties. As I've said, you didn't have to have been around in the sixties to know what life was like back then. However, there are any amount of people around who were adults or young adults in the sixties who could, I am sure, bring better perspective to a documentary dealing with that subject.

I am glad I played in the era of football that I did. Likewise, I'm glad I worked in the era of television broadcasting that I did. I still occasionally appear on television, but I'm pleased I don't have to depend on it for a living anymore. Though much of what appears on our screens is dross, television continues to produce good programmes and there are still decent folk working in the medium. Which is why, when asked to appear on television, I cherry pick.

There is not much humour in football today, which I find sad. One of the areas where wit and humour is still prevalent is on the sporting after-dinner circuit. It is no coincidence that the former players who now work that circuit played at a time when there was a lot of fun and laughter in football. Today's top players earn so much money they will never need to work on the after-dinner circuit, but I'm not sure they would be able to do it anyway. They don't appear to possess the wit, humour and funny stories.

Can you imagine David Beckham or Paul Scholes taking to their feet at a dinner and rattling off hilarious stories and witty comments about their time under Sir Alex Ferguson and Sven Göran Eriksson? No, neither can I.

Should you ever want to find out what a particular era was like, rather than read a history or sociology book, you would be better off looking at the newspaper cartoons of the day. Cartoons capture what life was like in a certain era in a way that no history book ever can.

These days you rarely see cartoons about football, which says much about what sort of game it is now. When I was a player, football was a popular subject for cartoonists. Most provincial newspapers and a good many match programmes carried cartoons that told the story of the previous game in a

humorous way. The players appeared in caricature with small
bodies and enlarged heads. Wherever possible the opposition
would be represented by animals or birds in keeping with their
nickname. Thus Norwich players appeared as canaries,
Newcastle as magpies and Leicester City were foxes. The
cartoonists rarely signed their work with their own name,
preferring to form their initials into an acronym, such as PAK
(Bristol Rovers), ROL (Sunderland Football Echo), BEE
(Accrington Stanley) and MAC (Leicester City). These
cartoons were indicative of the time. People took their football
seriously, but the game was also seen as being fun.

Charles Buchan's Football Monthly, the most popular football
magazine of its time, ran a whole page of cartoons. Sporting
Sam, the little rotund man who shared all the fantasies of us
sporting people, was a regular feature in the *Sunday Express* for
over forty-five years. Roy Ullyett's football cartoons adorned
the sports pages of the *Daily Express*. Bill Tidy's work featured
in several match programmes as well as in countless
newspapers and magazines. One of Bill's cartoons I particularly
remember referred to Desmond Hackett of the *Daily Express*.

It was common for a newspaper to flag up a journalist
assigned to a particular game by employing sandwich-board
men outside the ground on match day. Bill Tidy's cartoon
featured a down-and-out standing outside a ground with the
sandwich-board hooked over his shoulders displaying the
message 'Desmond Hackett is here today!' The sandwich-
board man is seen being confronted by a football supporter
who sympathetically says, 'Hello, Desmond, lad . . . things not
so good?'

It's a funny cartoon but Bill Tidy also captures an aspect of
football at that time. Sandwich-board men were a common
sight outside grounds, especially on the occasion of an
important match. There was no saturation coverage of football
by television or radio. Newspapers were a supporter's prime

source for news about a game. When a newspaper sent one of its top writers to report on a match, supporters knew the game in question was a big one. Tidy's depiction of the fan perfectly captures supporters of the sixties. He is seen wearing a heavy overcoat and flat cap but also wears a collar and tie. Mistaking the down and out for Desmond Hackett suggests a certain naivety, but football was a simple game back then. The cartoon depicts football as fun because it was seen to be fun. Tidy captured all that in this single cartoon.

That football was once fertile ground for cartoonists says much about the humour that was attached to the game in the past. Football is now seen as a very serious business by managers, coaches, players, directors and television. This attitude has passed on to many supporters, whose serious attitude to matches involving their team often detracts from their enjoyment of watching football. One only has to look at the faces of supporters when a TV camera pans the crowd to know this is true. Invariably supporters are seen sitting with solemn faces that are wracked with tension and nerves. They endure the match rather than enjoy it. Their only release from this pent-up state is a goal for their team, or the final whistle should their team have won. Compare this contemporary image to film or photographs of supporters of the past. In time gone by, when a camera was pointed at a section of the crowd the response of the supporters was to laugh and wave. Should that happen now, what we invariably see are snarling fans with hands and fingers gesticulating aggressively.

In my playing days, home or away, just as Spurs were about to take to the pitch for a game, Bill Nicholson's final words to us as a team were always the same. 'Go out and enjoy your-selves. Go out and entertain. Go out and win,' he'd say. Today I listen to pundits on television praising an away team by saying, 'They did a great job. They silenced the home crowd, which is what you've got to do.' I think such a statement is a damning indictment of football today. Teams should set out to entertain the supporters who have paid hard-earned money to watch them, not numb their sensibilities.

The serious manner in which many supporters now watch a football match has led to the demise of what we used to call 'the wag in the crowd'. Of course supporters still make funny remarks at matches, but in my opinion the 'wags' are a dying breed. Too often these days supporters will simply hurl abuse at opposing players. When I played away games for Chelsea or Spurs I rarely suffered abuse and vitriol. The comments of home fans were often witty and occasionally clever. I can recall a match at Everton at the beginning of the 1968–9 season. I was in the Everton penalty area, at the Gladwys Street End, waiting for Jimmy Roberston to take a corner when I heard someone shout, 'Greaves, you're over the hill!' When Jimmy's corner came across, Alan Gilzean nodded the ball back to me and I volleyed it into the net. Goodison Park fell silent.

'Okay, so you're not over the hill,' boomed the same Gladwys Street voice, 'but you've got a bloody good view of the valley!'

In the fifties, the Newcastle centre forward Jackie Milburn was loved by the home fans who affectionately dubbed him 'Wor Jackie'. When I was a Chelsea player Newcastle United had an inside forward called George Hannah. The Newcastle fans took to calling Hannah 'Wor Palindrome'. It's that sort of imaginative wit I no longer hear when attending matches these days.

Football has changed, but it is good that it has. I have always seen football as being a celebration of life. Without change life would be unchallenging, sterile, without colour, spectacle and spirit. Those qualities are the very essence of the game.

In writing my autobiography, I have not only attempted to tell the story of my life so far, but also that of football, particularly in my time as a player. I have also given my views on all manner of subjects. I hope you will now have a good idea of what I am like as a person and feel you know me. In telling my story that is what I set out to do. How successful I have been in this, only you, the reader, will know.

Should you look at the index in Paolo Di Canio's autobiography, under Di Canio, you will find the following: argument with Atkinson 191–3; argument with Burns 161–2; argument with Capello 151–3; argument with Ferguson (Ian) 175–6; argument with Trapattoni 127–30; argument with Wilson 200. In my opinion that not only offers an insight into the character of Paolo Di Canio who, on his day, is a wonderful player, but it also serves as an indication of how much conflict there is in the game today. At no point in the index of Di Canio's autobiography is there any reference to 'having a joke with so and so', or 'having fun with Celtic or West Ham teammates'. I enjoyed a lot of fun as a footballer, simply because the game was more fun back then. Football was also more physical, but for all that there was less conflict between those involved in the game.

My days as a footballer are long gone. My career as television presenter is also history. I still have my column with the *Sun* and enjoy that very much. I make the occasional appearance on TV and radio. I also keep myself busy with the occasional theatre tour and after-dinner speaking. For relaxation I like to take the dogs for a daily walk and get out into the garden. I have always been a keen gardener. A few years ago I had the honour of having a rose named after me. The rose was originally developed at a garden centre in Colchester. Warley Rose Garden in Essex acquired the rights to develop and produce this rose and asked if they could name it after me. I was only too pleased to say 'Yes'. To the best of my knowledge Warley Rose Garden no longer produces 'Jimmy Greaves' and, sadly, I no longer have an example in my own garden. According to other gardeners 'Jimmy Greaves' is still available and from time to time appears in rose catalogues. To date, I haven't come across it. So if you know where I can acquire the 'Jimmy Greaves' rose, let me know!

My after-dinner speaking takes me to all corners of the United Kingdom. I drive to sporting dinners, and as I prefer to be with my family I drive back the same night. Sometimes this involves a long journey which gives me much time for thought. Often on the minutiae of life, such as the passing of those little cardboard trays you used to get with Bounty bars. They used to make a good bookmark. Other sights you no longer see are boys playing football with their underpants hanging down below their football shorts. I wonder how many kids today receive a warning from their mum not to eat an orange in a cinema 'in case you swallow a pip and an orange tree grows in your stomach'? How many kids today finish a school exam question in mid-sentence in an attempt to con the examiner into thinking they knew the answer but just ran out of time? Do today's kids have arguments about whose house they are going to play outside? And how many use a washing line as a cowboy's lasso?

There was a simple naivety to life when I was a kid and I'm glad there was. Life was much less complicated, more convivial, less crass and not so opportunistic. These days even a blessed event in someone's life is seemingly an opportunity for self-promotion and money making. When the Beckhams issued a press release about the news of the impending birth of their second child, it also had a paragraph about Posh's new record. In the days following the events of 11 September, as people struggled to come to terms with what had happened, one journalist wondered how the media could ever again waste its time slavishly following the antics of uncharismatic celebrities with nothing meaningful to say for themselves. Two years on, the cult of the so-called celebrity shows no let-up, especially on television when there is a compliant production team to make a documentary that can be sold cheaply to a broadcaster to publicise a solo album.

Having got this far, the reader will have formed an opinion about the sort of person I am. In 1958 Orson Welles made a film called *Touch of Evil*. It is a very atmospheric film in which Welles plays the part of a police chief with no scruples about framing those he knows to be guilty. Charlton Heston plays the part of an honest and upstanding narcotics investigator who clashes with the police chief over a murder. The police chief is convinced that the suspect he has brought in for questioning is the murderer, but can't prove his guilt. So the police chief fits him up by planting evidence. Charlton Heston discovers what the police chief has done and takes him to task. He considers him to be no better than the criminals he has put behind bars. The two men clash. The police chief is eventually killed. When Heston's narcotics agent further investigates the original murder, he discovers that the police chief was right all along. The suspect the chief fitted-up is indeed the murderer.

The final scene involves the local floozy, played by Marlene Dietrich, being asked for her opinion on the police chief with whom she once had a relationship. 'He was some sort of man,' says Dietrich. 'What does it matter what you say about people.'

Exactly.

I have been a professional footballer, a TV presenter and a newspaper columnist. I was once a hopeless alcoholic but no longer drink. I was a succesful businessman, then an unsuccessful businessman. I am a devoted and loving family man. I have travelled the world. I've been places and seen things, and I have seen places and been things. You have read my story and you will have formed an opinion about me. But I'm just 'some sort of man'.

In choosing chapter titles for this book, as a lover of music I thought it appropriate to choose titles of songs popular during the period. Song titles that were also in keeping with what was happening in my life at the time. I chose a forties song, 'Once upon a Time', as the title for my opening chapter. I thought that appropriate as I felt I had a story to tell. I have now told my story to date. I'm in my early sixties. God willing, I still have a lot of life yet to live. So, while this is my story so far, all being well, it is far from . . .

CHAPTER TWENTY

STARRY-EYED SURPRISE

. . . The end.

CAREER RECORD

Jimmy Greaves played in 516 Football League matches and scored 357 goals, all in the First Division (Premiership equivalent):

Chelsea (1957–61)	124 goals
AC Milan (1961)	9 goals
Tottenham Hotspur (1961–70)	220 goals
West Ham United (1970–1)	13 goals

He scored 35 goals in the FA Cup:

Chelsea	3 goals
Tottenham Hotspur	32 goals

And 7 in the League Cup:

Chelsea	2 goals
Tottenham Hotspur	5 goals

13 goals in European Competitions:

Chelsea

Inter Cities Fairs Cup	3 goals (4 appearances)

Tottenham Hotspur

European Cup Winners' Cup	10 goals (12 appearances)

44 goals at full International level
England
Total

44 goals (57 appearances)
465 goals

Jimmy Greaves also scored:
13 goals for England Under 23s (12 appearances)
6 goals in Inter-League matches
2 goals in the Charity Shield (for Tottenham Hotspur)
2 goals for England v Young England
1 goal for England v The Football League
2 goals for The Rest of Europe XI

He was the leading First Division goal scorer a record six times:

Chelsea	1958–9	32 goals
	1960–1	41 goals
Tottenham Hotspur	1962–3	37 goals
	1963–4	35 goals
	1964–5	29 goals
	1968–9	27 goals

His average score per First Division game was 0.69.
He scored 25 hat-tricks or more in 25 First Division matches.
He was his club's leading goalscorer in 12 of the 14 seasons in which he played First Division football.
His total tally of goals in senior games from 1957 to 1971 is 491 goals.

He scored his League goals against the following clubs:

Nottingham Forest 24	Blackburn Rovers 14
Burnley 19	Manchester United 13
Blackpool 18	Newcastle United 13
Wolverhampton Wanderers 17	Fulham 12
Birmingham City 17	Arsenal 11
West Bromwich Albion 16	Aston Villa 11
West Ham United 16	Everton 11
Leicester City 15	Liverpool 11
Manchester City 15	Leeds United 10

Preston North End 10
Sunderland 10
Sheffield United 9
Ipswich Town 9
Sheffield Wednesday 8
Stoke City 7
Southampton 6
Bolton Wanderers 5
Coventry City 5
Portsmouth 5

Tottenham Hotspur 5
Chelsea 4
Cardiff City 2
Derby County 2
Luton Town 2
Leyton Orient 1
Northampton Town 1
Queens Park Rangers 1

Jimmy Greaves scored on his debut for every senior team he played for:
Chelsea v Tottenham Hotspur at White Hart Lane, 23 August 1957
England Under 23s v Bulgaria at Stamford Bridge, 25 September 1957
England v Peru in Lima, 17 May 1959
AC Milan v Botafogo at San Siro Stadium, 7 June 1961
Tottenham Hotspur v Blackpool at White Hart Lane, 16 December 1961
West Ham United v Manchester City at Maine Road, 20 March 1970

At 21 years of age he became the youngest player in the history of English football to score 100 League goals.
Aged 23, he scored his 200th League goal to equal the record set by Dixie Dean of Everton.

England Career

1958–9 (Chelsea)

Date	Opponent	Venue	Score	Goals
17 May 1959	v Peru	Lima	1-4	(1 goal)
24 May 1959	v Mexico	Mexico City	1-2	
28 May 1959	v USA	Los Angeles	8-1	

1959–60

Date	Opponent	Venue	Score	Goals
17 Oct 1959	v Wales	Cardiff	1-1	(1 goal)
28 Oct 1959	v Sweden	Wembley	2-3	
11 May 1960	v Yugoslavia	Wembley	3-3	(1 goal)
15 May 1960	v Spain	Madrid	0-3	

1960–1

Date	Opponent	Venue	Score	Goals
8 Oct 1960	v Northern Ireland	Belfast	5-2	(2 goals)
19 Oct 1960	v Luxembourg	Luxembourg	9-0	(3 goals)

26 Oct 1960	v Spain	Wembley	4-1	(1 goal)
23 Nov 1960	v Wales	Wembley	5-1	(2 goals)
15 April 1961	v Scotland	Wembley	9-3	(3 goals)
21 May 1961	v Portugal	Lisbon	1-1	
24 May 1961	v Italy	Rome	3-2	(1 goal)
27 May 1961	v Austria	Vienna	1-3	(1 goal)

1961–2 (Tottenham Hotspur)

14 April 1962	v Scotland	Glasgow	0-2	
9 May 1962	v Switzerland	Wembley	3-1	
20 May 1962	v Peru	Lima	4-0	(3 goals)
31 May 1962	v Hungary	Rancagua	1-2	
2 June 1962	v Argentina	Rancagua	3-1	(1 goal)
7 June 1962	v Bulgaria	Rancagua	0-0	
10 June 1962	v Brazil	Vina del Mar	1-3	

1962–3

3 Oct 1962	v France	Sheffield	1-1	
20 Oct 1962	v Northern Ireland	Belfast	3-1	(1 goal)
21 Nov 1962	v Wales	Wembley	4-1	(1 goal)
27 Feb 1963	v France	Paris	2-5	
6 April 1963	v Scotland	Wembley	1-2	
8 May 1963	v Brazil	Wembley	1-1	
29 May 1963	v Czechoslovakia	Bratislava	4-2	(2 goals)
5 June 1963	v Switzerland	Basle	8-1	

1963–4

12 Oct 1963	v Wales	Cardiff	4-0	(1 goal)
23 Oct 1963	v Rest of World	Wembley	2-1	(1 goal)
20 Nov 1963	v Northern Ireland	Wembley	8-3	(4 goals)
6 May 1963	v Uruguay	Wembley	2-1	
17 May 1964	v Portugal	Lisbon	4-3	
24 May 1964	v Rep. of Ireland	Dublin	3-1	(1 goal)
30 May 1964	v Brazil	Rio de Janeiro	1-5	(1 goal)
4 June 1964	v Portugal	São Paulo	1-1	
6 June 1964	v Argentina	Rio de Janeiro	0-1	

1964–5

3 Oct 1964	v Northern Ireland	Belfast	4-3	(3 goals)
21 Oct 1964	v Belgium	Wembley	2-2	
9 Dec 1964	v Holland	Amsterdam	1-1	(1 goal)

10 April 1965	v Scotland	Wembley	2-2	(1 goal)
5 May 1965	v Hungary	Wembley	1-0	(1 goal)
9 May 1965	v Yugoslavia	Belgrade	1-1	

1965–6

2 Oct 1965	v Wales	Cardiff	0-0	
20 Oct 1965	v Austria	Wembley	2-3	
4 May 1966	v Yugoslavia	Wembley	2-0	(1 goal)
29 June 1966	v Norway	Oslo	6-1	(4 goals)
3 July 1966	v Denmark	Copenhagen	2-0	
5 July 1966	v Poland	Chorzow	1-0	
11 July 1966	v Uruguay	Wembley	0-0	
16 July 1966	v Mexico	Wembley	2-0	
20 July 1966	v France	Wembley	2-0	

1966–7

15 April 1967	v Scotland	Wembley	2-3	
24 May 1967	v Spain	Wembley	2-0	(1 goal)
27 May 1967	v Austria	Vienna	1-0	

In his 57 International appearances, England won 30, drew 13 and lost 14.

Tottenham Hotspur Career

1961–2

Dec 16 (h) Blackpool	5-2	42,374	(3 goals)
Dec 23 (a) Arsenal	1-2	63,440	
Dec 26 (a) Chelsea	2-0	51,282	(1 goal)
Dec 30 (h) Chelsea	5-2	44,630	
Jan 13 (a) Cardiff C.	1-1	33,606	
Jan 20 (h) Man Utd	2-2	55,225	(2 goals)
Feb 3 (a) Wolves	1-3	45,687	
Feb 10 (h) Nottm Forest	4-2	42,710	
Feb 21 (a) Aston Villa	0-0	49,892	
Feb 24 (h) Bolton W.	2-2	36,470	(1 goal)
Mar 3 (a) Man City	2-6	31,706	(2 goals)
Mar 14 (h) Ipswich T.	1-3	51,098	(1 goal)
Mar 17 (a) Burnley	2-2	46,810	(1 goal)
Mar 24 (h) Everton	3-1	47,343	(1 goal)

Apr 7 (h) Sheffield Wed.	4-0	40,846	(2 goals)
Apr 9 (h) Sheffield Utd	3-3	49,030	(1 goal)
Apr 17 (a) Fulham	1-1	43,355	(1 goal)
Apr 20 (h) Blackburn R.	4-1	55,183	(1 goal)
Apr 21 (h) West Brom. A.	1-2	53,512	
Apr 23 (a) Blackburn R.	1-0	23,301	(1 goal)
Apr 28 (a) Birmingham C.	3-2	29,614	(2 goals)
Apr 30 (a) Leicester C.	3-2	23,929	(1 goal)

FA Cup

Jan 6 (a) Birmingham C.	3-3	46,096	(2 goals)
Jan 10 (h) Birmingham C. (replay)	4-2	62,917	(1 goal)
Jan 27 (a) Plymouth A.	5-1	40,040	(2 goals)
Feb 17 (a) West Brom. A.	4-2	53,539	(2 goals)
Mar 10 (h) Aston Villa	2-0	64,000	
Mar 31 (n) Man Utd (semi-final)	3-1	65,000	(1 goal)
May 5 (n) Burnley (final)	3-1	100,000	(1 goal)

European Cup

Mar 21 (a) Benfica	1-3	86,000	
Apr 5 (h) Benfica	2-1	64,448	

In March and April 1962, Jimmy Greaves played 18 games for Spurs and England over this two-month period.

1962–3

Aug 18 (h) Birmingham C.	3-0	51,140	(1 goal)
Aug 20 (a) Aston Villa	1-2	55,630	
Aug 25 (a) West Ham Utd	6-1	32,527	(2 goals)
Aug 29 (h) Aston Villa	4-2	55,650	(2 goals)
Sep 1 (h) Manchester C.	4-2	48,758	(1 goal)
Sep 8 (a) Blackpool	2-1	31,786	
Sep 12 (h) Wolves	1-2	61,412	
Sep15 (h) Blackburn R.	4-1	43,014	
Sep 19 (a) Wolves	2-2	48,166	(2 goals)
Sep 22 (a) Sheffield Utd	1-3	38,355	(1 goal)
Sep29 (h) Nottm Forest	9-2	49,075	(4 goals)
Oct 13 (a) West Brom. A.	2-1	32,753	
Oct 24 (h) Man Utd	6-2	51,314	(3 goals)
Oct 27 (a) Leyton O.	5-1	30,967	

Nov 3 (h) Leicester C.	4-0	52,361	(2 goals)
Nov 10 (a) Fulham	2-0	39,961	
Nov 17 (h) Sheffield Wed.	1-1	42,390	
Nov 24 (a) Burnley	1-2	44,478	(1 goal)
Dec 1 (h) Everton	0-0	60,626	
Dec 8 (a) Bolton W.	0-1	20,737	
Dec 15 (a) Birmingham C.	2-0	36,623	(1 goal)
Dec 22 (h) West Ham Utd	4-4	44,650	
Dec 26 (h) Ipswich T.	5-0	34,822	(3 goals)
Jan 19 (h) Blackpool	2-0	25,710	(2 goals)
Feb 23 (a) Arsenal	3-2	59,980	
Mar 2 (h) West Brom. A.	2-1	41,193	
Mar 9 (a) Man Utd	2-0	53,416	
Mar 16 (a) Ipswich T.	4-2	23,679	(2 goals)
Mar 23 (a) Leicester C.	2-2	41,622	(1 goal)
Mar 27 (h) Leyton O.	2-0	40,260	(1 goal)
Mar 30 (h) Burnley	1-1	46,536	(1 goal)
Apr 8 (a) Sheffield Wed.	1-3	43,368	
Apr 12 (a) Liverpool	2-5	54,463	
Apr 13 (h) Fulham	1-1	45,951	(1 goal)
Apr 15 (h) Liverpool	7-2	53,727	(4 goals)
Apr 20 (a) Everton	0-1	67,750	
Apr 27 (h) Bolton W.	4-1	40,965	(1 goal)
May 4 (h) Sheffield Utd	4-2	42,886	(1 goal)
May 11 (a) Man City	0-1	27,784	
May 18 (a) Nottm Forest	1-1	27,995	
May 20 (a) Blackburn R.	0-3	22,867	

European Cup Winners' Cup

Oct 31 (h) Glasgow Rangers	5-2	58,859	
Dec 11 (a) Glasgow Rangers	3-2	80,000	(1 goal)
Mar 5 (a) Slovan Bratislava	0-2	32,000	
Mar 14 (h) Slovan Bratislava	6-0	61,504	(2 goals)
Apr 24 (a) OFK Belgrade (sf)	2-1	45,000	
May 15 (n) Atletico Madrid (F)	5-1	40,000	(2 goals)

FA Cup

Jan 3 (h) Burnley	0-3	32,756	

Charity Shield

Aug 1 (a) Ipswich T.	5-1	20,179	(2 goals)

1963–4

Aug 24 (a) Stoke City	1-2	40,638	
Aug 28 (a) Wolves	4-1	41,488	(2 goals)
Aug 31 (h) Nottm Forest	4-1	49,407	(3 goals)
Sep 4 (h) Wolves	4-3	51,851	
Sep 7 (a) Blackburn R.	2-7	20,949	(1 goal)
Sep 14 (h) Blackpool	6-1	38,138	(3 goals)
Sep 16 (a) Aston Villa	4-2	36,643	(2 goals)
Sep 21 (a) Chelsea	3-0	57,401	
Sep 28 (h) West Ham Utd	3-0	51,667	
Oct 2 (h) Birmingham C.	6-1	37,649	(3 goals)
Oct 5 (a) Sheffield Utd	3-3	33,606	(1 goal)
Oct 15 (a) Arsenal	4-4	67,857	(1 goal)
Oct 19 (h) Leicester C.	1-1	50,521	
Oct 26 (a) Everton	0-1	65,386	
Nov 2 (h) Fulham	1-0	42,023	(1 goal)
Nov 9 (a) Man Utd	1-4	57,513	
Nov 16 (h) Burnley	3-2	42,222	
Nov 23 (a) Ipswich T.	3-2	25,014	
Nov 30 (h) Sheffield Wed.	1-1	39,378	
Dec 7 (a) Bolton W.	3-1	18,394	(1 goal)
Dec 14 (h) Stoke C.	2-1	36,776	(2 goals)
Dec 21 (a) Nottm Forest	2-1	23,888	(1 goal)
Dec 26 (a) West Brom. A.	4-4	37,189	(2 goals)
Dec 28 (h) West Brom. A.	0-2	47,863	
Jan 11 (h) Blackburn R.	4-1	43,953	(3 goals)
Jan 18 (a) Blackpool	2-0	23,955	(1 goal)
Jan 25 (h) Aston Villa	3-1	36,394	(1 goal)
Feb 1 (h) Chelsea	1-2	51,007	(1 goal)
Feb 8 (a) West Ham Utd	0-4	36,838	
Feb 15 (h) Sheffield Utd	0-0	30,833	
Feb 22 (h) Arsenal	3-1	57,261	(1 goal)
Feb 29 (a) Birmingham C.	2-1	28,433	(1 goal)
Mar 7 (h) Everton	2-4	41,926	
Mar 21 (h) Man Utd	2-3	56,292	(1 goal)
Mar 27 (h) Liverpool	1-3	57,022	
Mar 28 (a) Fulham	1-1	30,388	(1 goal)

Apr 4 (h) Ipswich T.	6-3	27,115	
Apr 13 (a) Sheffield W.	0-2	26,628	
Apr 18 (h) Bolton W.	1-0	32,507	(1 goal)
Apr 21 (a) Burnley	2-7	16,660	(1 goal)
Apr 25 (a) Leicester C.	1-0	26,441	

FA Cup

Jan 4 (h) Chelsea	1-1	49,382	
Jan 8 (a) Chelsea (r)	0-2	70,123	

European Cup Winners' Cup

Dec 3 (h) Man Utd	2-0	57,447	
Dec10 (a) Man Utd	1-4	48,639	(1 goal)

1964–5

Aug 22 (h) Sheffield Utd	2-0	45,724	(1 goal)
Aug 25 (a) Burnley	2-2	21,661	(1 goal)
Aug 29 (a) Everton	1-4	55,148	
Sep 2 (h) Burnley	4-1	43,326	
Sep 5 (h) Birmingham C.	4-1	34,809	(1 goal)
Sep 9 (a) Stoke C.	0-2	36,329	
Sep 12 (a) West Ham Utd	2-3	36,730	(2 goals)
Sep 16 (h) Stoke C.	2-1	34,821	(1 goal)
Sep 19 (h) West Brom. A.	1-0	36,993	(1 goal)
Sep 26 (a) Man Utd	1-4	53,362	
Sep 28 (a) Blackpool	1-1	26,436	
Oct 5 (h) Fulham	3-0	32,908	(1 goal)
Oct 10 (h) Arsenal	3-1	55,959	(1 goal)
Oct 17 (a) Leeds Utd	1-3	41,164	(1 goal)
Oct 24 (h) Chelsea	1-1	52,927	
Oct 31 (a) Leicester C.	2-4	29,167	(1 goal)
Nov 7 (h) Sunderland	3-0	36,677	(1 goal)
Nov 14 (a) Wolves	1-3	28,728	
Nov 21 (h) Aston Villa	4-0	29,724	(1 goal)
Nov 28 (a) Liverpool	1-1	41,198	(1 goal)
Dec 5 (h) Sheffield Wed.	3-2	24,019	(2 goals)
Dec12 (a) Sheffield Utd	3-3	19,325	(1 goal)
Dec 19 (h) Everton	2-2	41,994	(2 goals)
Dec 26 (a) Nottm Forest	2-1	42,056	
Dec 28 (h) Nottm Forest	4-0	56,693	(1 goal)

Jan 2 (a) Birmingham C.	0-1	33,833	
Jan 16 (h) West Ham Utd	3-2	50,054	(2 goals)
Jan 23 (a) West Brom. A.	0-2	23,718	
Feb 6 (h) Man Utd	1-0	58,639	
Feb 13 (a) Fulham	1-4	27,708	(1 goal)
Feb 23 (a) Arsenal	1-3	48,367	
Feb 27 (h) Leeds Utd	0-0	42,350	
Mar 10 (a) Chelsea	1-3	51,390	
Mar 13 (h) Blackpool	4-1	27,257	(1 goal)
Mar 20 (a) Sunderland	1-2	44,394	(1 goal)
Mar 27 (h) Wolves	7-4	25,974	
Apr 3 (a) Aston Villa	0-1	24,930	
Apr 16 (h) Blackburn R.	5-2	36,497	(2 goals)
Apr 17 (a) Sheffield Wed.	0-1	21,843	
Apr 19 (a) Blackburn R.	1-3	14,026	
Apr 24 (h) Leicester C.	6-2	32,427	(2 goals)

FA Cup

Jan 9 (a) Torquay Utd	3-3	20,000	
Jan 18 (h) Torquay Utd (r)	5-1	55,081	(3 goals)
Jan 30 (h) Ipswich T.	5-0	43,992	(3 goals)
Feb 20 (a) Chelsea	0-1	63,205	

Glasgow Charity Challenge Cup

Aug 1 (a) Glasgow Select XI	2-4	58,768	

1965-6

Aug 25 (h) Leicester C.	4-2	39,876	(1 goal)
Aug 27 (h) Blackpool	4-0	36,882	(2 goals)
Sep 1 (a) Leicester C.	2-2	28,463	(1 goal)
Sep 4 (a) Fulham	2-0	28,718	
Sep 8 (h) Leeds Utd	3-2	48,156	(2 goals)
Sep 11 (h) Arsenal	2-2	53,962	
Sep 15 (a) Leeds Utd	0-2	41,920	
Sep 18 (h) Liverpool	2-1	46,925	
Sep 25 (a) Aston Villa	2-3	29,856	
Oct 6 (h) Sunderland	3-0	37,364	(1 goal)
Oct 9 (a) Everton	1-3	40,022	
Oct 16 (h) Man Utd	5-1	58,051	(1 goal)
Oct 23 (a) Newcastle Utd	0-0	42,430	

Oct 30 (h) West Brom. A.	2-1	43,658	(2 goals)
Jan 29 (h) Blackburn R.	4-0	34,573	(1 goal)
Feb 5 (a) Blackpool	0-0	13,103	
Feb 19 (h) Fulham	4-3	32,244	
Mar 8 (a) Arsenal	1-1	51,824	
Mar 12 (a) Liverpool	0-1	50,760	
Mar 19 (h) Aston Villa	5-5	28,371	(1 goal)
Mar 26 (a) Sunderland	0-2	27,828	
Apr 2 (h) Nottm Forest	2-3	27,593	
Apr 8 (h) West Ham Utd	1-4	50,635	
Apr 16 (h) Northampton T.	1-1	29,749	(1 goal)
Apr 23 (a) Stoke C.	1-0	19,112	(1 goal)
Apr 25 (a) West Ham Utd	0-2	32,232	
Apr 30 (h) Burnley	0-1	29,337	
May 7 (a) West Brom. A.	1-2	22,586	
May 9 (a) Blackburn R.	1-0	7,256	(1 goal)

FA Cup

Jan 22 (h) Middlesbrough	4-0	37,349	
Feb 12 (h) Burnley	4-3	50,611	
Mar 5 (a) Preston N. E.	1-2	36,792	(1 goal)

1966–7

Aug 20 (h) Leeds Utd	3-1	43,844	(1 goal)
Aug 24 (a) Stoke C.	0-2	34,683	
Aug 27 (a) Newcastle Utd	2-0	35,780	
Aug 31 (h) Stoke C.	2-1	37,908	(1 goal)
Sep 3 (h) Arsenal	3-1	56,271	(2 goals)
Sep 6 (a) Sheffield Utd	1-2	21,650	(1 goal)
Sep 10 (h) Man Utd	2-1	56,295	(1 goal)
Sep 17 (a) Burnley	2-2	25,184	(1 goal)
Sep 24 (h) Nottm Forest	2-1	34,405	(1 goal)
Oct 1 (a) Fulham	4-3	28,628	(1 goal)
Oct 8 (a) Man City	2-1	32,551	
Oct 15 (h) Blackpool	1-3	36,459	
Oct 26 (a) Chelsea	0-3	54,191	
Oct 29 (h) Aston Villa	0-1	31,014	
Nov 5 (a) Blackpool	2-2	16,524	
Nov 12 (h) West Ham Utd	3-4	57,157	(1 goal)
Nov 19 (a) Sheffield Wed.	0-1	32,376	

Nov 26 (h) Southampton	5-3	35,736	(1 goal)
Dec 3 (a) Sunderland	1-0	32,733	
Dec 10 (h) Leicester C.	2-0	41,089	(1 goal)
Dec 17 (a) Leeds Utd	2-3	29,852	(1 goal)
Dec 26 (a) West Brom. A.	0-3	37,969	
Dec 27 (h) West Brom. A.	0-0	39,129	
Dec 31 (h) Newcastle Utd	4-0	27,948	(2 goals)
Jan 7 (a) Arsenal	2-0	49,851	
Jan 14 (a) Man Utd	0-1	57,365	
Jan 21 (h) Burnley	2-0	42,187	(1 goal)
Feb 4 (a) Nottm Forest	1-1	41,822	(1 goal)
Feb 11 (h) Fulham	4-2	43,961	(1 goal)
Mar 18 (h) Chelsea	1-1	49,553	(1 goal)
Mar 22 (a) Everton	1-0	50,108	(1 goal)
Mar 25 (a) Leicester C.	1-0	27,711	
Mar 27 (h) Everton	2-0	46,917	
Apr 1 (h) Liverpool	2-1	53,135	(2 goals)
May 3 (h) Sunderland	1-0	33,936	(1 goal)
May 6 (a) Liverpool	0-0	40,845	
May 9 (a) West Ham Utd	2-0	35,758	(1 goal)
May 13 (h) Sheffield Utd	2-0	44,912	(1 goal)

FA Cup

Jan 28 (a) Millwall	0-0	41,260	
Feb 1 (h) Millwall (r)	1-0	58,189	
Feb 18 (h) Portsmouth	3-1	57,910	(1 goal)
Mar 11 (h) Bristol C.	2-0	54,610	(2 goals)
Apr 8 (a) Birmingham C.	0-0	51,500	
Apr 12 (h) Birmingham C. (r)	6-0	52,304	(2 goals)
Apr 29 (n) Nottm Forest (sf)	2-1	55,000	(1 goal)
May 20 (n) Chelsea (F)	2-1	100,000	

Football League Cup

Sep 14 (a) West Ham Utd	0-1	34,068	

Tay Challenge

Oct 10 (a) Dundee	3-2	10,058	(2 goals)

Friendship Bowl

Nov 23 (h) Polish Select XI	2-1	21,028	(1 goal)

1967–8

Date	Result	Attendance	Goals
Aug 19 (a) Leicester C.	3-2	32,552	
Aug 23 (h) Everton	1-1	53,809	
Aug 26 (h) West Ham Utd	5-1	55,831	(2 goals)
Aug 29 (a) Everton	1-0	57,790	
Sep 2 (a) Burnley	1-5	23,337	(1 goal)
Sep 6 (h) Wolves	2-1	44,408	(1 goal)
Sep 9 (h) Sheffield Wed.	2-1	43,317	
Sep 16 (a) Arsenal	0-4	62,936	
Sep 23 (a) Man Utd	1-3	58,779	
Sep 30 (h) Sunderland	3-0	36,017	(2 goals)
Oct 7 (h) Sheffield Utd	1-1	33,233	(1 goal)
Oct 14 (a) Coventry C.	3-2	38,008	(2 goals)
Oct 25 (h) Nottm Forest	1-1	40,928	(1 goal)
Oct 28 (a) Stoke C.	1-2	27,144	
Nov 4 (h) Liverpool	1-1	47,682	
Nov 11 (a) Southampton	2-1	29,902	
Nov 18 (h) Chelsea	2-0	53,981	
Nov 25 (a) West Brom. A.	0-2	29,033	
Dec 2 (h) Newcastle Utd	1-1	34,494	
Dec 9 (a) Man City	1-4	35,792	(1 goal)
Dec 16 (h) Leicester C.	0-1	26,036	
Dec 23 (a) West Ham Utd	1-2	32,122	
Jan 17 (a) Sheffield Wed.	2-1	31,610	(1 goal)
Jan 20 (h) Arsenal	1-0	57,885	
Feb 3 (h) Man Utd	1-2	57,690	
Feb 26 (a) Sheffield Utd	2-3	27,008	(1 goal)
Mar 1 (h) West Brom. A.	0-0	31,318	
Mar 16 (a) Nottm Forest	0-0	37,707	
Mar 23 (h) Stoke C.	3-0	29,530	
Mar 30 (h) Burnley	5-0	26,494	(2 goals)
Apr 6 (h) Southampton	6-1	41,834	(2 goals)
Apr 12 (h) Leeds Utd	2-1	56,587	(1 goal)
Apr 13 (a) Chelsea	0-2	53,049	
Apr 17 (a) Leeds Utd	0-1	48,933	
Apr 20 (h) Coventry C.	4-2	36,175	(2 goals)
Apr 27 (a) Newcastle Utd	3-1	30,281	
Apr 29 (a) Liverpool	1-1	41,688	(1 goal)
May 4 (h) Man City	1-3	51,242	(1 goal)
May 11 (a) Wolves	1-2	40,929	(1 goal)

FA Cup

Jan 31 (h) Man Utd (r)	1-0	57,200	
Feb 17 (h) Preston N. E.	3-1	47,088	(2 goals)
Mar 9 (h) Liverpool	1-1	54,005	(1 goal)
Mar 12 (a) Liverpool (r)	1-2	53,658	

FA Charity Shield

Aug 12 (a) Man Utd	3-3	54,106	

European Cup Winners' Cup

Sep 20 (a) Hajduk Split	2-0	25,000	(1 goal)
Sep 27 (h) Hajduk Split	4-3	38,623	
Nov 29 (a) O. Lyonnais	0-1	10,997	
Dec 13 (h) O. Lyonnais	4-3	41,895	(2 goals)

Glasgow Challenge

Aug 5 (n) Glasgow Celtic	3-3	57,333	(2 goals)

1968–9

Aug 10 (h) Arsenal	1-2	56,280	(1 goal)
Aug 17 (a) Everton	2-0	56,570	(1 goal)
Aug 21 (h) West Brom. A.	1-1	35,746	
Aug 24 (h) Sheffield Wed.	1-2	30,542	
Aug 28 (a) Man Utd	1-3	62,649	(1 goal)
Aug 31 (a) Chelsea	2-2	48,412	(1 goal)
Sep 7 (h) Burnley	7-0	30,167	(3 goals)
Sep 14 (a) West Ham Utd	2-2	35,802	(1 goal)
Sep 17 (a) Coventry C.	2-1	40,950	
Sep 21 (h) Nottm Forest	2-1	37,386	(1 goal)
Sep 28 (a) Newcastle Utd	2-2	30,469	
Oct 5 (h) Leicester C.	3-2	36,622	(3 goals)
Oct 9 (h) Man Utd	2-2	56,205	
Oct 12 (a) Man City	0-4	38,019	
Oct 19 (h) Liverpool	2-1	44,122	(2 goals)
Oct 26 (a) Ipswich T.	1-0	30,251	
Nov 2 (h) Stoke C.	1-1	33,308	(1 goal)
Nov 9 (a) Leeds Utd	0-0	38,995	
Nov 16 (h) Sunderland	5-1	29,072	(4 goals)
Nov 23 (a) Southampton	1-2	28,384	(1 goal)
Dec 7 (a) Wolves	0-2	30,846	

Dec 14 (h) Man City	1-1	28,462	
Dec 21 (a) Liverpool	0-1	43,843	
Jan 11 (a) Stoke C.	1-1	21,729	
Jan 18 (h) Leeds Utd	0-0	42,396	
Jan 29 (h) QPR	3-2	38,766	
Feb 1 (a) Sunderland	0-0	22,251	
Feb 15 (a) QPR	1-1	30,013	(1 goal)
Feb 22 (h) Wolves	1-1	35,912	
Mar 8 (h) Everton	1-1	44,882	
Mar 18 (h) Ipswich T.	2-2	21,608	(1 goal)
Mar 22 (h) Chelsea	1-0	47,349	
Mar 24 (a) Arsenal	0-1	43,972	
Mar 29 (a) Burnley	2-2	14,547	
Apr 2 (h) Newcastle Utd	0-1	22,528	
Apr 4 (h) Coventry C.	2-0	35,034	
Apr 7 (a) West Brom. A.	3-4	24,173	(2 goals)
Apr 12 (a) Nottm Forest	2-0	22,920	(1 goal)
Apr 19 (h) West Ham Utd	1-0	50,970	(1 goal)
Apr 22 (h) Southampton	2-1	29,201	(1 goal)
Apr 29 (a) Leicester C.	0-1	35,833	
May 12 (a) Sheffield Wed.	0-0	28,582	

FA Cup

Jan 3 (a) Walsall	1-0	18,779	(1 goal)
Jan 25 (h) Wolves	2-1	48,985	(1 goal)
Feb 12 (h) Aston Villa	3-2	49,986	(2 goals)
Mar 1 (a) Man City	0-1	48,872	

Football League Cup

Sep 4 (a) Aston Villa	4-1	24,775	
Sep 25 (h) Exeter C.	6-3	25,798	(3 goals)
Oct 16 (h) Peterborough Utd	1-0	28,378	(1 goal)
Oct 30 (h) Southampton	1-0	35,198	
Nov 20 (a) Arsenal (sf)	0-1	55,237	
Dec 4 (h) Arsenal (sf2)	1-1	55,923	(1 goal)

1969–70

Aug 9 (a) Leeds Utd	1-3	35,804	(1 goal)
Aug 13 (h) Burnley	4-0	35,920	(1 goal)

Aug 16 (h) Liverpool	0-2	50,474	
Aug 19 (a) Burnley	2-0	19,485	
Aug 23 (a) Crystal P.	2-0	39,494	
Aug 27 (h) Chelsea	1-1	47,661	
Aug 30 (h) Ipswich T.	3-2	33,333	(1 goal)
Sep 6 (a) West Ham Utd	1-0	40,561	
Sep 13 (h) Man City	0-3	41,644	
Sep 16 (a) Arsenal	3-2	55,280	
Sep 20 (a) Derby C.	0-5	41,826	
Sep 27 (h) Sunderland	0-1	30,523	
Oct 4 (a) Southampton	2-2	23,901	(1 goal)
Oct 7 (a) Liverpool	0-0	46,518	
Oct 11 (h) Wolves	0-1	36,736	
Oct 18 (h) Newcastle Utd	2-1	33,287	(2 goals)
Oct 25 (a) Stoke C.	1-1	19,569	
Nov 1 (h) Sheffield Wed.	1-0	31,656	
Nov 8 (a) Nottm Forest	2-2	24,034	(1 goal)
Nov 15 (h) West Brom. A.	2-0	28,340	
Nov 22 (a) Man Utd	1-3	53,053	
Dec 6 (a) Coventry C.	2-3	28,443	
Dec 13 (a) Man City	1-1	29,216	
Dec 17 (h) Everton*	0-0	28,494	
Dec 20 (h) West Ham Utd	0-2	28,375	
Dec 26 (h) Crystal P.	2-0	32,845	
Dec 27 (a) Ipswich T.	0-2	24,658	
Jan 10 (h) Derby Co.	2-1	38,645	(1 goal)
Jan 17 (a) Sunderland	1-2	13,993	

* Abandoned 29 minutes – floodlight failure.

FA Cup

Jan 3 (a) Bradford C.	2-2	23,000	(1 goal)
Jan 7 (h) Bradford C. (r)	5-0	36,039	(2 goals)
Jan 24 (h) Crystal P.	0-0	43,948	
Jan 28 (a) Crystal P. (r)	0-1	45,980	

Football League Cup

Sep 3 (a) Wolves	0-1	34,017	

1972–3

Jimmy Greaves Testimonial

| Oct 17 (h) Feyenoord | 2-1 | 45,799 | (1 goal) |

INDEX